# Workplace Skills for Success with AutoCAD® 2008
## BASICS
## A Layered Learning Approach

**Gary Koser, P.E.**

*Indian River Community College*

**Dean Zirwas**

*Indian River Community College*

PEARSON

Prentice
Hall

Upper Saddle River, New Jersey
Columbus, Ohio

Library of Congress Control Number: 2007921361

T
385
K67
2008

**Editor in Chief:** Vernon R. Anthony
**Acquisitions Editor:** Jill Jones-Renger
**Editorial Assistant:** Yvette Schlarman
**Development Editor:** Karen Fortgang, bookworks publishing services
**Production Editor:** Louise N. Sette
**Production Supervision:** Karen Fortgang, bookworks publishing services
**Design Coordinator:** Diane Ernsberger
**Art Coordinator:** Janet Portisch
**Cover Designer:** Jason Moore
**Production Manager:** Deidra M. Schwartz
**Director of Marketing:** David Gesell
**Marketing Manager:** Jimmy Stephens
**Marketing Coordinator:** Alicia Dysert

This book was set by Aptara, Inc. It was printed and bound by Bind-Rite Graphics. The cover was printed by Coral Graphic Services, Inc.

Certain images and materials contained in this publication were reproduced with the permission of Autodesk, Inc. © 2007. All rights reserved. Autodesk and AutoCAD are registered trademarks of Autodesk, Inc., in the U.S.A. and certain other countries.

**Disclaimer:**
The publication is designed to provide tutorial information about AutoCAD® and/or other Autodesk computer programs. Every effort has been made to make this publication complete and as accurate as possible. The reader is expressly cautioned to use any and all precautions necessary, and to take appropriate steps to avoid hazards, when engaging in the activities described herein.

Neither the author nor the publisher makes any representations or warranties of any kind, with respect to the materials set forth in this publication, express or implied, including without limitation any warranties of fitness for a particular purpose or merchantability. Nor shall the author or the publisher be liable for any special, consequential or exemplary damages resulting, in whole or in part, directly or indirectly, from the reader's use of, or reliance upon, this material or subsequent revisions of this material.

Pearson Education Ltd.
Pearson Education Singapore Pte. Ltd.
Pearson Education Canada, Ltd.
Pearson Education—Japan

Pearson Education Australia Pty. Limited
Pearson Education North Asia Ltd.
Pearson Educación de Mexico, S.A. de C.V.
Pearson Education Malaysia Pte. Ltd.

PEARSON
Prentice
Hall

10 9 8 7 6 5 4 3 2 1
ISBN-13: 978-0-13-612701-7
ISBN-10:    0-13-612701-0

From Gary with Love, Honor, and Thankfulness to
Katrina, Cheryl, Larry, and Grace

From Dean with Love and Thankfulness to
Jackie, Taylor, Elliot, and Rylee

# THE NEW AUTODESK DESIGN INSTITUTE PRESS SERIES————

Pearson/Prentice Hall has formed an alliance with Autodesk® to develop textbooks and other course materials that address the skills, methodology, and learning pedagogy for the industries that are supported by the Autodesk® Design Institute (ADI) software products. The Autodesk Design Institute is a comprehensive software program that assists educators in teaching technological design.

## Features of the Autodesk Design Institute Press Series

**JOB SKILLS**—Coverage of computer-aided drafting job skills, compiled through research of industry associations, job websites, college course descriptions, and the Occupational Information Network database, has been integrated throughout the ADI Press books.

**PROFESSIONAL** and **INDUSTRY ASSOCIATION INVOLVEMENT**—These books are written in consultation with and reviewed by professional associations to ensure they meet the needs of industry employers.

**AUTODESK LEARNING LICENSES AVAILABLE**—Many students ask how they can get a copy of the AutoCAD® software for their home computer. Through a recent agreement with Autodesk®, Prentice Hall now offers the option of purchasing textbooks with either a 180-day or a 1-year student software license agreement for AutoCAD. This provides adequate time for a student to complete all the activities in the book. The software is functionally identical to the professional license, but is intended for student personal use only. It is not for professional use.

For more information about this book and the Autodesk Student Portfolio, contact your local Pearson Prentice Hall sales representative, or contact our National Marketing Manager, Jimmy Stephens, at 1(800)228-7854 x3725 or at Jimmy_Stephens@prenhall.com. For the name and number of your sales rep, please contact Prentice Hall Faculty Services at 1(800)526-0485.

This text presents a layered learning approach to using AutoCAD. That is, it is designed around a concept of layering the simple fundamental information used to create basic drawings, and then revisiting topics through project-based learning while increasing the difficulty of the drawings being created. Rather than discussing all commands in a sequence, this book uses a "Draw-Modify-Dimension-Print" cycle.

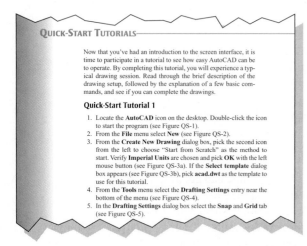

A "Quick-Start" section at the beginning of the book allows users to get up to speed in no time to create AutoCAD drawings.

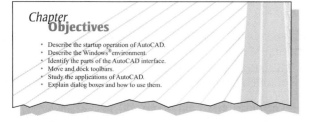

Chapter Objectives, a bulleted list of learning objectives for each unit, provide users with a roadmap of important concepts and practices that will be introduced in the unit.

Key Terms are boldfaced and italicized within the running text, briefly defined in the margin, and defined in more detail in the Glossary at the end of the book to help students understand and use the language of the computer-aided drafting world.

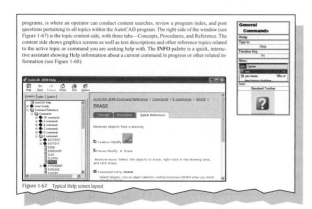

Figure 1-67  Typical Help screen layout

Command Grids appear in the margin, alongside the discussion of the command. These grids provide a visual of the action options using the Toolbar, Pull-Down Menu, Command Line, or Command Alias, ensuring that the student is in the right place at the right time and correctly following the authors' direction.

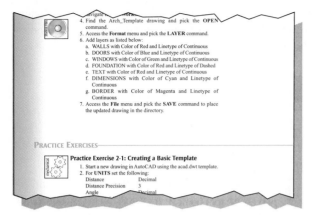

4. Navigate to... work
4. Find the Arch_Template drawing and pick the **OPEN** command.
5. Access the **Format** menu and pick the **LAYER** command.
6. Add layers as listed below:
   a. WALLS with Color of Red and Linetype of Continuous
   b. DOORS with Color of Blue and Linetype of Continuous
   c. WINDOWS with Color of Green and Linetype of Continuous
   d. FOUNDATION with Color of Red and Linetype of Dashed
   e. TEXT with Color of Red and Linetype of Continuous
   f. DIMENSIONS with Color of Cyan and Linetype of Continuous
   g. BORDER with Color of Magenta and Linetype of Continuous
7. Access the **File** menu and pick the **SAVE** command to place the updated drawing in the directory.

**PRACTICE EXERCISES**

**Practice Exercise 2-1: Creating a Basic Template**
1. Start a new drawing in AutoCAD using the acad.dwt template.
2. For **UNITS** set the following:
   Distance            Decimal
   Distance Precision  3
   Angle               Decimal

**Discipline Icons**, placed in the margin alongside Tutorials and Practice Exercises, identify the discipline to which the exercise applies. These icons allow instructors to quickly identify homework assignments that will appeal to the varying interests of their students and give students the opportunity to work on projects that have the most interest and relevance to their course of study.

---

**Drawing Status Bar**

The drawing status bar is located on the right end of the status bar. This area has a series of icons used to control the drawing's **Scale Annotations** (Figure 1-59).

In AutoCAD 2008, annotations can be scaled automatically for various layout viewports as well as model space. When annotation objects are created, they are scaled to the active annotation scale. This will size all the entities to the proper relationship for that viewport. The icons in the drawing status bar will turn automatic scaling on or off. You will be able to set the annotation scale and the visibility of the annotation objects. Other icons in this area lock the positions of the toolbars and

**A New to AutoCAD 2008** icon flags features that are new to the 2008 version of the Auto-CAD software, creating a quick "study guide" for instructors who need to familiarize themselves with the newest features of the software to prepare for teaching the course.

---

When a toolbar is in a floating mode, its shape can be reconfigured, based on the number of icons on the toolbar (see Figures 1-43 and 1-44). To dock a floating toolbar, grab the blue title bar with the left mouse button depressed and drag it to where you wish to dock it. When the toolbar gets to the docked location the ghost image of the toolbar will change shape, at which time you will let go of the mouse button and dock the toolbar in that location. Toolbars provide a faster way of executing frequently used commands. There is a learning curve required to identify which picture or icon will execute which commands, but once you are familiar with the program, you will become adept at executing commands using the toolbars.

**Note:**
For the novice user, it may be beneficial to use the pull-down menus to execute commands initially. This will familiarize you with the organization of commands built into the software.

Figure 1-43   AutoCAD toolbar as a single row

Figure 1-44   AutoCAD toolbar as a double row

**Drawing Area and Scroll Bars**

drawing area: The large center area of the screen where the drawing is created.

The next area of the interface is the largest. This black (or white) window is known as the *drawing area.* This is where you will develop your drawings. The background color is black as the default (see Figure 1-45), but this can easily be changed to any color you desire by accessing the **Screen Display** tab of the **OPTIONS** command.

**FOR MORE DETAIL**   The drawing area may at times contain tool palettes with blocks for inserting, commands for certain operations, hatch patterns, and entity properties for modifications. These palettes are discussed in Unit 11.

**Note** and **For More Detail** boxes highlight additional helpful information for the student as tips, warnings, or higher-level references.

---

The size of the drawing area is established in units and based on the template chosen. On the initial startup the size of the area is 12 units by 9 units. You can adjust this area to equal any size required to create your drawings in full-size units or at full size.

All drawings created in a CAD world are full size. The traditional drafting scale is applied during the creation of layout space for printing purposes.

It is not uncommon to have a drawing area of 100′ × 150′, 24″ × 18″, or 3 km × 2 km. These sizes might be used to represent af small, single-family, residential lot, a part in an airplane, or a subdivision. The physical size of the window itself does not change. A user can adjust the **Drawing LIMITS** to control the value, in specific units of measurement, to have the drawing area represent an area large enough to handle the design at a full scale. When working with larger

**Job Skills** boxes relate specific unit content to the job skills necessary for success in the workplace.

---

**CHAPTER TEST QUESTIONS**

**Multiple Choice**
1. An arrow to the right of an entry in the pull-down menu means
   a. Window to follow
   b. Cascading menu to follow
   c. Command execution
   d. Dialog box to follow
   c. Delete
   d. Enter

2. What does the ellipsis to the right of an entry in the pull-down menu mean?
   a. Window to follow
   b. Cascading menu to follow
   c. Command execution
   d. Dialog box to follow

3. The Space bar in the AutoCAD program will act as another ___ key.

4. To stop or cancel a command in AutoCAD press the ___ key.
   a. Cancel
   b. Escape
   c. Delete
   d. Enter

5. The double grab bar on the side of a tool ___ a toolbar.
   a. Float
   b. Close
   c. Dock
   d. Delete

**End-of-unit** material, easily located by shading on page edges, includes:

- Tutorials
- Practice Exercises
- Chapter Test Questions
- Chapter Projects

to help students check their own understanding of important unit concepts.

**Exercises** placed throughout the units provide step-by-step walk-through activities for the student, allowing immediate practice and reinforcement of newly learned skills.

**Chapter Projects** are contextual projects and additional research-type questions for extra credit or for use as additional assignments at the end of the unit.

**CD icons** in the margins alongside Exercises, Practice Exercises, and Tutorials direct students to the Student Data Files on the CD bound into the textbook.

# Preface

## From the Authors

Helping learners to become productive quickly within a 2D drawing environment is the primary goal of *Workplace Skills for Success with AutoCAD® 2008: BASICS*. We use a layering approach in this text, first orienting the learner to the commands needed to complete fundamental drawings successfully, and then gradually increasing the difficulty of the drawings being created through project-based learning. Instead of presenting all commands in a sequence, this text is designed around the "Draw-Modify-Dimension-Print" cycle.

This text is designed for a typical semester of instructor presentation and drawing lab time. By limiting the drawing lab time, instructors can complete each unit in one week. Expanding the coverage with contextual projects can fill a traditional semester term. Each unit consists of command content and presentation materials, as well as drawing activities and projects. Discipline-oriented practice activities are placed in each appropriate unit, emphasizing the unit's content. These practice tasks and activities are from the three major computer-aided drafting disciplines: architectural, mechanical, and civil. This gives the instructor and students a variety of project-based exercises to show application of the unit's content.

Various methods are used to reinforce the concepts and skills. In some cases, an immediate tutorial or exercise is used. For more complicated concepts, a higher-level tutorial is presented. In many units, practice exercises offer learners an additional chance to practice their skills.

Through this layered-learning approach, learners build a foundation of skills based on a logical sequence and repetition, driven toward the end results of developing workplace skills and creating industry-style drawings in a timely fashion.

## Features of This Text

- Words shown in ***bold italic*** are key terms the learner should know.
- **Note** boxes present hints, tips, and tricks to enhance productivity.
- **For More Detail** boxes provide a higher level of information to use as background, reference, or research.
- **Exercise** items are quick tutorials to show a command or present a concept.
- **Tutorials** are either generic or discipline-specific. Disciplines include mechanical engineering, architectural, and civil engineering.
- **Practice Exercises** are learner-oriented with minimal instructions. Some are discipline-specific as noted above.
- **Chapter Test Questions** include Multiple Choice, Matching, and True or False questions.
- **Chapter Projects** are contextual and may involve research. They may also be assigned by the instructor for different learning styles or for extra credit.
- **Job Skills** icons appear alongside material that relates specific chapter content to the job skill necessary for success in the workplace.

## Recommended Learning Path

We recommend that learners use the following method:

- Read the overview section and give particular attention to unit objectives.
- Listen to the instructor's presentation about the topics in the unit.
- Participate in class discussions.
- Work through the **Exercises** carefully.
- Complete the **Practice Exercises** and **Tutorials** with an awareness of ways to increase productivity.

- Answer the **Chapter Test Questions** and verify the answers using AutoCAD.
- Read and use your text materials to apply the **Chapter Projects** and other references provided by your instructor.
- Present additional examples of the concepts learned to your class.

## Instructor Resources

The Online Instructor's Manual provides answers to unit exercises and tests and solutions to end-of-unit problems; drawing files to get learners started; and lecture-supporting PowerPoint® slides.

To access supplementary materials online, instructors need to request an instructor access code. Go to **www.prenhall.com,** click the **Instructor Resource Center** link, and then click **Register Today** for an instructor access code. Within 48 hours after registering you will receive a confirming email including an instructor access code. Once you have received your code, go to the site and log on for full instructions on downloading the materials you wish to use.

OneKey—All instructor and student online course materials for this book are delivered in one Web-based course system—OneKey.

OneKey Blackboard—Prentice Hall's online content, combined with Blackboard's popular tools and interface, result in robust Web-based courses that are easy to implement, manage, and use—taking your courses to new heights in student interaction and learning.

OneKey WebCT—Course-management tools within WebCT include page tracking, progress tracking, class and student management, gradebook, communication, calendar, reporting tools, and more. Gold Level Customer Support, available exclusively to adopters of Prentice Hall courses, is provided free of charge on adoption and provides you with priority assistance, training discounts, and dedicated technical support.

## Student Resources

Companion Website—A Companion Website at **www.prenhall.com/koser** includes an interactive study guide.

## Acknowledgments

We want to thank the individuals whose contributions helped shape this textbook.

Chris Chamberlain
Delaware Technical and Community College, DE

James Freygang
Ivy Tech Community College, IN

Jerry M. Gray
West Georgia Technical College, GA

Dorothy Gerring
Pennsylvania College of Technology, PA

DeDe Griffith
Lee College, TX

JoBeth Halpin
Triton College, IL

Carol Hoffman
The University of Alabama, AL

Paul Lekang
North Dakota State College of Science, ND

Philip A. Leverault
Milwaukee Area Technical College, WI

Seymour Rosenfeld
Westchester Community College, NY

James Kevin Standiford
Arkansas State University, AR

Mel L. Whiteside
Butler Community College, KS

## Supplements

**PowerPoint Presentation**
Craig Stinchcomb
Terra Community College, OH

**Companion Website**
Craig Stinchcomb
Terra Community College, OH

**BlackBoard/WebCT**
Craig Stinchcomb
Terra Community College, OH

## Reviewers

David A. Probst
Pennsylvania College of Technology

Randal Reid
Chattahoochee Technical College

Katherine Spencer
Design Institute of San Diego

Ken Stupka
Wharton County Junior College

Michael (Fox) Sutton
Art Institute of California-San Diego

Gerald E. Vinson
Texas A & M University

| Text Element | Example |
|---|---|
| **Key terms**—Boldface and italic on first mention (first letter lowercase, as it appears in the body of the text). Brief definition in margin alongside first mention. Full definition in Glossary at back of book. | Views are created by placing ***viewport*** objects in the paper space layout. |
| **AutoCAD commands**—Bold and uppercase | Start the **LINE** command. |
| **Toolbar names, menu items, and dialog box names**—Bold and follow capitalization convention in AutoCAD toolbar or the menu (generally first letter capitalized). | The **Layer Manager** dialog box<br><br>The **File** menu |
| **Toolbar buttons and dialog box controls/ buttons/input items**—Bold and follow the name of the item or the name shown in the AutoCAD tooltip. | Choose the **Line** tool from the **Draw** toolbar.<br><br>Choose the **Symbols and Arrows** tab in the **Modify Dimension Style** dialog box.<br><br>Choose the **New Layer** button in the **Layer Properties Manager** dialog box.<br><br>In the **Lines and Arrows** tab, set the **Arrow size:** to **.125.** |
| **AutoCAD prompts**—Dynamic input prompts are italic. Command window prompts use a different font (Courier New). This makes them look like the text in the command window. Prompts follow capitalization convention in AutoCAD prompt (generally first letter capitalized). | AutoCAD prompts you to *Specify first point:*<br><br>`Specify center point for circle or [3P/2P/Ttr (tan tan radius)]:` |
| **Keyboard input**—Bold with special keys in brackets. | Type **3.5 <Enter ↵>.** |

# Contents

# AutoCAD Introduction and Overview

## Chapter Objectives

- Describe the startup operation of AutoCAD.
- Describe the Windows® environment.
- Identify the parts of the AutoCAD interface.
- Move and dock toolbars.
- Study the applications of AutoCAD.
- Explain dialog boxes and how to use them.

## INTRODUCTION

This book was developed to provide a basic understanding of the drawing process using *computer-aided drafting (CAD)* systems.

**computer-aided drafting (CAD):** The process of producing engineering documentation through a computer.

## THE WORLD OF AUTOCAD

Over the past 30 years the continued development of computer-aided drafting systems has made CAD a major component in the design and drafting process. According to Daratech, Inc., a research firm on computer trends and policies, currently over 70 percent of all engineered drawings are produced by AutoCAD systems. Future CAD enhancements and integration are expected to increase the CAD influence in all aspects of designing, building, managing, and communicating. Every year CAD systems add more design capabilities, are reduced in cost, become more integrated to production, and increasingly use the Internet to communicate design.

Computer-aided drafting and design (CADD) systems are being used extensively in many fields, including architectural engineering (see Figure 1-1); mechanical engineering (see Figure 1-2); civil engineering and surveying, landscape, architecture (see Figure 1-3), and the environment; structural engineering (see Figure 1-4); utility and infrastructure design; and manufacturing. Basically, any industry that uses a drawing is using CAD or CADD systems.

This book focuses on the initial drawing commands and the accurate placement of drawing entities. Since most of the CAD/CADD systems around the world are based on the product called AutoCAD® that was developed and is distributed by Autodesk®, Inc., this book will use AutoCAD as its base. Knowledge of AutoCAD drawing commands should be useful for other CAD systems that provide similar methods and techniques needed for precise work.

It is the authors' hope that students will gain a basic knowledge in using these accurate drawing methods and be able to apply this knowledge to other drawings in other disciplines.

**Figure 1-1**    Office building in layout space

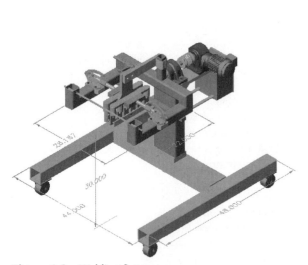

**Figure 1-2**    Welding fixture

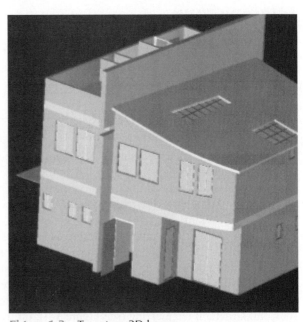

**Figure 1-3**    Two-story 3D house

## INDUSTRY USES OF AUTOCAD

The following are typical scenarios of CAD projects and drawings for your information and as an introduction to the possible uses of computer-aided drafting and design.

### Scenario 1—Architecture

You work for an architectural engineering consulting firm that is to draw a new office building in your area (see Figures 1-5 and 1-6). The architect has determined the basic dimensions of the

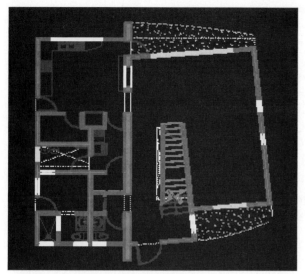

Figure 1-4    Two-story house floor plan

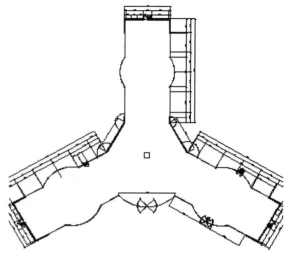

Figure 1-5    Office building floor plan

building and located the stairs, elevators, and office space. You must draw this plan accurately and quickly. As you look at the building layout, the symmetry shows that drawing one wing and arraying it around the center of the building will speed production. Using CAD makes it possible to draw the building in a few hours and create a 3D model for rendering.

## Scenario 2—Civil Engineering

You work for the department of transportation. Your task is to draw a new road along the river. The survey crew has completed the topographic survey shown in Figure 1-7 using radial methods. Therefore, you have a file of angles and distances to each survey point. You must locate the points accurately for a proper design. Using the CAD system with units set for Surveyors, you enter the bearings and distances to create the points. The Civil software, based on the points, develops a Triangular Irregular Net, which leads to the creation of the contours. The contours show points of equal elevation and aid in the placement of the road, intersections, and drainage (see Figure 1-8).

Figure 1-6    Office building rendering by Autodesk 3D VIZ

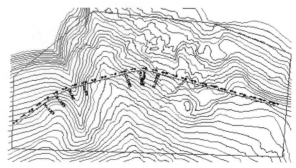

Figure 1-7    Civil engineering contours

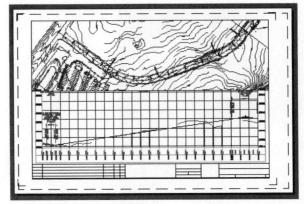

**Figure 1-8**  Civil engineering street design

## Scenario 3—Landscape Design

You work for a landscaping firm and are to design a playground in an existing park (see Figures 1-9 and 1-10). The park authority has given you information based on state plane coordinates (an absolute coordinate system that links to the Geographic Information System). Your work must result in a file that can be imported into the GIS and can be used by the construction company.

**Figure 1-9**  Landscape plan

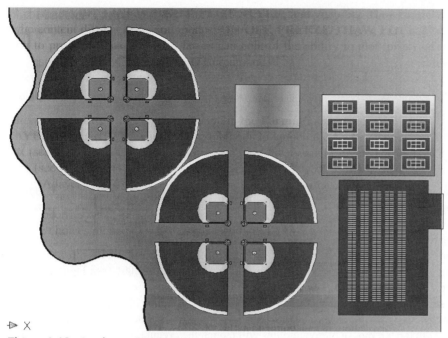

Figure 1-10    Landscape 3D view

## Scenario Four—Mechanical Engineering

You work for an industrial design development firm. Your client is applying for a patent on a toll road wireless transponder (see Figure 1-11). The client has given you an artist's sketch of the object and has requested a physical 3D model. Your office must develop the 3D model and extract the 2D production drawings for the patent application. Your model must be a compatible file to be printed with a 3D Rapid Prototyping printer.

Figure 1-11    View of proposed case

## AutoCAD and the Windows Environment

As is most software today, AutoCAD *software* is based on Microsoft® Windows®. Windows has supported AutoCAD through several versions of its *operating system,* with the most current version of the Windows operating system being the common platform. Because of this, a solid working knowledge of a Windows program such as Microsoft® Word, Excel®, or PowerPoint® is helpful. Though this is not required, you will increase your knowledge of your Windows operating system by running AutoCAD software. If you feel your knowledge of Windows is limited, consider taking an entry-level Windows operating class at a local community college or technical center. All file management actions such as **NEW, OPEN, SAVE, SAVE**

software: Programs that control the operations of a computer and its peripherals.

operating system: The code that runs all commands for the computer system.

file management: The process of saving, copying, moving, and deleting the files produced by a computer system.

directory: A listing of files.

**Figure 1-12**   XP Start button

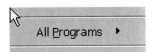

**Figure 1-13**   All Programs menu

icon: A small picture used to launch a command.

desktop: The initial screen of a Windows operating system.

**Figure 1-14**   Autodesk submenu

AutoCAD

**Figure 1-15**   AutoCAD desktop icon

**AS,** and **CLOSE** work as typical Windows-based commands. This is also true for edit action commands such as **CUT, COPY, PASTE, MATCHPROP,** and so on. This means that any experience you have from current or previous versions of Windows will help in your *file management* procedures.

From launching the program to printing drawing files, you will find the experience of navigating the *directory* structure on your hard disk and managing files similar to other programs you have already used.

## STARTING AUTOCAD

After successfully installing the AutoCAD software, you will have two basic options to launch the program and start a drawing session. The first method to start the software is through the traditional programs menu in the corner of the Windows environment. With the left mouse button pick the **Start** button (see Figure 1-12). Next you pick the **All Programs** (see Figure 1-13) selection and look for the **Autodesk/AutoCAD** listing. After picking the **Autodesk** group, you will have one more cascading menu from which you pick **AutoCAD 2008** (see Figure 1-14). The previous selections are made with a left mouse button click.

A second method to launch the program is to use the *icon* placed on the Windows *desktop* through the installation procedure. Locate the icon that looks similar to Figure 1-15. Double-click on the icon with the left mouse button and this will launch the executable file to start the program. Both methods will take you to the same place—a new drawing session within the AutoCAD environment.

## AUTOCAD INTERFACE

Upon beginning an AutoCAD session, you may find the screen interface a bit overwhelming. There can be several different looks to the interface depending on how the last user left the program. AutoCAD will open up based on the settings of the last user's session or on an AutoCAD workspace.

### AutoCAD Workspaces

Over the years various forms of the interface have been created and used based on commands such as **PREFERENCES, OPTIONS,** and currently **WORKSPACE.** The Windows environment as well stores the current interface, set up as Profiles. You can also use these commands to customize the interface for your particular style and application. These commands are presented in Unit 11 of this book.

Upon entering AutoCAD 2008 for the first time the interface will appear with a perspective viewpoint and two command panels (see Figure 1-17). This book is based on the AutoCAD Classic Workspace as defined in AutoCAD 2008 software and shown in Figure 1-16. This basic look has been the same for many previous versions of AutoCAD. This gives you the best chance to understand and use any release of AutoCAD.

If the AutoCAD interface does not match Figure 1-16, access the **WORKSPACE** command (see Figures 1-18 and 1-19) and choose the **AutoCAD Classic** option. This will change the interface to look similar to Figure 1-16 with the **Sheet Manager** and **Tools Palettes.** You can turn off these palettes by picking the **x** in the top area of the palette's title bar.

If the screen still shows a 3D perspective view, access the **View** menu and use the **3D Views** options to change to a **Top** view (see Figure 1-20). If the grid lines are still present, access the **View** menu and use the **Visual Styles** options to change to a **2D Wireframe** style (see Figure 1-21). This should result in the AutoCAD Classic screen used as the basis in the following sections.

### Identification of Interface Areas

The interface can be divided into several subareas or windows.

New to 2008 is a workspace called **2D Drafting & Annotation** (Figure 1-22). This new workspace is geared toward the 2D drafting and annotation process. It utilizes a dashboard component that can have a variety of control panels strictly related to the 2D environment.

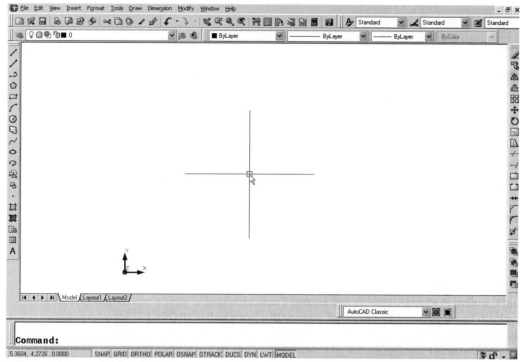

**Figure 1-16**    AutoCAD basic screen

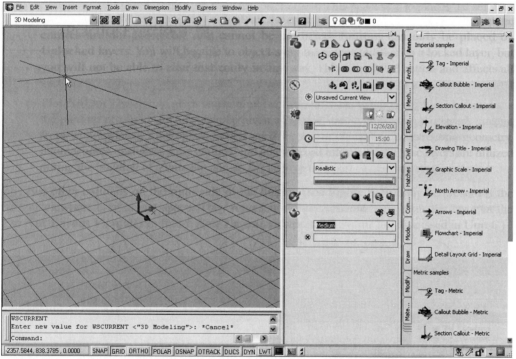

**Figure 1-17**    The typical AutoCAD 3D modeling workspace showing the dashboard and tool palette on the right and 3D perspective view window on the left

## The Dashboard

The ***dashboard*** related to the 2D Drafting & Annotation workspace (Figure 1-23) contains a set of control panels that are organized by commands. These panels are completely customizable allowing the arrangement of the dashboard to match your preferences. A right click on any area of the dashboard will bring up a context-sensitive menu with a **Control panels** option (Figure 1-24).

dashboard: The dashboard is a palette of command icons organized by specific tasks connected to the 3D modeling workspace.

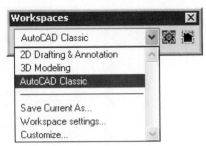

**Figure 1-18**   Workspace drop-down to change workspace

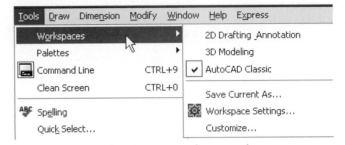

**Figure 1-19**   Workspace menu to change workspace

**Figure 1-20**   The View menu to modify to the Top view

**Figure 1-21**   The View menu for the 2D Wireframe Visual Styles

This menu selection will list the control panels available. The check marks represent the control panels currently on the dashboard (Figure 1-25).

Several panels have an expanded panel that becomes visible with additional information when working within the active control panel. As with tool palettes, the dashboard can be docked on the left or right side of the screen. When you are ready to use the control panel, all you need to do is click on the control panel's title bar and the panel will expand showing the slide-out portion of the panel that will contain additional commands. If you click on the icon for the panel, you will activate that panel and display an additional tab-based menu to the right of the dashboard.

### Title Bar

At the top of the screen is a windows bar (typically blue) known as the title bar indicating that you are in the AutoCAD program (see Figure 1-26). On the left side of this top bar, the name of the current file is listed in brackets. The file location may precede the name. On the right side of this title bar there are three icons typical of the Windows environment. These icons are

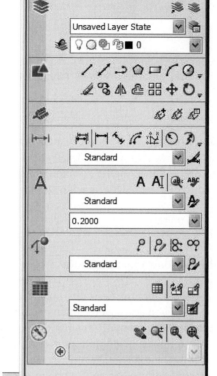

**Figure 1-23**   The dashboard for the 2D Drafting Workspace

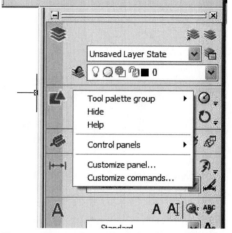

**Figure 1-24**   The right-click menu on the dashboard

**Figure 1-22**   Workspace drop-down showing new workspace for 2D Drafting and Annotation

**Figure 1-25**   Menu showing control panel options for the dashboard

**Figure 1-26**   AutoCAD title bar, left side

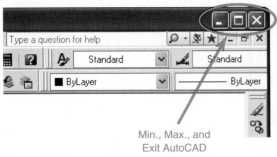

Min., Max., and
Exit AutoCAD

**Figure 1-27**    AutoCAD title bar, right side

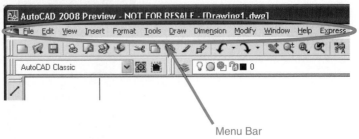

Menu Bar

**Figure 1-28**    Typical AutoCAD menu bar

used to **Minimize, Maximize,** and **Exit,** respectively, the AutoCAD software (see Figure 1-27). You can change the AutoCAD window to any size by pulling the edges of the current window. The first two buttons aid in sizing the window quickly, and the third exits the program. If drawings have been edited, AutoCAD will request confirmation to save changes before closing the software.

## Menu Bar

**Figure 1-29**    Draw menu

This contains the pull-down menus for the program. Each word represents a file folder and a series of commands.

When you make a selection from this menu bar (see Figure 1-28) a menu will drop down, exposing a series of related commands, submenus, and dialog boxes. The most used commands and options can be found in the pull-down menus. Beginning users will need to get used to the organization of the command within the pull-down menu areas. This familiarity will come with experience but at this point in the learning curve, new users should merely become acquainted with a few graphical features in the pull-down menus.

First, notice how the placement of the toolbar icons in the menus shown helps you connect each icon to the corresponding command. (This was new in the 2006 version.)

As you look at a pull-down menu such as the **Draw** menu in Figure 1-29, you will see several small black triangles. Each triangle indicates that there is a submenu known as a cascading menu (see Figure 1-30). You must make a selection from the menu that cascades out to the right (or left, depending on screen position) of the original selection. The actual commands are located on the last menu. Any text to the left (or right) of the last menu is considered organizational and not an actual command.

A second graphical feature is an *ellipsis,* a series of three periods following a word (see Figure 1-31). This symbol indicates a dialog box related to the command selected.

*Dialog boxes* appear as floating windows on the screen (see Figure 1-32). You need to address the information in the dialog box and either accept or cancel the dialog before you will have access to the main program interface again. Dialog boxes allow you to randomly input information related to the command chosen, and in some cases, preview what would be the results of the input prior to accepting the change. We will present more information on the various fields within a dialog box later in this unit.

At the right side of the menu bar there is a second set of the Windows **Minimum, Maximum,** and **Close** icons (see Figure 1-33). This set of buttons is for the individual drawing file you have open during the current drawing session. When using AutoCAD you can have multiple drawing files open at a single time. This set of buttons will help you navigate through multiple open drawing files.

## InfoCenter

In the upper right corner of the menu bar you will find a feature new to AutoCAD 2008. This area is known as **InfoCenter** (Figure 1-34).

This area gives you several options to access help-related topics. You obtain help by selecting the **Search** icon and typing in your question. The program will then search multiple locations for your answer and display them as links for you to choose the type of help you are looking

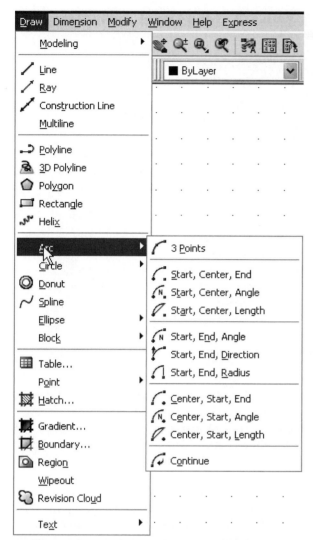

**Figure 1-30**    Draw menu with cascading menu

**Figure 1-31**    Draw menu with ellipsis

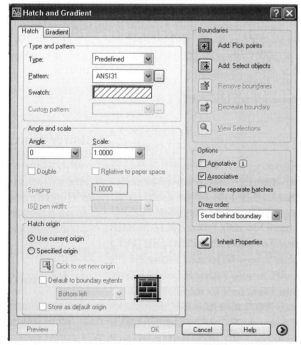

**Figure 1-32**    Hatch and Gradient dialog box

Min., Max., and
Exit Drawing

**Figure 1-33**    Draw Session
Upper Right Icons

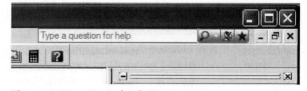

**Figure 1-34**    Typical InfoCenter area

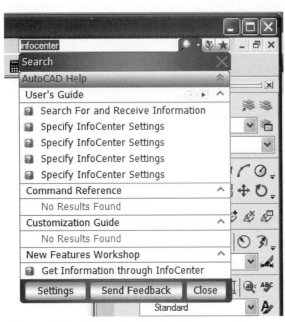

Figure 1-35   InfoCenter showing search results

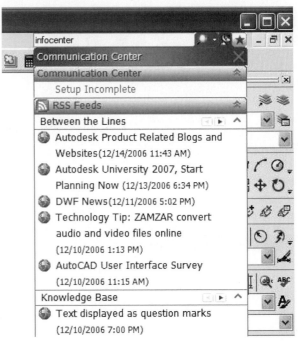

Figure 1-36   InfoCenter showing communication option

for (Figure 1-35). Answers may come from several locations such as the command reference guide, the customization guide, or the user reference guide.

The next item on the menu bar is a **Communication Center** icon (satellite dish), which will list a variety of announcements from several locations related to product updates and subscription programs along with articles and tips on productivity and knowledge-based command enhancements (Figure 1-36).

The final item on the **InfoCenter** menu bar is an icon (star) that accesses the **Favorites**, a location similar to the Favorites list of any Web browser. This is the area in which you save topics that you want to revisit. You can add links to the **Favorites** from the **Communication Center** by clicking on the star icon to the right of the help topic. This will place the link in the **Favorites** list under the appropriate area based on where it comes from (Figure 1-37).

## Toolbars

toolbar:  A collection of icons representing various commands or operations.

***Toolbars,*** located below the menu bar, show a series of icons, representing AutoCAD commands or operations (see Figures 1-38, 1-39, and 1-40). You can select one of these icons with a left mouse

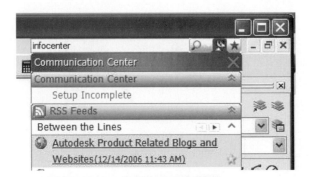

Figure 1-37   InfoCenter saving information

Figure 1-38   AutoCAD Standard, Layers, Properties, and Style toolbars

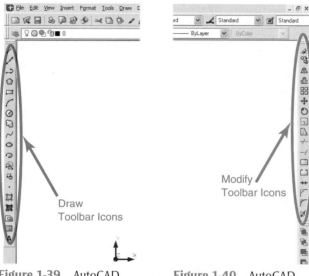

**Figure 1-39** AutoCAD Draw toolbar, on left screen

**Figure 1-40** AutoCAD Modify toolbar, on right screen

button and the program will execute the AutoCAD command related to that icon. AutoCAD 2008 has over 30 predefined toolbars available. The initial startup screen shows six. Four are located at the top of the screen, with the other two on the left and the right side of the drawing area. Each of these toolbars is organized with similar commands common to the title of the toolbar. Unlike the pull-down menu, not all commands can be found on a toolbar and you have the option of what toolbars you want displayed, and at what location. Toolbars can be docked on any of the four sides of the screen, or they may be left undocked, or floating around the drawing area (see Figure 1-41). Each docked toolbar has a double bar located on the left edge known as a grab bar (see Figure 1-42). Selecting this grab bar while holding down the left mouse button and using a dragging motion will allow the user to undock a toolbar, changing the toolbar's status from docked to floating.

**FOR MORE DETAIL**    For more on the docking of toolbars see the video in the Companion Website.

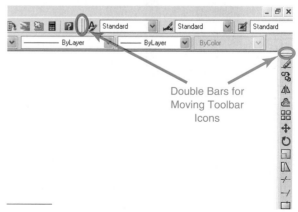

Double Bars for Moving Toolbar Icons

**Figure 1-41** AutoCAD toolbar undocked (floating)

**Figure 1-42** AutoCAD toolbar docked with grab bar area highlighted

When a toolbar is in a floating mode, its shape can be reconfigured, based on the number of icons on the toolbar (see Figures 1-43 and 1-44). To dock a floating toolbar, grab the blue title bar with the left mouse button depressed and drag it to where you wish to dock it. When the toolbar gets to the docked location the ghost image of the toolbar will change shape, at which time you will let go of the mouse button and dock the toolbar in that location. Toolbars provide a faster way of executing frequently used commands. There is a learning curve required to identify which picture or icon will execute which commands, but once you are familiar with the program, you will become adept at executing commands using the toolbars.

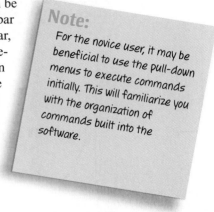

**Note:** For the novice user, it may be beneficial to use the pull-down menus to execute commands initially. This will familiarize you with the organization of commands built into the software.

**Figure 1-43**    AutoCAD toolbar as a single row

**Figure 1-44**    AutoCAD toolbar as a double row

## Drawing Area and Scroll Bars

drawing area: The large center area of the screen where the drawing is created.

The next area of the interface is the largest. This black (or white) window is known as the ***drawing area.*** This is where you will develop your drawings. The background color is black as the default (see Figure 1-45), but this can easily be changed to any color you desire by accessing the **Screen Display** tab of the **OPTIONS** command.

**FOR MORE DETAIL**    The drawing area may at times contain tool palettes with blocks for inserting, commands for certain operations, hatch patterns, and entity properties for modifications. These palettes are discussed in Unit 11.

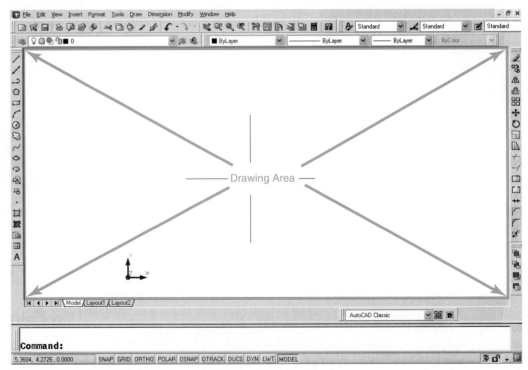

**Figure 1-45**    AutoCAD drawing area in white

The size of the drawing area is established in units and based on the template chosen. On the initial startup the size of the area is 12 units by 9 units. You can adjust this area to equal any size required to create your drawings in full-size units or at full size.

All drawings created in a CAD world are full size. The traditional drafting scale is applied during the creation of layout space for printing purposes.

It is not uncommon to have a drawing area of 100′ × 150′, 24″ × 18″, or 3 km × 2 km. These sizes might be used to represent af small, single-family, residential lot, a part in an airplane, or a subdivision. The physical size of the window itself does not change. A user can adjust the **Drawing LIMITS** to control the value, in specific units of measurement, to have the drawing area represent an area large enough to handle the design at a full scale. When working with larger values for your drawing limits, you will need to use a series of viewing commands such as **ZOOM** and **PAN** to manipulate the view within the drawing area window.

Along the right side and the bottom of the drawing window are two slider boxes known as *scroll bars* (see Figure 1-46). You can slide the screen left or right or up and down by clicking on the arrows within the scroll bar boxes.

The drawing area can also display two visual drawing aids. Using the **GRID** command, you can turn on a *grid*. In AutoCAD 2006 and earlier versions this is a series of equally spaced

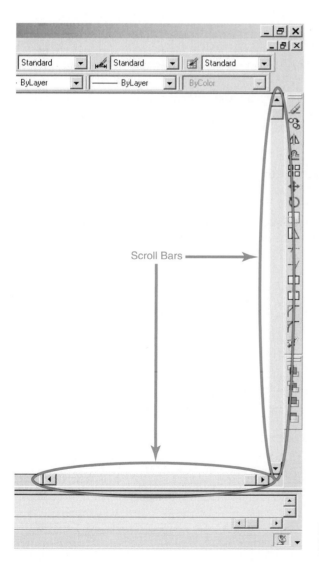

**Figure 1-46**   AutoCAD drawing area highlighting the scroll bars

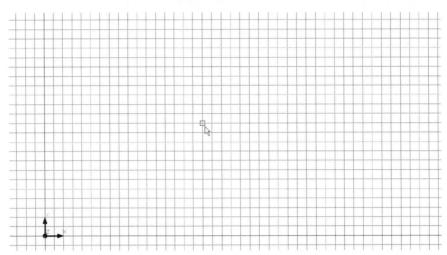

**Figure 1-47**    AutoCAD drawing area with grid

dots. In AutoCAD 2007 it is shown as grid lines (see Figure 1-47). Then, located in the lower left corner of the drawing area is the ***user coordinate system (UCS) icon*** (see Figure 1-48). The **UCSICON** command gives information related to 3D space orientation and coordinate input. Both of these drawing aids are invisible to the plotting process, which means they do not print.

### Model Space and Layout Space Tabs

Directly below the drawing area, to the lower left of the screen, there are three buttons used to switch between *model space* and *layout* or *paper space* (see Figure 1-49). *Model space* refers to the space where a drawing or design is created; *layout space* controls the views of a drawing or design for the production of printed pages.

### Command Line

The ***command line*** is typically located below the drawing area (see Figure 1-50). Its function is to communicate with the user through questions and statements based on the commands currently active, and it is much like a toolbar.

Its default location is below the drawing area, but like toolbars, it can be undocked to a floating style or repositioned somewhere else on the edges of the drawing area (see Figure 1-51).

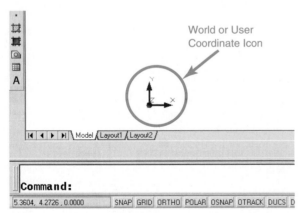

**Figure 1-48**    AutoCAD drawing area with coordinate system icon

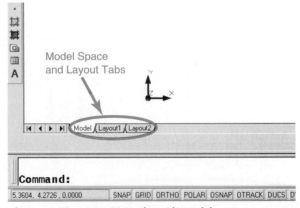

**Figure 1-49**    AutoCAD tabs with model

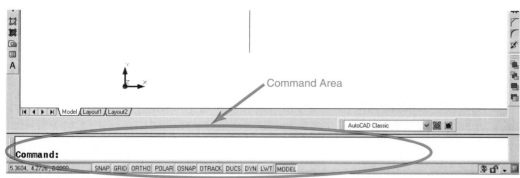

**Figure 1-50**    Command line

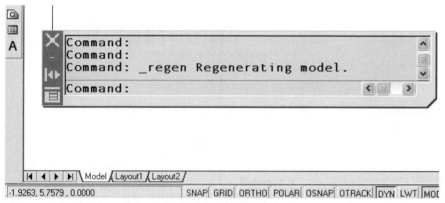

**Figure 1-51**    Command line area floating or undocked

One difference between toolbars and the command line area is that when the command line window is undocked and floating, the window can have a transparency value. This value allows the drawing geometry behind the command line window to be seen. The most current line of information in the command line area is the bottom line. By default, the command line shows three lines of text. This can be adjusted to other values based on your preferences, but three lines are recommended for seeing AutoCAD responses, answer options, and error messages. All the lines are recorded in a text window, available through pressing the **F2** key (see Figure 1-52). The **F2** function key will turn a ***text screen*** window on and off, showing all the contents of the command line since the beginning of the current drawing session.

**text screen:** A window that shows the history of the commands used.

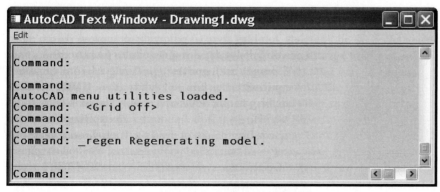

**Figure 1-52**    Text window available through the F2 key toggle

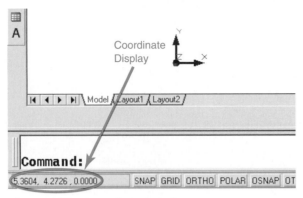

**Figure 1-53**    Status line—coordinate area

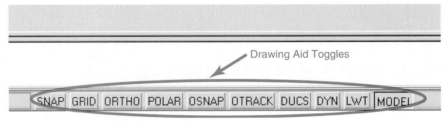

**Figure 1-54**    Status line—drawing aid toggle area

Commands can be typed directly onto the command line and executed by hitting the **Enter** key from this point. Previous commands and operations may be "copied and pasted" at the command line and executed again. Any typing that occurs on the command line must be followed by pressing the **Enter** key to execute the command.

### Status Bar

**status bar:** A series of read-outs and on/off buttons, for drawing aids, located on the bottom of the screen.

The bottom area of the interface is the ***status bar*** located under the command line window. The status bar houses a series of on/off buttons or toggles referred to as *drawing aids.* On the left end of the status bar there is a coordinate or display readout (see Figure 1-53). When coordinate display is turned on, the current position of the cursor will read out as X, Y, and Z coordinates. Other variations of this information are available by cycling with left mouse picks in this area. To the right on this status bar is a series of drawing aid buttons, including **SNAP** and **GRID.** The button labeled **DUCS** was new for 2007 (see Figure 1-54). These buttons act as toggle switches to turn these drawing aids on or off. When a drawing aid is *on,* the button appears in a depressed or sunken mode. At the right end of the status bar there is a small downward pointing arrow that will bring up a short menu (see Figure 1-55). This menu controls what buttons will be visible on the status bar. You can customize which buttons are available by selecting them in the pop-up menu.

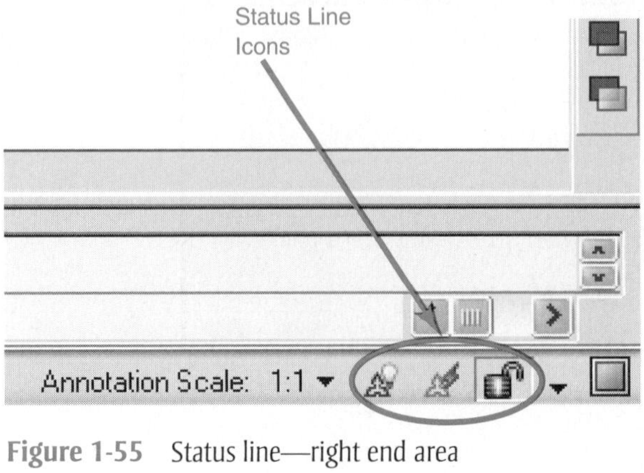

**Figure 1-55**    Status line—right end area

## Dynamic Input (Heads Up Input)

This feature, which was added in the 2006 version, lets the command prompt be linked to the cursor rather than left in a fixed location. This is called Dynamic Input and it will be shown in the related commands. This is an addition to the drafting tools settings. The status of your operation is shown with the other "toggles" in the status line. Dynamic Input allows you to have the command line follow wherever the cursor goes. A series of small windows will appear at the cursor location, providing information based on the current command (see Figure 1-56). The **Tab** key will switch the input fields (see Figure 1-57) while the down arrow key will show any options available for the current command (see Figure 1-58).

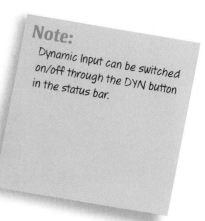

Note:
Dynamic Input can be switched on/off through the DYN button in the status bar.

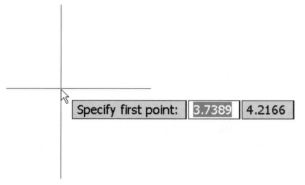

**Figure 1-56**   Start of line command in Dynamic Input

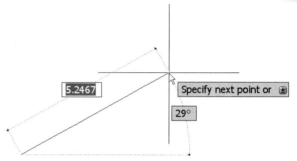

**Figure 1-57**   Typical Dynamic Input display

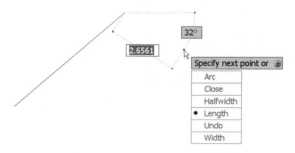

**Figure 1-58**   Options available in a Dynamic Input command

## Drawing Status Bar

The drawing status bar is located on the right end of the status bar. This area has a series of icons used to control the drawing's **Scale Annotations** (Figure 1-59).

In AutoCAD 2008, annotations can be scaled automatically for various layout viewports as well as model space. When annotation objects are created, they are scaled to the active annotation scale. This will size all the entities to the proper relationship for that viewport. The icons in the drawing status bar will turn automatic scaling on or off. You will be able to set the annotation scale and the visibility of the annotation objects. Other icons in this area lock the positions of the toolbars and

**Figure 1-59**

windows, control the CLEANSCREEN operation (which will hide/unhide all toolbars and windows), and allow you to select the elements you want displayed in the status bar area (Figure 1-60).

These tools are specific to model space and layout space. Different icons will appear depending on what space you are in.

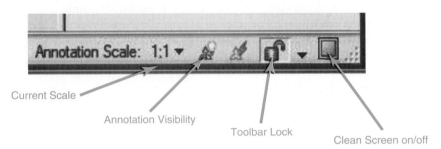

Current Scale

Annotation Visibility

Toolbar Lock

Clean Screen on/off

**Figure 1-60**

## DIALOG BOXES, FUNCTION/SPECIALTY KEYS, AND HELP FILES

**dialog box:** A window that appears on top of the drawing screen for random input of a command.

**radio buttons:** Buttons used to select an option in a dialog box.

*Dialog boxes* appear as windows during a drawing session. As mentioned earlier, some commands in the pull-down menus are followed by an ellipsis. When you select one of these commands, a dialog box will appear. You will then have an opportunity to set values and make selections related to the command. There are several styles or methods for inputting this information.

Numerical fields require you to single-click, or swipe across the current value, turning the field blue (see Figure 1-61). Then you can change the value through keyboard entry. You can also make choices from a *drop-down list*, which requires you to click on the black triangle (see Figure 1-62). You can select from a list of options called *radio buttons* (see Figure 1-63), or toggle check marks in boxes to activate or deactivate the option (see Figure 1-64).

These methods give you the ability to address any area of the dialog box at any time. Along with the previous methods, dialog boxes can contain a series of buttons or commands that will launch other dialog boxes. Remember, you must address the topmost dialog box and either accept or cancel this box before moving back through the remaining dialog boxes and back to the main interface. Some dialog boxes have an option to preview the results of the current values. By testing the values through the preview window, you can make changes to the values before actually placing the entities in the drawing file.

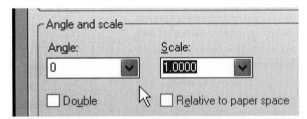

**Figure 1-61**    Dialog box with numerical field highlighted

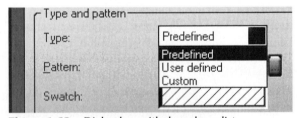

**Figure 1-62**    Dialog box with drop-down list

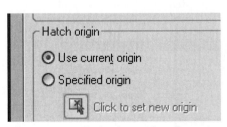

**Figure 1-63**    Dialog box with radio buttons

**Figure 1-64**    Dialog box with check boxes

Across the top of the keyboard is a row of *function keys.* This series of **F1** through **F12** keys are programmable for functions within AutoCAD. Generally they are used as on/off toggles. Table 1-1 shows the function keys and their actions.

**function keys:** Typically 12 programmable keys across the top of the keyboard.

| | |
|------|---------------------|
| F1   | Help                |
| F2   | Text Screen         |
| F3   | Object Snap         |
| F4   | Tablet              |
| F5   | Isoplane Options    |
| F6   | Coordinate Display  |
| F7   | Grid Display        |
| F8   | Ortho Mode          |
| F9   | Snap Mode           |
| F10  | Polar Tracking      |
| F11  | Object Tracking     |
| F12  | Dynamic Commands    |

**Table 1-1**   Function Keys

## Specialty Keys

Along with the function keys, AutoCAD uses the functionality of the control keys. It has a series of combination **CTRL** and character keystrokes that perform predefined commands. To execute a control keystroke function, both the **CTRL** key and the character must be depressed at the same time. Several of these combinations are the same in all Windows-based programs; **CTRL+S** for **SAVE** and **CTRL+C** for **COPY to CLIPBOARD** are examples. Others are unique to AutoCAD software. Table 1-2 lists the typical control keystroke combinations used within AutoCAD. Figure 1-65 shows the typical location of the **CTRL** (control) key for most keyboards.

Control Key

**Figure 1-65**   The control key

## Esc, Delete, and Arrow Keys

Certain keys have specific commands attached to them. For example, the **Esc** key will end, stop, or cancel any currently active command. A few commands require the user to select the **Esc** key twice to cancel. Most commands cancel after a single **Esc** keystroke. The **Delete** key can act as an **ERASE** function. You can select an entity on the screen and hit the **Delete** key to erase the entity from the file. Finally, the **Arrow** keys typically located between the alpha keyboard and the numeric keypad can be used to nudge entities around the drawing environment. See Figure 1-66 for a typical location of these keys.

| Key Code | Command | Key Code | Command | Key Code | Command |
|---|---|---|---|---|---|
| Ctrl+0 | CleanScreen | Ctrl+1 | Properties Palette | Ctrl+2 | Design Center |
| Ctrl+3 | Tool Palettes | Ctrl+4 | Sheet Set Manager | Ctrl+5 | Info Palette |
| Ctrl+6 | dbConnect | Ctrl+7 | Markup Set Manager | Ctrl+F4 | Closes Drawing |
| Ctrl+A | Selects All Objects | Ctrl+B | Snap Toggle | Ctrl+C | Copy to Clipboard |
| Ctrl+D | Dynamic UCS Toggle | Ctrl+E | Isoplane Toggle | Ctrl+F | Osnap Toggle |
| Ctrl+G | Grid Toggle | Ctrl+L | Ortho Toggle | Ctrl+K | Hyperlink |
| Ctrl+N | Starts New Drawing | Ctrl+O | Open Drawing | Ctrl+P | Plot/Print Dialog |
| Ctrl+Q | Exit/Quit AutoCAD | Ctrl+R | Cycles through Viewports | Ctrl+S | Save Drawing |
| Ctrl+T | Tablet Toggle | Ctrl+V | Paste from Clipboard | Ctrl+U | Polar Toggle |
| Ctrl+W | Object Tracking Toggle | Ctrl+X | Cut to the Clipboard | Ctrl+Z | Undo |

**Table 1-2**   Typical Control Key Commands

| Single-Character Aliases (Typical) | |
|---|---|
| A | ARC |
| B | BLOCK |
| C | CIRCLE |
| D | DIMSTYLE |
| E | ERASE |
| F | FILLET |
| G | GROUP |
| H | BHATCH |
| I | INSERT |
| J | JOIN |
| L | LINE |
| M | MOVE |
| O | OFFSET |
| P | PAN |
| R | REDRAW |
| S | STRETCH |
| T | MTEXT |
| V | VIEW |
| W | WBLOCK |
| X | EXPLODE |
| Z | ZOOM |

**Table 1-3**   Single-Character Command Aliases

**Figure 1-66**   Useful keys

## Command Aliases

Command aliases are an alternate method of launching a command. Most aliases are one to three keystrokes followed by the **Enter** key. For example, **L** initiates the **LINE** command, **E** begins the **ERASE** command, and so on (see Table 1-3). This shortcut method of invoking a command saves on the time it takes to track down a command in the traditional pull-down menu area or to find an icon. Not all commands have an alias alternative. A complete list of command aliases is stored in a text file named acad.pgp, which can also be modified to the operator's desires. This list can be found in Appendix C along with other character aliases available in AutoCAD.

## Online Help Files

Help files can be found in the pull-down menu option of **Help;** by typing in the command **HELP;** or by touching **F1.** From this menu a traditional help window, similar to all Windows-based programs, is where an operator can conduct content searches, review a program index, and post questions pertaining to all topics within the AutoCAD program. The right side of the window (see Figure 1-67) is the topic content side, with three tabs—Concepts, Procedures, and Reference. The content side shows graphics screens as well as text descriptions and other reference topics related to the active topic or command you are seeking help with. The **INFO** palette is a quick, interactive assistant showing Help information about a current command in progress or other related information (see Figure 1-68).

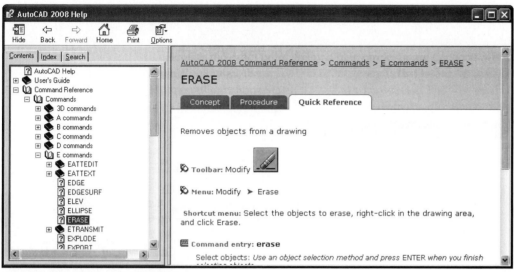

**Figure 1-67** Typical Help screen layout

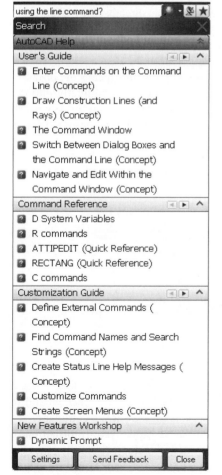

**Figure 1-68** INFO palette

## Online Resource

In the same **Help** pull-down menu, there are several live links to Autodesk websites that have information addressing product support, training, and customizing AutoCAD plus access to AutoCAD user groups (see Figure 1-69). If you have an active Internet connection, selecting one of these menu choices will launch an Internet session taking you to the link location. There are many Internet sites devoted to AutoCAD, and several links will start you in the right direction with additional help and links related to users' questions.

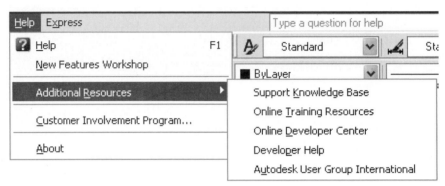

**Figure 1-69**    Additional Resources submenu

## Command Line Details

As mentioned earlier, the command line is a window where operators can directly type in AutoCAD commands. This window will then display command prompts and messages regarding the active commands (see Figure 1-70). The most current line is located at the bottom of the window, allowing preceding lines of text to scroll upward and out of the command line display onto the text screen. When the word **Command** is shown in the active command line, this means the program is ready and waiting for an instruction. Any command or alias can be entered directly into the command line. To execute the typed command you must press the **Enter** key on the keyboard. Once a command is in operation the command line will communicate with you through a series of statements about the current command.

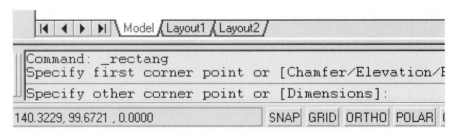

**Figure 1-70**    Command prompt area with command in action

There are two visual clues to some of the information seen in the command line. Once a command is in operation there will be information that is displayed in square brackets and in parentheses. Information inside the square brackets will be options for the current commands. To execute an option, you must type in the letter(s) of the word that is capitalized. Information in parentheses is referred to as default information. To accept any default value you simply press the **Enter** key on the keyboard.

## Mouse Operations

Most input devices these days are three-button mouse devices. In some cases the middle button is replaced with a wheel programmed to perform certain viewing or display commands. The left button is the pick, select, or input button. When it is depressed, the command highlighted by the cursor executes. This is the case if the arrow is on a word in a menu or on an icon in a toolbar. The right button is used for a context-sensitive pop-up menu (see Figures 1-71 and 1-72). Depending on where the arrow is when the right mouse button is depressed, different menus will display.

If you hold the **CTRL** key down and then depress the right mouse button an **Object Snap** menu appears at the location of the cursor (see Figure 1-73).

Demonstrate an efficient use of previous commands by using the **Recent Input.** This can be found on a right-click menu.

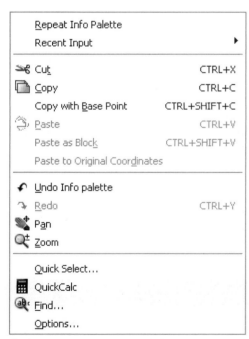

**Figure 1-71**   Typical right-click menu

**Figure 1-72**   Typical right-click menu when a command is active

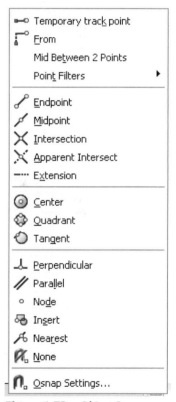

**Figure 1-73**   Object Snap right-click menu

AutoCAD has preprogrammed the center button for viewing commands. By rolling the wheel you will perform a **ZOOM** command, which changes the magnification of the drawing. When you roll the wheel up you perform a **ZOOM IN** command. When you roll the wheel down, you perform a **ZOOM OUT** command. When you are using the wheel, the current location of the cursor will be the center of the **ZOOM** operation. A third display command known as **PAN** (no change in magnification, just movement based on the cursor movement) is executed when you push down on the wheel and keep the wheel depressed as you move the mouse around.

## SUMMARY

In this unit we introduced you to the concept of CAD/CADD (computer-aided drafting and design), explained the operation of the AutoCAD software, and presented an overview of its applications and functions in the Microsoft® Windows® operating system environment. First, you were presented with typical examples of AutoCAD drawings generated for projects in the fields of architecture, civil engineering, landscape design, and mechanical engineering. Then, you learned about AutoCAD functions in the Windows operating system environment: the Windows-based file management commands **(NEW, OPEN, SAVE, SAVE AS,** and **CLOSE),** and the edit action commands **(CUT, COPY, PASTE,** and **MATCHPROP).** Subsequently,

you were shown the basics of the AutoCAD workspace and its features (basic screen, title bar, dashboard and control panels, menu bar and drop-down menus, dialog boxes, InfoCenter, toolbars, drawing area and scroll bars, model space and layout space tabs, command line, status bar, Dynamic Input, and drawing status bar). Finally, you learned how to access AutoCAD commands and options through dialog boxes, check boxes, radio buttons, function/specialty keys (**F1** through **F12** keys, **CTRL, Esc, Delete,** and **Arrow**), command aliases, and mouse operations, as well as how to obtain help from the pull-down menu, live Autodesk website links, and command line details.

## QUICK-START TUTORIALS

Now that you've had an introduction to the screen interface, it is time to participate in a tutorial to see how easy AutoCAD can be to operate. By completing this tutorial, you will experience a typical drawing session. Read through the brief description of the drawing setup, followed by the explanation of a few basic commands, and see if you can complete the drawings.

### Quick-Start Tutorial 1

1. Locate the **AutoCAD** icon on the desktop. Double-click the icon to start the program (see Figure QS-1).
2. From the **File** menu select **New** (see Figure QS-2).
3. From the **Create New Drawing** dialog box, pick the second icon from the left to choose "Start from Scratch" as the method to start. Verify **Imperial Units** are chosen and pick **OK** with the left mouse button (see Figure QS-3a). If the **Select template** dialog box appears (see Figure QS-3b), pick **acad.dwt** as the template to use for this tutorial.
4. From the **Tools** menu select the **Drafting Settings** entry near the bottom of the menu (see Figure QS-4).
5. In the **Drafting Settings** dialog box select the **Snap** and **Grid** tab (see Figure QS-5).

AutoCAD

**Figure QS-1**

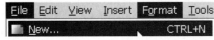

**Figure QS-2**

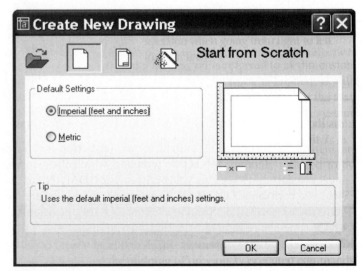

**Figure QS-3a**

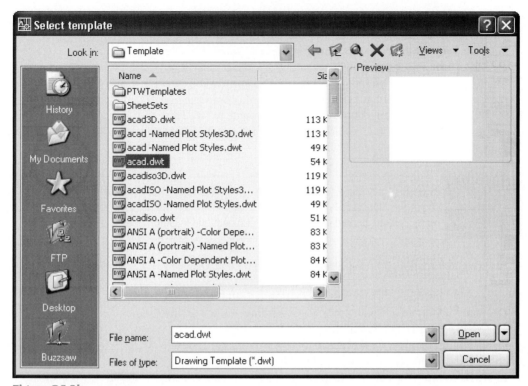

**Figure QS-3b**

**Figure QS-4**

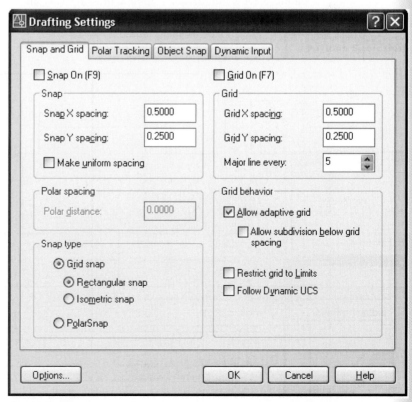

**Figure QS-5**

6. In the **Snap** section, change the **Snap Y spacing** value to **.25**. This is done by double-clicking the current value, which will highlight with a blue box, and typing in the new value. Be sure the **Make uniform spacing** box does not have a check mark in it. The **Snap type** should be set to **Rectangular snap.** Also be sure the **Grid behavior** area has no check marks for this drawing.

7. In the **Grid** section, change the **Grid Y spacing** value to **.25**. This is done by double-clicking the current value, which will highlight with a blue box, and typing in the new value.

**FOR MORE DETAIL**    New users may find it helpful to read the command descriptions for a better understanding of the LINE and ERASE commands. That information can be found at the end of this tutorial. More detailed information can also be found in Unit 3 of this book.

8. Place a check mark in both the **Snap On (F9)** and **Grid On (F7)** boxes.

9. Accept all the changes made in the dialog box by selecting the **OK** button. You should now see a series of dots, known as the grid, in the lower left corner of the screen.

10. Double-click the wheel on the mouse to perform a **Zoom Extents** command, which repositions the grid to fill the drawing area.

11. In the **Draw** menu, select the **LINE** command (see Figure QS-6). Create the drawing QS-1 shown in Figure QS-7, drawing each line as shown from grid point to grid point. The pointing device will snap to each grid point due to the drafting settings. Every line may need the user to restart the **LINE** command. This may require the occasional use of the **ERASE** command, which is found in the **Modify** menu shown in Figure QS-8.

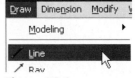

**Figure QS-6**

12. When the drawing is complete you will want to save your work. Go to the **File** menu and select **SAVE** (see Figure QS-9). You should enter a unique name for the drawing file, and press the **Enter** key (see Figure QS-10).

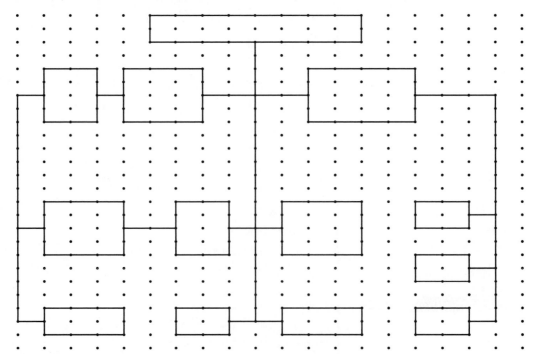

**Figure QS-7**    Drawing QS-1

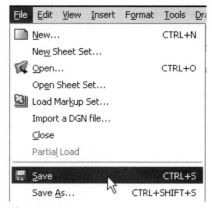

**Figure QS-8**        **Figure QS-9**

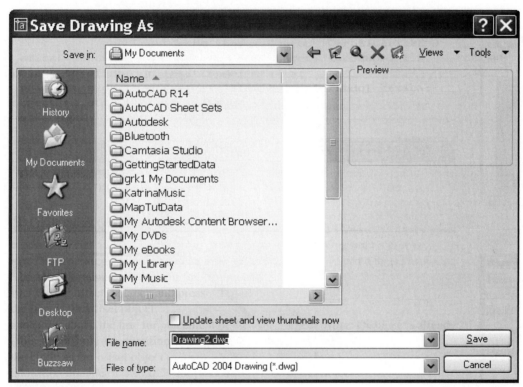

**Figure QS-10**

## Quick-Start Tutorial 2

The following is a second quick-start tutorial with an architectural flair. This will require the user to change the unit type along with adjustments to both X and Y values in the Snap and Grid areas. Follow the steps below to complete the drawing.

1. Locate the **AutoCAD** icon on the desktop (refer back to Figure QS-1). Double-click the icon to start the program.
2. From the **File** menu select **New** (see Figure QS-11).
3. From the **Create New Drawing** dialog box, pick the second icon from the left to choose "Start from Scratch" as the method to start. Verify **Imperial** units are chosen and pick **OK** with the left mouse button (see Figure QS-12a). If the **Select template** dialog box appears (see Figure QS-12b) pick the **acad.dwt** template as the template to use for this tutorial.

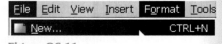

**Figure QS-11**

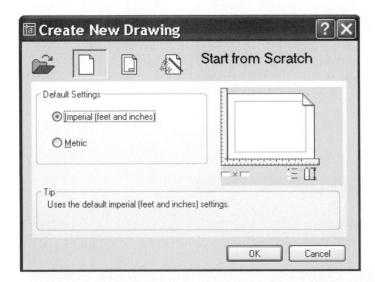

**Figure QS-12a**

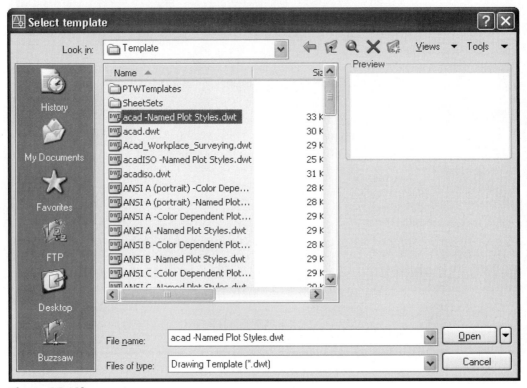

**Figure QS-12b**

4. In the **Format** menu (see Figure QS-13) select **Units . . .** near the bottom of the menu.
5. In the **Drawing Units** dialog box (see Figure QS-14), locate the drop box for the **Length Type** and change the units to **Architectural.**
6. From the **Format** menu select **Drawing Limits**. Enter a value of 0,0 for the lower left-hand corner and a value of 10′,15′ for the upper right-hand corner.
7. From the **View** menu select the **Zoom** cascading menu. From the **Zoom** cascading menu select **All.**
8. From the **Tools** menu select **Drafting Settings . . .** near the bottom of the menu (see Figure QS-15).
9. In the **Drafting Settings** dialog box select the **Snap and Grid** tab (see Figure QS-16).

Figure QS-13

Figure QS-14

10. In the **Snap** section, change the **Snap X spacing** and **Snap Y spacing** values to 2″. This is done by double-clicking the current value, which will highlight with a blue box, and typing in the new value. Be sure the **Make uniform spacing** box does not have a check mark in it. The **Snap type** should be set to **Rectangular snap.** Also be sure the **Grid behavior** area has no check marks for this drawing.

11. In the **Grid** section, change the **Grid X spacing** and **Grid Y spacing** values to 4″. This is done by double-clicking the current value, which will highlight with a blue box, and typing in the new value.

Figure QS-15

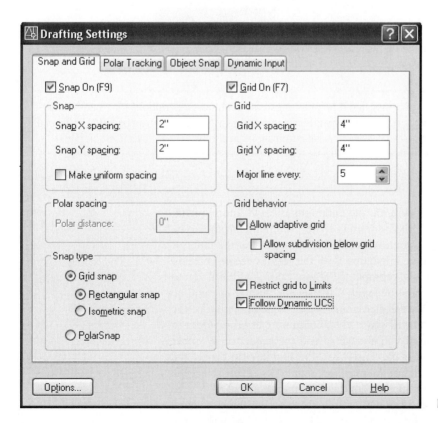

Figure QS-16

12. Place a check mark in both the **Snap On (F9)** and **Grid On (F7)** boxes. Accept all the changes made in the dialog box by selecting the **OK** button. You should now see a series of dots, known as the grid, in the lower left corner of the screen.

13. In the **Draw** menu, select the **LINE** command (see Figure QS-17) and create the drawing in Figure QS-18 with each line as shown. You may need to restart the command with every line. This may require the occasional use of the **ERASE** command, which is found in the **Modify** menu (see Figure QS-19).

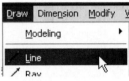

Figure QS-17

14. When the drawing is complete you will want to save your work. Go to the **File** menu and select **SAVE** (refer back to Figure QS-9). You may enter a name for the drawing file (refer to Figure QS-10), and press the **Enter** key to complete the save operation.

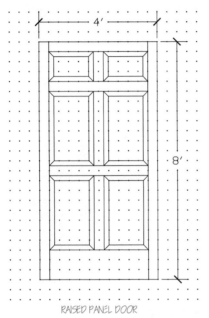

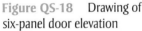

**Figure QS-18**    Drawing of six-panel door elevation

**Figure QS-19**

> **FOR MORE DETAIL**   New users may find it helpful to read the command descriptions for a better understanding of the LINE and ERASE commands. That information can be found at the end of this tutorial. More detailed information can also be found in Unit 3 of this book.

## LINE Command

Lines are created by specifying the endpoints of each line segment. After executing the **LINE** command the command prompt (see Figure QS-20) will ask you to **Specify first point.** After the input of the first point by picking a location with the left mouse or entering coordinates, the command prompt (see Figure QS-21) will ask you to **Specify next point.** Upon the input of the second point a line will be created between the two selected points. After the completion of the first line, the command will stay active, continuing to prompt you to **Specify next point** until you choose to end the sequence by either pressing the space bar or the **Enter** key, the **Esc** key (to cancel the operation), or a right mouse button (see Figure QS-22) to select the **ENTER/CANCEL** command from the right mouse menu.

The **LINE** command has two options from within the command, **Close** and **Undo.** Options to a command are displayed within the

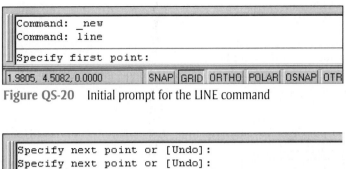

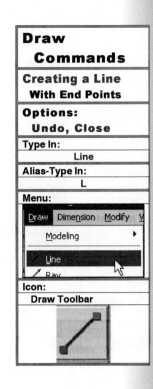

Figure QS-20    Initial prompt for the LINE command

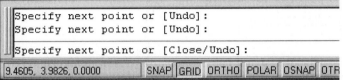

Figure QS-21    Succeeding prompts for the LINE command

Figure QS-22    Right mouse menu

square brackets in the prompt line. To execute a command's option you will identify the capital letter from the word in the prompt line and type in that letter, followed by an **Enter** key. After two or more line segments are created you can execute the **Close** option to create one more line segment that will close the shape back to the first selected endpoint that started the sequence. This will end the command.

When the **Undo** option is executed from within the **LINE** command the last point of input will be released and allow the user to re-specify the endpoint of that line segment. Be aware that continuous execution of the **Undo** function will step back through all endpoints specified during this line activity.

## ERASE Command

The **ERASE** command is used to delete entities from the drawing file. As with all modify commands, after the selection of the command you will be prompted to **Select objects** (see Figure QS-23). After the selection of entities is completed and the **Enter** key is hit the selected entities will be erased from the drawing file and screen. An alternative method to the **ERASE** command is to select an entity when a command is not in progress and press the **Delete** key on the keyboard, thus removing the entity from the drawing file. Remember the program is in neutral when the prompt line reads "Command." This is when a user can use the alternative method mentioned above.

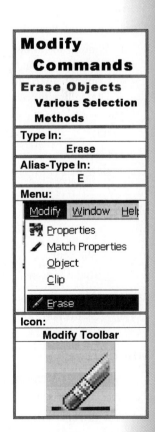

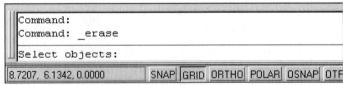

Figure QS-23    Erase command prompt

## Selecting Objects

Upon entering into any modify command the prompt of **Select objects** will appear in the command line and the screen cursor will be replaced by a small square known as a *pick box* (see Figure QS-24). This pick box is referred to as a *single-selection pick box* and is used to select the single entity that is below the box when a left mouse click is executed. By moving the pick box over any object on the screen and left-clicking you select that entity and place it into the current selection set. Selected objects will appear in a dashed form to signify they are part of the currently selected set for modification. You may continue to select other objects that need to be placed into the selection set by simply moving the pick box over other entities and using a left mouse click. This process will continue until you complete your selections and finish the selection process by hitting the **Enter** key or the right mouse button for a menu to stop the selection or to cancel the selection.

```
Select objects: 1 found
Select objects: 1 found, 2 total
Select objects:
5.8603, 3.9334, 0.0000    SNAP GRID ORTHO POLAR OSNAP OTR
```

**Figure QS-24**    Select objects prompts in ERASE command

## CHAPTER TEST QUESTIONS

### Multiple Choice

1.  An arrow to the right of an entry in the pull-down menu means
    a. Window to follow
    b. Cascading menu to follow
    c. Command execution
    d. Dialog box to follow

2.  What does the ellipsis to the right of an entry in the pull-down menu mean?
    a. Window to follow
    b. Cascading menu to follow
    c. Command execution
    d. Dialog box to follow

3.  The Space bar in the AutoCAD program will act as another _____ key.
    a. Cancel
    b. Escape
    c. Delete
    d. Enter

4.  To stop or cancel a command in AutoCAD, you would press the _____ key.
    a. Cancel
    b. Escape
    c. Delete
    d. Enter

5.  The double grab bar on the side of a toolbar is used to _____ a toolbar.
    a. Float
    b. Close
    c. Dock
    d. Delete

### Matching

a. _____ F2
b. _____ Shortcut
c. _____ Radio buttons
d. _____ Alias
e. _____ Status bar

1.  Used to select an option in a dialog box
2.  Function key that flips the text screen and graphic screen
3.  Alternate method of launching a command
4.  An icon on the desktop to start a program
5.  Contains drawing aids

### True or False

1.  True or False: The center wheel on a mouse can be used for viewing control.

2.  True or False: All the commands in the pull-down menus can be found in a toolbar.

3.  True or False: The look of the AutoCAD interface is set at the factory and cannot be changed.

4.  True or False: The ORTHO drawing aid will produce objects perpendicular to each other.

5.  True or False: A right click on the mouse will bring up a context-sensitive menu.

## CHAPTER PROJECTS

1. Which icon in the Standard toolbar will fly out to show more options?
2. What is shown at the bottom of the File menu immediately above EXIT?
3. Check with technical firms in your area to learn which CAD software and which CAD standards they are using.
4. Examine Microsoft Office software. Find the common icons that are in both the AutoCAD and the Office products and create a list. Are the actions the same in both programs?
5. Invite a speaker to talk about the use of CAD software in the projects he or she is involved with.
6. Research the history and report on prominent buildings in the community. Make a display board of drawings used in the construction, if possible.
7. Take pictures of structures during construction to see the progression from foundations to columns to beams to walls and compare the pictures to the drawings. Put the pictures in a display.

8. Fill in the identifying names in Figure 1-74. See this figure on the Student CD.

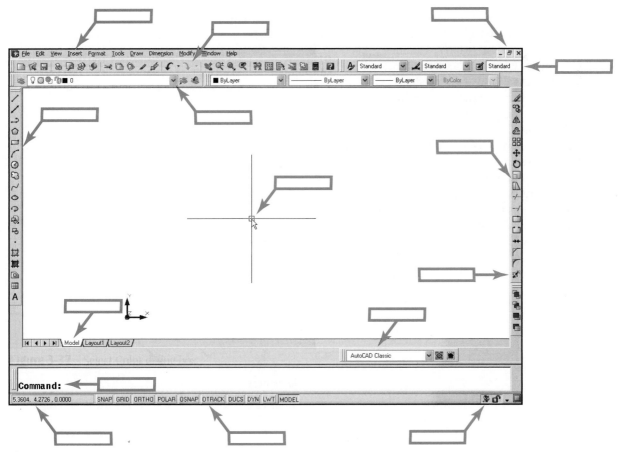

**Figure 1-74**   Screen view with leaders

## PRACTICE EXERCISE

1. Start AutoCAD using the Desktop icon or menus.
2. Examine each of the menus to learn the location of commands and when submenus or dialog boxes will appear.
3. Move the mouse slowly over various icons to see the command name (tooltip) for that icon.
4. Pick the **File** menu and choose **OPEN** (see Figure 1-75).
5. Using the drop-down area at the top of the **Select File** dialog box, find the student CD.

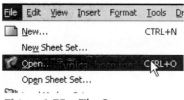

**Figure 1-75**    File, Open

6. Scroll through the list of drawing files (.dwg) and choose one to open by picking the **Open** button in the lower right of the dialog box:
   a. **Architectural Drawings**—8th Floor, Hotel, Hummer, Stadium, Taisei, Willhome, Campus, Kitchen, or Stadium North
   b. **Building Services**—8th Floor
   c. **Civil Drawings**—Hotel or SPCA Site Plan
   d. **Facilities Management**—Db_samp
   e. **Landscaping**—SPCA Site Plan
   f. **Mechanical**—Oil Module, Welding Fixture 1, Welding Fixture Model, Chevy, Truck Model, or Watch
   g. **Presentation**—Hotel, Hummer, Stadium, Welding Fixture Model, Campus, Chevy, Kitchen, Stadium North, or Truck Model
   h. **Process Piping**—Oil Module
   i. **Structural**—MKMPlan or Oil Module
7. Practice using the mouse wheel to **PAN** and **ZOOM** on these drawings.
8. Access various commands and watch the command line for instructions. Pressing the **Esc** key will cancel any operation.
9. To end your work session on a drawing, go to the **File** menu and pick **CLOSE.** Pick the answer **No,** so that no modifications are saved at this time. If you want to open and examine another drawing, go back to Step 4.
10. To end your AutoCAD session, go to the **File** menu and pick **EXIT.** If a drawing is active, answer **No** to the prompt in the command line so that no modifications are saved at this time. The program then ends.

# Creating and Working with AutoCAD Files

**2**

## Chapter Objectives

- Understand the concepts of file management.
- Identify the file extensions used in AutoCAD.
- Use ANSI and ISO drawing templates.
- Create user-defined templates for various engineering disciplines.

## INTRODUCTION

Now that you have completed a quick tutorial, we turn to the drawing file setup and the file management process. By creating templates you can begin each new design with the same approach to the process of completing a drawing. These templates will be the foundation of the drawing process in any engineering discipline.

## FILE MANAGEMENT

File management is the saving, storage, archiving, and organization of the product created in a drawing session. AutoCAD drawings produce a file with a *.dwg* file extension. Security and organization are two main issues when saving or archiving drawing files.

**.dwg:** The file extension used for all valid AutoCAD drawing files.

 Since most computers use Windows as the operating system, the file management commands that are within the AutoCAD program are the same ones found in any Windows-based program. Commands such as **NEW, OPEN, SAVE, SAVE AS,** and **CLOSE** are the basic operations related to file management. These commands can be found in the **File** pull-down menu (see Figure 2-1) and on the left end of the **Standard** toolbar (see Figure 2-2). Procedures for each of these commands are executed only on the single file that is currently active, even though AutoCAD has the ability to have multiple drawing files open at one time. These commands allow users to name files, save files, retrieve files, and manipulate the locations where files are stored. It is considered good practice to store drawing files in various folders referred to as *directories*. Drawing files should never be saved in folders containing any of the AutoCAD system files. Making a separate subdirectory or folder on your local hard drive and saving files into that folder will help secure your drawing files, as well as the program system files. Beginning users need to develop day-to-day habits regarding the management of the files they work with.

CAD operators are responsible for the tracking of their daily work within the company file management system. This would include revision versions as well as archived files from past projects.

Figure 2-1     File menu

Figure 2-2     Icons for file
management

## BEGINNING A NEW DRAWING SESSION

**template:** A predefined series
of variables saved in a file for
the purpose of starting a new
drawing file.

Use the **NEW** command to open the *template* dialog box (see Figure 2-3). You can then
choose a basic, generic AutoCAD template or one of several preprogrammed templates established for various engineering disciplines. After accepting a style of template, you will exit
the dialog box by clicking on the **OPEN** button, thus starting a new drawing session. All new
drawing sessions are temporarily named DRAWING1.dwg and any sequential new drawing
sessions are named DRAWING2.dwg, DRAWING3.dwg, and so on. You should rename this
drawing and store it in the correct folder or directory using the **SAVE** or **SAVE AS** commands. If the system variable **STARTUP** is set to a value of 1, executing the **NEW** command
will result in the **Create New Drawing** dialog box (see Figures 2-5, 2-6, and 2-7). You may
also choose to change the **STARTUP** field through the **Options** dialog box under the **System**
tab (see Figure 2-4), which starts this dialog box. This **Create New Drawing** dialog box has
three choices available. You may **Start from Scratch** (see Figure 2-5), **Use a Template** (see
Figure 2-6), or **Use a Wizard** (see Figure 2-7).

**ANSI** (American National
Standards Institute): A govern-
ment-controlled series of
standards for engineering.

The **Start from Scratch** option (see Figure 2-5) will allow you to select either imperial or
metric units, and then it will launch a session based on the standard default **acad.dwt** template.

The **Use a Template** option allows you to select from one of over 60 predefined templates
(see Figure 2-6). These templates are based on sheet sizes and drafting standards such as
*ANSI* (American National Standards Institute) or *ISO* (International Standards Organization)
practices.

**ISO** (International Standards
Organization): An internation-
ally controlled series of standards for engineering, manufacturing, and other technical
issues.

In addition, standard templates are included from various international countries.

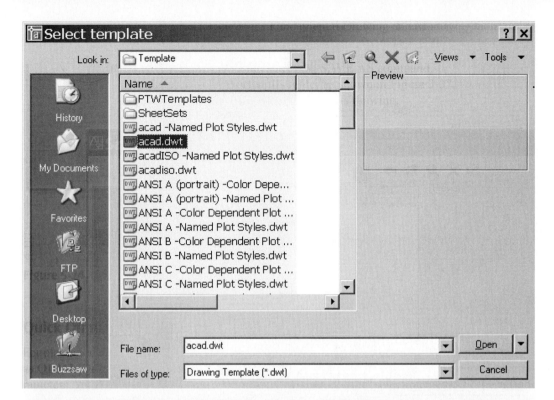

**Figure 2-3** Select template dialog screen

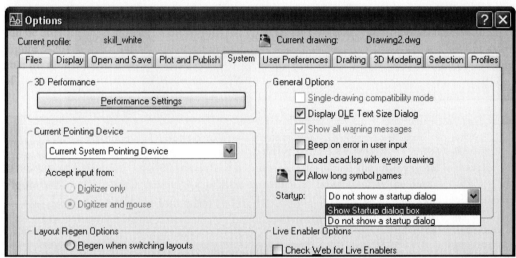

**Figure 2-4** Drop-down choices for Startup in the System tab of the OPTIONS command

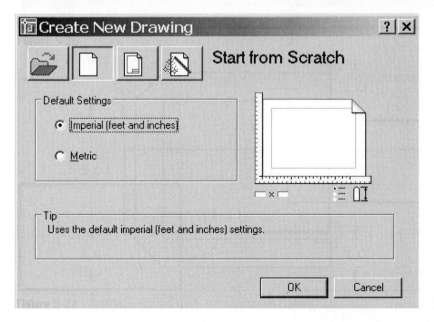

**Figure 2-5** Create New Drawing screen—Start from Scratch

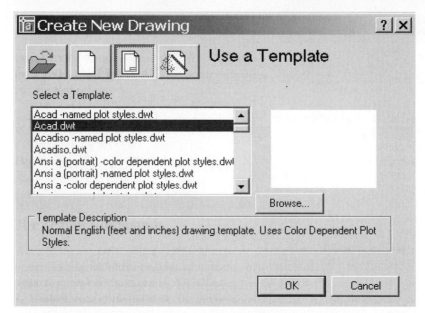

Figure 2-6  Starting a new drawing with a template

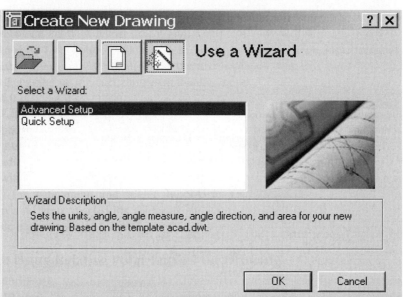

Figure 2-7  Starting a new drawing with the Wizard

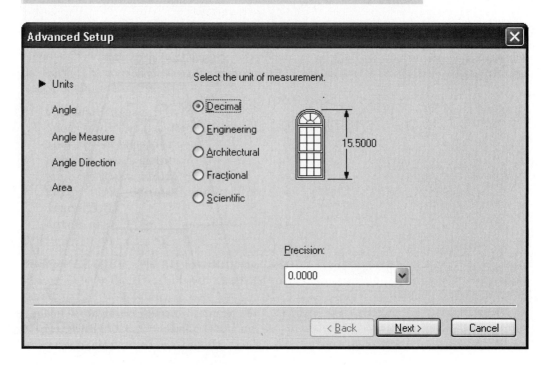

Figure 2-8  Wizard Screen for Units

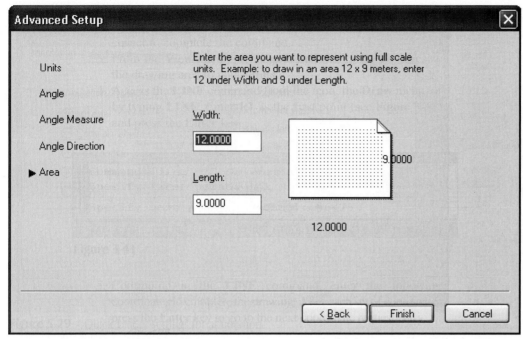

**Figure 2-9**    Wizard Screen for Distances

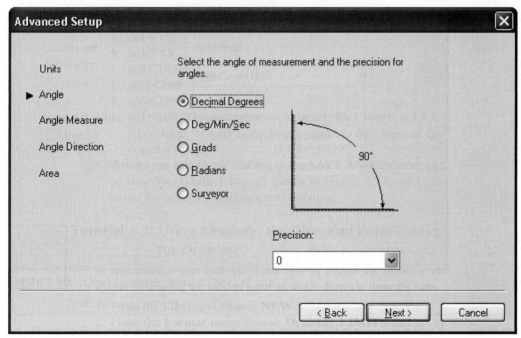

**Figure 2-10**    Wizard Screen for Angle

The **Use a Wizard** option (see Figure 2-7) has two choices, **Quick Setup** and **Advanced Setup.** The *Wizard* uses a series of dialog boxes with options to establish settings used in controlling the drawing's input methods and overall environment. **Quick Setup** allows you to set the type of **UNITS** used, along with the size or **LIMITS** of the drawing area (see Figures 2-8 and 2-9). The **Advanced Setup** asks the same two questions as the **Quick Setup,** along with additional questions related to type of angles, angle measurement, and angle direction (see Figures 2-10, 2-11, and Figure 2-12). Your selections are established along with the default acad.dwt template file for the new drawing.

**Wizard:** A tool that uses a step-by-step routine to establish drawing settings.

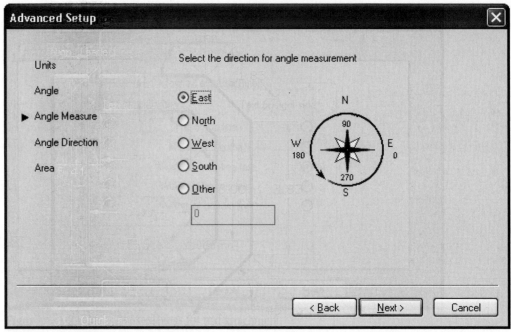

**Figure 2-11**   Wizard Screen for Angle Measure

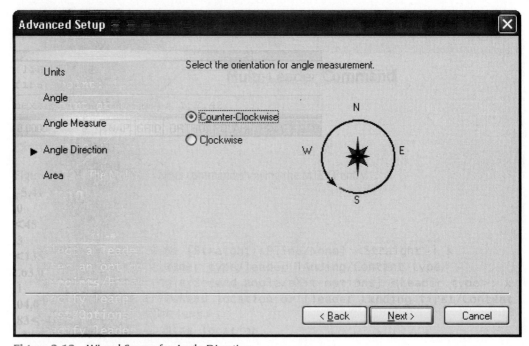

**Figure 2-12**   Wizard Screen for Angle Direction

## SAVING FILES

You have three options for saving your work: **SAVE, QSAVE,** and **SAVE AS.** The first time a **SAVE** command is executed, the **Save Drawing As** dialog box appears (see Figure 2-13). At this time you can navigate the system drives to go to a specific directory and rename the drawing file (see Figure 2-14). Remember, AutoCAD will place a generic name such as Drawing1.dwg, Drawing2.dwg, and so forth, on all files that have not yet been saved. It is to your advantage to invoke a **SAVE** command as soon as possible. Once an initial **SAVE** command has been completed, any future execution of a **SAVE** command will result in the execution of

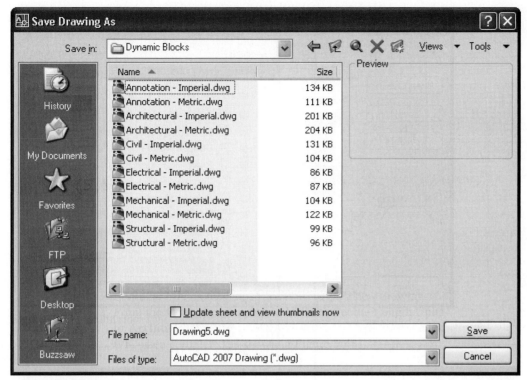

**Figure 2-13**    Save Drawing As dialog box

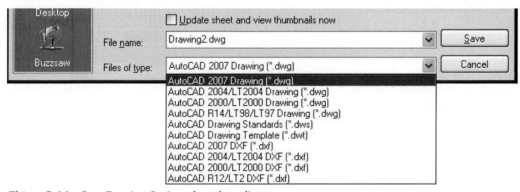

**Figure 2-14**    Save Drawing Options drop-down list

a **QSAVE** command. This command will simply update the previously saved file to the current status of the file. If you would like to change the location the file is saved in or change the name of the saved file, you must invoke the **SAVE AS** command. **SAVE AS** will allow you to change the name of the file, the location it is being saved in, and the format in which it is saved. Upon execution of the **SAVE AS** command, the existing file will become a copy (with an extension suffix of *.bak* as explained next). When a new name is entered, it will result in an automatic closure of the previous file you were working on.

**.bak:** A standard file name extension used by many programs to be the last saved version of a document, spreadsheet, or drawing before the most recently saved version.

## Auto Saved and Backup Files

AutoCAD does have an automatic save function. This system variable, **SAVETIME,** is set by default to save the active drawing every 120 minutes. It can be changed in the **Options** dialog box under the **Open and Save** tab. There you will find a check box to activate the feature, along with a time field for Minutes Between Saves. It is a good practice to reduce the time field to approximately 10 to 15 minutes (see Figure 2-15). You can do a great deal of work in 120 minutes that you may not want to do over in case of a system crash, power failure, or similar problem. Individual user habits or established office practices will vary when related to this issue. It is important to note that the **Auto Saved** file (typically with a default extension suffix of .sv$ or .ac$) is

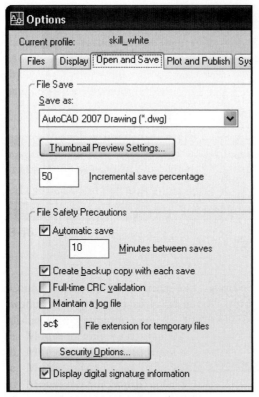

Figure 2-15    Savetime Options dialog box

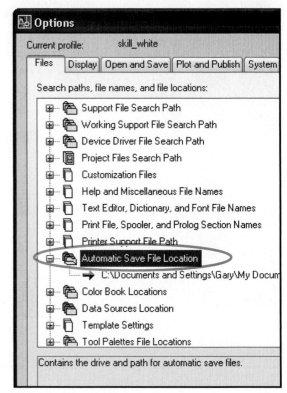

Figure 2-16    Automatic Save File Location dialog box

not saved in the same location as the drawing file saved with the **QSAVE** command. Check the file path location in the **Options** dialog box under the **Files** tab to find the location of automatically saved files (see Figure 2-16).

Along with automatic file saving, each time an existing file is opened, a backup copy of the original file is created or updated if the file already exists. This feature is also controlled in the **Options** dialog box shown above. The file will be created in the same directory as the AutoCAD .dwg file. The only difference is that its file name will have a .bak extension. This file can be renamed through typical Windows procedures to have a .dwg extension, if needed, to recover the file as a valid AutoCAD drawing file.

## OPENING A DRAWING

The **OPEN** command will allow you to retrieve an existing AutoCAD drawing file. After executing the command you will be presented with the **Select File** dialog box (see Figure 2-17). In this dialog box you will be able to navigate your system drives to locate directories and select a drawing file. Most valid AutoCAD drawing files will show a thumbnail preview in the upper right area of the dialog box. By default, this dialog box filters for drawing files with a .dwg file extension. At the bottom of the dialog box there is a field for file types, which can be changed to search for other types of files such as .dxf (data exchange files), .dwt (template files), or .dws (drawing standards files) (see Figure 2-18). Once the file is located and selected, you can select the **Open** button in the lower right area of the dialog box to retrieve the data from the file.

A second method to opening files is to select the file from the Windows Explorer program. Any valid AutoCAD drawing file (one with a .dwg extension) can be located through the Explorer; then you can double-click with the left mouse button on the file to launch the AutoCAD software and open the contents of the drawing file selected (see Figure 2-19). A third method of

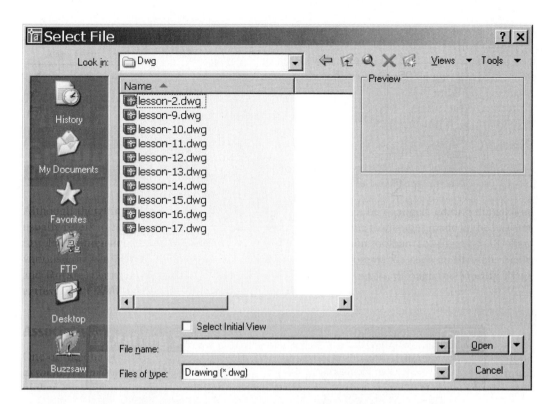

Figure 2-17    Open Drawing dialog box

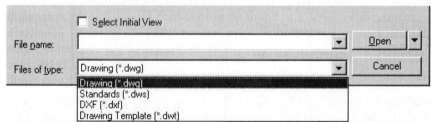

Figure 2-18    File type drop-down for open drawing

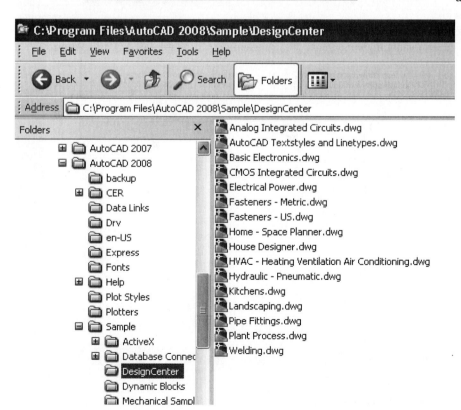

Figure 2-19    Explorer dialog showing AutoCAD files

**Smith House Drawings**

**Figure 2-20**    AutoCAD desktop icon to open a drawing directly

**Figure 2-21**

accessing an AutoCAD drawing is to set up a desktop icon (see Figure 2-20) by either using the AutoCAD icon as a base with the drawing name specified or placing the drawing name on the desktop as an icon directly (see Figure 2-21).

## Working with Multiple Drawing Sessions

As mentioned earlier, AutoCAD is capable of having several drawings open in a single session. This is referred to as a *Multiple Design Environment* (MDE). Drawings can be viewed in several arrangements. A single floating window is the default mode (see Figure 2-23).

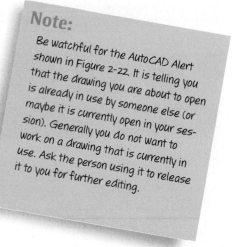

*Note:*
Be watchful for the AutoCAD Alert shown in Figure 2-22. It is telling you that the drawing you are about to open is already in use by someone else (or maybe it is currently open in your session). Generally you do not want to work on a drawing that is currently in use. Ask the person using it to release it to you for further editing.

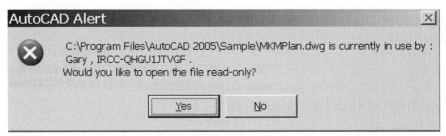

**Figure 2-22**    Read-only/open file warning

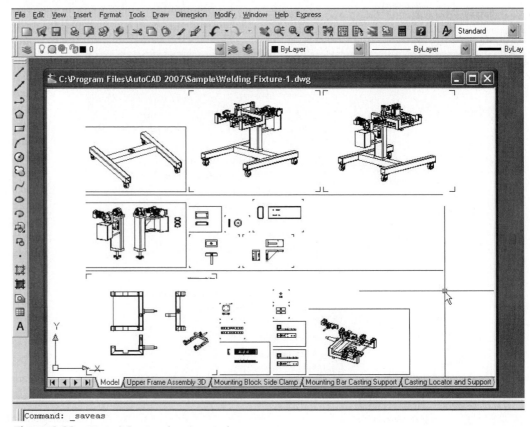

**Figure 2-23**    Typical floating drawing window

**Figure 2-24**   Multiple drawings in a cascade format

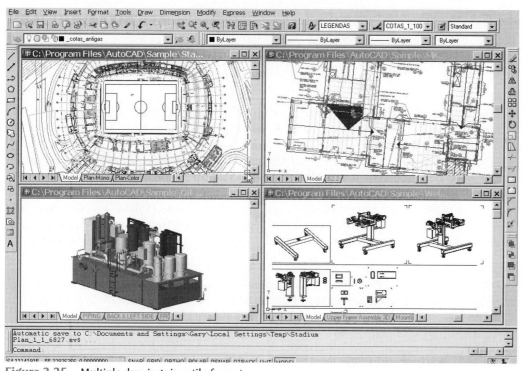

**Figure 2-25**   Multiple drawings in a tile format

Drawings can also be *cascaded* (see Figure 2-24), exposing the title bar of each file, *tiled horizontally,* or *tiled vertically* on the screen (see Figure 2-25). You can navigate through multiple active drawing files by selecting the name of the drawing from the **Window** menu (see Figure 2-26). If one of the other display modes is active, you may simply click on the title bar of the drawing you want to activate. Switching drawings when the multiple drawings are tiled requires you only to move the cursor into the file and click anywhere within that drawing's viewport. If the system variable **TASKBAR** is set to a value of 1, each open drawing will appear as an icon on the Windows taskbar. Simply selecting the icon from the bottom taskbar will activate that drawing.

**Figure 2-26**  Window menu showing open drawings     **Figure 2-27**  Edit menu     **Figure 2-28**  Cut, Copy, Paste icons

There are several commands or actions that can take place between multiple drawings.

Users will often share information between drawings through drag-and-drop techniques. This can be easily accomplished when drawings are tiled vertically or horizontally.

The traditional Windows commands of **CUT, COPY,** and **PASTE** are available from the **Edit** menu (see Figure 2-27), by the combination control keystrokes shown on the menu, and on the Standard toolbar (see Figure 2-28).

The **COPY with BASE POINT** and the **PASTE SPECIAL** commands ensure that the transfer of objects maintains their accuracy as related to their specific drawings. These commands are discussed further in later units.

The use of the DesignCenter (Unit 8) and the tool palettes (Unit 11) allows you to transfer definition-based content such as **Layers, Blocks, Text Styles, Linetypes, Dimension Styles, Layouts,** and **Properties** from one file to another with drag-and-drop operation, as well as the commands above.

Demonstrate the use of **Copy with Base Point** when using the Windows versions of the **Cut, Copy, Paste** sequence. This will increase the accuracy of your placement no matter what the destination file format is.

## CLOSING AND EXITING

The **CLOSE** command will end your currently active drawing file session. This command will affect the current file while leaving you still in the AutoCAD program. In most cases the execution of a **CLOSE** command will produce an AutoCAD alert window asking if you would like to save the file (see Figure 2-29). Selecting Yes will produce the **Save As** dialog box (see Figure 2-13), while selecting No will close the session and discard all changes made during the drawing session. The **CLOSE** command is found in two locations, the **File** menu and the **Window** menu. If there are multiple drawing files open, you may choose the **CLOSE ALL** selection under the **Window** menu to close all the files currently opened. To close the drawing session and exit the program, use the **EXIT** command in the **File** menu. As in the **CLOSE** command, the **EXIT** command will also produce the **Save As** dialog box if changes have been made to the drawing.

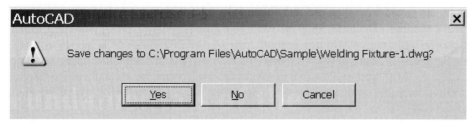

Figure 2-29    AutoCAD alert about saving

## DRAWING UNITS

Next we will create the environment of a typical drawing session. The following commands are all found in the **Format** menu (see Figure 2-30). Initially you should address selecting units and establishing of drawing limits, and developing and executing a layering scheme. Addressing these commands when beginning a new file will help organize and control the creation of the drawing entities.

First and foremost, you need to select the type of units with which you will be working. The **UNITS** command will launch the **Drawing Units** dialog box (see Figure 2-31). Here you can address the type or style of input units you will use for both linear input (see Figure 2-32), as well

Figure 2-30    Format menu

Figure 2-31    Drawing Units dialog box

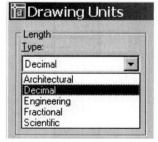

Figure 2-32    Length units drop-down list

as angular input (see Figure 2-33). By default, the linear units are set to decimal input with four-place precision (see Figure 2-34). Other choices found in the **Length** drop-down list include **Architectural** (see Figure 2-35), **Engineering** (see Figure 2-36), **Fractional** (see Figure 2-37), and **Scientific** (see Figure 2-38).

Keep in mind that the **Decimal** style is used for imperial units (feet or inches) as well as metric units. All the styles have a precision value. This controls the accuracy of a number when displayed in various inquiry commands. It does not influence dimensions, as they are controlled by the dimension style. The default precision the program starts with is four-place accuracy. Familiarize yourself with the precision options and format, as they relate to each input style.

Angular inputs are addressed on the right side of the **DRAWING UNITS** dialog box. Once again, they will default to a **Decimal** input style with four-place accuracy (see Figure 2-39). Other angle input choices are **Degree/Minutes/Seconds** (see Figure 2-40), **Grads** (see Figure 2-41), **Radians** (see Figure 2-42), and **Surveyor's Units** (see Figure 2-43), and are found under the **Type** drop-down arrow. Each of these styles has a precision field to control the accuracy of the display of input information. Refer to these figures as examples of the angular input styles and their related precision controls.

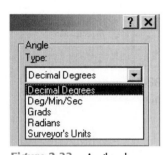

**Figure 2-33**   Angles drop-down list

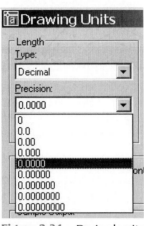

**Figure 2-34**   Decimal units precision

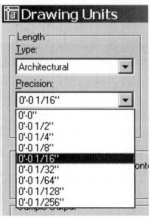

**Figure 2-35**   Architectural units precision

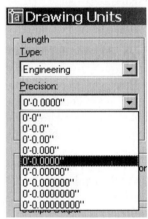

**Figure 2-36**   Engineering units precision

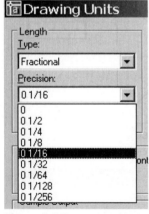

**Figure 2-37**   Fractional units precision

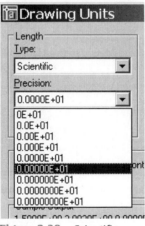

**Figure 2-38**   Scientific units precision

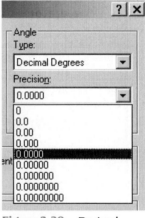

**Figure 2-39**   Decimal angle units precision

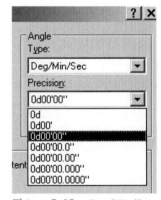

**Figure 2-40**   Deg/Min/Sec angle units precision

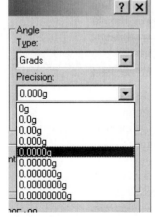

**Figure 2-41**   Grads angles

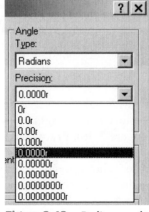

**Figure 2-42**   Radians angle precision

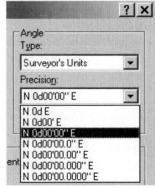

**Figure 2-43**   Surveyor's angle units precision

## DRAWING LIMITS

Now that a selection has been made for your input units, you can start to develop the drawing area. The command **LIMITS** establishes an electronic drawing zone in which to produce the drawing. This zone is created by establishing the lower left corner and the upper right corner of the area. The points of the drawing limits are established with absolute coordinates (x, y) where the first number is a horizontal distance and the second number is vertical distance from the origin in a Cartesian coordinate system.

These values are entered in the current **UNITS** settings. This area should be large enough to accept all the entities required for the drawing in *full size*. Typical default drawing limits are 12 units by 9 units. This could be used for small mechanical parts or electronic components. For most situations the lower left limit should be **0,0** (see Figure 2-44) so that you are always in positive X and Y coordinates. If you are going to do a typical residential floor plan, more appropriate upper right input might be 100'-00" × 75'-00" (see Figure 2-45), whereas a civil application required for a subdivision could be upwards of 10,000'-00" × 10,000'-00".

**full size:** Drawing something in a 1 unit = 1 unit scale such as 1" = 1" or 1' = 1' or 1 m = 1 m.

**Note:**
Drawings should be made at full size or with actual dimensions. Scaling the drawing to fit the paper is done when the plotter device and paper size are chosen in the *PLOT* command.

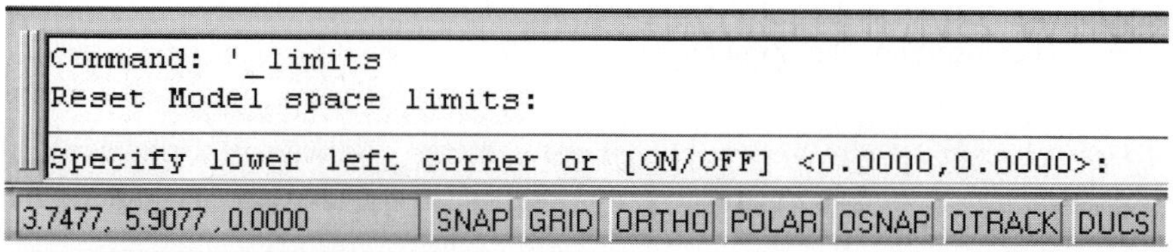

```
Command: '_limits
Reset Model space limits:

Specify lower left corner or [ON/OFF] <0.0000,0.0000>:

3.7477, 5.9077 , 0.0000        SNAP  GRID  ORTHO  POLAR  OSNAP  OTRACK  DUCS
```

**Figure 2-44**   Limits command line 1

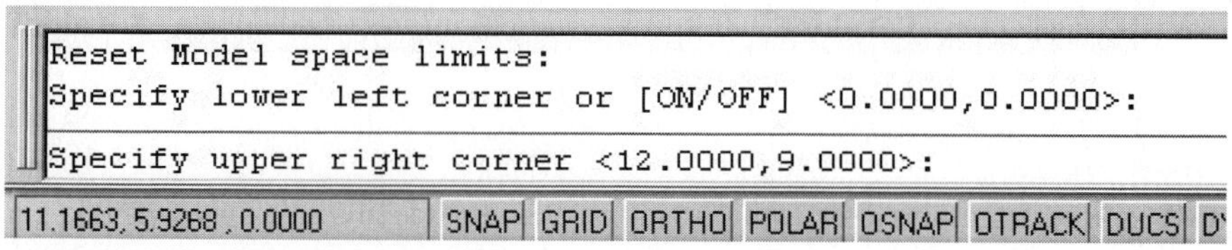

```
Reset Model space limits:
Specify lower left corner or [ON/OFF] <0.0000,0.0000>:

Specify upper right corner <12.0000,9.0000>:

11.1663, 5.9268 , 0.0000        SNAP  GRID  ORTHO  POLAR  OSNAP  OTRACK  DUCS  D
```

**Figure 2-45**   Limits command line 2

For architectural and engineering unit formats, a single quote or foot mark (') is used; otherwise AutoCAD will assume the input unit is in inches. For the scientific format the **E** must be inputted to complete the precision.

Controlling the drawing **LIMITS** will help when it comes to certain **View** commands, the display of a grid, and for plotting of the files.

## LAYER CONCEPTS AND SETTINGS

The layering of a drawing file is a concept relating to the organization and control of drawing entities. *Layers* are like clear overlay sheets to which entities or drawing elements can be attached. These overlays can control certain properties of an entity attached to the layer as well as the visual display of the layer's content.

**layer:** A property attached to an entity for an organizational and control purpose.

**FOR MORE DETAIL**

Various organizations including many government agencies require the use of the U.S. National CAD Standards for drawings (www.nationalcadstandard.org). This standard includes Layering Guidelines and Sheet Naming Conventions as developed by the American Institute of Architects (www.aia.org) and the Construction Specifications Institute (www.csinet.org).

The general concept of layers is to assemble similar entities on individual layers. For instance, you may have an individual layer for object lines, hidden lines, centerlines, dimensions, text, and so on. Although there are layering standards in place throughout the various industries, the development and implementation of a layering scheme is up to the user. Layering practices are not automated in standard AutoCAD. You must continuously be aware of the concepts involved with layering, as well as the commands, in order to maintain the organizational advantages of a properly layered drawing file.

There are no limitations to the number of layers in a drawing file. The initial default layer is named **0** (see Figures 2-46 and 2-47). Each layer must have a unique name. When you first create a layer, a generic default name of Layer1 is assigned to it. Any sequential layers are named Layer2, Layer3, and so on. You can rename layers immediately following their creation, or at a later time. To do that, slowly double-click on the layer name in the **Layer Properties Manager** (see Figure 2-48) and enter into a rename procedure. Layers will address the properties of

**Figure 2-46**    Layers toolbar displaying the current layer

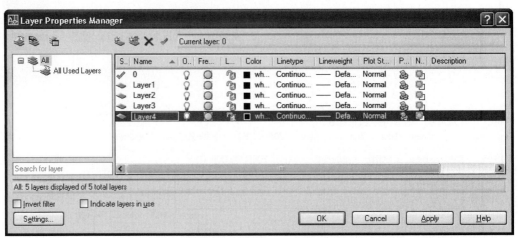

**Figure 2-47**    The Layer Properties Manager for a New Drawing shows layer 0 as the initial layer in model space

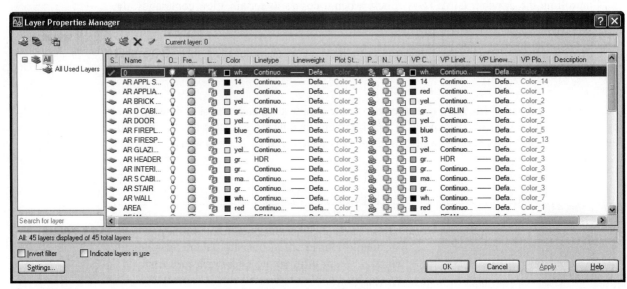

**Figure 2-48**    Layer Properties Manager dialog box when in layout space

**COLOR, LINETYPE, LINEWEIGHT, PLOT STYLE,** and visibility. They control the visibility of the content display in several modes: **ON/OFF, FREEZE/THAW, LOCK/UNLOCK.** In addition to properties and displays, layers can control the ability to plot (print) information from user-designated layers using the **PLOT** command.

## Layer Setup

The creation and control of layers can be found in the **Format** menu under LAYERS . . . as well as the **LAYER** command. Use one of these methods to launch the **Layer Properties Manager** dialog box (see Figure 2-48). From this dialog box, new layers can be created by picking the **New Layer** icon (see Figure 2-49). This will add a layer named Layer1 to the manager window (see Figure 2-50). A layer's color can be changed by picking the color box (see Figure 2-51). This will

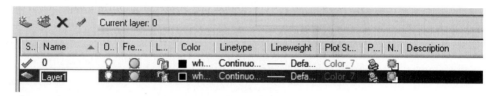

**Figure 2-49**   New Layer     **Figure 2-50**   New Layer naming area in model space
icon

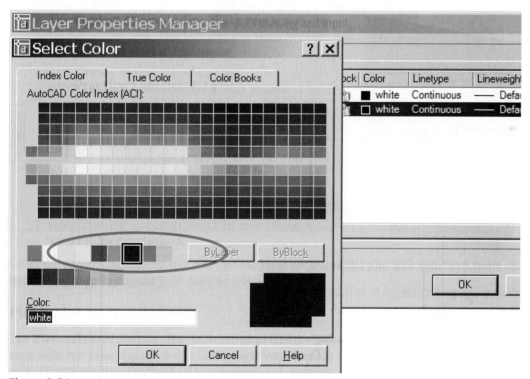

**Figure 2-51**   Color selection

bring up the color selection window. The linetype field allows you to assign a specific linetype to all entities attached to the layer (see Figure 2-52). Keep in mind that you may have to load the linetype first in order to have the style available for assignment. The next property is lineweight (see Figure 2-53). As with the other properties, a lineweight can be assigned to all entities attached to a layer. Depending on your template selection, the plot style property may be available for selection (see Figure 2-54). As mentioned earlier, the second advantage of a properly layered drawing file is the ability to control the display of a layer's content (see Figure 2-55). **On/Off,**

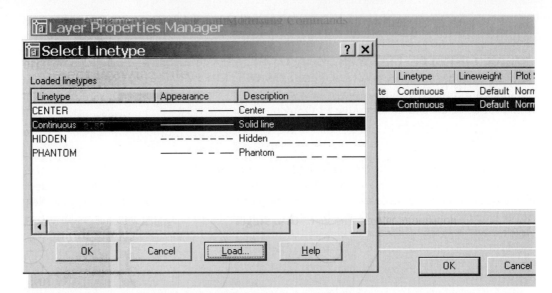

**Figure 2-52** Linetype selection

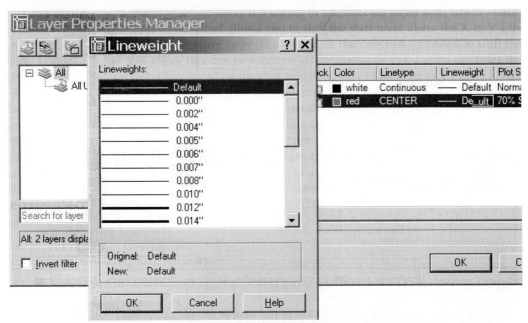

**Figure 2-53** Lineweight selection

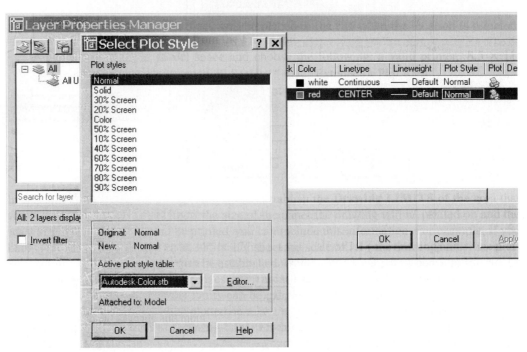

**Figure 2-54** Plot style selection

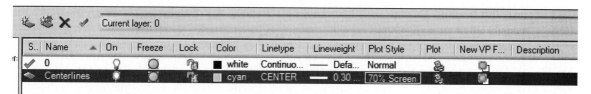

**Figure 2-55**   Completed layer for use in model space

**Freeze/Thaw, Lock/Unlock,** and **Plot** are the options to control the visibility of a layer's content. These controls are accessible through the **Layer Properties Manager,** or by using the pull-down field in the **Layers** toolbar. In both areas the user will have a series of icons to toggle these options on or off. The options and their results are as follows:

- **On/Off** When a layer is **On,** the lightbulb is bright or yellow. When a layer is turned **Off** (dark lightbulb), the entities attached to that layer are invisible. This is a global activity, as this setting affects all model and layout space viewports. Keep in mind that the entities on these layers are still in the regeneration calculations for the drawing, so no time is saved during a regeneration of the drawing.

- **Freeze/Thaw** When a layer is available, it is **Thawed** and the sun is bright or yellow. This option is similar to **On/Off,** in that it too will remove layer entities from the visual display. This is also a global layer operation on the left side, meaning it will freeze objects in all viewports. **Freeze** is similar to **Off** and is represented by the snowflake. The advantage of this option is that it will remove "frozen entities" from the calculations required by a regeneration of the drawing file, thus speeding up redraw and regeneration time. This option does have a higher level of protection than the **On/Off** option for the layer entities.

- **Lock/Unlock** When a layer is **Locked,** all the entities on that layer remain visible, but the entities are not accessible and cannot be modified. Entities can only be placed on **Unlocked** layers. You will be able to object-snap to various entities on a locked layer, but you will not be able to alter that entity in any way. This is a global action and affects all viewports.

- **Plot/NoPlot** This option gives you control over which layers will be used for calculations in the plotting process. Any layer can be given a **NoPlot** status, preventing the layer's content from being printed. This option is best used for layers containing construction geometry, internal notes, sketches, scrap entities, and other record information. These layers are utilized during the building of a drawing and do not need to be a part of the final drawing.

Two other columns on the right side of the display (see Figure 2-56) may be present if the current viewport is in layout space. They represent a **Freeze/Thaw** toggle for the layer in the **Current Layout View** and in future **New Layout** viewports. (Layouts are discussed in Unit 6.)

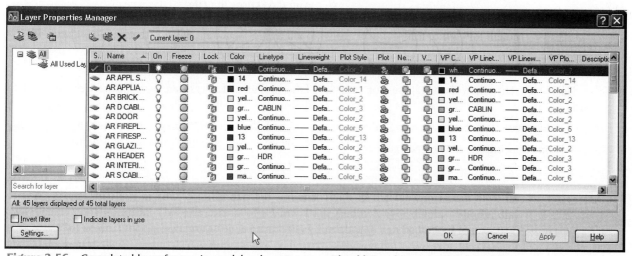

**Figure 2-56**   Completed layer for use in model or layout space with additional icons on the right side

# SUMMARY

In this unit we introduced you to the creation, saving, storage, archiving, and organization of drawing files in AutoCAD. You learned how to start a new drawing either from scratch, by using templates or the Wizards, and were introduced to the ANSI and ISO drafting standards on which the templates are based. You then learned how to manage drawing files with the **NEW, OPEN, SAVE, QSAVE, SAVE AS,** and **CLOSE** commands and the proper use of file directories and extensions. The process of working with several drawings open in a single session, or a Multiple Design Environment (MDE), was explained, as well as the selection of units and the establishment of drawing limits to create the environment of a drawing session. Last, we investigated the creation and use of layers, which are properties that are attached to entities in a drawing and that resemble clear overlay sheets. In general, the concept of layering in AutoCAD is the organization and control of drawing entities by assembling similar entities on individual layers.

# CHAPTER TEST QUESTIONS

## Multiple Choice

1. To save a drawing under a new name, what command would you use?

    a. Save
    b. Rename
    c. Quick Save
    d. Save As

2. A layering scheme will aid in a drawing's:

    a. Organization
    b. Content
    c. Accuracy
    d. File size

3. Which of the following is **not** a display function within layers?

    a. ON/OFF
    b. Freeze/Thaw
    c. Plot/NoPlot
    d. Lock/Unlock

4. To save a drawing file in a different format, what command would you use?

    a. Save
    b. Rename
    c. Quick Save
    d. SaveAs

5. Which of the following is **not** a valid drawing unit to work in?

    a. Scientific
    b. Fractional
    c. Object-based
    d. Architectural

## Matching

a. _____ .dwg
b. _____ .bak
c. _____ .dwt
d. _____ .sv$
e. _____ .dws

1. AutoCAD drawing template
2. AutoCAD backup file
3. AutoCAD Auto save file
4. AutoCAD drawing file
5. AutoCAD drawing standards

## True or False

1. True or False: Users can start a new drawing file from a drawing wizard.

2. True or False: Drawing area is the same as drawing limits.

3. True or False: Only one drawing file can be open at a time.

4. True or False: Layers can have properties attached to them.

5. True or False: All file management commands are similar to the ones used in other Windows-based programs.

# CHAPTER PROJECTS

## Chapter Project 2–1

Describe the differences between manual drafting and CAD.

## Chapter Project 2–2

Research the various standards used by AutoCAD (AIA, U.S. National CAD, British, DIN, and JIS) and others. Which is most appropriate for your drawings and why?

## Chapter Project 2–3

Examine the **Select File** dialog box. How could you search for and find a file? Research and explain the differences in the left column icons for History, My Documents, Favorites, and Desktop. What is the fastest way to find a drawing?

# TUTORIALS

## Tutorial 2-1: Starting a New Drawing from Scratch

1. Start AutoCAD.
2. Access the **File** menu and pick the **NEW** command.
3. Pick the Start from Scratch icon.
4. AutoCAD will complete the initial setup.
5. Access the **File** menu and pick the **SAVE** command.
6. Using the system drive drop-down at the top of the dialog box, navigate to your **Workskills** folder.
7. Enter the name "Scratch" in the location and save the drawing.

## Tutorial 2-2: Starting a New Drawing with Advanced Setup

1. Start AutoCAD.
2. Access the **File** menu and pick the **NEW** command.
3. Pick the Use a Wizard icon.
4. Pick the Advanced Setup option.
5. On the screens pick the following options:
   a. Decimal units
   b. Surveyor angles
   c. East as angle measurement
   d. Counterclockwise as angle direction
   e. Area with 15 for length and 12 for width
   f. Pick **Finish** and AutoCAD will complete the setup.
6. Access the **File** menu and pick the **SAVE** command.
7. Using the system drive drop-down at the top of the dialog box, navigate to your **Workskills** folder.
8. Enter the name "Wizard" in the location and save the drawing.

## Tutorial 2-3: Starting a New Drawing Directly with a Template

1. Start AutoCAD.
2. Access the **File** menu and pick the **NEW** command.
3. Pick the Use a Template icon.
4. Pick the Architectural, English units, named plot style.dwt template from the list displayed.
5. Pick **OK** and AutoCAD will complete the setup.
6. Access the **File** menu and pick the **SAVE** command.
7. Using the system drive drop-down at the top of the dialog box, navigate to your **Workskills** folder.
8. Enter the name "Arch_Template" in the location and save the drawing.

### Tutorial 2-4: Opening a Drawing and Adding Layers

1. Start AutoCAD.
2. Access the **File** menu and pick the **OPEN** command.
3. Using the system drive drop-down at the top of the dialog box, navigate to your **Workskills** folder.
4. Find the Arch_Template drawing and pick the **OPEN** command.
5. Access the **Format** menu and pick the **LAYER** command.
6. Add layers as listed below:
   a. WALLS with Color of Red and Linetype of Continuous
   b. DOORS with Color of Blue and Linetype of Continuous
   c. WINDOWS with Color of Green and Linetype of Continuous
   d. FOUNDATION with Color of Red and Linetype of Dashed
   e. TEXT with Color of Red and Linetype of Continuous
   f. DIMENSIONS with Color of Cyan and Linetype of Continuous
   g. BORDER with Color of Magenta and Linetype of Continuous
7. Access the **File** menu and pick the **SAVE** command to place the updated drawing in the directory.

## PRACTICE EXERCISES

### Practice Exercise 2-1: Creating a Basic Template

1. Start a new drawing in AutoCAD using the acad.dwt template.
2. For **UNITS** set the following:

   Distance                Decimal
   Distance Precision      3
   Angle                   Decimal
   Angle Precision         0.000
   Drag and Drop           Feet

3. For **LIMITS** set the following:

   Lower Left       −20, −20
   Upper Right      220, 220

4. For **LINETYPES** add the following:
   BORDER
   CENTERLINE
   DASHED
   PHANTOM
5. For **LAYERS** add the following:
   PART with Color of Red and Linetype of Continuous
   ASSEMBLY with Color of Blue and Linetype of Continuous
   LINES with Color of Green and Linetype of Continuous
   CENTERLINES with Color of Cyan and Linetype of Centerlines
   HIDDEN with Color of Magenta and Linetype of Dashed
   PHANTOM with Color of Blue and Linetype of Phantom
   TEXT with Color of Red and Linetype of Continuous
   DIMENSIONS with Color of Cyan and Linetype of Continuous
   BORDER with Color of Magenta and Linetype of Continuous
6. Save as a **Template** file type using the **SAVE AS** command with the name ACAD_Template in your **Workskills** folder.

## Practice Exercise 2-2: Creating a Basic Architectural Template

1. Start a new drawing in AutoCAD using the Architectural, English units, color plot style.dwt template.
2. For **UNITS** set the following:
   Distance                Architectural
   Distance Precision      1/8″
   Angle                   Deg, Min, Sec
   Angle Precision         0d00′00″
   Drag and Drop           Inches
3. For **LIMITS** set the following:
   Lower Left              −10, −10
   Upper Right             180, 120
4. For **LINETYPES** add the following:
   BORDER
   CENTERLINE
   DASHED
5. For **LAYERS** add the following:
   WALLS with Color of Red and Linetype of Continuous
   DOORS with Color of Blue and Linetype of Continuous
   WINDOWS with Color of Green and Linetype of Continuous
   FOUNDATION with Color of Red and Linetype of Dashed
   TEXT with Color of Red and Linetype of Continuous
   DIMENSIONS with Color of Cyan and Linetype of Continuous
   BORDER with Color of Magenta and Linetype of Continuous
6. Save as a **Template** file type using the **SAVE AS** command with the name ACAD_Building in your **Workskills** folder.

## Practice Exercise 2-3: Creating a Basic Roadway Design Template

1. Start a new drawing in AutoCAD using the acad.dwt template.
2. For **UNITS** set the following:
   Distance                Decimal
   Distance Precision      3
   Angle                   Decimal
   Angle Precision         0.000
   Drag and Drop           Feet
3. For **LIMITS** set the following:
   Lower Left              −100, −100
   Upper Right             5000, 5000
4. For **LINETYPES** add the following:
   BORDER
   CENTERLINE
   DASHED
   PHANTOM
5. For **LAYERS** add the following:
   ROADWAY with Color of Red and Linetype of Continuous
   DRAINAGE with Color of Blue and Linetype of Continuous
   SIDEWALKS with Color of Green and Linetype of Continuous
   CENTERLINES with Color of Cyan and Linetype of Centerlines
   PIPES with Color of Magenta and Linetype of Dashed
   WATERLINES with Color of Blue and Linetype of Phantom
   TEXT with Color of Red and Linetype of Continuous
   DIMENSIONS with Color of Cyan and Linetype of Continuous
   BORDER with Color of Magenta and Linetype of Continuous
6. Save as a **Template** file type using the **SAVE AS** command with the name ACAD_CIVIL in your **Workskills** folder.

# Fundamental Drawing and Modifying Commands

# 3

## Chapter Objectives

- Use the Cartesian coordinate system.
- Define the "World" coordinate system in AutoCAD.
- Explain input methods.
- Demonstrate Object Snap functions.
- Use drawing aids.
- Use the basic selection methods.
- Create and modify basic entities.

## INTRODUCTION

Now that we have established a few variables within our template file, it's time to create and modify a few basic entities. All CAD systems have the ability to create lines, circles, arcs, text, and so on. The difference between CAD systems is in the methods and options when creating and modifying entities. The draw-modify-dimension-print cycle is a standard approach to the completion of a drawing in a basic AutoCAD system.

Accuracy within the AutoCAD system relies on understanding the *Cartesian coordinate system.* AutoCAD has several input methods that help you create the accurate entities. Understanding the various input methods will ensure accuracy when creating and modifying drawing entities.

Cursor control, drawing aids, and the use of input methods as they relate to the Cartesian coordinate system are the foundation of the accuracy required for creating these entities. Let us first take a look at how each of the basic entities are created and then we will explore the various input methods available to accurately control the creation of these entities. All the following commands can be found on the **Draw** menu (see Figure 3-1) or the **Draw** toolbar (see Figure 3-2).

**Cartesian coordinate system:** A three-dimensional system where the X direction is horizontal, the Y direction is vertical, and the Z direction is coming out of the paper toward the reader.

## ELEMENTARY ENTITIES

### Line

Lines are created by specifying the endpoints of each line segment. After executing the **LINE** command the command prompt will ask you to Specify first point. After the input of the first point the command prompt will ask you to Specify next point. Upon the input of the second point a line will be created between the two selected points. After the completion of the first line the

**Note:**
A review of geometric definitions related to Cartesian coordinates, geometric shapes, and the right-hand rule will help you understand the terms used in the creation of entities in CAD systems.

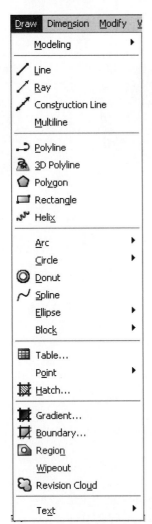

**Figure 3-1**   Draw menu

**Draw**

/ / ⊃ ○ □ ⌒ ⊘ ⊗ ⌒ ○ ○ 🔲 🔲 · 📷 📷 📷 📷 A

**Figure 3-2**   Draw toolbar

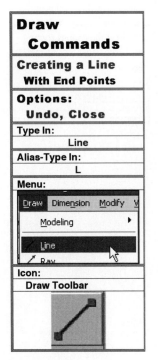

command will stay active, continuing to prompt you to `Specify next point` until you choose to end the sequence by either pressing the **Enter** key, the right mouse button to select a command from the pop-up menu, or the **Esc** key to cancel.

The **LINE** command has two options from within the command. Remember that options to a command are displayed within the square brackets in the prompt line. To execute a command's option you will identify the capital letter from the word in the prompt line and type in that letter, followed by the **Enter** key. After two or more line segments are created you can execute the **Close** option to create one more line segment that will close the shape back to the first selected endpoint or beginning point for the command. The second option is the **Undo** command. When the **Undo** option is executed from within the **LINE** command the last point of input will be released and allow you to respecify the endpoint of the line. Be aware that continuous execution of the **Undo** function will step back through all endpoints specified during the active line sequence.

### Exercise 3-1: Create a Line

- Start AutoCAD and begin a new drawing.
- Select the LINE command from the Draw menu or Draw toolbar.
- Select a location on the screen with the left mouse button to establish the first endpoint of the line.
- Move the cursor to a new location and establish the other endpoint of the line with the left mouse button.

■ Continue moving around the screen drawing lines by clicking on the left mouse button.
■ To finish the command simply hit the Enter key.

## Circle

There are six different ways to create a circle. The two basic methods require an input for the **Center Point** of the circle and a second input for either a **Radius** or **Diameter** value. By default a rubber-band line will appear after the selection of the center point. You can establish the value of the second input by dragging the rubber-band line out to the desired length or by typing in a numeric value.

- **Center radius** The first point will establish the center point for the circle while the second input will be used as the radius for the circle.

- **Center diameter** The first point will establish the center point for the circle while the second input will be used as the diameter for the circle.

**FOR MORE DETAIL**   Additional options for creating a circle will be presented in Unit 7.

## Exercise 3-2: Create a Circle

■ Start AutoCAD and start a new drawing or continue with the drawing from the previous exercise.
■ Select the CIRCLE command from the Draw menu and Center, Radius on the cascading menu.
■ Select a location on the screen with the left mouse button to establish the center point of the circle.
■ Drag the cursor to a new location to establish the radius of the circle and select that point with the left mouse button.
■ Select the CIRCLE command from the Draw menu and Center, Radius on the cascading menu.
■ Select a location on the screen with the left mouse button to establish the center point of the circle.
■ Key in a value of three followed by the Enter key for the value of the circle radius.

## Arc

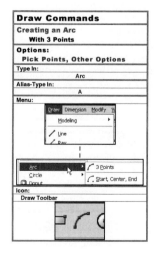

Although there are 11 ways to create an arc, most of the methods are based on prompting the user for start points, endpoints, and center points in various orders. The simplest and quickest way to create an arc is with the **3 Point** method. By selecting three points on the screen you will be creating an arc that passes through all three selected points with the two points farthest apart as the start point and the endpoint.

**FOR MORE DETAIL**   Additional options for creating an arc will be presented in Unit 7.

## Exercise 3-3: Create an Arc

■ Start AutoCAD and start a new drawing or continue with the drawing from the previous exercise.
■ Select the ARC command from the Draw menu and 3 Point on the cascading menu or Draw toolbar.

regular polygon: A multi-sided closed figure where all sides are equal and interior angles are equal.

inscribe: To construct an entity inside a circle.

circumscribe: To construct an entity on the outside of a circle.

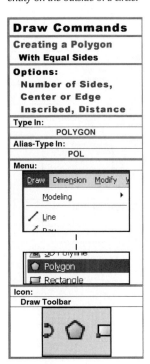

- Select a location on the screen with the left mouse button to establish the first endpoint of the arc.
- Drag the cursor to a new location to establish the second point of the arc and select that point with the left mouse button.
- Move the cursor to a third location to establish the remaining endpoint of the arc. Select that point with the left mouse button.

## Rectangle

The **Rectangle (RECTANG)** command will prompt the user to specify the First Corner Point and the Other Corner Point. This will control the creation of the **Rectangle** by opposite corners. All four lines of the rectangle created will be joined together as one entity. Options for the **Rectangle** command include **Chamfer, Elevation, Fillet, Thickness,** and **Width**. These options can be executed to establish beveled (**Chamfer**) or rounded (**Fillet**) corners. The **Elevation** and **Thickness** options are related to the creation of a three-dimensional rectangle and the **Width** option will create the lines that give the rectangle a wider line value. We will learn more about these options in Unit 7.

### Exercise 3-4: Create a Rectangle

- Start AutoCAD and start a new drawing or continue with the drawing from the previous exercise.
- Select the Rectangle command from the Draw menu or Draw toolbar.
- Select a location on the screen with the left mouse button to establish the first corner of the rectangle.
- Drag the cursor to a new location to establish the diagonal corner of the rectangle. Select that point with the left mouse button.

## Polygon

The **POLYGON** command produces a multisided **regular polygon** in the drawing. This command uses a series of prompts that you will be required to answer. Polygons are based on a center point and a radius or edge. They will then be constructed either **inscribed** within the circle or **circumscribed** about the outside of the circle.

The radius value can be considered across the flats (circumscribed) or across the corners (inscribed). The following is the sequence of prompts issued during the construction of the polygon.

```
Enter number of sides:
Specify center of polygon or [Edge]:
Enter an option [Inscribed in circle/Circumscribed about circle] <I>:
Specify radius of circle:
```

Be aware that if you make an input error during the sequence you will have to cancel the command (**Esc** key) and start it again. There is no method to back up through the sequence to change any previous inputs.

### Exercise 3-5: Create a Polygon

- Start AutoCAD and start a new drawing or continue with the drawing from the previous exercise.
- Select the POLYGON command from the Draw menu or toolbar.
- Enter the number of sides you want in your polygon.
- Specify a location on the screen for the center point of the polygon with the left mouse button.
- Type in an "I" followed by the Enter key to inscribe the polygon inside the circle.
- Drag the cursor out to specify the polygon radius.

## Point

A *point* is a location in space. Points have no physical characteristics such as length, width, or height. When you select the **POINT** command, the X, Y, and Z coordinates are recorded for that position. Since points have no physical characteristics, they can be displayed as a variety of graphic outputs. By default the point will show up as a dot on the screen. The system variable **PDMODE** controls the graphic display of a **Point.**

Figure 3-3 shows available point styles. Only one **Point** graphic output can be used in a drawing file. All **Points** in the drawing will have the same graphic output.

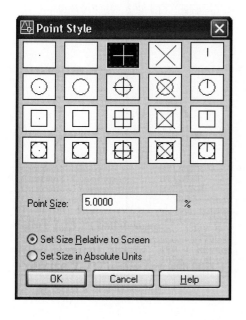

Figure 3-3    Point styles

## CREATING GRID AND SNAP CONTROLS

A *grid* is a series of dots spaced in a rectangular pattern on the screen. The rectangular pattern of dots will extend over the area you specify as the drawing limits (default area is from 0,0 to 9,12 in English units). Using the *grid* is similar to placing a sheet of graph paper under a drawing. The grid helps you align objects and visualize the distances between them. The visual display of the grid can be turned on or off in the status line and is transparent to the print process, meaning it will not plot.

*Snap* is a user-defined value that restricts the movement of the cursor based on the value to be found. The **On/Off** of **SNAP** can also be controlled through the status line. When **SNAP** is turned on, the cursor seems to adhere or "snap" to an invisible rectangular grid.

The combination of these two commands can produce a visual display of dots along with a controlled motion of the cursor, which can be useful for specifying precise input with the arrow keys or the pointing device. Though the **SNAP** and **GRID** settings can be equal, resulting in the cursor movement snapping to each grid dot, they can be set up in such a way that they have a proportional relationship to each other. You can change the grid and snap values in the **Tools** menu under **Drafting Settings** (see Figure 3-4). You can also right-click on the word **SNAP** or **GRID** in the status line and select **Settings** from the pop-up menu. If you zoom in or out of your drawing, you may need to adjust grid and snap spacing to be more appropriate for the new magnification.

Snap spacing does not have to match grid spacing. For example, you might set a wide grid spacing to be used as a reference but maintain a closer snap spacing for accuracy in specifying points. The **SNAP** and **GRID** spacing are based on X and Y values. If you change the X value, the Y value will change to match it. If you need a more rectangular look you may enter a new value for the Y field in the dialog box, resulting in a rectangular grid and/or snap.

There is also a setting in this dialog box referred to as **Snap type.** The choices are **Rectangle snap, Isometric snap,** and **Polar.** The selection of an isometric style will result in

grid: A symmetrically spaced pattern.

snap: The ability to exactly choose a known location.

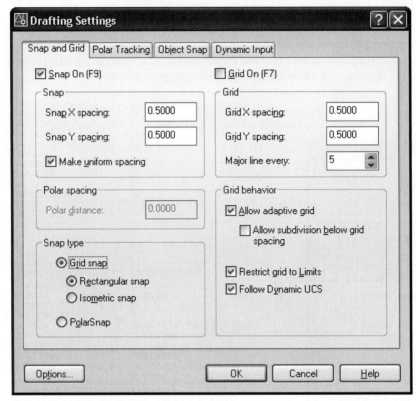

**Figure 3-4**   The Drafting Settings dialog box

the rotation of the grid and snap values to an isometric receding axis in both directions (approximately 35°). Refer to Figures 3-5 and  3-6 to see the difference in the styles available.

The Snap type area lets you select a rectangular grid, isometric grid, or polar grid as the basic layout for placement of lines. The grid behavior area is self-explanatory as to these grid options.

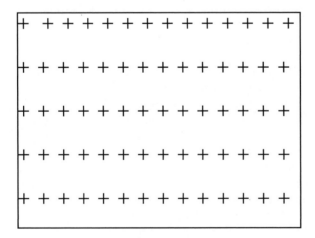

**Figure 3-5**   A rectangular grid display

## PRECISION INPUT METHODS

There are several different input methods available to you at any given time for the precise location of an object. Based on information you are working with, one method may be more beneficial than another, but all are available for use at any time and in any combination. The bottom line regarding input methods is to maintain the level of accuracy, while doing a minimal amount of

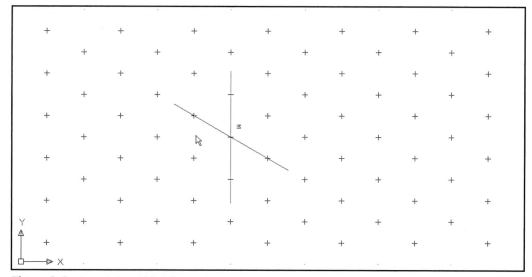

**Figure 3-6**    Isometric grid for drawing

mathematical calculation. Input can be done through ***direct distance entry,*** the ***absolute coordinate system,*** the ***relative coordinate system,*** and the ***relative polar coordinate system.*** These methods offer a wide choice of philosophies and are the most common styles.

Some of these methods work in a formula style meaning there is a specific syntax that needs to be followed, i.e., **X,Y** or **@X,Y** or **@DISTANCE<ANGLE.** The @ (at) symbol implies the method of input is floating origin based. The < (less than) symbol indicates the information is a polar angle. Other input methods benefit from the use of drawing aids or object snaps to increase the accuracy of the input.

> Mastery of the Cartesian coordinate system and its relationship to data entry is essential to a drawing's accuracy.

## Cartesian Coordinates

AutoCAD draws only on an X-Y plane that is initially defined by the ***world coordinate system (WCS)*** and is shown by the X-Y icon in the lower left corner of the drawing screen. In this configuration, the positive X axis is horizontal, the positive Y axis is vertical, and the positive Z axis is coming out of the screen toward the operator (see Figure 3-7).

There is an ability to redefine the X-Y plane's orientation by defining a ***user coordinate system (UCS).*** This method repositions the drawing's origin at some other location or orientation to a drawing's entities. The point at which the X and Y axes intersect is called the ***origin*** and is assigned a coordinate value of **0** for **X** and **0** for **Y,** expressed as **0,0.** Values are assigned from the

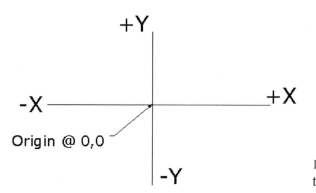

**Figure 3-7**    The X and Y axes showing the origin

**direct distance entry:** Input method that works on a mouse direction and an input of the distance value.

**absolute coordinate system:** Input method based on an X, Y, and Z value related to a fixed origin.

**relative coordinate system:** Input method based on an X, Y, and Z value related to a floating or moving origin.

**relative polar coordinate system:** Input method based on an angle and a distance related to a floating or moving origin.

**world coordinate system:** Base location of the fixed origin position typically 0,0,0 and the relationship of the XY plane.

**user coordinate system:** An alternate position of the Cartesian coordinate system based on user input.

**origin:** The fixed position of a Cartesian coordinate system. The origin has an X,Y value of 0,0.

origin with the appropriate sign (+ or −) based on the direction from the origin. Movement to the right and upward is positive and the movement to the left and downward is negative.

## Cursor Control

*Cursor control* refers to the movement of the screen pointer or crosshairs. The cursor movement is generated by mouse movement or in some cases use of the arrow keys on a keyboard. A left click on a location or an entity will be considered an input. Although with the free movement of the cursor it is rather hard to control the exact input, the use of several different ***drawing aids*** in combination can ensure a great deal of accuracy. As mentioned in the previous section, the use of a grid and snap will help control cursor movement.

When you need to attach to a specific point on an existing entity you can use ***Object Snap*** mode to find that exact location.

The drawing aid known as ***ORTHO*** is used to create entities perpendicular to one another. ***Tracking*** with **Polar** and **Object** options is yet another method used to invoke snap angles and information filters using **X** and **Y** values from entities on the screen (see Figure 3-8).

| SNAP | GRID | ORTHO | POLAR | OSNAP | OTRACK | DUCS | DYN | LWT | MODEL |

**Figure 3-8** Cursor control toggles at the base of the screen, also known as the status line

## Direct Distance

**Direct Distance** uses a mouse direction and a typed input distance to specify the location. With **Direct Distance** input, you can quickly specify a point relative to the last point you entered. At any AutoCAD prompt asking for a point location, you can point the mouse's rubber-band line in the direction needed and enter a numeric value through the keyboard, followed by the **Enter** key. This will create a line or entity in the direction of the mouse with the length equal to the value typed in. The **ORTHO** and **Polar Snap** drawing aids can be used in conjunction with direct distance to increase accuracy in mouse direction.

## Absolute Coordinate System

Absolute coordinate values are based on a fixed position location from the base known as the origin (**0,0**). The origin is where the X and Y axes intersect in the Cartesian coordinate system. Use an absolute coordinate when you know the precise **X** and **Y** values of the point coordinate. For example, the coordinate **3,4** specifies a point **3** units along the X axis and **4** units along the Y axis from the origin. To use absolute coordinate values to specify a point location, enter an **X** value and a **Y** value separated by a comma. The syntax looks like this: **X,Y** followed by the **Enter** key (see Figure 3-9).

The **X** value is the positive or negative distance, in units, along the horizontal axis. The **Y** value is the positive or negative distance, in units, along the vertical axis. All absolute coordinate input is related to the current position of the origin. To calculate X and Y movement it will be necessary to know the **X,Y** values of the previous inputted point. Remember to add values when moving to the right and upward, and subtract values when moving to the left and downward.

**drawing aids:** Series of on/off toggles such as SNAP, GRID, ORTHO, and POLAR that assist with input.

**Object Snap mode:** Method for selecting predefined positions on an object.

**ORTHO:** A drawing aid to create objects at right angles.

**tracking:** A way to locate points relative to other points on the drawing.

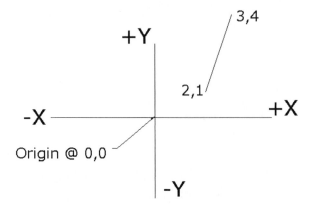

**Figure 3-9** Using absolute coordinates

## Relative Coordinate System

Relative coordinate input is related to a floating origin. Relative coordinate values are based on the last point entered as if it was a temporary origin value of **0,0.** Movement can then be calculated as if it was moving from the temporary origin located at the last point of input (see Figure 3-10). As in the absolute coordinate system, **X** movement is horizontal and **Y** movement is vertical. Use a relative coordinate when you know the position of a point in relation to the previous point. To specify a relative coordinate, precede the coordinate with an @ sign. For example, the coordinate **@3,4** specifies a point **3** units along the X axis and **4** units along the Y axis from the last point specified.

> **Note:**
> You could also include the third dimension (Z) as the height of the entity, making the entry X,Y,Z for a true 3D drawing.

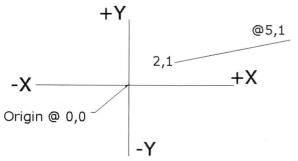

**Figure 3-10**    Using relative coordinates for placement of line

You must keep in mind the syntax required for relative input and the positive and negative values of the input, since this will control the direction of the movement from the origin. This input method should eliminate the need to add and subtract values from the previous point of input.

## Polar Coordinate System

Polar coordinate input is based on an angle and a distance. By default, the direction of east equals **0** degrees and angles increase in the counterclockwise direction (a positive angle value) and decrease in the clockwise direction (a negative angle value) (see Figure 3-11). For example, entering **@1<315** is the same as entering **@1<-45.** The angle conventions for the current drawing are set within the **Format** menu under the **UNITS** command. Polar coordinates can be entered as either absolute (measured from the origin) or relative to the previously entered point. To specify a relative coordinate, precede the coordinate with a @ sign. The correct syntax would look like this; **distance<angle** or **@distance<angle** (see Figure 3-12). The first number will be taken as a distance and the second number will be taken as the angle. These two values need to be separated by the less than (<) sign, which in turn treats the numeric input as polar coordinate values.

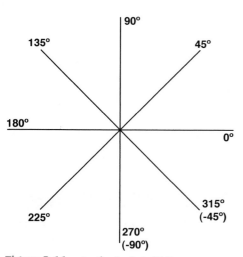

**Figure 3-11**    Angles in AutoCAD

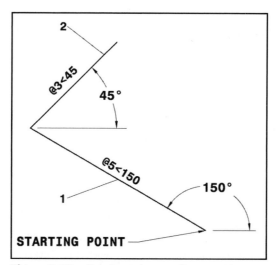

**Figure 3-12**    Relative polar coordinate entries

Mastery of the various drawing aids found on the status line will increase efficiency, accuracy, and productivity.

## PRECISION DRAFTING CONTROLS

Precision drafting controls are referred to as drawing aids. We have already covered two drawing aids known as **GRID** and **SNAP. Object Snap, Object Tracking, Polar Tracking,** and **ORTHO** are the remaining drawing aids available when the program is asking for an input. Like **GRID** and **SNAP** all these aids are easily toggled on or off from the status line below the drawing area (see Figure 3-8), and a right click on the button will access a setting command to adjust the values of the option. The most used of these aids is **Object Snap. Object Snap** is the best way to attach new elements to existing entities in the drawing by "snapping" or linking to a specified location on an existing object already in the drawing file. Using the cursor control input method without object snap will generally not be accurate depending on the level of zoom applied. Even with maximum zoom, one's eye is no match for the accuracy of a CAD system. Therefore snapping is an important tool for drawing accurately. Auto-CAD offers a wide range of snap options for use in a drawing as discussed in the following sections.

A drawing's integrity is based on accurate placement of geometry. In today's CAD/CAM world there is no room for run-ons (overshoots) or gaps (undershoots) between entities. Operators must use Object Snap to ensure accuracy in their work.

### Object Snap

**Object Snap (OSNAP)** constrains a point specification to exact locations, such as a midpoint or an intersection, on existing objects. Using **Object Snap** is a quick way to locate an exact position on an object without having to know the coordinate or draw construction geometry. For example, you can use **Object Snap** to draw a line from the center of a circle to the midpoint of an existing line segment. You can specify an object snap whenever AutoCAD prompts for a point. Let's take a look at the most common **Object Snap** functions (see Figures 3-13 and 3-14).

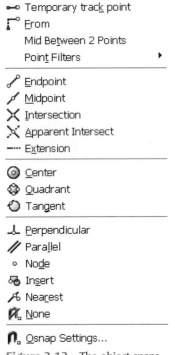

Figure 3-13  The object snaps available from the Right Mouse menu

Figure 3-14  Object Snap toolbar

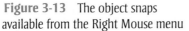

- **Endpoint** Endpoint will snap to the endpoint of either a line or an arc or to any vertex on a polyline.
- **Midpoint** Midpoint will snap to the midpoint of either a line or an arc or to the midpoint of any segment on a polyline.
- **Center** Center will snap to the center point of either a circle or an arc.
- **Quadrant** Quadrant will snap to the 0, 90, 180, or 270 degree point on a circle or an arc.
- **Intersection** Intersection will connect to the exact location where two existing entities cross in a geometric plane or in space (apparent intersection).
- **Perpendicular** Perpendicular will snap to a point that would be at a right angle to the entity selected.
- **Tangent** Tangent will calculate the exact point where a line, circle, or arc connects with a second line, circle, or arc. Remember the definition of tangency is that two entities touch in one point and only one point.
- **Node** Node is the function that will snap to a point entity.
- **Nearest** Nearest is the function that will connect an entity to another entity at the closest location selected. This function is a little less accurate than other methods, but it will ensure that the two entities do connect in space without leaving a gap or an overshoot of the object.

**FOR MORE DETAIL** Though this is not a complete list of the **Object Snap** functions, we will visit the more advanced methods in future units.

When an **Object Snap** function is active, AutoCAD displays a marker and a tooltip whenever you move the cursor over or near an active snap point (see Figure 3-15). This feature provides a visual clue that indicates which object snaps are in effect. Each object snap has a unique symbol identifying the function as shown in Figure 3-16.

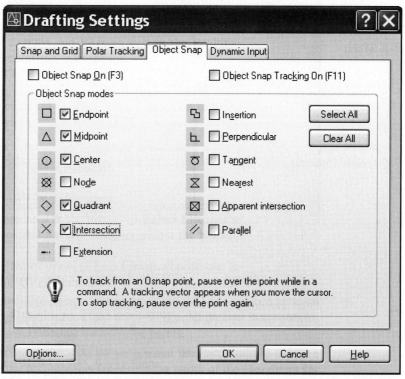

**Figure 3-15** Tooltip and symbol for Object Snap

**Figure 3-16** The Object Snap tab on the Drafting Settings dialog box showing the marker symbols

There are a variety of ways to turn on object snaps. If you choose an individual object snap from the toolbar shown in Figure 3-13 or enter the object snap name on the command line, the object snap stays in effect only for the next point you specify. You also can set a **Running Object Snap,** with one or more object snaps that remain in effect as you work. This is done by accessing the **Drafting Settings** dialog box (see Figure 3-16) from the **Status line** (see Figure 3-8) with a right mouse click to **Settings** or the **Tools** menu. Select the **Object Snap** tab. A choice of **NONE** in the right-click menu or toolbar will turn off both single and running object snaps for the next input.

When you specify an object snap, the cursor changes to an object snap target box. When you select an object, AutoCAD snaps to the eligible snap point closest to the center of the target box. If you need to use the same object snap repeatedly, you can set it as a **Running Object Snap,** which means it stays on until you turn it off. For example, you might set **Center** as a **Running Object Snap** if you need to connect the centers of a series of circles with a line. As with single object snaps, the aperture, or target box, identifies the object snap position with a graphic symbol. When you turn on multiple running object snaps, AutoCAD uses the object snap most appropriate to the object you select. If two potential snap points fall within the selection area, AutoCAD snaps to the eligible point closest to the center of the target box.

## Object Tracking

**Object Tracking** allows you to hover over an existing object snap position and track from that position at a specified angle. Object tracking is used in combination with **Object Snaps.** By default, object tracking will track in a horizontal or vertical direction from the object snap position. This feature can also be set to track in the increments of the **Polar Tracking** angle setting (see Figure 3-17). This aid filters out the X or Y value of the position and makes that value available to input the next position. You will notice the dotted "tracking" line when the cursor passes over a valid object snap position. You can then move down the tracking line to select a position along the line for the next input.

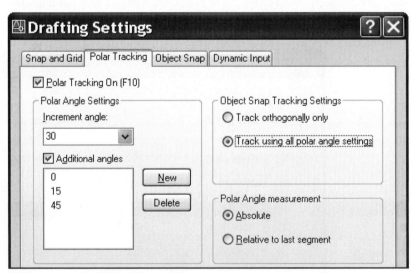

**Figure 3-17**    Polar Tracking settings tab in the Drafting Settings dialog box

## Polar Tracking

**Polar Tracking** is sometimes referred to as **Angle Snap.** This drawing aid allows you to specify an angle as an incremental value (again, see Figure 3-17). When active the cursor will snap to the angle's value in an incremental fashion as the cursor is moved around the drawing screen.

If the **Polar Tracking** value is set for 45°, the function will snap to 45, 90 135, 180, 225, and so on around the drawing screen. When the cursor is in the range of the angle value (or a multiple of the value) a dotted "tracking" line appears along with a display of the current distance and angle.

## Ortho

**ORTHO** is a drawing aid that creates entities that are perpendicular to previous entities regardless of the screen cursor's position. This function will only track cursor movement that is parallel to the world or a user-defined coordinate system X or Y axis. When active, ORTHO generates all inputs perpendicular to the previously inputted position. This function cannot be used in conjunction with the **Polar Tracking** drawing aid.

## OBJECT SELECTION METHODS

Now that we have discussed the creation of a few basic entities, we need to focus on modifying entities that are on the screen. AutoCAD in general is a command-driven program. This means you pick a command (verb) first and then the entities (noun) for the operation. When working with the series of commands found in the **Modify** menu you will always be prompted to `Select objects` as part of the command sequence.

There are nine different ways of selecting entities within AutoCAD. Let's take a look at some of the basic selection methods.

### Single Selection

Upon entering into any modify command the prompt of `Select objects` will appear in the prompt line and the screen cursor will be replaced by a small square known as a *pick box*. This is referred to as a **single selection** pick box and is used to select the single entity that is below the box when a left click is executed (see Figure 3-18). By moving the pick box over any object on the screen and left-clicking you select that entity and place it in the current selection set. Selected objects will appear in a dashed or highlighted form to signify they are part of the current selection set. You may continue to select other objects that need to be placed in the selection set by simply moving the box over other entities and left-clicking. This process will continue until you complete your selections and finish the selection process by hitting the **Enter** key.

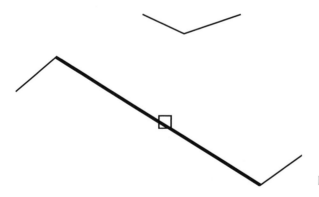

**Figure 3-18**   Pick box single selection

This selection method will select only one entity at a time even if there are multiple entities under the pick box. After completing the selection process you will be prompted for additional information regarding the command originally executed. When the **Modify** command is completed, all the entities in the selection set will be affected.

### Window Selections

Other selection methods allow for the selection of multiple entities in one selection operation. When you are being prompted to `Select objects` and there is no entity under the pick box, you can select that position and start a selection method known as *implied windowing*. Implied windowing will allow you to create a box on the screen to encompass all entities you wish to select (see Figure 3-19). If the movement away from the initial selection point is to the right, a ***window selection*** is in effect. If the movement is to the left, a ***crossing window*** is executed.

window selection: A selection method where only the entities completely inside the selection window are selected.

crossing window: A rectangular area drawn to select objects within its borders.

**Figure 3-19**   Implied window selection when going from left to right (solid line)

The window selection box will appear as a solid box with a light blue background, indicating the window method is active. The window selection method requires that the complete entity must be within the window to be selected. Only entities that are completely inside the window are placed in the selection set. After completing the window you will remain in the select object mode to make other selections. As previously mentioned you must complete the selection process by hitting the **Enter** key. This window method will select all entities, even those that lie directly on top of others.

### Crossing Window Selection

As in the previous method, an implied window is invoked when a left click is made and there is not an entity under the pick box. When you make a move to the left of the initial point a crossing window will appear. The crossing window is displayed as a dashed box with a green background (see Figure 3-20). Any entity that is touched by the crossing style window or is completely inside the crossing style window will be placed in the selection set. As mentioned before, after completing the crossing window you will remain in the select object mode to make other selections. Again you must complete the selection process by hitting the **Enter** key. This crossing window method will select all entities, even those entities that lie directly atop others.

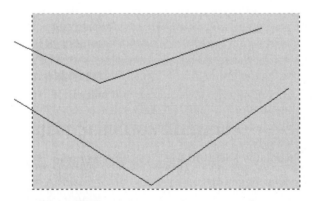

**Figure 3-20**   Implied crossing window selection when going from right to left (dashed line)

| **FOR MORE DETAIL** | Although there are many other selection methods, these three selection methods are sufficient for basic operations. We will be looking at the other methods in Unit 7. |
|---|---|

## ELEMENTARY MODIFYING OF ENTITIES

One of the biggest advantages of a CAD system is the ability to modify existing geometry for other uses. Even though the erasing of objects and the undoing of previously executed commands are part of the **Modify** menu, most modifying commands are used to either alter existing geometry or create more geometry from existing entities currently in the drawing file. As a general rule of thumb you will spend more time in the **Modify** menu than in the **Draw** menu. This may not be the case for all users, but an efficient production session will more likely than not adhere to this concept. If entities already exist, use those entities rather than create a new set of entities from scratch. All of the following modify commands can be found in the **Modify** menu or the **Modify** toolbar (see Figures 3-21 and 3-22).

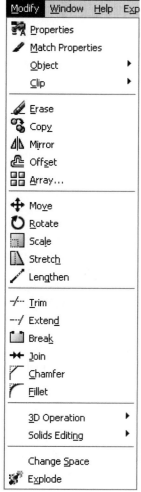

**Figure 3-21**    Modify menu

**Figure 3-22**    Modify toolbar

| Modify Commands |
| --- |
| **Erase Objects** |
| **Various Selection Methods** |
| **Type In:** |
| Erase |
| **Alias-Type In:** |
| E |
| **Menu:** |
| **Icon:** |
| **Modify Toolbar** |

## Erase

The **ERASE** command is used to delete entities from the drawing file. Like all modify commands, after the selection of the command you will be prompted to `Select objects`. After the selection of entities is completed and **Enter** is hit, the selected entities are erased from the drawing file. An alternative method to the **ERASE** command is to select an entity when a command is not in progress and hit the **Delete** key on the keyboard, thus removing the entity from the drawing file. Remember, the program is in "neutral" when the prompt line reads `Command`. This is when you can use the alternative method mentioned above.

### Exercise 3-6: Practice the ERASE Command

- Start a new drawing.
- From the Draw menu pick the LINE command and create a rectangle with diagonal absolute coordinates of 1,1 and 4,4.
- From the Modify menu access the ERASE command.
- Select two lines with the pick box and press the Enter key to remove the objects.

**Modify Commands**

| Move Objects |
| Various Selection Methods |

**Type In:**
Move

**Alias-Type In:**
M

**Menu:**

Modify  Window  Help  Express
- Properties
- Match Properties
- Change to ByLayer
- Object ▸
- Clip ▸

- Annotative Object Scale ▸

- Erase
- Copy
- Mirror
- Offset
- Array…

- Move
- Rotate
- Scale

**Icon:**
**Modify Toolbar**

## Move

The **MOVE** command allows you to select entities and physically move the entities from one location to another. This command will prompt you to select objects. After the selection of objects is completed you will be prompted for a base point that will be used as a control point and a second point or displacement value used as the new location for all the selected entities. Remember that a second point can be established through any of the input methods described earlier. The use of a precise input method will greatly increase the accuracy of the move.

### Exercise 3-7: Practice the MOVE Command

■ Start a new drawing.
■ From the Draw menu pick the LINE command and create a rectangle with diagonal absolute coordinates of 1,1 and 4,4.
■ From the Modify menu access the MOVE command.
■ Select two lines with the pick box and press the Enter key to complete the selection process.
■ Pick a base point for the start of the move.
■ Pick the position for the objects to be located after the move.
■ Notice the objects are in the new location only.

## Copy

The **COPY** command is similar to the **MOVE** command. This command also prompts you to Select objects. After the selection of objects is completed, you will be prompted for a base point to be used as a control point and a second point or displacement value used as the new location for all the selected entities. The difference between the two commands is that the original selected entities will remain in their original location and a second copy of the selected entities will go to the new location specified. Once a second point is specified, you will be able to place multiple copies of the selection set in as many locations as needed by simply left-clicking in a new location. Keep in mind, the selection of a base point and a related second point can be accurately positioned with the use of an **Object Snap** drawing aid or any other input method described earlier.

### Exercise 3-8: Practice the COPY Command

■ Start a new drawing.
■ From the Draw menu pick the LINE command and create a rectangle with diagonal absolute coordinates of 1,1 and 4,4.
■ From the Modify menu access the COPY command.
■ Select two lines with the pick box and press the Enter key to complete the selection process.
■ Pick a base point for the start of the copy.
■ Pick the position for the objects to be located after the move.
■ Notice the objects are in the new location as well as the original positions.

## Offset

The **OFFSET** command produces a copy of the object selected (source object) a specified distance away or through a selected point. First you are prompted to Specify offset distance, where you can key in a specified distance. Next you Select a source object. Last, you are asked to Specify point on side to offset to determine both the direction the offset copy will be produced, and the established distance away.

CAD operators should always look for an opportunity to use and modify geometry already created. This will increase speed and consistency during the drawing session.

If you enter a null response (by pressing <**Enter**>) to the Specify offset distance prompt, the **Through** option is invoked. In this option you select a source object and then specify a point somewhere on the screen through which the offset copy is produced. In both cases a copy of the source object and all the source object's properties are created at the specified location.

There are two options within the **OFFSET** command (see Figure 3-23). The **Erase** option has a **YES** or **NO** value. If this option is **YES** the original source object is deleted when the second point or side of object is selected. The second option addresses the **Layer** function. As mentioned earlier, in default mode, **OFFSET** makes a copy of the selected source object with all the same properties. The **Layer** option has a value of **Current** or **Source.** If this option is set to **Current** the new object created is placed on the current or active layer. If the option is set to **Source,** the new object created retains the layer of the original source object. (The **Layer** option was new in the 2006 version.)

The **Multiple** option will keep the most recently created object active, so you can continue to the **OFFSET** command from that object.

Modify Commands

Copy Objects
**Various Selection Methods**

Type In:
Copy

Alias-Type In:
CO or CP

Menu:

Icon:
**Modify Toolbar**

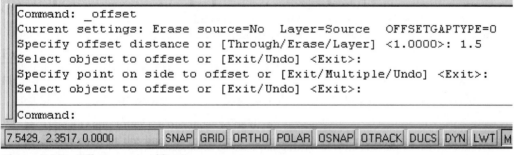

```
Command: _offset
Current settings: Erase source=No  Layer=Source   OFFSETGAPTYPE=0
Specify offset distance or [Through/Erase/Layer] <1.0000>: 1.5
Select object to offset or [Exit/Undo] <Exit>:
Specify point on side to offset or [Exit/Multiple/Undo] <Exit>:
Select object to offset or [Exit/Undo] <Exit>:

Command:

7.5429, 2.3517, 0.0000    SNAP  GRID  ORTHO  POLAR  OSNAP  OTRACK  DUCS  DYN  LWT  M
```

**Figure 3-23**    Offset command lines

**Exercise 3-9:** Create Offset Objects

- Start a new drawing.
- From the Draw menu place a line and a circle in the drawing.
- From the Modify menu pick the OFFSET command.
- Enter 0.5 for the offset distance and press <Enter>.
- Pick the line as the offset object.
- Pick a location above the line for placement of the offset object. *Note:* Distance is already set so this step is only for direction. The command continues to be available.
- Pick the circle as the offset object.
- Pick a location outside of the circle for placement of the offset object.
- Press <Enter> to stop the command.

## Mirror

The **MIRROR** command flips a series of selected objects in a symmetrical fashion over a defined mirror line (see Figure 3-24). After selecting the objects to work with and pressing **Enter,** you are prompted to Specify first point of mirror line: and Specify second point of mirror line:. After the first mirror point is chosen, a rubber-band view moves, as does the cursor, until a second mirror point is chosen. Once the second point of the mirror line is established you are prompted to Erase source object? Yes/No <N>. Answering **Yes** to this question and pressing the **Enter** key erases the original source objects, leaving only the mirrored version of the objects; this action is rarely used.

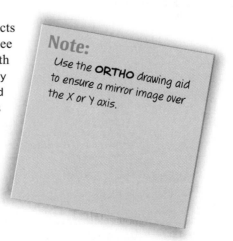

**Note:**
Use the **ORTHO** drawing aid to ensure a mirror image over the X or Y axis.

**Modify Commands**

Offset an Object

**Options:**
**Distance, Through, Side to Offset, Erase, Layer, Multiple, Undo**

Type In:
Offset

Alias-Type In:
O

Menu:

Icon:
Modify Toolbar

**Modify Commands**

**Mirror Objects**

**Options:**
**Mirror Line, Erase
Source Objects**

**Type In:**
Mirror

**Alias-Type In:**
MI

**Menu:**

**Icon:**
**Modify Toolbar**

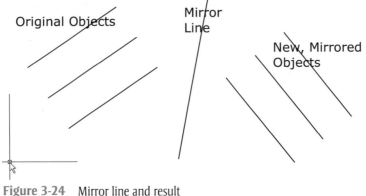

**Figure 3-24**    Mirror line and result

**Exercise 3-10:** Create a Mirror Object

- Start a new drawing.
- From the Draw menu place three lines in the drawing.
- From the Modify menu pick the MIRROR command.
- Select two of the lines as the objects to be mirrored and press <Enter> to end the selection process.
- For the "First point" use an ENDpoint Object Snap to select one end of the line not chosen above.
- Move the mouse to the other end of this line and watch the rubber banding of the mirrored object.
- For the "Second point" use an ENDpoint Object Snap on the other end of the line not chosen.
- Answer No to the question regarding the erasing of objects.

## Arrays

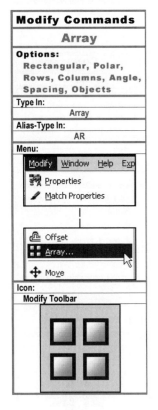

**Modify Commands**

**Array**

**Options:**
**Rectangular, Polar,
Rows, Columns, Angle,
Spacing, Objects**

**Type In:**
Array

**Alias-Type In:**
AR

**Menu:**

**Icon:**
**Modify Toolbar**

An **ARRAY** creates a copy of the selected objects in a patterned format. There are two types of arrays, **Rectangular** and **Polar**. A **Rectangular Array** produces copies based on a rectangle or orthogonal pattern. A **Polar Array** produces copies based on a center point and a circular pattern. The controls for both are found in the **Array** dialog box (see Figure 3-25) under the **Modify** menu and on the **Modify** toolbar. When you select the radio button near the top of the dialog box corresponding to the type of array you want to produce, the dialog box screen reflects the information needed for that particular option.

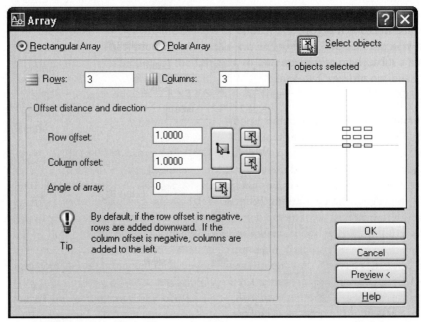

**Figure 3-25**    Array dialog box for rectangular arrays

*Rectangular Array*    Rectangular arrays (see Figure 3-26) form a pattern based on two dimensions. The **Rows** dimension is parallel to the X axis, and the **Columns** dimension is parallel to the Y axis. You need to select the objects you want to pattern and establish the number of **Rows** and **Columns** needed for the array. Then you enter the distance between **Rows** and the distance between **Columns.** Keep in mind that the distance between rows or columns is from the lower left corner of one object to the lower left corner of the next object or from one center to the other center. This distance is made up of the distance across the object, as well as the distance between the objects. The direction in which the pattern will form is based on the positive or negative values of the **Rows** and **Columns** distances. For example, two positive values produce an array in the first quadrant (positive X and Y), while two negative values produce an array in the third quadrant (negative X and Y). The remaining field in the dialog box is for the **Angle** of the array. The **Angle** value rotates the array around the lower left point of the pattern. After you have entered the required information in the dialog box, you can execute the **Preview** button to see the results of the values inputted. If you like the preview results you can **Accept** the input or return back to the **Array** dialog box through the **Modify** button.

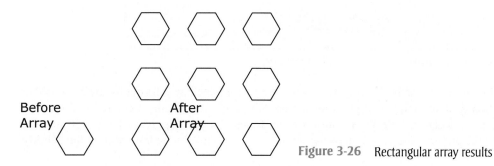

Figure 3-26    Rectangular array results

## Exercise 3-11: Creating a Rectangular Array

- ■ Start a new drawing.
- ■ From the Draw menu pick the RECTANGLE command and create a rectangle with diagonal absolute coordinates of 0,0 and 2,1.
- ■ From the Modify menu access the ARRAY command.
- ■ Verify the top button is set to the Rectangular option.
- ■ Set the following parameters in the dialog box:
  - Rows: 5
  - Columns: 4
  - Row Offset: 2
  - Column Offset: 3
- ■ In the upper right area of the dialog box, pick the Select objects icon and choose the rectangle in the drawing.
- ■ With the left mouse button, pick the Preview option from the lower right command area.
- ■ If the array looks correct, pick Accept from the options provided. If it does not look correct, make the appropriate changes and preview it again.

*Polar Array*    Polar arrays are based on the number of copies needed, a center point, and an angle to fill. You begin by selecting the **ARRAY** command and switching the radio button near the top of the dialog box to **Polar Array** (see Figure 3-27). Next you select the objects you want to pattern and establish the center point around which the pattern will be produced. This can be done by coordinate entry, or by clicking on the **Pick center** button and selecting a point from the drawing screen. Finally, choose the **Method** by which the array is calculated from the drop-down list in the center of the dialog box. There are three methods available, as follows:

- Total number of items (including the original) and Angle to fill
- Total number of items (including the original) and Angle between items
- Angle to fill and Angle between items

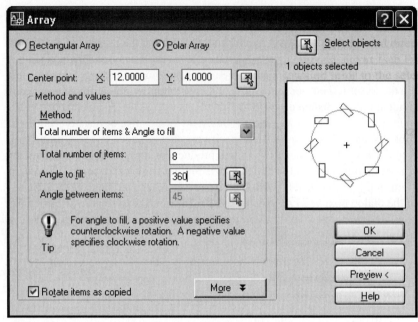

**Figure 3-27**   Polar Array dialog with rotate items selected

Depending on which method you choose, you need to complete the information by establishing the Number of items and the Angle information. When all information is entered in the dialog box you can execute the **Preview** button to see the results (see Figure 3-28). If you like the results of the preview you can **Accept** the input or return to the dialog box through the **Modify** button.

Items that are arrayed may be rotated as they are copied or held with the same orientation as the original based on the check box in the lower left corner of the **Polar Array** dialog box.

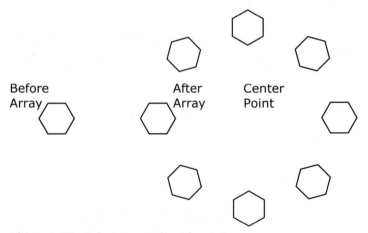

**Figure 3-28**   Polar array results with rotation

## Exercise 3-12: Creating a Polar Array

- Start a new drawing.
- From the Draw menu pick the CIRCLE command and create a circle with center coordinates of 0,0 and a radius of 0.4.
- From the Modify menu access the Array command.
- Verify the top button is set to the Polar option.
- Set the following parameters in the dialog box:
  - Center Point: 3,3
  - Method: Total number and Angle to fill
  - Number: 8
  - Angle: 360

- In the upper right area of the dialog box, pick the Select objects icon and choose the circle in the drawing.
- With the left mouse button, pick the Preview option from the lower right command area.
- If the Array looks correct, pick Accept from the options provided. If it does not look correct, make the appropriate changes and preview it again.

## Rotate

The **ROTATE** command will spin or rotate the selected entities around a specified base point. After your selection of the entities is complete, you will be prompted for a base point, which is the control point the entities rotate around. After selecting a base point you can then specify a rotation value in degrees (see Figure 3-29) or use a **Reference** option to reference two points on the screen, which move that line to a specific rotated position. Remember that 0° points to the east on the polar coordinate system, and 0° is also the default location for the **ROTATE** command. The second option is **Copy.** This option will leave the original selection set of objects in place and create a copy of the objects at the specified rotation and base point.

Modify Commands
Rotate Objects
Various Selection Methods
Type In:
Rotate
Alias-Type In:
R
Menu:
Modify  Window  Help
Properties
Match Properties
Move
Rotate
Scale
Icon:
Modify Toolbar

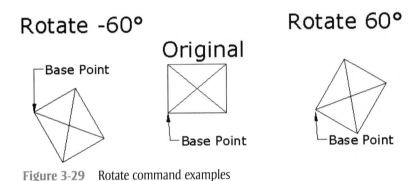

**Figure 3-29**    Rotate command examples

### Exercise 3-13: Practice the ROTATE Command

- Start a new drawing.
- From the Draw menu pick the LINE command and create a rectangle with diagonal absolute coordinates of 1,1 and 4,4.
- From the Modify menu access the ROTATE command.
- Select two lines with the pick box and press <Enter> to complete the selection process.
- Pick a base point for the start of the rotation.
- Pick the location for the objects to be located after the rotation by moving the mouse. A left mouse click will set the new location.
- Notice the objects are in the new location only.

## Scale

The **SCALE** command allows you to increase or decrease the size of the selected objects proportionally in all three directions. This scale operation will be in reference to a user-defined base point. Like all the previous commands, you need to select the objects to work with. After finishing the selection process, you will be prompted for a base point. This is the point the object will grow to, or grow away from. After the definition of the base point you will enter a scale factor, or you can also move the mouse to dynamically view the scaled size.

The current size of the selected objects is considered a factor of 1.0 (see Figure 3-30). Any number larger than 1.0 will increase the size of the objects proportionally; for example, entering a 2 will scale to twice the current size or entering a 4 will scale to four times the current size. Any number under 1.0 will reduce the size of the selected objects by the percentage entered; for instance, inputting 0.5 will reduce the selected set to one-half the current size or inputting 0.25 will reduce it to one-fourth the current size. For the most accuracy, a rational number should be entered at the Scale Factor prompt.

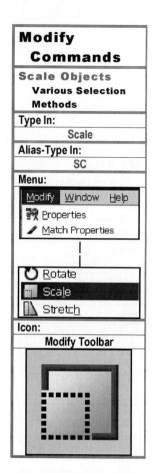

**Modify Commands**

**Scale Objects**
Various Selection Methods

**Type In:**
Scale

**Alias-Type In:**
SC

**Menu:**

**Icon:**
Modify Toolbar

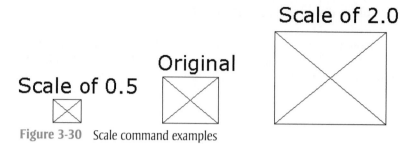

**Figure 3-30**  Scale command examples

The **SCALE** command has two options. The **Reference** option allows you to dynamically select two points on the current entity with the mouse and then enter a value for the new **Reference Length,** which will set the scale factor for the selected set. The second option is the **Copy** option. This will leave the original selection set of objects in place and create a copy of the objects at the specified scale factor and the base point.

### Exercise 3-14: Practice the SCALE Command

- Start a new drawing.
- From the Draw menu pick the LINE command and create a rectangle with diagonal absolute coordinates of 1,1 and 4,4. Also draw the diagonals using the LINE command.
- From the Modify menu access the SCALE command.
- Select the lines that make up the rectangle and press <Enter> to complete the selection process.
- Select the lower left corner of the rectangle for the base point.
- Enter a value of 3.0 for the scale factor and press <Enter>. This will triple the size of the original rectangle.
- Repeat the SCALE command and this time enter a scale factor value of 0.5. This should reduce the size of the rectangle by one-half.

### Undo/Redo

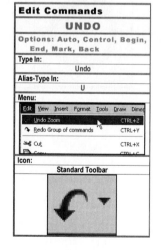

**Edit Commands**

**UNDO**

**Options: Auto, Control, Begin, End, Mark, Back**

**Type In:**
Undo

**Alias-Type In:**
U

**Menu:**

**Icon:**
Standard Toolbar

The **UNDO** command reverses the action of the last command executed. This is considered a basic modifying command even though it is not found in the Modify menu.

You will find this command in the **Edit** menu or in the **Standard** toolbar (see Figure 3-31) typically located under the pull-down menus. The **UNDO** command may act like an **ERASE** command but it is much more. When you invoke an **UNDO** command all the steps used during the execution of the command are also reversed. For example, if you turn on **ORTHO** during the execution of the command, **ORTHO** will be turned off when the **UNDO** command is executed. Multiple **UNDO** functions can be selected from the toolbar icon as you hold down the left mouse button and choose the command you want from the pop-up menu. To reverse an **UNDO** command you can choose the **REDO** command from the **Standard** toolbar. This will reverse the **UNDO** operation and restore the file to the status prior to the **UNDO** command. As with the multiple **UNDO** function there is a multiple **REDO** function that is executed in the same manner.

## ELEMENTARY OBJECT PROPERTIES

All entities created in a drawing file have a series of properties attached to them. These properties can be classified into three areas: general, entity-specific, and style-based. The general properties that are attached to all objects are **LAYER, COLOR, LINETYPE, LINETYPE SCALE,** and **LINEWEIGHT.** Entity-specific properties come in the form of geometry, such as the length of a line or the center point coordinates of a circle or arc. Style-based properties refer to a value that is part of a larger definition-based style. Examples include use of arrowheads in a dimension style, justification of a text string, or the rotation of a block insertion. Although most properties will be assigned and controlled by the user, the general properties assigned to entities in a new drawing session all have a default version related to layer 0. For instance, an entity is white in

**Figure 3-31**  The Undo and Redo arrows on the Standard toolbar

instance, an entity is white in color with a continuous linetype when attached to the layer 0. As mentioned earlier, part of the drawing setup is to establish a layering scheme for organizational purposes. This is where you start to address object properties by assigning some of the general properties to a layer, all the while maintaining awareness of the layer that is active. At this time, let's take a look at the general properties of every entity when it is created. All these properties can be controlled through the **Format** menu, the **Properties** toolbar, or the **PROPERTIES** command found in the **Modify** menu.

## Layer

Each entity is attached to a layer. Layers are identified by giving each one a unique name. An entity can only be attached to one layer at a time. Which layer an object is attached to is up to the user and depends on the current layering scheme. Remember that AutoCAD does not have an automatic layering feature and the organization of layers is defined by the user or individual office practices.

> An understanding of layering concepts and procedures is essential in a well-organized drawing file. Most offices will have established layering guidelines for operators to follow.

## Color

You can assign a color to an object by selecting the color through the **Select Color** dialog box (see Figure 3-32). This dialog box contains the standard AutoCAD colors along with tabs that address a color index, a tab for mixing True Color, and a tab for color books like the PANTONE® series of colors.

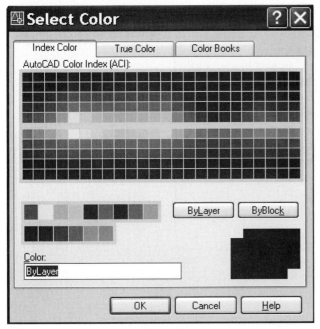

Figure 3-32    Select Color dialog box

## Linetype

This property controls the noncontinuous linetype patterns loaded into the drawing file. By default, linetype is set to continuous. If a noncontinuous pattern such as center or hidden is needed, you must first load the linetype definition from the **Linetype Manager** dialog box (see Figure 3-33) and then assign the linetype property to a specific pattern and to an entity or layer.

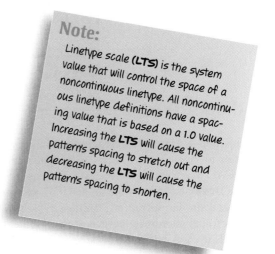

Note:

Linetype scale (**LTS**) is the system value that will control the space of a noncontinuous linetype. All noncontinuous linetype definitions have a spacing value that is based on a 1.0 value. Increasing the **LTS** will cause the pattern's spacing to stretch out and decreasing the **LTS** will cause the pattern's spacing to shorten.

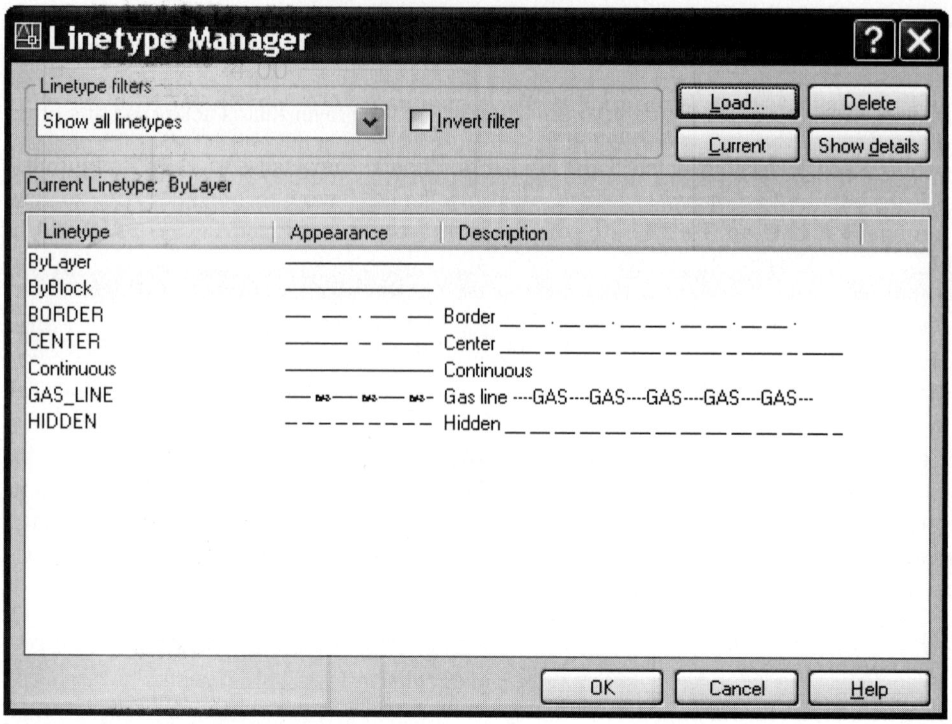

Figure 3-33    Linetype Manager dialog box

## Lineweight

The lineweight property refers to the width of the line when the entity is printed and can be scaled for the current drawing display. Lineweights can be established in English or metric values as shown in the **Lineweight Settings** dialog box (see Figure 3-34). This property is also available through a layering scheme.

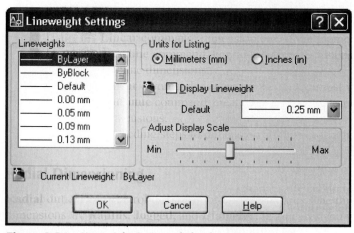

Figure 3-34    Lineweight Settings dialog box

## SUMMARY

In this unit we practiced creating and modifying such basic entities as lines, circles, arcs, rectangles, and polygons in AutoCAD. You were introduced to the various commands (found on the **Draw** and **Modify** menus and toolbars) used to perform these and similar operations. We then explained the basics of the Cartesian coordinate system as well as the different input methods used to precisely locate an object including grid and snap for cursor control, direct distance entry, the absolute and relative coordinate systems, and the relative polar coordinate system. You then learned about various precision drafting controls including **Object Snap (OSNAP)** functions, **Object Tracking, Polar Tracking,** and **Ortho.** Next we discussed some of the different methods used to select objects for Auto-CAD operations (single selection, window selection, and crossing window selection). You then proceeded to learn the modifying commands, focusing those used to either alter existing geometry (**OFFSET, MIRROR, ARRAY, ROTATE,** and **SCALE**) or create more geometry from existing entities. Finally, you learned the entity properties that are attached to all objects in AutoCAD: layer, color, linetype, linetype scale, and lineweight.

## CHAPTER TEST QUESTIONS

### Multiple Choice

1. Grid and Snap settings can be found in the _____ dialog box.

    a. Options
    b. Drafting Standards
    c. Properties
    d. Object Snap

2. Which of the following is **not** a valid input method?

    a. Absolute
    b. Relative coordinates
    c. Direct distance
    d. Object-based

3. The origin of the absolute coordinate system has a value of:

    a. 1,1
    b. 0,1
    c. 0,0
    d. 1,0

4. When using a modify command, users will be prompted to:

    a. List objects
    b. Select objects
    c. Draw the objects
    d. Assign objects

5. Which of the following is **not** a valid object property?

    a. Linetype
    b. Layer
    c. Color
    d. Coordinate

### Matching

a. _____ Absolute coordinates

b. _____ Relative coordinates

c. _____ Polar coordinates

d. _____ Direct distance

e. _____ Cursor control

1. Mouse movement

2. X,Y

3. @X,Y

4. Distance<angle

5. Mouse direction and a distance

### True or False

1. True or False: Only one input method can be active at a time.

2. True or False: The pick box is used for the selection of multiple objects.

3. True or False: ORTHO mode will lock cursor movement to the X or Y axis.

4. True or False: Polar tracking is referred to as angle snap.

5. True or False: A crossing window requires the object to be completely inside the window.

## CHAPTER PROJECTS

### Chapter Project 3–1

Your instructor will divide the class into groups. Then your group will measure one of the classroom buildings on campus and determine the spacing of support columns, beams, roof beams, and other information. Make a drawing and show the location of stairs and elevators. What method for input did you use?

### Chapter Project 3–2

Measure the building where you live and do the above.

### Chapter Project 3–3

Take a field trip to an office construction site or visit an existing building and check the drawings for accuracy and compare to the construction. How accurate do you need to be?

## TUTORIALS

## Tutorial 3-1: Using Absolute Coordinates to Draw

In this tutorial you will use AutoCAD to create the drawing in Figure 3-35 using the absolute coordinates shown to draw the lines.

1. From the **File** menu choose **NEW** to begin a new drawing.
2. From the **Format** menu choose **Drawing LIMITS** and enter **0,0** for the lower left corner and **11,8.5** for the upper right corner to complete the command.

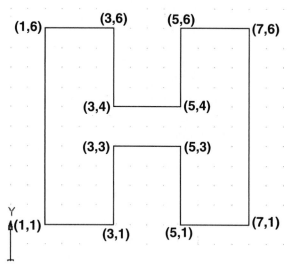

Figure 3-35

3. From the **View** menu, pick **Zoom** and then pick **All** to resize the drawing area to your limits.
4. Access the **LINE** command from the icon, the **Draw** menu, or by typing **LINE.** Enter **1,1** as the first point (see Figure 3-36) and press the **Enter** key.

```
Command: line
Specify first point: 1,1
Specify next point or [Undo]:
```
```
5.9909, 7.5757, 0.0000        SNAP GRID ORTHO POLAR OSNAP OTR
```

Figure 3-36    Start of LINE command

5. Continuing in the **LINE** command, enter the following coordinates to complete the drawing. After each set of coordinates press the **Enter** key to go to the next coordinate request entry:
   a. **1,6**
   b. **3,6**
   c. **3,4**
   d. **5,4**
   e. **5,6**
   f. **7,6**
   g. **7,1**
   h. **5,1**
   i. **5,3**
   j. **3,3**
   k. **3,1**
   l. **1,1** (This last entry could be a **C** for **Close** as this returns the end of the line segment to the origin of the drawing line).

6. Access the **File** menu and select the **SAVE AS** command. Maneuver to your **Workskills** folder as shown in Figure 3-37, enter the name **Tutorial 3-1,** and save this drawing.

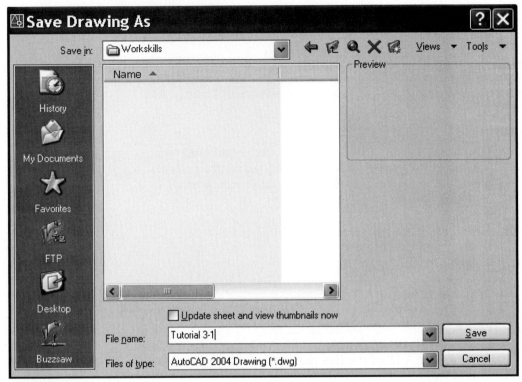

**Figure 3-37**

## Tutorial 3-2: Using Relative Coordinates to Draw

In this tutorial you will use AutoCAD to create the drawing in Figure 3-38 using the relative coordinates shown to draw the lines.

1. From the **File** menu choose NEW to begin a new drawing.
2. From the **Format** menu choose **Drawing LIMITS** and enter **0,0** for the lower left corner and **11,8.5** for the upper right corner to complete the command.
3. From the **View** menu, pick **Zoom** and then pick **All** to resize the drawing area to your limits.

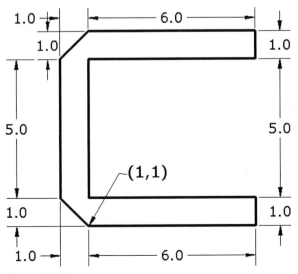

**Figure 3-38**

4. Access the **LINE** command from the icon, the **Draw** menu, or by typing **LINE.** Enter **1,1** as the first point (see Figure 3-39) and press the **Enter** key.

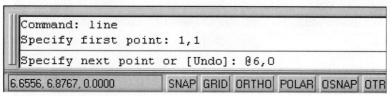

```
Command: line
Specify first point: 1,1

Specify next point or [Undo]: @6,0
```
| 6.6556, 6.8767, 0.0000 | | SNAP | GRID | ORTHO | POLAR | OSNAP | OTR |

Figure 3-39

5. Continuing in the **LINE** command, enter the following information to complete the drawing. After each set of coordinates press the **Enter** key to go to the next coordinate request entry:
   a. **@6,0**
   b. **@0,1**
   c. **@-6,0**
   d. **@0,5**
   e. **@6,0**
   f. **@0,1**
   g. **@-6,0**
   h. **@-1,-1**
   i. **@0,-5**
   j. **@1,-1** (This last entry could be a **C** for **Close** or a **1,1** as this returns the end of the line segment to the origin of the drawing line.)
6. Access the **File** menu and select the **SAVE AS** command. Maneuver to your **Workskills** folder as shown in Figure 3-37, enter the name **Tutorial 3-2,** and save this drawing.

## Tutorial 3-3: Using Relative Polar Entries for Drawing

In this tutorial you will use AutoCAD to create the drawing in Figure 3-40 using the relative coordinates shown to draw the lines.

1. From the **File** menu choose **NEW** to begin a new drawing.

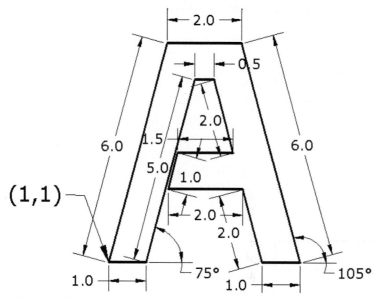

Figure 3-40

2. From the **Format** menu choose **Drawing LIMITS** and enter **0,0** for the lower left corner and **11,8.5** for the upper right corner to complete the command.
3. From the **View** menu, pick **Zoom** and then pick **All** to resize the drawing area to your limits.
4. Access the **LINE** command from the icon, the **Draw** menu, or by typing **LINE.** Enter **1,1** as the first point (see Figure 3-41) and press the **Enter** key.

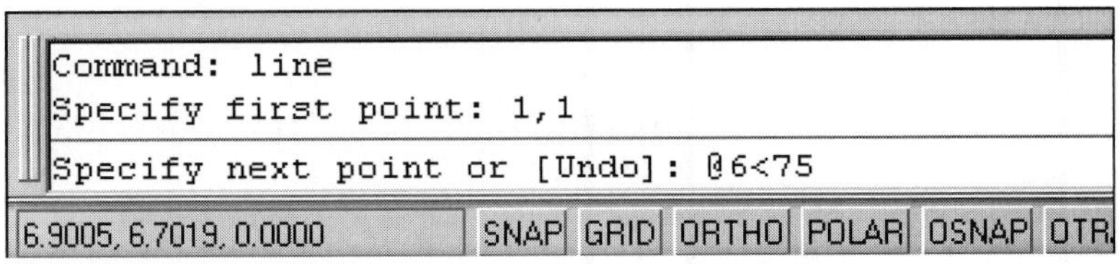

```
Command: line
Specify first point: 1,1

Specify next point or [Undo]: @6<75
```
```
6.9005, 6.7019, 0.0000          SNAP GRID ORTHO POLAR OSNAP OTR
```

**Figure 3-41**

5. Continuing in the **LINE** command, enter the following coordinates to complete the drawing. After each set of coordinates press the **Enter** key to go to the next coordinate request entry:
   a. **@6<75**
   b. **@2<0**
   c. **@6<-75**
   d. **@1<180**
   e. **@2<105**
   f. **@2<180**
   g. **@1<75**
   h. **@1.5<0**
   i. **@2<105**
   j. **@.5<180**
   k. **@5<255**
   l. **@1<180** (This last entry could be a **C** for **Close** or a **1,1** as this returns the end of the line segment to the origin of the drawing line.)
6. Access the **File** menu and select the **SAVE AS** command. Go to your **Workskills** folder as shown in Figure 3-37, enter the name **Tutorial 3-3,** and save this drawing.

## Tutorial 3-4: Using Absolute, Relative, and Polar Entries for Drawing

In this tutorial you will use AutoCAD to create the drawing in Figure 3-42 using the various input methods shown to draw the lines.

1. From the **File** menu choose **NEW** to begin a new drawing.
2. From the **Format** menu choose **Drawing LIMITS** and enter **0,0** for the lower left corner and **11,8.5** for the upper right corner to complete the command.
3. From the **View** menu, pick **Zoom** and then pick **All** to resize the drawing area to your limits.
4. Access the **LINE** command from the icon, the **Draw** menu, or by typing **LINE.** Enter **1,1** as the first point (see Figure 3-43) and press the **Enter** key.
5. Continuing in the **LINE** command, enter the following coordinates to complete the drawing. After each set of coordinates press the **Enter** key to go to the next coordinate request entry:
   a. **1,7.42**
   b. **@1,0**

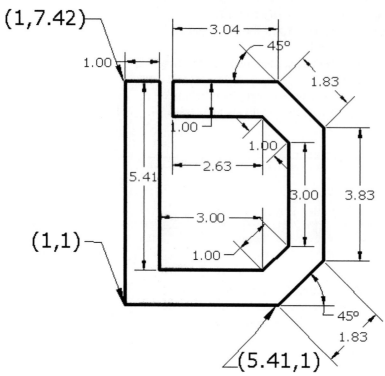

**Figure 3-42**

```
Command: line
Specify first point: 1,1
Specify next point or [Undo]: 1,7.42
6.2358, 5.9155, 0.0000        SNAP GRID ORTHO POLAR OSNAP OTR
```

**Figure 3-43**

    c. **@0,-5.41**
    d. **@3,0**
    e. **@1<45**
    f. **@0,3**
    g. **@1<135**
    h. **@-2.63,0**
    i. **@0,1**
    j. **@3.04,0**
    k. **@1.83<-45**
    l. **@0,-3.83**
    m. **5.41,1**
    n. **1,1** (This last entry could be a **C** for **Close** as this returns the end of the line segment to the origin of the drawing line.)

6. Access the **File** menu and select the **SAVE AS** command. Go to your **Workskills** folder as shown in Figure 3-37, enter the name **Tutorial 3-4,** and save this drawing.

## Tutorial 3-5: Using Direct Distance Entries for Drawing

In this tutorial you will use AutoCAD to create the drawing in Figure 3-44 using the relative coordinates shown to draw the lines.

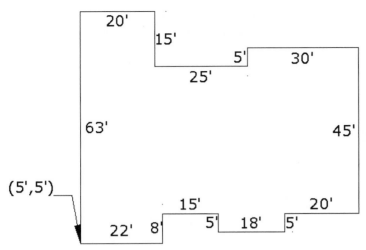

Figure 3-44

1. From the **File** menu choose **NEW** to begin a new drawing.
2. From the **Format** menu choose **UNITS.** Set the Length Units to **Architectural** and the Length Precision to **0″-0″** and pick **OK** when completed as shown in Figure 3-45.

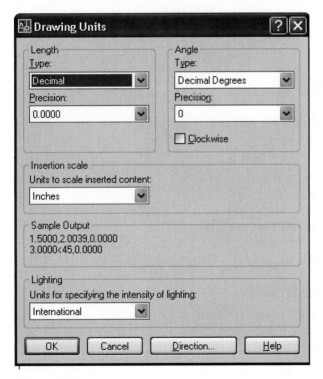

Figure 3-45

3. From the **Format** menu choose **Drawing LIMITS** and enter **0,0** for the lower left corner and **100′,80′** for the upper right corner to complete the command. Remember that **UNITS** are set to Architectural and the foot mark (single quote) is required input for most distances. Otherwise, AutoCAD will consider the distance input to be in inch units.
4. From the **View** menu, pick **Zoom** and then pick **All** to resize the drawing area to your limits.

5. From the status area at the bottom of the screen, pick **ORTHO** and turn it on. This will allow the drawing of objects in only a horizontal or vertical orientation.
6. Access the **LINE** command from the icon, the **Draw** menu, or by typing **LINE**. Enter **5′,5′** as the first point (see Figure 3-46) and press the **Enter** key.

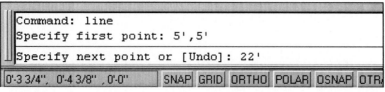

```
Command: line
Specify first point: 5',5'
Specify next point or [Undo]: 22'
```
0'-3 3/4",  0'-4 3/8"  ,0'-0"      SNAP  GRID  ORTHO  POLAR  OSNAP  OTR

Figure 3-46

7. Continuing in the **LINE** command, enter the distances below while moving the mouse in the proper direction. After each distance entry press the **Enter** key to go to the next request entry:
   a. **Mouse** moving **East**; enter **22′**
   b. **Mouse** moving **North**; enter **8′**
   c. **Mouse** moving **East**; enter **15′**
   d. **Mouse** moving **South**; enter **5′**
   e. **Mouse** moving **East**; enter **18′**
   f. **Mouse** moving **North**; enter **5′**
   g. **Mouse** moving **East**; enter **20′**
   h. **Mouse** moving **North**; enter **45′**
   i. **Mouse** moving **West**; enter **30′**
   j. **Mouse** moving **South**; enter **5′**
   k. **Mouse** moving **West**; enter **25′**
   l. **Mouse** moving **North**; enter **15′**
   m. **Mouse** moving **West**; enter **20′**
   n. **Mouse** moving **South**; enter **63′** (This last entry could be a **C** for **Close** or a **5′,5′** as this returns the end of the line segment to the origin of the drawing line.)
8. Access the **File** menu and select the **SAVE AS** command. Go to your **Workskills** folder as shown in Figure 3-37, enter the name **Tutorial 3-5,** and save this drawing.

## Tutorial 3-6: Using Object Snaps for Drawing

In this tutorial you will use AutoCAD to create the additional lines shown in Figure 3-47 using the drawing from the previous tutorial in Figure 3-44 as the base drawing or access this figure from the Student CD.

1. From the **File** menu choose **OPEN** to access the drawing **Tutorial 3-5** from your **Workskills** folder to begin the session.
2. From the **Tools** menu choose **Drafting Settings.**
3. Select the **Object Snaps** tab and place check marks in the boxes for **ENDpoint, MIDpoint,** and **INTersection** (see Figure 3-48).
4. Access the **LINE** command from the icon, the **Draw** menu, or by typing **LINE.** Add the lines to the drawing as follows:
   a. **Line 1**—pick the **MIDpoint** of the 43′ wall and connect to the **MIDpoint** of the 63′ wall.

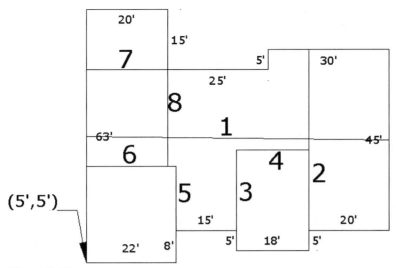

Figure 3-47

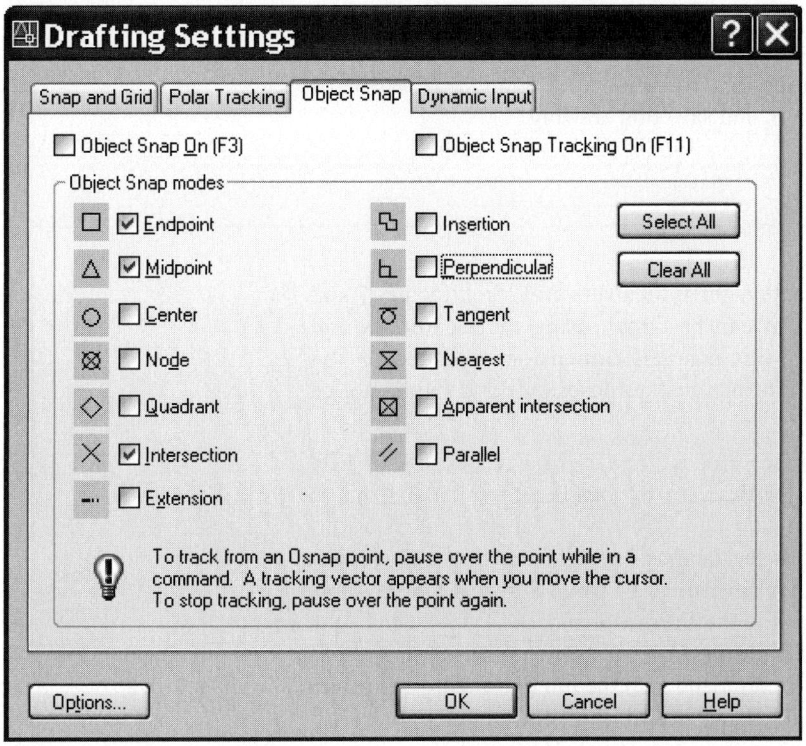

**Drafting Settings**

Snap and Grid | Polar Tracking | Object Snap | Dynamic Input

☐ Object Snap On (F3)          ☐ Object Snap Tracking On (F11)

Object Snap modes

☐ ☑ Endpoint          ☐ ☐ Insertion          [Select All]

△ ☑ Midpoint          ☐ ☐ Perpendicular     [Clear All]

○ ☐ Center            ○ ☐ Tangent

⊠ ☐ Node             ⋉ ☐ Nearest

◇ ☐ Quadrant          ⊠ ☐ Apparent intersection

✕ ☑ Intersection       ∕∕ ☐ Parallel

⋯ ☐ Extension

⚠ To track from an Osnap point, pause over the point while in a command. A tracking vector appears when you move the cursor. To stop tracking, pause over the point again.

[Options...]          [OK]  [Cancel]  [Help]

Figure 3-48

b. **Line 2**—pick the **ENDpoint** at the south end of the line, type **PER** (see Figure 3-49), and press the **Enter** key to connect to the 30′ wall at a right angle or 90° to complete the line.

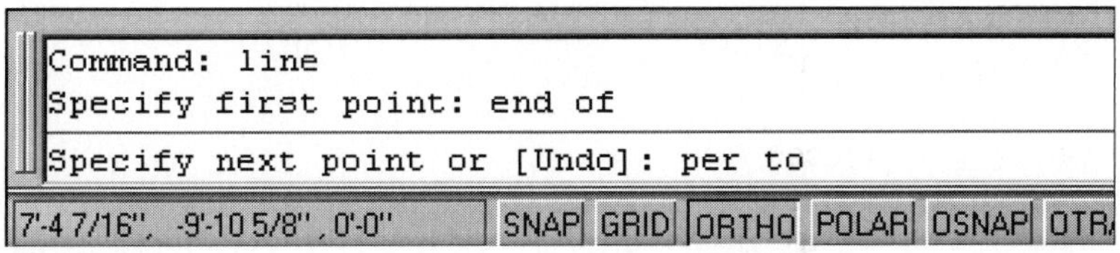

```
Command: line
Specify first point: end of
Specify next point or [Undo]: per to
```
7'-4 7/16", -9'-10 5/8", 0'-0"     SNAP GRID ORTHO POLAR OSNAP OTR/

Figure 3-49

     c. **Line 3**—pick the **END**point at the south end of the line. Move the mouse due north (be sure ORTHO is on), enter **20′,** and press the **Enter** key for a direct distance input.

     d. **Line 4**—continuing from **Line 3** move to **Line 2,** type **PER,** and press the **Enter** key to connect to the wall at a right angle or 90° to complete the line.

     e. **Line 5**—pick the **END**point at the south end of the line. Move the mouse due north (be sure ORTHO is on), type **16′,** and press the **Enter** key for a direct distance input.

     f. **Line 6**—continuing from **Line 5** move to the 63′ wall, type **PER,** and press the **Enter** key to connect to the wall at a right angle or 90° to complete the line.

     g. **Line 7**—pick the **END**point at the east end of the wall, move to the 63′ wall, type **PER,** and press the **Enter** key to connect to the wall at a right angle or 90° to complete the line.

     h. **Line 8**—pick the **END**point at the north end of the wall, move to **Line 6,** type **PER,** and press the **Enter** key to connect to the wall at a right angle or 90° to complete the line.

5. Access the **File** menu and select the **SAVE AS** command. Go to your **Workskills** folder as shown in Figure 3-37, enter the name **Tutorial 3-6,** and save this drawing.

## PRACTICE EXERCISES

Figures 3-50 to 3-69 represent typical general, architectural, and mechanical drawings that can be drawn using the techniques and commands explained in this chapter. Dimensions and text on the drawings are given for informational purposes only and should not be drawn at this time.

- To begin the drawing process for each drawing, access the **File** menu and pick **NEW.** (Use the acad.dwt template if this is requested.)
- Then set the **Units** for the drawing if the drawing will use feet and inches or **Architectural** as **UNITS** for the input. This command is found in the **Format** menu.
- Next set **LIMITS** for the drawing to resize the screen to hold the drawing. This command is in the **Format** menu. The lower left corner should be set to 0,0 with the upper right set to numbers just beyond the maximum X,Y of the figure.
- Then process the **ZOOM ALL** commands using the keyboard, **View** menu, or icon. This will resize the screen to view the complete drawing as described by the limits.
- Access the **LINE** command to begin drawing the figure.
- Remember to save your drawing every 10 to 15 minutes to avoid losing your work. Save the drawings in your **Workskills** folder with the figure number as the file name.

## Practice Exercise 3-1

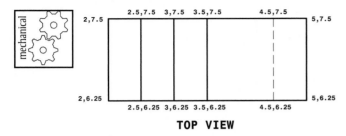

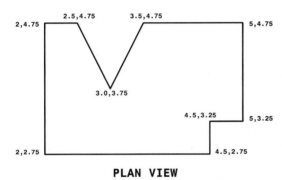

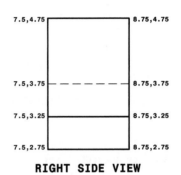

**Figure 3-50**    Practice Exercise 3-1 drawing and input

## Practice Exercise 3-2

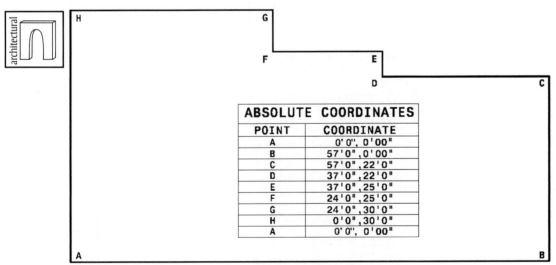

**Figure 3-51**    Practice Exercise 3-2 drawing and input with architectural units

## Practice Exercise 3-3

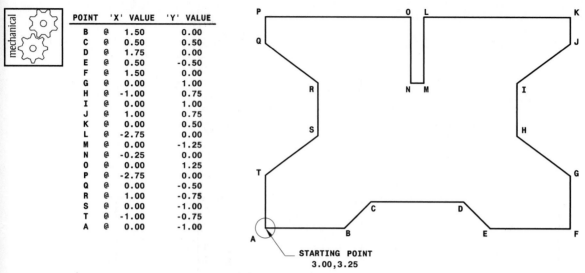

| POINT | | 'X' VALUE | 'Y' VALUE |
|-------|---|-----------|-----------|
| B | @ | 1.50 | 0.00 |
| C | @ | 0.50 | 0.50 |
| D | @ | 1.75 | 0.00 |
| E | @ | 0.50 | -0.50 |
| F | @ | 1.50 | 0.00 |
| G | @ | 0.00 | 1.00 |
| H | @ | -1.00 | 0.75 |
| I | @ | 0.00 | 1.00 |
| J | @ | 1.00 | 0.75 |
| K | @ | 0.00 | 0.50 |
| L | @ | -2.75 | 0.00 |
| M | @ | 0.00 | -1.25 |
| N | @ | -0.25 | 0.00 |
| O | @ | 0.00 | 1.25 |
| P | @ | -2.75 | 0.00 |
| Q | @ | 0.00 | -0.50 |
| R | @ | 1.00 | -0.75 |
| S | @ | 0.00 | -1.00 |
| T | @ | -1.00 | -0.75 |
| A | @ | 0.00 | -1.00 |

STARTING POINT
3.00,3.25

Figure 3-52    Practice Exercise 3-3 drawing and input

## Practice Exercise 3-4

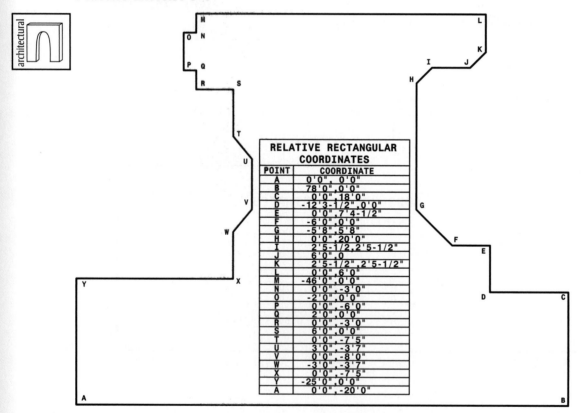

| RELATIVE RECTANGULAR COORDINATES | |
|-------|-------|
| POINT | COORDINATE |
| A | 0'0", 0'0" |
| B | 78'0",0'0" |
| C | 0'0",18'0" |
| D | -12'3-1/2",0'0" |
| E | 0'0",7'4-1/2" |
| F | -6'0",0'0" |
| G | -5'8",5'8" |
| H | 0'0",20'0" |
| I | 2'5-1/2,2'5-1/2" |
| J | 6'0",0 |
| K | 2'5-1/2",2'5-1/2" |
| L | 0'0",6'0" |
| M | -46'0",0'0" |
| N | 0'0",-3'0" |
| O | -2'0",0'0" |
| P | 0'0",-6'0" |
| Q | 2'0",0'0" |
| R | 0'0",-3'0" |
| S | 6'0",0'0" |
| T | 0'0",-7'5" |
| U | 3'0",-3'7" |
| V | 0'0",-8'0" |
| W | -3'0",-3'7" |
| X | 0'0",-7'5" |
| Y | -25'0",0'0" |
| A | 0'0",-20'0" |

Figure 3-53    Practice Exercise 3-4 drawing and input with architectural units

## Practice Exercise 3-5

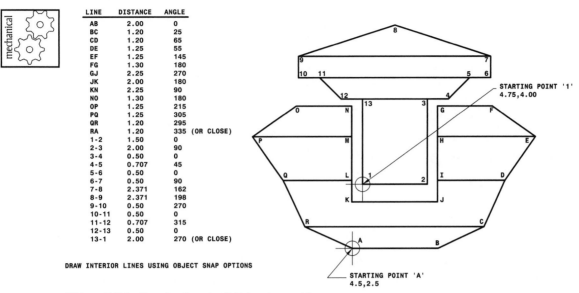

| LINE | DISTANCE | ANGLE |
|------|----------|-------|
| AB | 2.00 | 0 |
| BC | 1.20 | 25 |
| CD | 1.20 | 65 |
| DE | 1.25 | 55 |
| EF | 1.25 | 145 |
| FG | 1.30 | 180 |
| GJ | 2.25 | 270 |
| JK | 2.00 | 180 |
| KN | 2.25 | 90 |
| NO | 1.30 | 180 |
| OP | 1.25 | 215 |
| PQ | 1.25 | 305 |
| QR | 1.20 | 295 |
| RA | 1.20 | 335 (OR CLOSE) |
| 1-2 | 1.50 | 0 |
| 2-3 | 2.00 | 90 |
| 3-4 | 0.50 | 0 |
| 4-5 | 0.707 | 45 |
| 5-6 | 0.50 | 0 |
| 6-7 | 0.50 | 90 |
| 7-8 | 2.371 | 162 |
| 8-9 | 2.371 | 198 |
| 9-10 | 0.50 | 270 |
| 10-11 | 0.50 | 0 |
| 11-12 | 0.707 | 315 |
| 12-13 | 0.50 | 0 |
| 13-1 | 2.00 | 270 (OR CLOSE) |

DRAW INTERIOR LINES USING OBJECT SNAP OPTIONS

STARTING POINT '1'
4.75,4.00

STARTING POINT 'A'
4.5,2.5

**Figure 3-54**    Practice Exercise 3-5 drawing and input

## Practice Exercise 3-6

| RELATIVE POLAR COORDINATES | |
|------|-----------|
| POINT | COORDINATE |
| A | 0'0",0'0" |
| B | 3'6"<315 |
| C | 7'0"<0 |
| D | 3'6"<45 |
| E | 39'3"<180 |
| F | 29'3"<90 |
| G | 38'5-1/2"<180 |
| H | 26'6"<135 |
| I | 20'0"<225 |
| J | 20'0"<315 |
| K | 10'0"<270 |
| L | 6'0"<0 |
| A | 9'8-1/2"<270 |

**Figure 3-55**    Practice Exercise 3-6 drawing and input with architectural units

## Practice Exercise 3-7

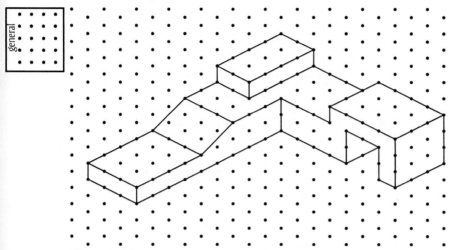

**Figure 3-56** Practice Exercise 3-7 drawing and input using the Isometric Snap and Grid at Y = .5

## Practice Exercise 3-8

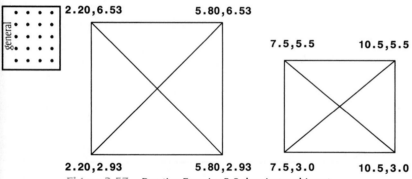

**Figure 3-57** Practice Exercise 3-8 drawing and input

**Practice Exercise 3-9**

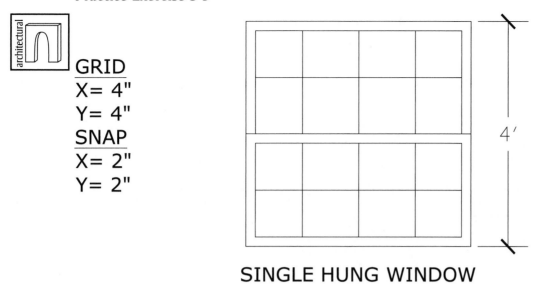

GRID
X= 4"
Y= 4"
SNAP
X= 2"
Y= 2"

SINGLE HUNG WINDOW

Figure 3-58    Practice Exercise 3-9 drawing and input

**Practice Exercise 3-10**

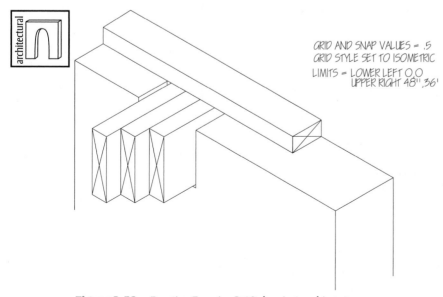

GRID AND SNAP VALUES = .5
GRID STYLE SET TO ISOMETRIC
LIMITS = LOWER LEFT 0,0
            UPPER RIGHT 48",36'

Figure 3-59    Practice Exercise 3-10 drawing and input

## Practice Exercise 3-11

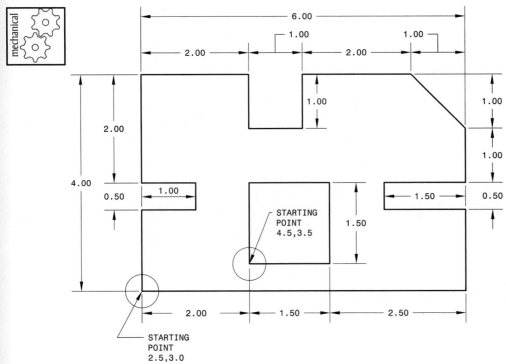

Figure 3-60     Practice Exercise 3-11 drawing and input

## Practice Exercise 3-12

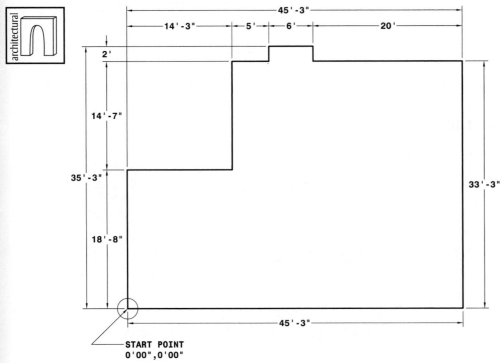

Figure 3-61     Practice Exercise 3-12 drawing and input

## Practice Exercise 3-13

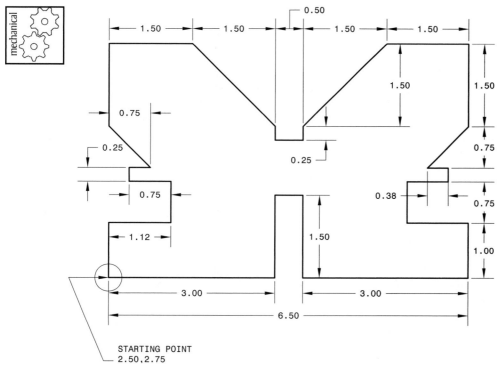

**Figure 3-62**   Practice Exercise 3-13 drawing and input

## Practice Exercise 3-14

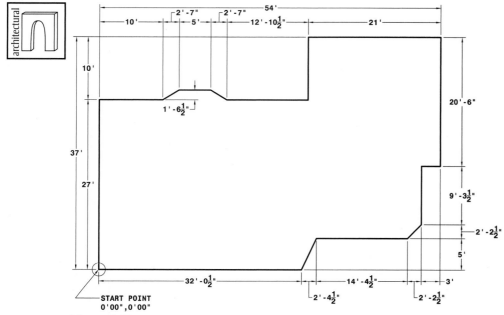

**Figure 3-63**   Practice Exercise 3-14 drawing and input

## Practice Exercise 3-15

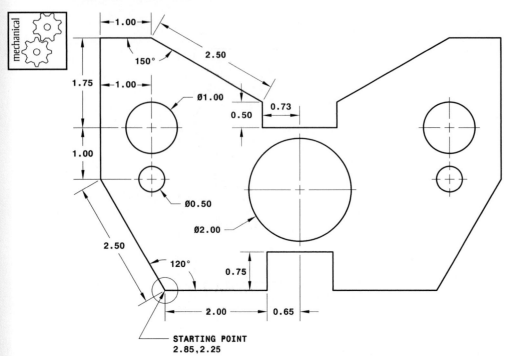

**Figure 3-64**    Practice Exercise 3-15 drawing and input

## Practice Exercise 3-16

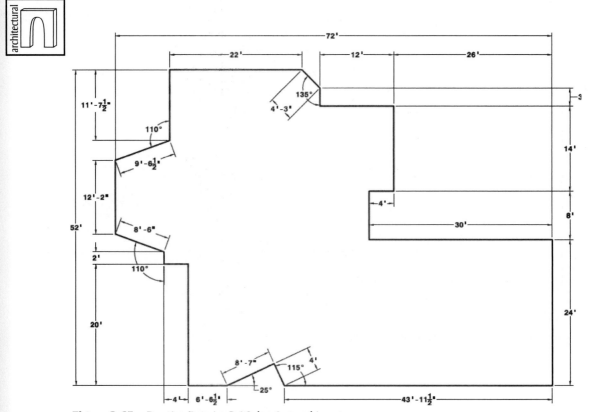

**Figure 3-65**    Practice Exercise 3-16 drawing and input

## Practice Exercise 3-17

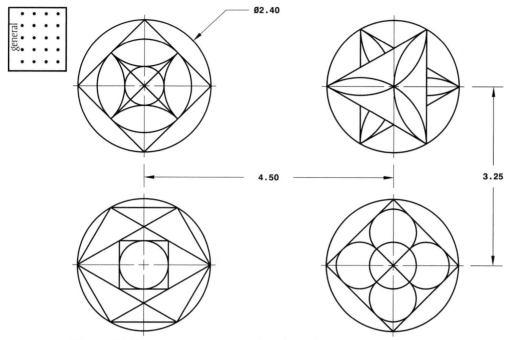

**Figure 3-66**    Practice Exercise 3-17 drawing and input

## Practice Exercise 3-18

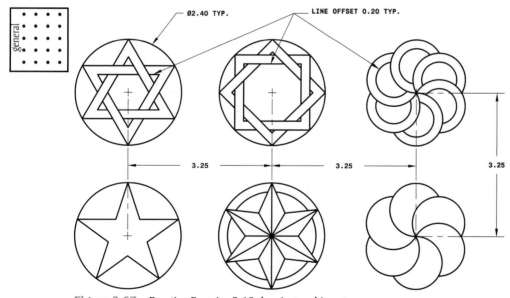

**Figure 3-67**    Practice Exercise 3-18 drawing and input

**Practice Exercise 3-19**

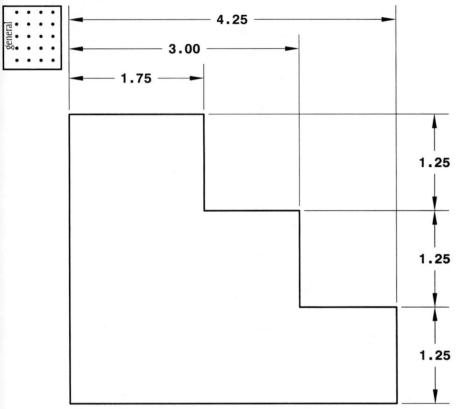

Figure 3-68     Practice Exercise 3-19 drawing and input

**Practice Exercise 3-20:**

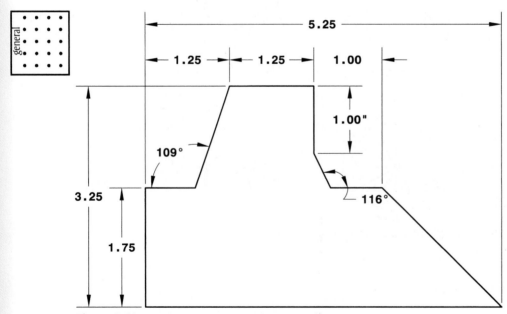

Figure 3-69     Practice Exercise 3-20 drawing and input

# Fundamental Viewing and Inquiry Commands

## 4

## Chapter Objectives

- Understand drawing regeneration.
- Use real-time mouse control.
- Understand view control commands.
- Retrieve information from entities.
- Perform inquiries related to the **DISTANCE** and **AREA** commands.

## INTRODUCTION

AutoCAD has no limitations on the size of the environment in which a drawing is created. Whether you are working on a circuit board, a floor plan, or a bridge, all entities that make up a drawing should be drawn in real-world units at full size. No matter how big the drawing is, you have to be able to move around the entire file to look at various parts of the drawing. You need to view the whole drawing—the extents—as well as the smallest detail in it.

## VIEWING A DRAWING

Your ability to control the display is found in the **View** menu (see Figure 4-1). Commands such as **ZOOM IN, ZOOM OUT,** and **PAN** give you complete control of the drawing area display. **ZOOM** refers to the computer's ability to magnify the screen similar to the way a camera lens can zoom in on a subject being photographed. **PAN** gives you the ability to move across the drawing at the current magnification to a part of the drawing that is presently off the screen to better see that area to add or revise entities. When a television camera shows the crowd at a football game, it is panning by moving along an invisible path and keeping the same magnification.

View commands can be performed at virtually any time and from several locations. The **View** menu (see Figure 4-1) houses many of the commands that pertain to the screen display. Other locations include the **Zoom** toolbar (see Figure 4-2), a section of the **Standard** toolbar (see Figure 4-3), the **View** toolbar (see Figure 4-4), the scroll bars, a mouse wheel, and the command line. Depending upon where you execute the viewing command from, it can be a *transparent command.*

A transparent command is one that can be executed during the activity of another command; it does not disrupt or cancel the original command. When the viewing command is

**transparent command:** A command that can be executed from within an active command; when completed the initial command resumes.

Figure 4-1    View menu

Figure 4-2    Zoom toolbar

Figure 4-3    View icons in the Standard toolbar

Figure 4-4    The View toolbar

completed, you are returned to the original command in progress with no interruptions to that sequence.

## REDRAW versus REGEN

Before we get into the actual viewing commands, you need to understand the differences between **REDRAW** and **REGEN** (regeneration) (see Figure 4-5). Both of these commands will in essence refresh the screen display. *Regeneration* is a more comprehensive version of the process. *REDRAW* removes the display from the screen and paints the display back on based on the last recorded memory of the display.

**REGEN** removes the display from the screen and sends all information in the drawing database back to the central processing unit (CPU) to reprocess the file before it paints the display back on the screen. This is why a **REGEN** is considered a more comprehensive version of the drawing database restoration. **REDRAW** is seen as a quicker screen refresh command. Both of these commands are found at the top of the **View** menu. If you are working in a multiple *viewport* configuration (see Figure 4-6), you may choose to invoke a **REGENALL** command to regenerate all viewports. This will cause regeneration to be processed in all viewports in the same command.

regeneration: The process of calculating the screen image and displaying the results.

REDRAW: The process of displaying the screen image based on the last recorded memory.

viewport: Display of a drawing in an AutoCAD session.

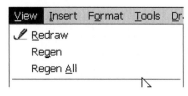

Figure 4-5    View menu with Redraw and Regen

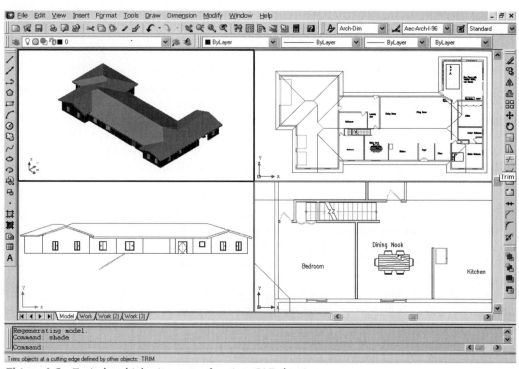

Figure 4-6    Typical multiple viewports of an AutoCAD drawing

## REALTIME PAN AND ZOOM

The quickest way to zoom and pan around a drawing is with the mouse wheel. If you do not have a wheel on the mouse, invoking the **ZOOM Realtime** command (see Figure 4-7, right icon) gives your left mouse button the ability to change magnification of the drawing by moving vertically (up for **ZOOM IN,** down for **ZOOM OUT**). Without a mouse wheel the **PAN Realtime** command (see Figure 4-7, left icon) allows the left mouse to move the drawing around the display area. When the **PAN** command is moving to the edge of the window, it will continue to move the drawing in that direction until the mouse button is released.

If your system is equipped with a mouse that has a wheel in between the left and right mouse buttons or a rocker-type middle mouse button, AutoCAD assigns the **PAN Realtime** and **ZOOM Realtime** features to this button. By rolling the wheel up (typically away from the user), a **ZOOM IN** command will be executed. By rolling the wheel down (typically toward the user), a **ZOOM OUT** command is invoked. The center of the **ZOOM** operation is based on the location of the cursor or crosshair as you spin the wheel. To use the **PAN Realtime** you must press and hold down the wheel, at which time the screen cursor will change to a "hand" icon, signifying the **PAN** command is in effect. As you move the mouse, the drawing will move in the same direction.

*Note:*

*If you do not have a mouse with a wheel, the authors highly recommend this minimal investment as a productive tool that will quickly be a valuable aid in creating AutoCAD drawings.*

A major advantage of executing the viewing commands with the mouse is that these commands are performed as a transparent version of the command. Furthermore, by double-clicking the wheel, a **ZOOM EXTENTS** command is executed, modifying the magnification to show the extents of all entities currently in the drawing and available for viewing.

When using the mouse for **ZOOM** and **PAN** operations, there are limitations to the level of magnification that can be viewed. The amount of magnification will go up only to the point of change that does not require a regeneration of the entire drawing database. A symbol may appear to indicate that you have reached this limit. If this limit is reached simply **REGEN** the drawing file and a new set of magnification boundaries will be generated.

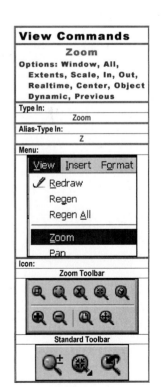

## ZOOM

Under the **View** menu you will find the word Zoom. This entry leads to a cascading menu of various *zoom* options (see Figure 4-8), all of which perform some type of screen magnification modification. Most of the versions found here are considered full versions of the command and can cause an automatic regeneration of the drawing database, which may be time-consuming. We will discuss some of these options now and reserve others for later unit topics.

### Zoom Window

**Zoom Window** (see Figure 4-9) prompts you to construct a window by establishing first one corner and then the opposite, diagonal corner. The area in which the window is created becomes the next magnification of the drawing screen. The actual magnification is calculated based on the longest side of the window while the proper aspect ratio of the X and Y screen dimensions is maintained.

### Zoom All

The **Zoom All** (see Figure 4-10) option calculates the largest screen magnification possible as it relates to the current **Drawing Limits.** If drawing entities exist outside the **Drawing Limits** the

zoom: To reduce or increase magnification of the screen image.

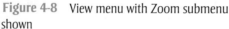

Figure 4-8   View menu with Zoom submenu shown

Figure 4-9   The Zoom Window icon

**Zoom All** command calculates the magnification based on the location of all the entities regardless of their location in the drawing. This is not a transparent command and may result in a regeneration of the drawing file.

Figure 4-10   Zoom All icon

### Zoom Extents

The **Zoom Extents** (see Figure 4-11) option is similar to the previous option in that it will calculate the largest magnification possible based on all the entities in the drawing file, regardless of the current drawing limits. If a **Zoom Extents** produces what appears to be a blank screen you need to look carefully around the top or right edge of the screen for any entities. These entities are located far from the main drawing and need to be erased. You can then execute a second **Zoom Extents** command to produce a more accurate display. Remember that **Zoom Extents** brings all objects in the drawing file into the display no matter where they are in space. This is not a transparent command and may result in a regeneration of the drawing file.

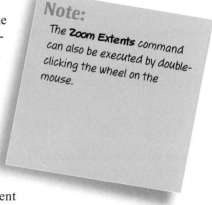

**Note:**
The **Zoom Extents** command can also be executed by double-clicking the wheel on the mouse.

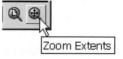

Figure 4-11   Zoom Extents icon

## Zoom Previous

The **Zoom Previous** (see Figure 4-12) option returns the screen display to the previous zoom magnification you were last working with. This command can step you back (up to ten times) through a series of previous display screens by repeating the command.

**Figure 4-12**   Zoom Previous icon

## PAN

*Pan* gives you the ability to slide the current screen display in all four directions to expose parts of the drawing file that may be just off the screen. In the **View** menu there is a cascading menu with the various **PAN** operations (see Figure 4-13). Except for **Pan Realtime,** these commands move a specific direction and distance. If you hold down the left mouse and drag the hand icon around the screen when using the **PAN Realtime** command (see Figure 4-14), the display will move in accordance with the mouse movement, keeping the current zoom magnification.

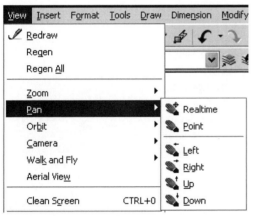

**Figure 4-13**   View Pan menu

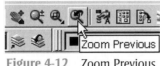

**Figure 4-14**   The Pan Realtime icon

It is essential for you to be able to move around a large drawing file by using a variety of viewing commands and techniques. A complete understanding of creating views and saving named views along with various ZOOM commands and the realtime PAN and ZOOM is necessary. This will keep the regeneration time during a drawing session to a minimum.

## DRAWING INQUIRY

You can access drawing file information through the *Inquiry* submenu found in the **Tools** menu (see Figure 4-15). This set of commands extracts information from the database pertaining to individual drawing entities as well as the complete drawing files. Commands such as **ID POINT, LIST, DISTANCE,** and **AREA** will give you information regarding the entities selected. The **TIME** and **STATUS** commands reveal summary information attached to the complete drawing file. **Set Variable** has to do with basic AutoCAD settings that are discussed later.

**pan:** The ability to slide the screen or shift the screen display around with no change in magnification.

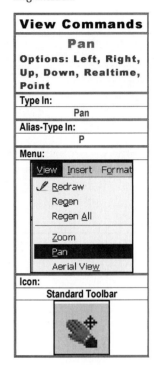

**inquiry:** The process of retrieving information from a drawing file.

When you execute a drawing inquiry, the information requested shows up in the text window. Remember that the **F2** function key is used to toggle or flip the user between the text window and the AutoCAD graphics screen. Entity-based inquiries can also be made from the **Inquiry** toolbar (see Figure 4-16).

Figure 4-16    The Inquiry toolbar showing the List icon

**Figure 4-15**    Tools menu with Inquiry submenu

## List

The **LIST** command (see Figure 4-17) will prompt you to `Select objects`. After the selection set is chosen, the text screen will display all information about the selected entities individually. The type of entity and its general properties as well as geometry-specific information such as the length, projected lengths, and coordinates of the start point and endpoint of lines, center coordinates and radius of circles, vertex coordinates, length, and area of polylines, and more will be read from the drawing database (see Figure 4-17). Geometry-based information will differ depending on the type of entity selected.

## ID Point

The **ID Point** command (see Figure 4-18) will present in the text window the absolute coordinates (X, Y, and Z) of the location selected and is shown in the current drawing units (see Figure 4-19). The location may be selected with a mouse pick or you can use any of the **Object Snap** options to ensure accuracy.

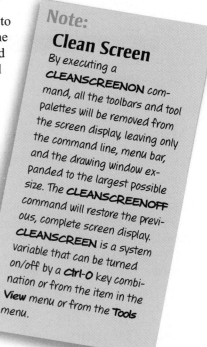

**Note:**

**Clean Screen**

By executing a **CLEANSCREENON** command, all the toolbars and tool palettes will be removed from the screen display, leaving only the command line, menu bar, and the drawing window expanded to the largest possible size. The **CLEANSCREENOFF** command will restore the previous, complete screen display. **CLEANSCREEN** is a system variable that can be turned on/off by a *Ctrl-0* key combination or from the item in the **View** menu or from the **Tools** menu.

## Distance

The **DISTance** command (see Figure 4-20) calculates the distance between any two points selected in the drawing file. The value returned will be in the currently established drawing units and in two forms. One is the actual or true distance between the two points and the polar

```
█ AutoCAD Text Window - Drawing5.dwg                    _ □ x
Edit
                CIRCLE      Layer: "0"
                            Space: Model space
                    Handle = 8D
            center point, X=   -5.0428  Y=   17.2634  Z=    0.0000
            radius   14.1977
    circumference   89.2068
            area   633.2660

                LINE       Layer: "0"
                            Space: Model space
                    Handle = 92
            from point, X= -19.1787  Y=   34.1186  Z=    0.0000
              to point, X=   9.9726  Y=   34.1186  Z=    0.0000
        Length =  29.1514,  Angle in XY Plane =      0
                    Delta X =  29.1514, Delta Y =      0.0000, Delta Z =    0.0000

                LWPOLYLINE  Layer: "0"
                            Space: Model space
                    Handle = 93
            Open
    Constant width    0.0000
Press ENTER to continue:
            area   40.5933
            length  121.3430

        at point  X=   21.7606  Y=   37.3019  Z=   0.0000
        at point  X=   43.5843  Y=   37.3019  Z=   0.0000
        at point  X=   43.5843  Y=   54.4920  Z=   0.0000
        at point  X=   69.3905  Y=   54.4920  Z=   0.0000
        at point  X=   69.3905  Y=   35.2327  Z=   0.0000
        at point  X=   92.1700  Y=   35.2327  Z=   0.0000
        at point  X=   92.1700  Y=   49.7170  Z=   0.0000

Command:
```

Figure 4-17    LIST command text window

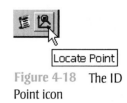

Figure 4-18    The ID Point icon

```
█ AutoCAD Text Window - Drawing5.dwg              _ □ x
Edit
Command: id Specify point:   X = 21.7606     Y = 37.3019     Z = 0.0000

Command: id Specify point:   X = 43.5843     Y = 37.3019     Z = 0.0000

Command: id Specify point:   X = 92.1700     Y = 49.7170     Z = 0.0000

Command:
```

Figure 4-19    ID command text window

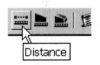

Figure 4-20    The Distance inquiry icon

angles from the principal planes (**in the XY plane** or the alpha angle, and **from the XY plane** or the beta angle). Also shown will be the projected or *delta distance* (Delta X, Delta Y, and Delta Z). Along with the distance values, the command will return angle information as well (see Figure 4-21). The angle **in the XY plane** and the angle **from the XY plane** will be expressed in the current angle settings.

delta distance: The projected distance in the horizontal or vertical planes between two points.

```
█ AutoCAD Text Window - Drawing5.dwg              _ □ x
Edit
Command: dist
Specify first point:  Specify second point:
Distance = 50.6370,  Angle in XY Plane = 20,  Angle from XY Plane = 0
Delta X = 47.6299,  Delta Y = 17.1901,   Delta Z = 0.0000

Command:   DIST Specify first point:  Specify second point:
Distance = 26.9944,  Angle in XY Plane = 212,  Angle from XY Plane = 0
Delta X = -22.7795,  Delta Y = -14.4842,   Delta Z = 0.0000

Command:
```

Figure 4-21    The Inquiry Distance command text window

**Figure 4-22**   Inquiry Area icon

## Area

The **AREA** command (see Figure 4-22) calculates the area of a closed figure or series of selected points. The value is expressed in the square of the current drawing distance units. For example, in architectural units (typically square inches) an alternate unit will typically be shown (such as square feet) in brackets. This command will also calculate the total perimeter of the selected entity or points.

The default input is to select a series of corner points. When the last point is selected, you hit **Enter** to close the figure and the program calculates the area (see Figure 4-23). To select a closed entity such as a circle or polygon, you should exercise the **Object** option by typing **O <Enter>.** Then you will be prompted to select the object. Remember that this is a single-selection process using the pick box. The object selected should represent a closed boundary area for best results. After selecting the object press **Enter** to conclude the command and see the result.

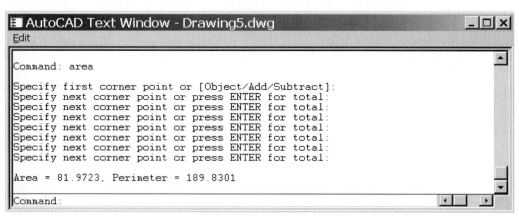

**Figure 4-23**   AREA command text window

## Time

The **TIME** command uses the clock within your computer system to keep track of information related to the drawing file (see Figure 4-24). Information on when the drawing file was first created, when the file was last updated, and total editing and elapsed times in the file are among the information displayed. All the information is in the 24-hour time format.

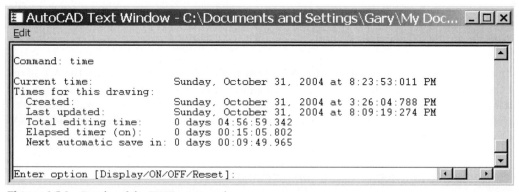

**Figure 4-24**   Results of the TIME command

You need to log the time spent on each project. The use of the TIME command will allow for accurate individual session times along with a total accumulation of time spent on the project.

## Status

The **STATUS** command displays information related to the drawing file through a variety of system variables. **Drawing LIMITS, GRID** and **SNAP** settings, and current **Property Settings** are included in the information displayed in the resulting text window (see Figure 4-25). The **STATUS** command also reports information about a file's size as well as disk space available (free), temporary disk space, available RAM memory, and swap file space available on the local disk drive.

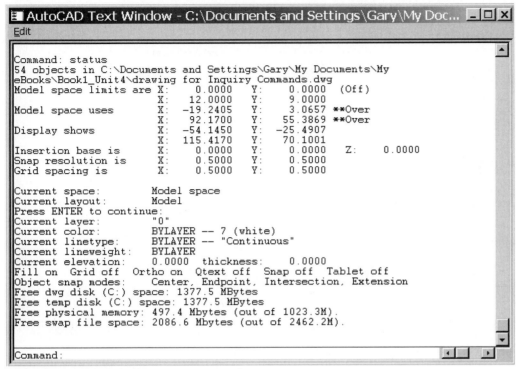

Figure 4-25    Results of the STATUS command

**Exercise 4-1:** Inquiries on a Drawing

- Open the Taisei Detail Plan drawing from the C:\Program Files\AutoCAD 2008\Sample folder or access this drawing from the Student CD.
- Using the TIME command, find the total elapsed time in this file.
- Using the LIST command, retrieve the name of the block that contains the bathtub and toilet.
- Zoom in on the upper right area of the drawing.
- What is the length of one of the red lines that form the "x" in the box?

# SYSTEM VARIABLE

The **SETVAR** command allows you to enter a *system variable* name, which in turn displays the current value as a default. Most of the system variables can be controlled through the command line by keying in the name of the variable. Options available may or may not be shown and often are just an **on/off** or **0/1** toggle. Some variables are also set in other command prompts or command options such as **Fillet Radius** or **Line Type Scale.**

To view all the current settings of the variables you can execute a **SETVAR** command followed by a question mark (**?**). For a complete list of the current variables and their values type an asterisk or star (**\***) as a wildcard input (see Figure 4-26). To change the variable setting type the variable name into the command line prompt. Then change the value through alphanumeric input as directed by the variable.

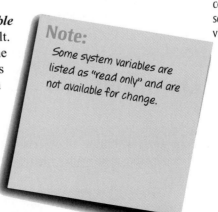

Note:
Some system variables are listed as "read only" and are not available for change.

system variable: A series of commands that control the settings for the operational environment.

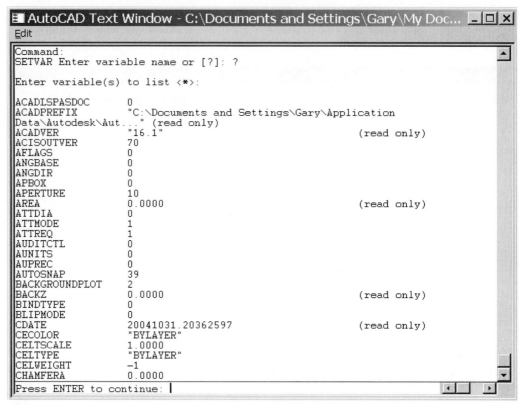

**Figure 4-26**    Typical SETVAR text window

## SUMMARY

The viewing and inquiry commands presented in this unit enable you to control the appearance of your drawing on the screen display regardless of how large the drawing is. We first looked at the **REDRAW** and **REGEN** (regeneration) commands, which refresh the screen display. This prepared us for the study of the viewing commands: Realtime **ZOOM** and Realtime **PAN**. The **ZOOM** command and its various options allow you to modify the screen display by changing the magnification of your drawing using either the mouse wheel or left mouse button. The various **PAN** operations, controlled by the left mouse button or mouse wheel, slide the screen display in all four directions, enabling you to expose any parts of your drawing that fall outside the screen display's viewing area. Next we examined the inquiry commands, **LIST, ID POINT, DISTANCE, AREA, TIME,** and **STATUS.** These commands obtain and display database information about individual drawing entities as well as information regarding the complete drawing file. Finally, we introduced the **SETVAR** command. This command displays the value of an individual system variable that you specify at the text prompt. This command can also show a list of the current settings of all system variables that control the operational environment.

## CHAPTER TEST QUESTIONS

### Multiple Choice

1. Which of the following commands will bring all objects in the drawing file into the display screen no matter where they are in space?

   a. Zoom All

   b. Zoom Dynamic

   c. Zoom Extents

   d. Zoom Arial

2. The wheel on the mouse can perform all the following viewing commands **except:**

   a. PAN

   b. Zoom In

   c. Zoom Window

   d. Zoom Extents

3. The DISTANCE command is found in the _____ menu.

   a. Inquiry
   b. Format
   c. Modify
   d. Input

4. The Cleanscreen command will:

   a. Remove all lost data
   b. Refresh the drawing view
   c. Remove all drawing blips
   d. Remove all toolbars

5. The LIST command will **not** show information about an object's:

   a. Properties
   b. Handle Number
   c. Coordinates
   d. System Variables

## Matching

a. _____ REGEN
b. _____ REDRAW
c. _____ ZOOM Window
d. _____ Transparent command
e. _____ SETVAR

1. Executed from within a command
2. System variable
3. Refresh of the screen
4. Recalculates the screen display
5. Defines the next area of the display

## True or False

1. True or False: Zoom Previous has no limit to the number of times it can go back.

2. True or False: The AREA command will also calculate the perimeter of the zone.

3. True or False: The DISTANCE command requires the user to Object Snap each point.

4. True or False: The TIME command shows when a drawing was created.

5. True or False: The STATUS command will display information related to the drawing file through system variables.

## CHAPTER PROJECTS

1. Using the Inquiry commands, find the "oldest" drawing in the AutoCAD Samples folder. Find the one with the least/most editing time. Which one has the smallest/largest file size? What are some of the block names in these drawings?

2. Using the Inquiry commands, examine your drawings from Unit 3. Which has the smallest/largest area? Which has the smallest/largest file size? Which took the least/most time to edit?

## TUTORIALS

### Tutorial 4-1

1. Open the **Wilhome** drawing file in the Samples folder of your AutoCAD program or access it from the Student CD (see Figure 4-27).

2. **ZOOM** into the kitchen area indicated by the circle using any of the **ZOOM** command options (see Figure 4-28).

3. Invoke the **LIST** command and select the following in order and view the various information:

   a. The Sink, the Stove, the Refrigerator
   b. One of the Green Upper Cabinet Lines
   c. One of the Cyan Text entities
   d. The Magenta Dimensions
   e. Other entities you may wish to examine.

4. Using the **AREA** command, pick points to calculate the area of the kitchen (see Figure 4-29).

5. **PAN** and **ZOOM** as needed to the upper right area of the house plan to show the GRAND Room. What is the area of this room?

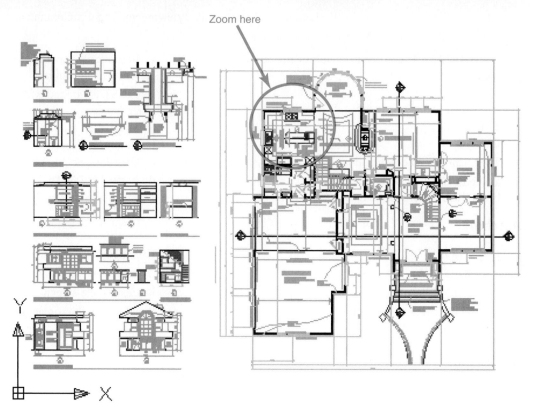

Zoom here

**Figure 4-27**

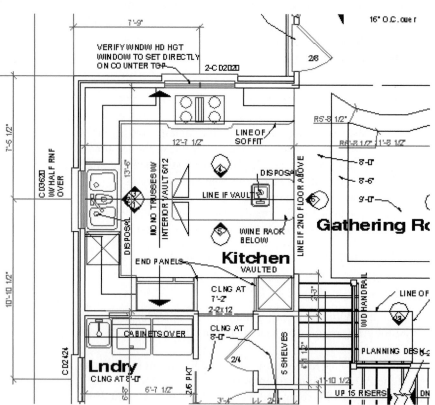

16" O.C. over

VERIFY WNDW HD HGT
WINDOW TO SET DIRECTLY
ON COUNTER TOP

2-C 02020

2/6

7'-9"

7'-5 1/2"

RS-8 1/2"

LINE OF SOFFIT

12'-7 1/2"

R6'-8 1/2" 1'-8 1/2"

C 0362W
W HALF RNF
OVER

13'-6"

MONO TRUSSES W/
INTERIOR VAULT 6/12

8'-0"

DISPOSAL

8'-6"

LINE IF VAULT

9'-0"

DISPOSAL

WINE RACK
BELOW

LINE IF 2ND FLOOR ABOVE

**Gathering Ro**

END PANELS

**Kitchen**
VAULTED

10'-10 1/2"

CLNG AT
7'-2"

LINE OF

WD HANDRAIL

2-2x12

CABINETS OVER

CLNG AT
8'-0"

5 SHELVES

PLANNING DESK

C 02424

**Lndry**
CLNG AT 8'-0"

2/4

2/6 PKT

6'-7 1/2"

3'-

UP 15 RISERS

DN

**Figure 4-28**

**Figure 4-29**

```
Command: area
Specify first corner point or [Object/Add/Subtract]: end of
Specify next corner point or press ENTER for total: end of
Specify next corner point or press ENTER for total: end of
Specify next corner point or press ENTER for total: end of
Specify next corner point or press ENTER for total:
Area = 25078.4 square in. (174.156 square ft.), Perimeter = 52'-10"

Command:
```

70'-9 1/2", 72'-2 1/2", 0'-0"  SNAP  GRID  ORTHO  POLAR  OSNAP  OTRACK  DUCS  DYN  LWT  MODEL

```
Edit

Select objects:

                  BLOCK REFERENCE   Layer: "MPFIXTURE"
                             Space: Model space
                      Handle = 356d
       Block Name: "KSINK-03"
                  at point, X=    58'-1"  Y=    65'-3"  Z=     0'-0"
    X scale factor:         1.0
Press ENTER to continue:
    Y scale factor:         1.0
    rotation angle: 90d0'0.0000"
    Z scale factor:         1.0
   Scale uniformly: No
   Allow exploding: Yes

                  ATTRIBUTE  Layer: "MPFIXTSPEC"
                           Space: Model space
                    Handle = 356e
            Style = "STANDARD"
            Font file = txt.shx
            center point, X=59'-6 1/2"  Y=    66'-3"  Z=     0'-0"
            height      0'-1"
            value American Standard
              tag MFR
       rotation angle 90d0'0.0000"
           width scale factor        1.0
       obliquing angle 0d0'0.0000"
           flags invisible   preset
       generation normal

Press ENTER to continue:
                  ATTRIBUTE  Layer: "MPFIXTSPEC"
                           Space: Model space
Press ENTER to continue:
```

Figure 4-30

Using the **LIST** command, are there any blocks in this room? (See Figure 4-30.) Using the **ID POINT** commands examine the corners of the room. What **UNITS** are in use in this drawing?

6. Using the **DISTance** command, check a few of the dimensions to verify correctness.
7. **CLOSE** the drawing and **do not save** any changes.

## Tutorial 4-2

1. Open the **Welding Fixture Model** drawing file (see Figure 4-31) in the Samples folder of your AutoCAD program or access it from the Student CD.
2. Use the **DISTance** command to verify the dimensions shown.
3. Use the **LIST** command to determine what objects other than **3D_Solids** are in the drawing.
4. Determine the units used in this drawing with the **STATUS** command.
5. Close the drawing and **do not save** any changes.

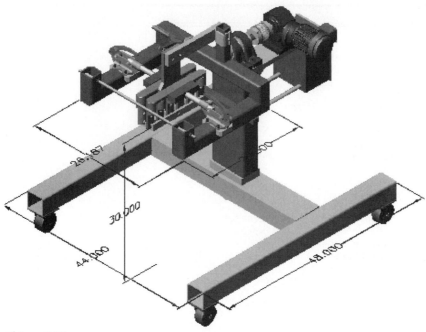

**Figure 4-31**

## Tutorial 4-3

1. Open the **Lots and Roads** drawing (see Figure 4-32) file from the Student CD.
2. Use the **DISTance** command to verify the lot line dimensions shown.

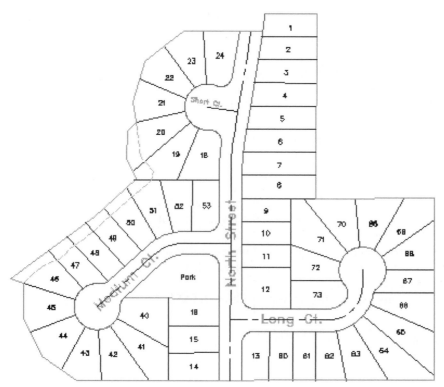

**Figure 4-32**   Typical subdivision layout

3. Use the **LIST** command to determine the length of the roadway centerlines.
4. Check various lot areas using the **AREA** command. Which lot is the biggest? Which is the smallest?
5. Determine the units used in this drawing with the **STATUS** command. Change units and repeat Steps 3 and 4.
6. Close the drawing and **do not save** any changes.

## PRACTICE EXERCISE

### Practice Exercise 4-1: PAN and ZOOM

1. Start **AutoCAD**.
2. Pick the **File** menu and choose **OPEN**.
3. Using the drop-down area at the top of the **Select File** dialog box, go to the AutoCAD Sample folder or access the Student CD.

4. Scroll through the list of drawing files (**.dwg**) and choose one to open by picking the **OPEN** button in the lower right of the dialog box:
   a. **Architectural Drawings**—8th Floor, Hotel, Hummer, Stadium, Taisei, or Wilhome
   b. **Building Services**—8th Floor
   c. **Civil Drawings**—Hotel or SPCA Site Plan
   d. **Facilities Management**—Db_samp
   e. **Landscaping**—SPCA Site Plan
   f. **Mechanical**—Oil Module, Welding Fixture 1, or Welding Fixture Model
   g. **Presentation**—Hotel, Hummer, Stadium, or Welding Fixture Model
   h. **Process Piping**—Oil Module
   i. **Structural**—MKMPlan or Oil Module
5. Practice using the mouse wheel to **ZOOM** and **PAN**, if you have one.
6. Use a mixture of **ZOOM** and **PAN** as well as the Realtime options to move around and examine the drawing.
7. When finished, **CLOSE** the drawing and answer **No** to saving your changes.
8. **EXIT** AutoCAD or return to **Step 4** and repeat this exercise using another drawing.

### Practice Exercise 4-2: Inquiry Commands

1. Start **AutoCAD**.
2. Pick the **File** menu and choose **OPEN**.
3. Using the drop-down area at the top of the **Select File** dialog box, go to the AutoCAD Sample folder or access the Student CD.

4. Scroll through the list of drawing files (**.dwg**), choose one to open, and pick the **OPEN** button in the lower right of the dialog box:

   a. **Architectural Drawings**—8th Floor, Hotel, Hummer, Stadium, Taisei, or Wilhome
   b. **Building Services**—8th Floor
   c. **Civil Drawings**—Hotel or SPCA Site Plan
   d. **Facilities Management**—Db_samp

e. **Landscaping**—SPCA Site Plan

   f. **Mechanical**—Oil Module, Welding Fixture 1, or Welding Fixture Model

   g. **Presentation**—Hotel, Hummer, Stadium, or Welding Fixture Model

   h. **Process Piping**—Oil Module

   i. **Structural**—MKMPlan or Oil Module

5. Use a mixture of **Inquiry** menu commands to examine the entities in the drawing and learn about the drawing.

6. When finished, **CLOSE** the drawing and answer **No** to the saving of changes.

7. Exit AutoCAD or return to Step 4 and repeat this exercise using another drawing.

# Elementary Dimensioning

## 5

## Chapter Objectives

- Identify the items that create a dimension.
- Define and describe the basic dimensioning concepts of size and shape description.
- Demonstrate the use of the standard dimensioning methods.
- Create, justify, and edit dimension annotations.
- Construct various dimension styles.

## INTRODUCTION

The general concept of dimensioning is to document the size and shape of a part or feature through the drawing file. The underlying result of a well-dimensioned drawing is that someone can manufacture, inspect, or assemble the part, build the house, or create the design based on the dimensions. This unit covers AutoCAD's ability to create annotations and to document the size and shape of a drawing.

## DIMENSIONING CONCEPTS

AutoCAD has a very extensive series of commands used for the description of a drawing's shape and size within the dimensioning commands. This series of commands utilizes over 70 system variables to control the look and placement of dimensions on a drawing. These settings form a **dimension style.** Creating the most common settings as a **DIMension STYLE** will make the dimensioning procedure quick and efficient.

**dimension style:** A collection of system variables that control the creation and look of a dimensional entity.

AutoCAD has an outstanding series of dimensioning tools that can be useful when you understand the concepts of size and shape description. There is no magic in the dimension commands; you must understand these concepts together with the dimensioning tools to create and successfully annotate a drawing.

This flexibility allows you to accommodate changes to a dimension style that reflect the standard practices adopted in any of the engineering disciplines. It should never be required of a production or construction worker to calculate or assume any dimension needed to fabricate the part. Although the rules and practices of dimensioning are important in the description of a drawing's shape and size, in this unit we are going to concentrate on the creation of the dimensioning elements. There will be some discussion on common dimensioning practices as they relate to the creation and placement of dimensions. If you need a complete description or explanation of a specific engineering's dimensioning practices you should research the topic of

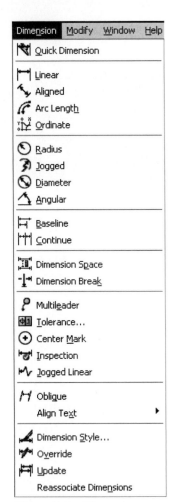

Figure 5-1    Dimension
menu

dimensioning standards through an engineering graphics textbook describing the graphic language used to communicate size and shape descriptions for the engineering discipline in which you are working.

| **FOR MORE DETAIL** | For more information on Drafting Standards and dimensioning, contact the American National Standards Institute (www.ansi.org) regarding Drafting Standard Y14. |
| --- | --- |

## DIMENSIONING TERMINOLOGY

AutoCAD has commands (see Figures 5-1 and 5-2) that produce dimensions in **Linear, Radial, Angular,** and **Ordinate** modes. **Linear** refers to the distance between two points, while **Radial** is a description of an arc or circle. **Angular** depicts the acute or obtuse angle between two lines. **Ordinate** is a feature-based dimensioning type relating all dimensions to a datum or fixed origin. The result of a dimension command is a series of lines, arrowheads or other similar terminators, and text that relate to the points or entities selected (see Figure 5-3). These dimension entities are blocked together with an associative quality so all parts of the dimension are treated as one entity. Furthermore, the dimension is associated to a location on the drawing. Changes made to the drawing will immediately update the dimension if any element within the dimension changes. The related elements will adjust accordingly, reflecting the new information.

Dimensioning uses several terms unique to the topic. The following definitions are related to the parts of a dimension as well as terms used in the geometric description of a drawing.

- **Dimension line** A dimension line is a graphic representation of the direction that is being described (see Figure 5-4). Dimension lines have a related piece of text giving the distance between the terminators attached to the ends of the dimension line. Dimension lines are offset parallel to the entities being dimensioned. Whenever possible, a dimension line should be placed between the views describing the object. Clarity and legibility are two of the main issues when placing dimensions and you should avoid placing dimensions on a drawing unless absolutely necessary. Dimension lines can be one thin solid line with the text placed above the line or they can have a break in the line with the text placed in the gap between the two parts of the dimension line. These conventions are based on the engineering discipline you are working in and controlled through the **Dimension Style Manager.**

- **Extension line** An extension line (see Figure 5-4) is used as a continuation of an edge or location of a feature. An extension line should never touch the object to which it is related. An extension line offset or gap distance is programmed into the creation of a dimension to ensure clarity. Extension lines will continue out past the last terminator used in the dimension sequence. This offset and continuation distance are controlled through dimension variables.

- **Dimension text** The numeric readout attached to a dimension is referred to as dimension text (see Figure 5-4). This text is generated at the time the dimension is created. It will read data from the entity or points selected and calculate the distance or value for the text description. The exact text style and placement is controlled through dimension system variables.

- **Terminators** This is a graphic representation of the intersection between the dimension line and the extension line. Terminators (see Figure 5-4) are commonly referred to as

Figure 5-2    The Dimension toolbar

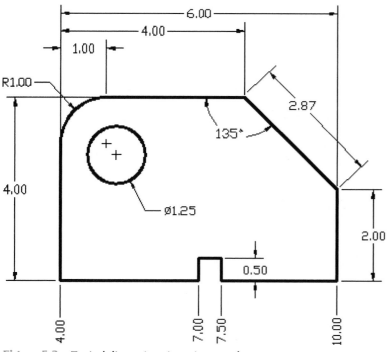

Figure 5-3    Typical dimensions in various modes

| Dimension Commands |
| --- |
| **Leader with Text** |
| **Type In:** |
| qleader |
| **Alias-Type In:** |
| LE |
| **Menu:** |
| Dimension  Modify  Wind |
| Quick Dimension |
| Linear |
| Continue |
| Leader |
| Tolerance... |
| **Icon:** |
| **Dimension Toolbar** |

arrowheads. Although other symbols such as architectural ticks, squares, and dots can be used, the arrowhead is the most often used termination symbol.

- **Leader** This is a series of entities that points to a specific location and has a note attached allowing the addition of any text string for the description of the detail (see Figure 5-4).

- **Continue dimensions** A style of linear dimensions that will string dimensions together in a continuous line (see Figure 5-5) from the end of one dimension to the beginning of the next linear dimension.

- **Baseline dimensions** A style of linear dimensions that uses a datum plane or baseline as a common reference point for all dimensions is known as a baseline style of dimensioning (see Figure 5-6).

- **Center mark** This is a series of lines organized as a plus sign that marks the center point of a circle or arc. The mark can be a simple plus sign (see Figure 5-6) or it can continue out past the circle or arc that is selected.

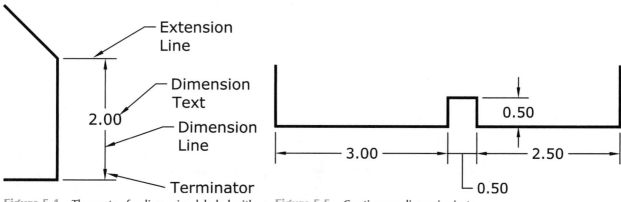

Figure 5-4    The parts of a dimension labeled with leaders

Figure 5-5    Continuous dimensioning

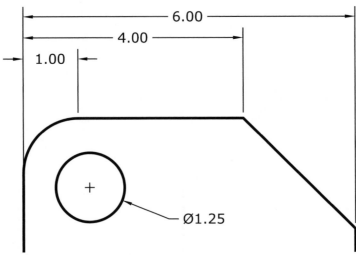

**Figure 5-6**   Baseline dimensions and diameter dimension with center mark

**aligned system:** A dimensional system where all the text entities are placed parallel to the dimension line and are read typically from the bottom or right-hand side of the document.

**unidirectional system:** A dimensional system where all the text entities are written parallel to the X axis and read from the bottom of the document.

## STANDARD PRACTICES

There are two recognized forms to the practice of dimensioning. These forms relate to the reading of the dimension text and are known as the ***aligned system*** and the ***unidirectional system.***

Certain industries like mechanical engineering prefer the unidirectional method over the aligned method. When choosing a system, you should refer to the common dimensioning practices for that industry and stay with that system's standard practices, keeping in mind that a key issue in dimensioning is clarity. Adjustments to a series of dimension variables can result in creating a dimension style used for either of these systems.

> Keep in mind the key issue in dimensioning a drawing is accuracy and clarity. The object's complete shape and size description is given through dimensional annotations and notes.

### Aligned System

This form aligns the text with the dimension line. The text figures are placed parallel to the dimension line and are read from the drawing sheet's bottom or right-hand edge (see Figure 5-7).

### Unidirectional System

This system rotates all text figures to be arranged horizontally no matter what angle the dimension line is traveling. This results in all text figures being read from the bottom of the drawing sheet (see Figure 5-8).

## DIMENSION STYLES

AutoCAD has over 70 dimension variables (see Appendix D) that can control the look of every part used in the creation of a dimension. You can establish values for these dimension variables; in turn, these create a look or style when placed in the drawing file. The basic AutoCAD drawing template has settings for a typical **Dimension Style** called Standard that works for small part drawings. This Standard Dimension Style provides a starting point for development of additional dimension styles to use in subsequent drawings. Some of these variables are numeric-based, such as **Text Height** or **Arrowhead Size;** others are simply **On/Off** or toggle variables; still other groups of variables control the placement of dimension features.

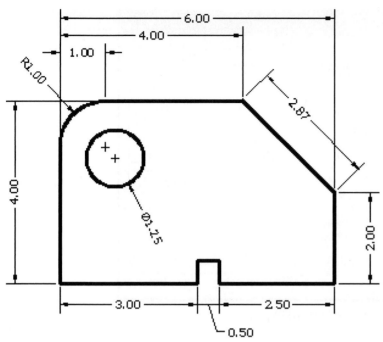

**Figure 5-7**    Aligned dimensions

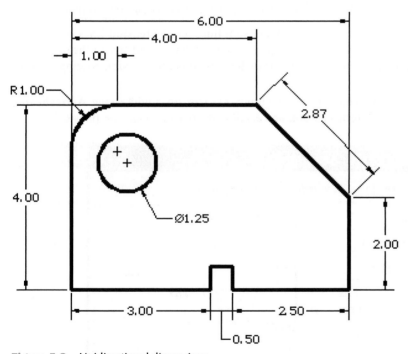

**Figure 5-8**    Unidirectional dimensions

## Dimension Style Manager

You can access the **Dimension Style Manager** (see Figure 5-9) through the **Format** menu, the **Dimension** menu, a **Dimension** toolbar icon, or by typing **DIMSTYLE,** an alias at the command prompt. This dialog box uses a series of buttons or tabs for modifying dimension variables along with the ability to save and load different combinations of the variables under previously saved style names known

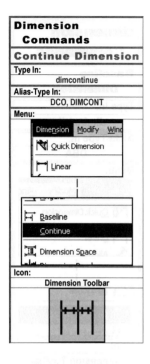

**Dimension Commands**

**Continue Dimension**

Type In:
dimcontinue

Alias-Type In:
DCO, DIMCONT

Menu:

Icon:
Dimension Toolbar

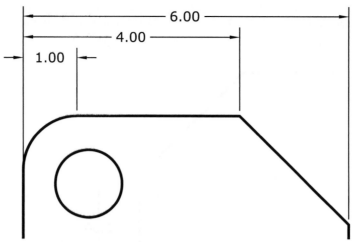

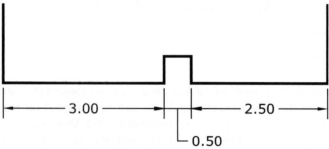

**Figure 5-19**   Typical baseline dimensioning

**Figure 5-20**   Continue dimensions

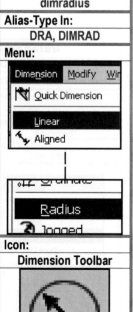

**Dimension Commands**

**Radius Dimension**

Options: Mtext, Text, Angle

Type In:
dimradius

Alias-Type In:
DRA, DIMRAD

Menu:

Icon:
Dimension Toolbar

**Exercise 5-1:** Creating Linear Dimensions

- Start a new drawing in AutoCAD.
- Draw at least three rectangles in the drawing area.
- Using the **Linear** command, dimension one of the topmost horizontal lines.
- Using the **Baseline** command, continue to create dimensions to describe the remaining top horizontal line dimensions.
- Using the **Linear** command, dimension the bottommost vertical line.
- Using the **Continue** command, create dimensions to describe the remaining bottom horizontal line dimensions.
- Repeat the preceding steps to dimension all the vertical lines.

## Radial Dimensioning

**Radial** dimensions control the sizing of circles and arcs. The three commands that create radial dimensions are **Radius, Jogged,** and **Diameter.** In all cases you will be prompted to Select arc or circle. Then you will be prompted for the location to place the dimension text. Depending on the type of dimension, the value of the **Radius** or **Diameter** of the entity selected will be displayed (see Figure 5-21). This routine also places the **Center Mark** according to the **Dimension Style** settings as shown in Figure 5-21.

The **Jogged** dimension command, which was new in the 2006 version, allows for the foreshortening of the radius dimension when the full length cannot be shown or would be confusing to the reader of the drawing.

## Angular Dimensioning

Angular dimensioning displays and will calculate the acute or obtuse angle between two entities (see Figure 5-22). To produce an **Angular** dimension, you are prompted with the following:

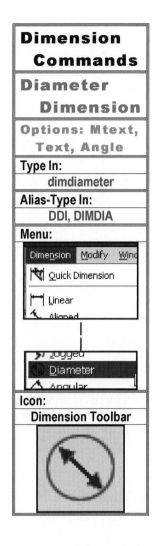

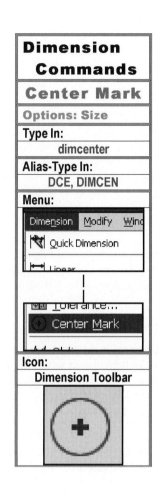

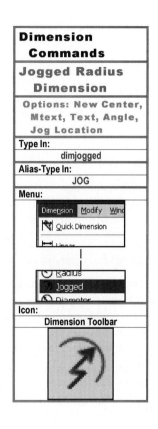

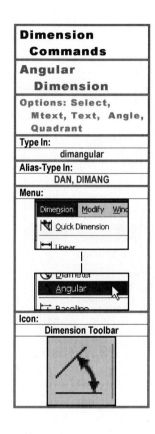

```
Select arc, circle, line, or <specify vertex>:
Select second line.
Specify dimension arc line location.
```

Depending on the placement of the dimension arc line and the text, you will see a readout of the acute or obtuse angle value. Extension lines will be placed according to the dimensional arc and the entities selected. When a circle is selected along with a second point the value can be greater than 180° depending on the placement of the dimensional arc.

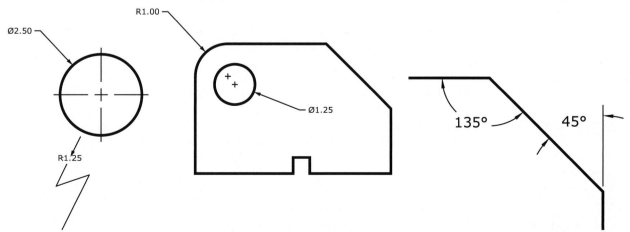

**Figure 5-21**   Radius, Jog, and Diameter dimensions with center marks          **Figure 5-22**   Angular dimensions

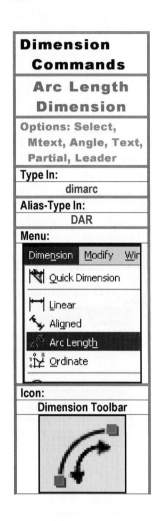

**Dimension Commands**

**Arc Length Dimension**

Options: Select, Mtext, Angle, Text, Partial, Leader

Type In:
dimarc

Alias-Type In:
DAR

Menu:

Icon:
Dimension Toolbar

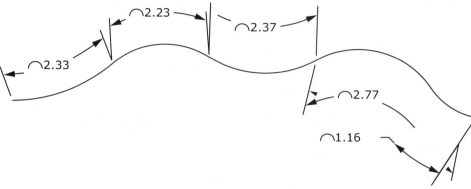

**Figure 5-23**    Typical arc length dimensioning

## Arc Length

This dimension, new in the 2006 version, calculates and displays the true length of an arc entity as an object from the beginning point of the arc to its ending point (see Figure 5-23). To produce an **Arc Length** dimension you are prompted with the following:

```
Select arc or polyline arc segment
Specify dimension arc line location
```

Depending on the settings of the symbol in the dimension style, you can place the dimension above or below the arc. Extension lines will be placed according to the dimension arc or the entity selected. At this time only arcs or arc segments from a polyline can be used.

### Exercise 5-2: Creating Angle, Radius, and Arc Dimension

- Start a new drawing in AutoCAD.
- Draw one circle, one rectangle with fillets, and one rectangle with chamfers.
- On the circle place a Diameter dimension on the inside and another on the outside of the circle.
- On each arc of the fillets place a Radius dimension on the inside and outside in the drawing area. Also place an Arc Length dimension on the inside and outside of each fillet.
- On each chamfer place an angular dimension at each end, alternating the acute and obtuse angles.

## Ordinate Dimensioning

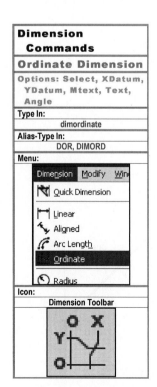

**Dimension Commands**

**Ordinate Dimension**

Options: Select, XDatum, YDatum, Mtext, Text, Angle

Type In:
dimordinate

Alias-Type In:
DOR, DIMORD

Menu:

Icon:
Dimension Toolbar

The **Ordinate** command creates a dimension that is the perpendicular distance from the current origin to the selected feature point. The dimension created will be parallel to either the X or the Y axis. Upon executing the command you will be prompted to Specify feature location. Although the word used is "feature," you can select any point shown in the drawing. This should be done with the aid of an **Object Snap** option to ensure accuracy. The next prompt will ask you to choose a location for text and leader placement as follows:

```
Specify leader endpoint or [Xdatum/Ydatum/Mtext/Text/Angle]:
```

The dimension produced will depend on which direction the mouse is dragged when selecting the leader's endpoint. If the desired results are not seen, you can exercise an **Xdatum** or **Ydatum** option to force the dimension to the correct datum plane. The dimension text will be calculated from the current datum origin to the feature or location selected (see Figure 5-24).

### Exercise 5-3: Creating Ordinate Dimensions

- Start a new drawing in AutoCAD.
- Draw at least three rectangles in the drawing area.
- Place Ordinate dimensions on all corners of the rectangles.

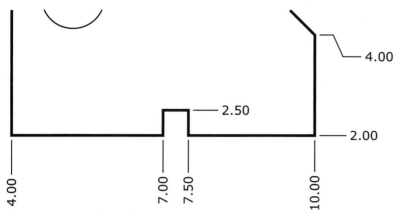

**Figure 5-24**    Ordinate dimension on object

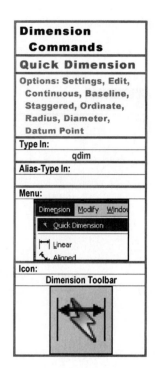

**Dimension Commands**

**Quick Dimension**

Options: Settings, Edit, Continuous, Baseline, Staggered, Ordinate, Radius, Diameter, Datum Point

Type In:
qdim

Alias-Type In:

Menu:
Dimension  Modify  Window
  Quick Dimension
  Linear
  Aligned

Icon:
Dimension Toolbar

## Quick Dimensioning

For placing many dimensions in a fast, single operation, AutoCAD developed a command known as **QDIM** (Quick Dimension). This command creates a series of dimensions based on certain parameters. You simply select—using a **Window, Crossing,** or other selection method—the entities of the drawing you want to be dimensioned. A series of dimensions will be created at each endpoint (see Figure 5-25) and/or center point of the entities in the selected area. These dimensions can be created in a **Baseline, Continuous, Staggered,** or **Ordinate** method of dimensioning (see Figure 5-26). The results of a **QDIM** command are shown in Figure 5-27. There are options available for dimensioning several circles or arcs as well as the ability to edit previously placed strings of quick dimensions.

```
Command:  QDIM
Associative dimension priority = Endpoint
Select geometry to dimension: Specify opposite corner: 8 found
Select geometry to dimension:
```

**Figure 5-25**    Quick Dimension basic command prompt

```
Specify dimension line position, or
[Continuous/Staggered/Baseline/Ordinate/Radius/Diameter/datumPoint/Edit/seTtings
] <Continuous>:

Command:
```
3.5764, 4.2181, 0.0000    SNAP  GRID  ORTHO  POLAR  OSNAP  OTRACK  DUCS  DYN  LWT  MODEL

**Figure 5-26**    Quick Dimension style command prompts

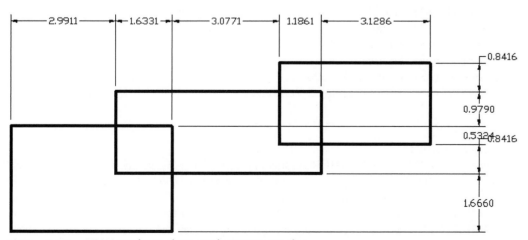

**Figure 5-27**    QDIM results on three overlapping rectangles

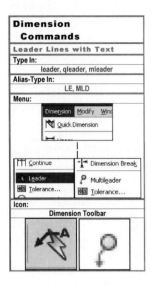

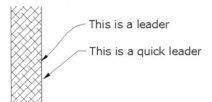

This is a leader

This is a quick leader

**Figure 5-28** Sample of leader commands

## The Leader Commands

A leader is a special object with text created through the dimensioning functions. In addition to dimensioning the shape and locations, dimensioning may include the addition of notes about the object's production, more specific information on materials, and other information needed for the proper creation of this object. These notes and directions may be connected to a particular location or may appear in the middle of an object. A leader contains four parts: an arrowhead or terminator, a leader line (straight or splined), a leader tail (sometimes called a shoulder), and a text or block entity. A leader (see Figure 5-28) generally will start at a specific location with the terminator (arrow, tick mark, squiggle, etc.), and proceed at an angle to the object, crossing into an open area on the drawing where the text is placed. The text can be single-line or multiline text depending on the user choices in the command.

*LEADER and Quick Leader*   The **LEADER** command is structured to simply create the leader line and place the text as shown by the prompts below. Only a few options are available including modifying the line from straight to splined. Text is entered in a single-line text mode and can be edited with a double-click on the text or with the modify commands.

```
Command: leader
Specify leader start point:
Specify next point:
Specify next point or [Annotation/Format/Undo]<Annotation>: f
Enter leader format option [Spline/STraight/Arrow/None]
<Exit>: s
Specify next point or [Annotation/Format/Undo] <Annotation>:
Enter next line of annotation text: This is a leader
Enter next line of annotation text:
```

The **Quick Leader (QLEADER)** command offers more options in the form of settings (see Figure 5-29, Figure 5-30, and Figure 5-31), which can be set in advance to speed the creation of the leader. The command prompts, as shown below, enable you to modify the settings for each leader. Settings are not saved.

```
Command: qleader
Specify first leader point, or [Settings] <Settings>:
Specify next point:
Specify next point:
Specify text width <0.0000>:
Enter first line of annotation text <Mtext>: This is a quick
leader
Enter next line of annotation text:
```

*Multiple LEADER*   The **MLEADER** command (see Figure 5-32) can be found in the dimension menu or on the 2D Annotation Dashboard. You have three options to create a leader: terminator first, tail first, or content first. You can access these options through the right-click menu. Content for the leader can come from an **MTEXT** dialog box or the insertion of a **BLOCK.** The **MLEADERSTYLE** command controls the format and display options of multileaders. These styles can be created and saved similar to other style editors. You will be able to access a leader's properties through the **Modify Properties** dialog box.

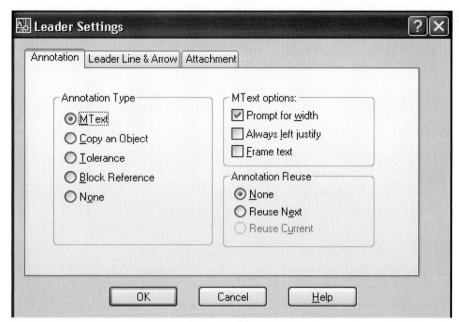

**Figure 5-29**   Quick Leader settings for annotation

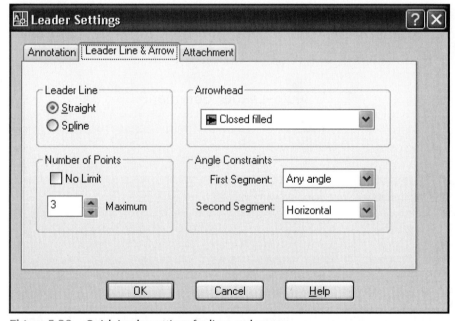

**Figure 5-30**   Quick Leader settings for lines and arrows

Other tools available for the editing of leaders include the removal of leader lines, creating a single leader that points to several items, and maintaining associativity between text objects and the other leader entities. In addition to these options, multileaders can be aligned with the **MLEADERALIGN** command (alias **MLA**) and collected into a single leader through the **MLEADERCOLLECT** command (alias **MLC**). These options can be found on the **MLEADER** dashboard panel or typed in as shown below. There is also a **MLEADEREDIT** command (alias **MLE**) to allow you to add or remove leader lines and terminators.

The command prompts are as follows:

```
Command: mleader
Specify leader arrowhead location or [leader Landing first/Content
first/Options] <Options>: o
Enter an option [Leader type/leader lAnding/Content type/
Maxpoints/First angle/Second angle/eXit options] <eXit options>: l
```

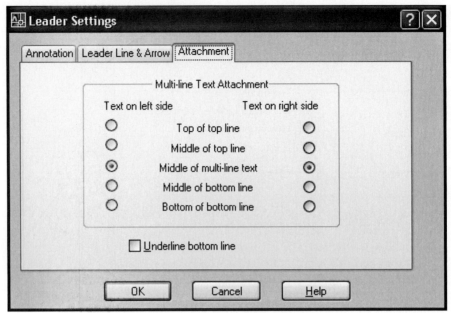

**Figure 5-31**    Quick Leader settings for text attachment

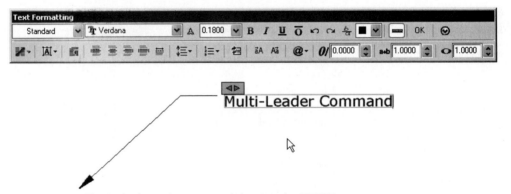

**Figure 5-32**    The Multiple Leader command showing the MTEXT entry

```
Select a leader type [Straight/sPline/None] <Straight>: s
Enter an option [Leader type/leader lAnding/Content type/
Maxpoints/First angle/Second angle/eXit options] <Leader type>: x
Specify leader arrowhead location or [leader Landing first/Content
first/Options] <Options>:
Specify leader landing location.
```

The **MLEADERSTYLE** command (Figure 5-33) controls the settings of the multileader. There are three tabs (see Figures 5-34, 5-35, and 5-36) that enable you to set the appearance that you want for the multileader. Multileader Styles can be stored and connected with an annotative scale that automatically scales objects based on layout scales for presentations or plotting.

**Exercise 5-4:** Placing a Leader

- Start a new drawing in AutoCAD.
- Draw a rectangle from coordinates 2, 2 to 4, 8.
- Type QLEADER <Enter> to activate the Quick Leader command.
- Use the midpoint of the right-side vertical line as the "First Leader Point" to start the leader to place the arrow.

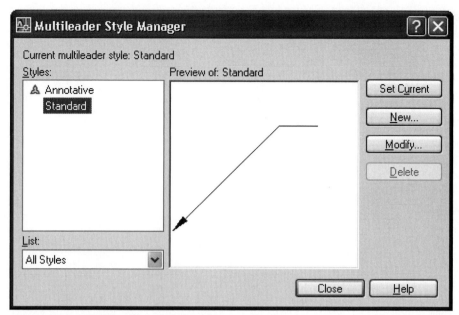

**Figure 5-33**    Multileader Style Manager

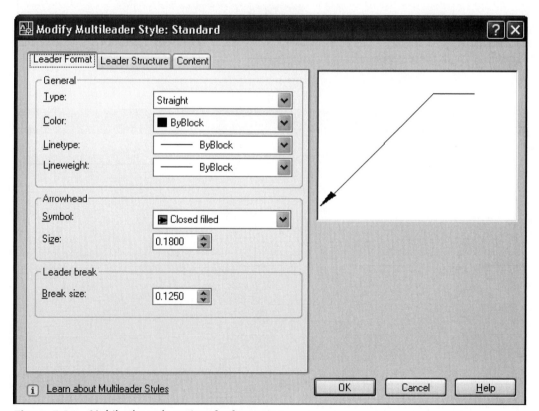

**Figure 5-34**    Multileader style settings for formatting

- Move up and to the right (a 45° angle) a short distance to establish the "Next Point" for the leader line.
- Press <Enter> to end the line inputs.
- Press <Enter> to bypass the entry for text width.
- Type 4" × 4" Wood Fence Post <Enter> to place the text in the drawing.
- Press <Enter> to complete the command.

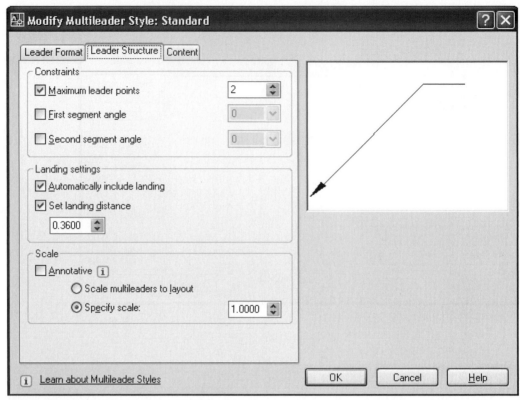

**Figure 5-35**   Multileader style settings for the structure

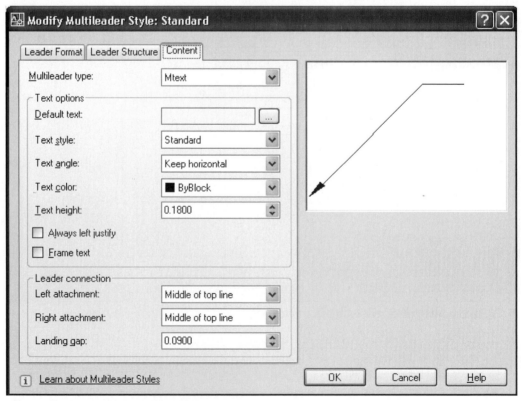

**Figure 5-36**   Multileader style settings for text

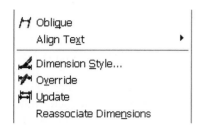

Figure 5-37    Menu items for editing dimensions

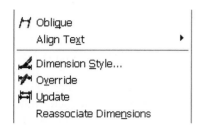

**Figure 5-38**    Toolbar icons for dimension editing

# EDITING DIMENSIONS

Although there are several entities within a dimension that can be changed, editing dimensions usually refers to changing the text value and related elements due to changes made to the base entity. The **Dimension** menu (see Figure 5-37) and the **Dimension** toolbar (see Figure 5-38) show various edit commands. Dimensions can be modified with commands such as **Stretch, Scale,** and **Rotate.** Dimensions can also be edited with **Grips** (see Unit 9), through the **Modify Properties** palette, and through the **Dimension Style Manager.**

## Associative/Nonassociative Dimensions

One of the qualities that makes editing dimensions easy is the ability to control a dimension's *associative property.* Dimensions can be linked to entities in a drawing, bringing a much higher level of intelligence to the dimension. At the same time AutoCAD gives you the ability to flag dimensions and text that have been edited and do not reflect the current drawing's dimension style. All these controls can be found in a series of dimension variables. When a dimension has an associative property all the dimensional entities are joined together as a single object and linked to the geometry of the object that is being selected. The system variable, **DIMASSOC,** has three settings that control the level of association available to a dimensional entity.

associative property: The ability to connect entities together and then make changes that will automatically be reflected in the dimension.

- By default this system variable is set to a value of **2.** This setting means that there is a full association between the dimension and the geometry. All elements of the dimension are joined as a single object, and control points are placed on the entities selected for the creation of the dimension. A no plot layer named "Defpoints" is created to hold these control points for associativity. If the geometry were to change, the dimension would also change, whether it was in the selected set or not.

- A **DIMASSOC** value of **1** creates a nonassociative relationship between the dimension and the geometry. This setting joins the elements of the dimension together but it does not have any connection to the geometry used to create the dimension. The geometry also has to be selected to have the changes affect the dimension.

- A **DIMASSOC** value of **0** constructs an exploded dimension. With this setting each element of the dimension is a separate object.

With the correct use of this variable, changes to an already dimensioned drawing should be relatively simple. Any modification of the geometry can be easily incorporated to reflect the changed dimension value.

## Updating Dimensions Through Dimension Styles

All dimension (system) variables that control the look of a dimension are part of a *dimension style.* Any changes to the dimension style will affect all the dimensions currently in the drawing file that are using that particular style. The variable **DIMASSOC** controls the automatic updating of dimensions in a drawing file. As mentioned earlier this associative property allows for changes to be passed through the geometry to the dimension. If only certain dimensions need to reflect the changes being made to the dimension style, you can use the **Update** icon (see Figure 5-29) from the **Dimension** toolbar or the **Dimension** menu (Figure 5-28) to select individual dimensions for updating.

# SUMMARY

This unit has introduced you to the basics of dimensioning in AutoCAD, the accurate and clear documentation of the size and shape of parts or features in drawings. First, we presented the concept of dimension styles, groups of system variables controlling the creation and appearance of dimensional entities that enable you to quickly and efficiently generate and place dimensions on objects in your drawing. We then provided definitions of several basic terms that are used in the topic of dimensioning together with some illustrative examples. You then learned about the two standard methods of dimensioning: the aligned system, which aligns the text with the dimension line, and the unidirectional system, which arranges all dimensional text horizontally regardless of the orientation of the dimension line. A discussion followed of the features of the **Dimension Style Manager** dialog box, which allows you to select and use a dimension style from several categories of dimension variables including **Lines, Symbols and Arrows, Text, Fit, Primary Units, Alternate Units,** and **Tolerances.** You then learned and practiced the commands used to create linear, radial, angular, and ordinate dimensions as well as leader lines and notes. Finally, we presented the concept of editing dimensions, a process in which the text value and related elements of the dimension are altered due to changes made to the base entity, as well as the use of the **STRETCH, SCALE,** and **ROTATE** commands, grips, and the associative property of dimensions (controlled by the **DIMASSOC** system variable) to edit and update dimensions in a drawing.

# CHAPTER TEST QUESTIONS

## Multiple Choice

1. Which dimension command will produce a string of in-line dimensions?

   a. Continue
   b. Baseline
   c. Ordinate
   d. Linear

2. A radial dimension is used on a:

   a. Line
   b. Rectangle
   c. Circle
   d. Polygon

3. Which dimension command will produce dimensions related to a feature?

   a. Angular
   b. Radial
   c. Linear
   d. Ordinate

4. Center marks are included with which type of dimensioning?

   a. Ordinate
   b. Radial
   c. Linear
   d. Angular

5. Which dimension command will produce a series of stacked dimensions?

   a. Continue
   b. Baseline
   c. Ordinate
   d. Linear

## Matching

a. _____ Dimension style
b. _____ Aligned system
c. _____ Leader
d. _____ Angular
e. _____ Associative dimension

1. Used to dimension an angle
2. Set of system variables for a dimension
3. Text-based pointer
4. Link between object and dimension
5. Text parallel to the dimension line

## True or False

1. True or False: Changes to a dimension style will affect only dimensions placed after the change.

2. True or False: Quick dimension will create a series of linear dimensions along an object.

3. True or False: AutoCAD can produce dimensions in primary as well as alternate units.

4. True or False: Dimension Style Manager will only control color and layer properties.

5. True or False: AutoCAD cannot produce a dimension to show an arc's length.

## CHAPTER PROJECTS

1.  Research the various dimensioning standards as defined by the following organizations:
    a.  ANSI (American National Standards Institute)
    b.  ISO (International Standards Organization)
    c.  BSI (British Standards Institute)
    d.  ASME (American Society of Mechanical Engineers)
2.  Create a list or set of rules for proper dimensioning of a drawing. Research various engineering and architectural graphics textbooks for guidelines and standards for dimensioning.
3.  What is *overdimensioning* and why is it considered wrong? Prepare a poster with examples to compare properly dimensioned items with overdimensioned ones.
4.  Prepare a report on Geometric Dimensioning and Tolerancing (GD&T) and include the history, standards of practices, symbology, and uses. Check with area machine shops and other companies that employ GD&T practices in their operation. Do AutoCAD's dimension styles fit these operations?

## PRACTICE EXERCISES

Using the drawings you created from Figures 3-49 to 3-68 in Unit 3, place dimensions using the techniques and commands explained in this chapter.

- First discuss the proper methods of placing dimensions, leaders, notes, etc. based on the ANSI Standards. Are there better places to put dimensions for more clarity and information? Are additional dimensions needed for proper construction of the part or figure?

- Create layers for dimension, notes, text, and other information as well as layers for object lines, centerlines, hidden lines, and other linetypes that may be used.

- Add dimensions, leaders, text, and other information to the drawings to make complete drawings.

- Save the completed drawing in the **Workskills** folder by adding a **-C5** to the end of the drawing name as an indication that dimensions are present.

# Fundamentals of the Printing Process

# 6

## Chapter Objectives

- Understand the difference between model space and layout space.
- Identify the basic plotting parameters.
- Establish plot settings for device, scale, output size, and orientation.
- Define sheet sizes and related scales.
- Create plots in both model space and layout space.

## INTRODUCTION

Plotting refers to the printing process. Within the AutoCAD software the printing process uses the term *plot*. All the commands in the **File** menu containing the term **Plot** (see Figure 6-1) refer to the printing process needed to produce hard copies (paper versions) of the electronic drawing files created in AutoCAD.

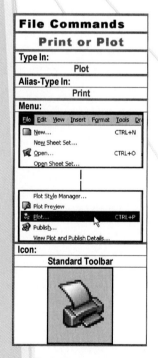

**Figure 6-1**    File menu highlighting Plot/print commands

## PLOTTING

plot: The process of printing
through a CAD system.

*Plot* is synonymous with print. Plotting is the same as printing and a plotter is the same as a printer. Prior to the boom of inkjet technology, the devices engineers used to print out their drawings were known as pen plotters. Historically, a plotter was bigger than a printer, with paper sizes up to 60″ wide. With the advancement of technology most printers are of the inkjet style. This process uses a variety of settings to control drawing data and develop a configuration understood by a plot device to print out the file on a standard engineering sheet size. What to plot, what size paper to plot on, and what drawing scale to use are all questions that will be addressed in the **Plot** process (see Figure 6-2).

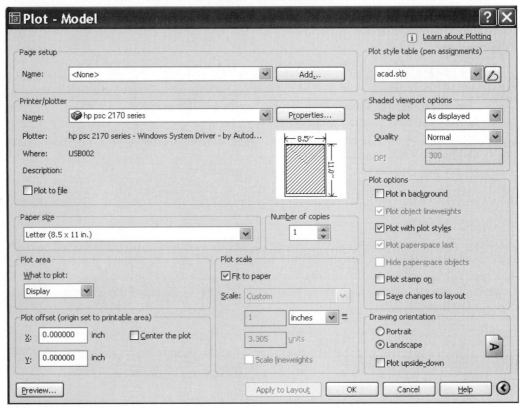

**Figure 6-2**   Plot/print dialog box

## TERMINOLOGY USED IN PLOTTING

As already mentioned, the term plot is synonymous with the term print. There are several terms and concepts used in the plotting process that you need to be familiar with. As we look at the overall procedure we will use terms we already know to describe the new terms needed to understand the plotting procedure.

To begin the process a printer (plotter) needs to be configured to your system (see Figure 6-3). Configuring a printer refers to the installation of the printer driver and the connection to the computer,

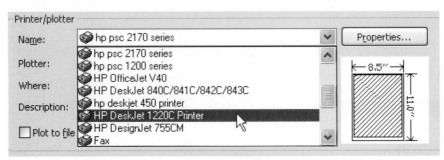

**Figure 6-3**   Choosing a plot device from the drop-down list

usually through a USB cable/port, and to a power source. The default system printer will show as the selected printer as you enter the **Plot** dialog box. Other printers may be available in the selection drop-down list. (The choices here will reflect printers configured in your Windows system.) Once your printer is in place, printing can be done from one of two worlds, model space or layout space.

- *Model space* (**MSPACE** or **MS** when on a layout) is the world in which the drawing is created or produced. **Model space** can be unlimited in size but, as mentioned earlier, *drawing limits* produce an electronic fence that can be helpful when calculating a plotting scale.

- *Layout space* (**PSPACE** or **PS**) is a highly flexible world allowing you to create various sheet sizes and combinations of drawing views and drawing scales with annotations that have a size relationship to the final printed sheet size. The controls of the drawing to be plotted are found in the **Plot** dialog box. Within the dialog box you will address several issues regarding sheet size (Tables 6-1 and 6-2), drawing scale, and plotting style.

**model space:** One of the two spaces in which entities can be created. A geometric model is created in a 3D coordinate space referred to as model space.

**drawing limits:** A defined area within model space used to control drawing size.

**layout space:** Used for creating finished views of a design with annotations and for printing or plotting, as opposed to doing design work.

| Sheet Sizes Drawing Area American National Standard | | |
|---|---|---|
| A | 8.5″ | 11″ |
| B | 11″ | 17″ |
| C | 17″ | 22″ |
| D | 22″ | 34″ |
| E | 34″ | 44″ |

**Table 6-1**   ANSI Sheet Sizes for Plotting

| Sheet Sizes Drawing Area (mm) International Standard | | |
|---|---|---|
| A4 | 210 | 297 |
| A3 | 297 | 420 |
| A2 | 420 | 594 |
| A1 | 594 | 841 |
| A0 | 841 | 1189 |

**Table 6-2**   ISO Sheet Sizes for Plotting

A *plot style* is a group of settings that control the characteristics such as color, linetype, lineweight, and visibility of a drawing entity for plotting. Although this can be done in other ways, using plot styles is a convenient method to achieve uniformity in printing drawings. *Drawing scale* is the ratio between the objects to be printed in the drawing area (true size) and the sheet size for plotting.

Traditionally this scale is 1″ = 1″ (full scale), ¼″ = 1′-0″ (architectural scale), 1 cm = 1 m (metric scale), or 1″ = 10′-0″ (civil scale). Once all the areas of the dialog box are addressed you can use the **Plot PREVIEW** command to see what the results of the current configuration will produce. The image that appears in the preview window is what will be printed when the data is sent to the printer to complete the process. The AutoCAD program refers to the **PREVIEW** window as "what you see is what you get" (WYSIWYG), meaning the image shown will be the drawing plotted. If you do not like what you see, simply return to the **Plot** dialog box (see Figure 6-2) and make adjustments to the print configuration.

**plot style:** The settings that control all the parameters of a plotted file.

**drawing scale:** A mathematical ratio between a design's real size and the printed drawing's sheet size.

Most engineering offices will have preestablished plot styles and plot scales based on the plotting equipment and common sheet sizes used in the office.

## PLOTTING FROM MODEL SPACE

When plotting from model space or **MSPACE,** you are able to set up one plotting scenario for the drawing. The **PLOT** command can be found in the **File** menu (see Figure 6-1) or in the **Standard** toolbar as an icon (see Figure 6-4). After executing the **PLOT** command you will establish plot settings in the **Plot** dialog box. In the simplest scenario you will select the following items from the **Plot** dialog box:

- Printer device
- Area of model space to plot

**Figure 6-4**   Plot icon

- Sheet size
- Drawing scale

### Elementary Controls of Plot Settings

We will examine each area of the dialog box separately. You need to remember that at any time during the establishment of the plot settings, you can select the **Preview** button in the lower left corner of the dialog box to see a preview of your current settings.

### Page Setup

All plotting scenarios can be named and saved as a **Page setup** (see Figure 6-5). By selecting a previously saved **Page setup** you are recalling a set of plotting variables as the basis or starting point of the current plotting scenario. The **Add** button on the right side will save the current plotting scenario to the list of previously saved page setups. Selecting a previously saved **Page setup** can be done through the drop-down arrow where the name is entered.

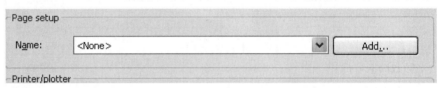

**Figure 6-5**    Page setup area of Plot dialog box

### Printer/Plotter

The print device is selected from the Printer/plotter area (see Figure 6-6). The **Name** drop-down list contains all the printers currently configured to the system as well as all .PC3 printer control file types. If a previous page setup is not chosen, the most recently used plotter will be listed here rather than the default printer. You should always verify this selection before proceeding.

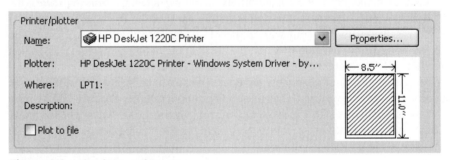

**Figure 6-6**    Plot device information

In the lower left corner of the **Printer/plotter** area th is a check box called **Plot to file.** If you check this box, stead of sending the plot data to the printer, you will create plot file (.plt) containing all the data needed to print the fil This file can then be printed at another location on a printe not currently connected to your system.

### Paper Size

This drop-down list contains the paper sizes available for the print device selected in the printer/plotter area. This list varies depending on the print device selected. The actual paper size is measured in length and width, with the length of the paper parallel to the X axis and

**Note:**
If you are plotting to a file for offsite reproduction, you must specify a plotter. Therefore, it is important to know the plotter to be used, and it must be configured before the plot file is made.

the width parallel to the Y axis. In this area you can also specify the number of copies to be printed (see Figure 6-7).

**Figure 6-7**   Paper size and copy information

## Plot Area

This section specifies what area of model space is used to calculate the **Plot area** (see Figure 6-8). There are four choices related to model space printing in AutoCAD 2008.

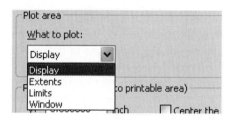

**Figure 6-8**   Plotting area

1. The **Display** option calculates the current screen dis┌ for the printed area. This includes any blank or open eas around the sides of the display.

2. The **Limits** option calculates the current drawin **LIMITS** (area) as the plot area. Any entities or par of entities located outside the current drawin; **LIMITS** are not included in the plot calculations.

3. The **Extents** option finds all entities in the drawing file and calculates the smallest area or window that encompasses all these entities for the plot calculation.

4. The **Window** option places you in the model space drawing screen to select an area (using a window) for the plot area.

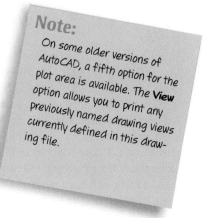

**Note:**
When using an **Extents** option, the preview window may show a very small drawing as a possible print; this is probably due to an entity drawn way out in model space. Look around the top and edges of the preview window for any stray entities that will need to be deleted and then reissue the plot command.

Of all the choices mentioned you will find the most control of the plot area with the **Limits** options if you have calculated your drawing limits correctly.

## Plot Scale

The **Plot scale** area contains the information to size the plot area selected (see Figure 6-9). Traditional engineering scale factors are listed in the **Scale** drop-down list, such as $1'' = 20'$ (civil), $1/8'' = 1'$ (architectural), and others. Selecting one of these scales results in the plot being calculated based on the ratio of the model space drawing units to the plotted units. There is also a check box to allow you to scale lineweights proportionally as well. When the box **Scale to fit** is selected, the plot scale is calculated so the plot will fit all drawing entities in the **Plot area** to the selected paper size. You can also create a custom scale by entering your own ratio for plotting scale.

**Note:**
On some older versions of AutoCAD, a fifth option for the plot area is available. The **View** option allows you to print any previously named drawing views currently defined in this drawing file.

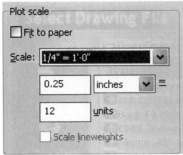

Figure 6-9    Plot scale setting

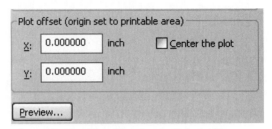

Figure 6-10    Plot offset/center information

## Plot Offset

All plotting instructions start from the lower left corner of the selected paper size, which is designated the origin of the plot. **Plot offset** allows you to shift the start point along the X or Y axis as needed. These values can be negative or positive based on the direction you need to shift the plot. The **Center the plot** check box can be selected for an automatic calculation to center the drawing on the current paper size based on the **Plot scale** and paper sheet size (see Figure 6-10). When these areas of the **Plot** dialog box have been addressed you have an option to preview the results of the **Page setup.** The **Preview** window shows the current results based on the parameters entered. Remember **WYSIWYG,** and if you like the preview, then pick the right mouse button to see a menu with the **PLOT** command to immediately send the plot to the specified printer. You can also press <**Enter**> or <**Esc**> to return to the **Plot** dialog box. This allows you to reset information and **Preview** again or pick **OK** to accept the settings and send the data to the print device. If you do not like the preview you can use <**Esc**> or <**Enter**> to return to the **Plot** dialog box to make adjustments in the settings and then produce another preview until the plot is correct.

### Exercise 6-1: Plotting from Model Space

- Either open the Quick-Start Tutorial Drawing QS–1 or access the QS–1 drawing from the Student CD.
- Verify that the Model tab at the bottom left of the drawing is selected.
- Add your name by creating a piece of text; place the text in the upper right area of the drawing.
- Select the PLOT command from the File menu.
- Plot the drawing in model space and choose the following: a valid printer, 8.5 × 11 paper size, Landscape orientation, Scale: 1″ = 1″, Extents for Plot Area.
- Preview the Plot. If it is OK, proceed to plot the drawing. If not, return to the Plot dialog box and modify the settings as needed.

## RELATIONSHIP BETWEEN DRAWING LIMITS AND PLOT SCALE

In the initial setup of the drawing file, you can establish the **Drawing LIMITS** of the area that you will be working in. If you know the size of the paper the drawing will be printed on and the scale at which the drawing will be printed, you can include this information. For example, if you know your file will be printed on an 11″ × 17″ sheet at a scale of 1:1 (one drawing unit = one plotted unit) **Drawing LIMITS** can then be established with the lower left corner at 0,0 and the upper right corner at 11,17. Since paper sizes and engineering scale factors have established standards and are consistent, drawing limits can be calculated for all combinations. Here's another example. A floor plan that is being plotted on a 24″ × 36″ sheet of paper at a scale factor of ¼″ = 1′-0″ (1:48) will have a set of **Drawing LIMITS** that are 0,0 for the lower left and 144′ × 96′

for the upper right. As long as the floor plan fits into the established drawing limits at full size, the entities will fit on the sheet at the calculated scale. See Tables 6-1 and 6-2 earlier in the chapter for a list of sheet sizes. Given scale factors and sheet sizes, **Drawing LIMITS** can be calculated. Although this list is not all-inclusive, it does cover the most common scenarios for the three major engineering disciplines.

## LAYOUT SPACE

Layout space (also known as paper space) is an alternative area of the program where finished views of a design can be arranged, annotations can be created, and various scaled plots can be located and plotted on the same sheet. Layout space is far more flexible for documenting a design. Layout space utilizes **VIEWPORTS** to display a particular view of the drawing. Zoom magnification can be used to adjust the drawing's scale based on the size of the sheet that it will be plotted on. Therefore each viewport can have its own scale assignment (as opposed to model space plotting where everything in the drawing is plotted at the same scale). There is virtually no limit to the number of **Layout Space** tabs that can be created in a drawing file; it depends on available memory. Although entities can be created in either model space or layout space, you can only work with the entities in the space they were created in. The exception is certain transmodal dimensions (drawn in layout space and associated to locations in model space). **Object Snap** positions can be determined from model space and used in layout space.

The simplest way to establish layout space is to begin a drawing session with a predefined AutoCAD template such as ANSI-A, ANSI-B, or Architectural. When you use the template option, the template includes a sheet size and sheet orientation. This process also places the selected titleblock and border on a layer named "Title Block." A viewport is created at the same time and placed on its own layer named "Viewport."

A thorough understanding of printing from layout space is advantageous when it comes to outputting drawing files. You have an array of options to choose from, and as you become familiar with those options you will begin to understand the potential of layout space.

### Exercise 6-2: Plotting from Layout Space

- Open the QSLayout 1 drawing from the Chapter 6 section of the Student CD.
- Select the ANSI A Title Block tab at the bottom left area of the screen.
- Add your name by creating a piece of text, and place the text in the titleblock area.
- Set the following parameters: 8.5 × 11 Portrait, Scale: 1″ = 1″, What to Plot? –Extents.
- Preview the plot. If it is OK, proceed to plot the drawing. If not, return to the Plot dialog box and modify the settings as needed.
- Save as HO-02 in your **Workskills** folder.

### Creating and Managing Viewports

A viewport can be considered a screen on which your drawing is displayed (see Figure 6-11). You can divide the screen into smaller screens by establishing the Viewport configuration using the **VIEWPORTS** command or other command options. Viewports can be created after the start of a drawing through the **View** menu. A typical Viewport configuration might consist of two vertical displays or four equally divided screens. Each of the viewports can have its own display configuration. This can consist of a **View, Pan, Zoom, Layer** display, **Shade,** display, and **Plot scale.** Once a configuration is established, the display can be **locked** to preserve the values established.

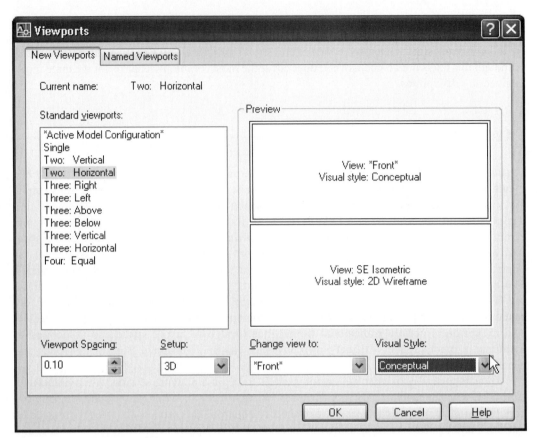

**Figure 6-11**     Viewports dialog screen

Demonstrate your understanding of customizing the viewport scale list to minimize the choice of scale options. This list can be unique to the primary plotting scales used in the office.

Model space viewports are "tiled": they must fill the display area, are rectangular, cannot overlap, and cannot have gaps in the coverage of the screen area. You will notice a thick line or border around the active viewport. When using multiple viewports in model space, you will switch from one viewport to another by moving the cursor into a viewport and clicking with a left mouse button.

Even though you may divide the model space world into multiple viewports, model space will only print the current or active **Viewport.** (Layout space will allow you to print multiple viewports at various scales; see Figures 6-12 and 6-13.)

To view a design through layout space, you will need to have a **Viewport.** The actual viewport object holds the scale information for the purpose of plotting. As mentioned earlier, only the entities created in layout space are eligible for selection and modification.

When a **Viewport** is created in layout space, you will be able to double-click inside the **Viewport** and enter the world of Floating model space. This alternate method of model space makes the objects created available while in the traditional layout space world. You will notice a thick line or border around the active viewport that is currently in Floating model space. To switch back and forth between the two worlds, there is a toggle button in the Status bar labeled **Model** or **Paper.**

**Note:**
You can switch viewports in the middle of the command without interrupting the active command.

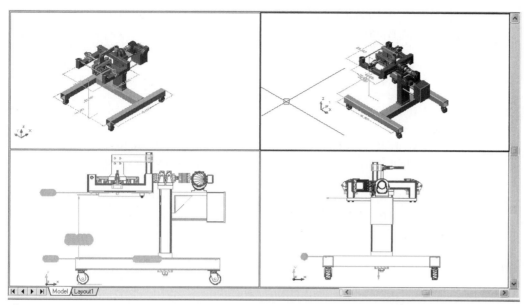

**Figure 6-12**    Four tiled viewports in model space; upper right is active and will be the only one plotted

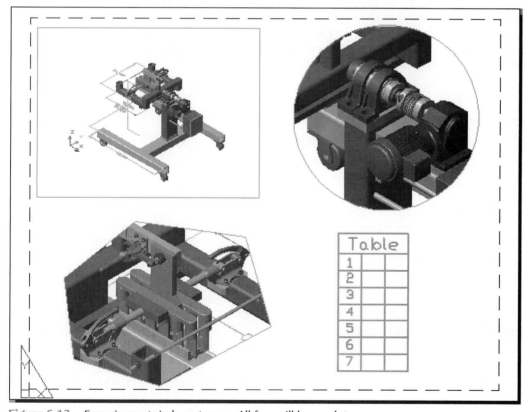

**Figure 6-13**    Four viewports in layout space. All four will be on plot

**Exercise 6-3:** Creating Layout Space Plots

■ Open the drawing HO-02 from Exercise 6-2 or from the Student CD.
■ Click on the Layout1 tab at the bottom of the drawing area.
■ Right-click on the Layout1 tab and select Page setup from the menu.

- Establish the layout page settings for the current plot device, paper size, plot area, plot scale, and drawing orientation.
- Insert your titleblock in the Layout Space (unless you have started with a drawing template that already has a titleblock).
- Using the Layer Manager, create a new layer named Viewports. Establish this layer with a "No Plot" value and set the layer to "current."
- Using the VIEWPORT command in the View menu, create a single viewport inside your titleblock.
- Double-click on the viewport object and establish a $1'' = 1''$ scale for the viewport in the Properties dialog box. Before leaving the dialog box, make sure you turn on the Lock Display option.
- Preview the plot. If it is OK, proceed to plot the drawing. If not, return to the Plot dialog box and modify the settings as needed.
- Save as HO-03 in your **Workskills** folder.

## Creating Annotations in Layout Space

Annotations consist of dimensions, leaders, and general notes that describe an object's size and shape. The creation of these entities can happen in either model space or layout space. You need to remember that objects created through a dimension or text based object have physical sizes. These objects will have to be sized based on the world they are created in. For example, text that has a height of 1/8″ would be difficult to read in a floor plan describing a 60′ wall. This is true for all parts of a dimension including terminators, gaps for extension lines, baseline dimension separation distance, and so on. Many times it is better to use multiple **Dimension Styles** to reflect annotations in viewports of varying scale than to modify individual parts of dimensions. The **Scale Factor** in the **Fit** tab of the **Dimension Style** dialog box is a quick way to factor the size of all parts of the annotations.

Applying all annotations in layout space allows you to control the sizes related to the sheet layout and not the model size.

When creating annotations in **Layout Space,** you must establish a variable within the **Dimension Style** to **Scale Dimensions to Layout.** This is found under the **Fit** tab within the **Dimension Style** dialog box.

An organized office uses an established series of Plot Styles defining the office's lineweight standards. Understanding plot style concepts from both the setup and application point of view will ensure a uniform look to all plotted files.

**Exercise 6-4:** Annotations in Layout

- Open drawing HO-03 from Exercise 6-3 or from the Student CD.
- Click on the Layout1 tab at the bottom of the drawing area.
- From the Format menu, select Dimension Style and the Modify button on the right.
- Under the Fit tab select the radio button next to Scale Dimensions to Layout.
- Create an overall linear dimension for both the X and Y directions. Note the sizes of the entities created. They should be proportionally correct for the drawing.

## SUMMARY

The topic of this unit was the process of plotting or printing a hard copy of an electronic drawing in the AutoCAD software. We first defined and distinguished the concepts of model space, the world in which the drawing is created for purposes of design, and of layout (paper) space, the space in which the design drawing is given a finished view with annotations that is suitable for plotting in a given sheet layout and size. You then learned and practiced plotting from model space using the **PLOT** command and the settings (page setup, printer/plotter, paper size, and plot area, scale, and offset) in the **Plot** dialog box. After an explanation of the relationship between drawing limits and plot scale in a drawing, you learned about the use of multiple viewports in model and layout space to display particular views of your drawing and practiced plotting a drawing from layout space.

## CHAPTER TEST QUESTIONS

### Multiple Choice

1.  The plot device refers to the:
    a. Paper
    b. File type
    c. Printer
    d. Port to send the information to

2.  Multiple viewports can only be printed:
    a. In model space
    b. In layout space
    c. Through the plot dialog box
    d. Through a .pc3 file format

3.  To print all objects on the selected paper, which scale option should you use?
    a. All
    b. 1 = 1
    c. Fit
    d. Full

4.  Plot offset will move the plot's:
    a. Titleblock
    b. Edges
    c. Dimensions
    d. Origin

5.  Plot style will control at least which two properties?
    a. Color and lineweight
    b. Layers and lineweight
    c. Line type and line weight
    d. Layers and colors

### Matching

a. _____ Display
b. _____ Window
c. _____ Extents
d. _____ View
e. _____ Limits

1.  Print the objects within the defined drawing area
2.  Print a named drawing view
3.  Print a user-defined window selection
4.  Print the current screen
5.  All objects regardless of where they are

### True or False

1.  True or False: What you see in the preview is what you get on the print.

2.  True or False: Sheet size and Drawing area mean the same thing.

3.  True or False: Plot style will control the color of the objects.

4.  True or False: Page setup will save the current configuration for future use.

5.  True or False: AutoCAD can make only one plot at a time.

## CHAPTER PROJECTS

1.  Visit a local consulting engineer, government office, manufacturing plant, or blueprinting company and see what type of plotter is used. What size paper is used most often? What are the typical scales used for plotting?

2.  Create a poster or chart showing the various architectural, engineering, metric, and mechanical scales related to the various paper sizes and showing the maximum size of the drawing object. For example: A scale of 1/4″ = 1′ on a D sheet can fit 144′ × 96′ model.

## PRACTICE EXERCISES

### Practice Exercise 6-1: Plot from Model Space

To practice plotting, use the drawings you created in the Quick-Start Tutorials, Unit 3, or Unit 5 and plot each of the mechanical drawings at a scale of 1″ = 1″, the architectural drawings at a scale of 1/4″ = 1′-0″ and the civil drawings at a scale of 1″ = 10′-0″. Be sure the tab at the lower left is set to Model.

Preview each drawing to be sure it is ready to plot.

### Practice Exercise 6-2: Plot from Model Space with Different Parameters

To practice plotting, use the drawings you created in the Quick-Start Tutorials, Unit 3, or Unit 5 and plot each of the drawings by varying the parameters regarding Plot scale, Plot area, Offsets and Centering, and Orientation. Be sure the tab at the lower left is set to Model. If possible vary the paper size and output device to gain more understanding of the possibilities for output.

Preview each drawing to be sure it is ready to plot.

### Practice Exercise 6-3: Plot from Layout Space

To practice plotting, use the drawings you created in the Quick-Start Tutorials, Unit 3, or Unit 5 and plot each in layout space using at least two viewports per sheet. Be sure the tab at the lower left is set to Layout1 or Layout2. The viewports should have different settings for the parameters regarding Plot scale, Plot area, Offsets and Centering, and Orientation. If possible vary the paper size and output device to gain more understanding of the possibilities for output.

Preview each drawing to be sure it is ready to plot.

# Intermediate Drawing and Modifying

**7**

## Chapter Objectives

- Expand the explanation and use of DRAW and MODIFY commands.
- Reinforce techniques through the draw-modify-dimension-print methods.
- Use advanced methods to select objects.
- Create, justify, and edit text annotations.
- Insert and edit hatch patterns.
- Use the built-in calculator through QuickCalc.

## INTRODUCTION

In Units 2 through 6 we covered a series of commands that reach across one of this textbook's core concepts. The draw-modify-dimension-print cycle is a standard approach to the completion of a drawing in a basic AutoCAD system with most engineering disciplines.

In the first units, we have covered a series of commands at an elementary level, trying to focus on a small amount of information needed to work through the draw-modify-dimension-print cycle. At this time you should feel comfortable with the various input methods available: the creating of lines, circles, and arcs, the concept of selecting objects and making simple modifications to these objects, the creation of size and shape description with dimensions, and the plotting process. It is understood that a complete mastery of these concepts and commands will take some practice.

Now it is time to revisit the draw-modify-dimension-print cycle to not only practice what we have learned, but also to look at an intermediate level of commands in each of these areas. Through the expansion of the command-based knowledge, you will have the opportunity to practice previous information covered at the elementary level, while learning new methods and procedures linked to your productivity in the workplace.

## BUILDING INTERMEDIATE ENTITIES

As we cover the creation of other types of entities, it is time to recognize that the **Draw** menu is not the only place to create more geometry. We will find out in this unit that the **Modify** menu has several commands to take existing geometry and make more geometry out of the user's selection set. Let's first look back at the **Draw** menu (see Figure 7-1) and **Draw** toolbar (see Figure 7-2) and cover a few options from commands we are already using, along with a few new commands to create other types of geometry.

**Figure 7-1** Draw menu

**Figure 7-2**    Draw toolbar

## Creating Circles

CIRCLE: A geometric shape with a constant radius.

There are four other options for creating a CIRCLE beyond the **Center/Radius** or **Center/Diameter** commands.

- The **2 Point** option (see Figure 7-3) allows you to select any two points on the screen and create a circle between the two points selected. Note that the distance between the two points selected is the diameter value of the circle created. Using this option you have no control over the placement of the center point for the circle.

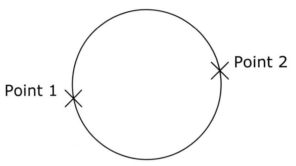

**Figure 7-3**    Circle created with 2 points

- Similar to the previous method, the **3 Point** option (see Figure 7-4) allows the selection of three points, and the circle is constructed passing through all three points. Once again there is no control over the placement of the center point for the circle created.

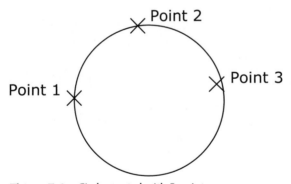

**Figure 7-4**    Circle created with 3 points

tangent: A place on a circle touched only at one point by an object and where the radius is perpendicular to the object.

- **Tan, Tan, Radius** (see Figure 7-5) is an option that is similar to the **2 Point** option. Two points are selected, and then the system prompts you for a radius to complete the circle. The difference is in the addition of the *tangent* object snap override to the cursor during the selection of the initial two points. This means instead of selecting two points in space (X,Y,Z location), you select two pieces of existing geometry that will be tangent to the circle. The objects the circle is tangent to should be selected close to the final tangent points, although the exact tangent point will be calculated when the circle's radius is entered.

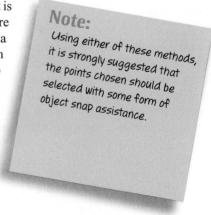

**Note:**
Using either of these methods, it is strongly suggested that the points chosen should be selected with some form of object snap assistance.

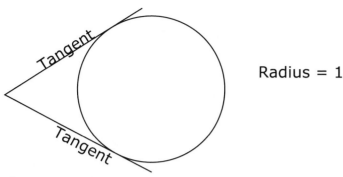

**Radius = 1**

**Figure 7-5**   Circle with tangents and radius

- The final option for the creation of circles is **Tan, Tan, Tan** (see Figure 7-6). This option uses the selection of three existing entities that are tangent to the circle. As with the **Tan, Tan, Radius** option, the selection of the entities should be close to the final tangent points. The actual value of the radius is calculated after the selection of the third entity. The circle is then created tangent to all three objects selected.

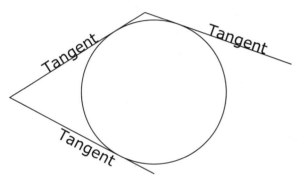

**Figure 7-6**   Circle with tangents

## Exercise 7-1: Creation of Circles with Tangent

- Start a new drawing.
- Using the LINE command, create three line segments in the drawing area.
- In the Draw menu select the CIRCLE command and then the Tan, Tan, Radius option from the cascading menu.
- Now select two of the line segments and enter a Radius value of 1. The selection of the lines should be approximately where you want the circle to be tangent. Notice that the Tangent object's snap override will be loaded to the cursor automatically. The actual location of the circle's center point and tangent points will be calculated upon the entry of the radius value.
- In the Draw menu select the CIRCLE command and then the Tan, Tan, Tan option from the cascading menu.
- Now select each of the line segments. The selection of the lines should be approximately where you want the circle and lines to be tangent. Notice that the Tangent object's snap override will be loaded to the cursor automatically. The actual location of the circle's center point and tangent points will be calculated upon the selection of the third entity.

## Arcs

There are 11 individual options for the construction of an *arc.* In Unit 3 we discussed the **3 Point** option (see Figure 7-7). The remaining ten options are a combination of various terms to describe the three points needed to construct an arc. By understanding the definition of the terms used to define the three points you will be able to construct arcs in a variety of methods.

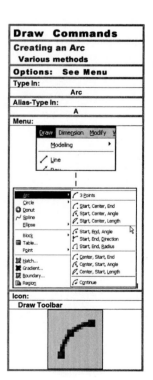

**Arc:** A portion of a circle.

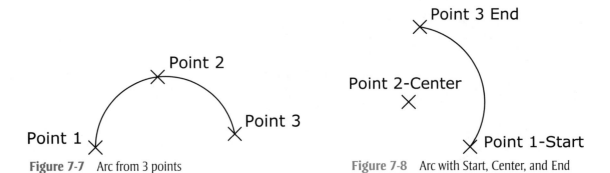

**Figure 7-7**    Arc from 3 points                    **Figure 7-8**    Arc with Start, Center, and End

- **Start** refers to the first endpoint of the arc while **End** describes the second endpoint of the arc (see Figure 7-8).
- **Center** defines the X,Y,Z location for the center point of the arc with the distance between the Center position and the Start position defining the radius value of the arc (see Figure 7-8).
- **Angle** refers to the included angle (see Figure 7-9) that describes the final point of the arc after the first two points define a line or leg of the included angle.
- **Radius** prompts you for a value of the radius (see Figure 7-10) to be used to describe the size of the arc.

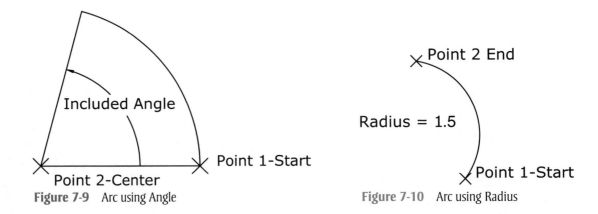

**Figure 7-9**    Arc using Angle                     **Figure 7-10**    Arc using Radius

- **Length** (see Figure 7-11) uses a value as defined by the chord distance or length of the arc. This input determines the included angle used to locate the final position of the arc.
- **Direction** uses the starting tangent direction (see Figure 7-12) as indicated by the pointing device to specify the direction of travel between the two points selected. Moving

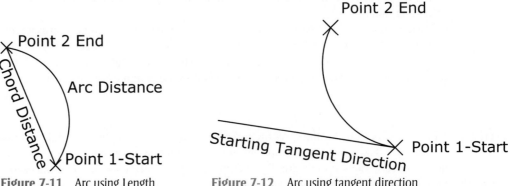

**Figure 7-11**    Arc using Length                    **Figure 7-12**    Arc using tangent direction

the cursor up from the start point to the endpoint draws a concave arc between the two points, while moving the cursor down draws a convex arc between the two points selected.

- **Continue** creates an arc tangent to the previous entity constructed (see Figure 7-13). This method only needs an endpoint to complete the construction of the new arc.

As you look at the different combinations available in the **Draw** menu to create arcs, you can select the appropriate combination to define the arc for its precise construction, given the information available.

Note:
Arcs are produced in a counter-clockwise direction from the start point to the endpoint.

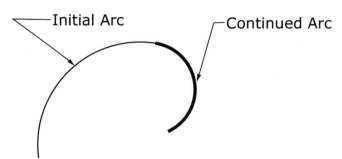

**Figure 7-13**    Continued arc

**Exercise 7-2:** Creating Arcs with Start, End, Radius

- Start a new drawing.
- Draw two line segments at any given angle to each other.
- In the Draw menu select the ARC command and then the Start, End, Radius option from the cascading menu.
- Select an endpoint of the first line as the start point.
- Select the closest endpoint of the second entity to establish the endpoint of the arc.
- Drag the mouse to establish the radius value.

## Ellipse

An *ellipse* is typically defined by a major and a minor axis. These axes are the longest and shortest line segments between the quadrant points of the shape. AutoCAD defines the axes for an ellipse from the center point of the ellipse in both the major (long) and minor (short) axis directions. The points for an ellipse can be entered using one of three methods.

- The **Center** method uses three points. The first point selected is the center point of the ellipse, the second point describes the distance and orientation of one axis, and the third point sets the distance for the remaining axis, which is perpendicular to the orientation of the first axis (see Figure 7-14).

ellipse:  A geometric shape with a varying radius.

| Draw  Commands |
|---|
| **Creating an Ellipse** |
| **Options: Center, Axis End, Rotation, Arc** |
| Type In: |
| Ellipse |
| Alias-Type In: |
| EL |
| Menu: |

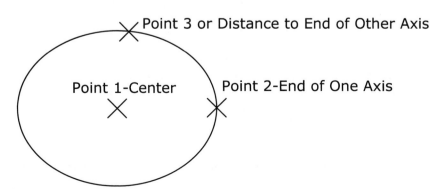

**Figure 7-14**    Ellipse with Center method

- The **Axis, End** is a method that uses the first two points to describe the complete length of one axis and then uses the third point selected to define the distance as a radial distance or half of the length for the remaining axis of the ellipse. This radial distance is the length of the line calculated from the location of the third point projected back to and perpendicular to the first axis created (see Figure 7-15).

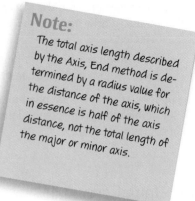

**Note:**
The total axis length described by the Axis, End method is determined by a radius value for the distance of the axis, which in essence is half of the axis distance, not the total length of the major or minor axis.

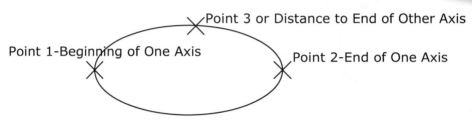

**Figure 7-15**    Ellipse using Axis and End option

- The **Arc** option is used to create a portion of an arc on an elliptical path or shape. You first input information to size the ellipse, following what you did for the **Axis, End** method. You select two points that define one complete length of an axis followed by a third point to define the radial distance for the second axis. After these three points are established you will be prompted for the start angle position and then for the end angle position or included angle. The elliptical arc is created in a counterclockwise direction from the start angle position to the end angle position (see Figure 7-16).

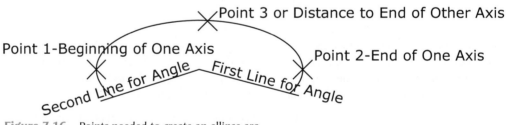

**Figure 7-16**    Points needed to create an ellipse arc

### Exercise 7-3: Create an Ellipse

- Start a new drawing.
- In the Draw menu select the ELLIPSE command and the Center option from the cascading menu.
- Select any point on the screen as the center point of the ellipse.
- Drag a line out in one direction to specify one-half the distance of the first ellipse axis.
- Drag a second line out of the center point to specify one-half the distance of the second axis for the ellipse.

**rectangle:** A four-sided geometric shape with equal opposite sides.

**polyline:** Multiple-line or arc segments joined as one entity.

### Rectangle

The **_rectangle_** command **(RECTANG)** creates a four-sided figure, through a two-point input, based on the opposite corners or a diagonal of the shape. This command results in a **_polyline_** being created. You are prompted for the `First corner point` and then for the `Other corner point`.

There are several options available prior to the selection of the first corner point. options of **Chamfer, Elevation, Fillet, Thickness,** and **Width** can be executed by tering the capital letter of any one of the options prior to picking the first point. Af picking the first point, additional options of **Area, Dimension,** and **Rotation** appear aid in setting the second point or diagonal point.

The following are brief descriptions of each of the options:

- **Chamfer** creates straight-line beveled corners based on the distances entered at the prompts. Only one value is entered for each of the chamfer distances and applied to all four corners (see Figure 7-17).

- The **Fillet** option creates rounded corners. After executing the **Fillet** option you can establish the **Radius** value. Only one value for radius is input and applied to all four corners (see Figure 7-18).

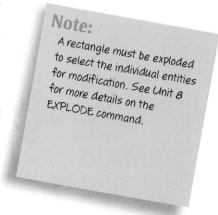

Note:
A rectangle must be exploded to select the individual entities for modification. See Unit 8 for more details on the EXPLODE command.

**Rectangle with
Chamfer Dist. 1=0.5
Chamfer Dist. 2=1**

**Figure 7-17**    Rectangle with Chamfer

**Rectangle with
Fillet Radius = 0.5**

**Figure 7-18**    Rectangle with Fillets

**Draw Commands**

**Creating a Rectangle With 2 Points**

**Options:**
Chamfer, Elevation, Fillet, Thickness, Width

**Type In:**
RECTANG

**Alias-Type In:**
REC

**Menu:**
Draw  Dimension  Modify
  Modeling ▸
  ∕ Line
  ⬠ Polygon
  ▭ Rectangle
  ⌇ Helix

**Icon:**
**Draw Toolbar**

- The **Elevation** option is used to create rectangles at some distance above or below the XY plane, which is typically given as an elevation of 0. This value allows you to establish a start position on the Z axis.

- The **Thickness** option establishes the end position on the Z axis or a height to the rectangle. For example, thickness is used to create the look of a building, as walls are created by this variable (see Figure 7-19).

**Figure 7-19**    Rectangle with Fillets and Thickness in a 3D isometric view

- The **Width** option establishes a value for the polyline width of the segments that make up the rectangle. This width can vary for the entities involved. This option is similar to adding a lineweight property value to the rectangle that results in a constant width per entity.

- The **Area** option aids in creating a precise area for the rectangle by inputting the value of the desired **Area** and either a **Length** or **Width** value to complete the needed information.

- **Dimension** requests the input of a **Length** and **Width,** leading to a request for the second point. The second point essentially becomes a directional pointer for the location of the rectangle.
- The **Rotation** allows you to specify or pick a location at any angle, which will rotate the rectangle to that orientation.

### Exercise 7-4: Creating a Rectangle

- Start a new drawing.
- From the Draw menu access the RECTANGLE command.
- Type an F to set the Fillet Radius for the corners of the rectangle.
- Enter .5 as the Radius value and press <Enter>.
- Pick a point in the Drawing area for one corner of the rectangle.
- Move the mouse and see the temporary view of the rectangle as the mouse is moved.
- Pick a second point for the rectangle, which will be diagonally across the rectangle from the first point.

### Hatching

The **HATCH** command (see Figure 7-20) fills an enclosed area with a vector-based pattern of lines, circular shapes, or a solid fill color with gradient. There are four items in the **Hatch** dialog box that need to be addressed in the creation of a hatched area. If we look at the simplest form of hatching, it includes the selection of a *hatch* pattern, the selection of a boundary area, and the scale and/or rotation of the hatch pattern in the hatch area.

**hatch:** Using a pattern of lines and shapes to fill a closed area of a drawing.

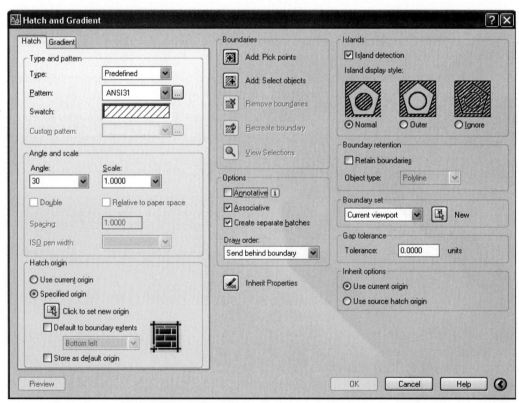

**Figure 7-20**    The complete Hatch dialog screen

Hatch patterns have the ability to link the pattern with the boundary entities through an associative property. After this link has been established through the **Hatch** dialog box (see Figure 7-20), the hatch pattern would adjust if the boundary were to be changed.

Patterns come from one of three sources. The **Type** drop-down list (see Figure 7-21) in the **Hatch** dialog box allows you to choose from a library of patterns from one of the three sources listed. Let's first take a look at the general types of a hatch pattern.

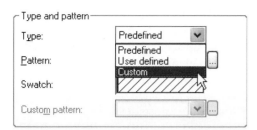

**Figure 7-21**    Type drop-down in HATCH command

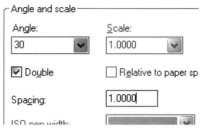

**Figure 7-22**    User-defined Hatch Pattern information

**User-defined** patterns (see Figure 7-22) take a simple line and pattern this entity based on a rotational and spacing value. The **Angle** field in the dialog box allows for input to establish the rotational value of the pattern. A value of 0° creates a lined pattern parallel to the X axis. Any positive value rotates the pattern in a counterclockwise direction; a negative value rotates the pattern clockwise. The **Spacing** field is the distance between lines in the pattern. This value is expected to be a positive numerical input. The check box for **Double,** when checked, creates the pattern at a 90° angle to the initial pattern.

**Predefined** patterns (see Figure 7-23) come in several categories. These include definitions of lines, circles, and arcs that are created through computer code to repeat the pattern until the designated closed areas are filled. Some of these patterns are based on ANSI or ISO drafting standards that have established cross-sectional symbols related to identifying materials; other predefined patterns have an architectural theme based on actual materials (i.e., block, brick, earth, grass, roof, concrete, etc.).

**Custom** patterns are defined by the user. These are often created in a computer language such as Visual Basic or AutoLISP®. You can create a pattern using any series of lines or symbols defined through a programmable language.

Once you have selected a pattern, you need to identify the **Boundary** area in which the hatch pattern will be placed. On the right side of the **Hatch** dialog box is a box labeled **Boundaries** (see Figure 7-24). There are two options for creating a boundary area along with

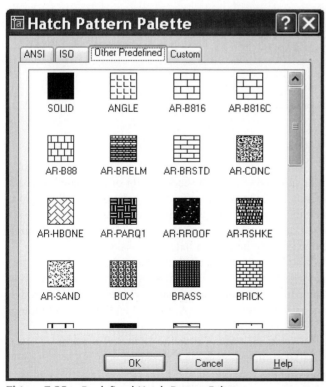

**Figure 7-23**    Predefined Hatch Pattern Palette

**Figure 7-24**    Boundaries area of the Hatch dialog box

one option to remove objects selected that define a boundary area. The easiest method to define a hatch boundary is to select an object or objects that define the boundary of the area. When you select the **Add: Select objects** button, the program sends you back to the drawing screen to select objects to make up the boundary area. Keep in mind the hatch pattern needs a closed area to define the boundary, and the pattern created will touch all parts of the objects selected. If the objects do not make up a clearly defined area, the hatch pattern may leak out of the closed boundary area in attempt to touch all parts of the objects selected.

The second method to define a hatch boundary is to select the **Add: Pick points** button from the **Bounda** area (see Figure 7-24). This selection again sends back to the drawing screen to select an internal pc among objects defining an area. The program then calc lates a closed boundary area based on the close object to the point selected and travels in a counter clockwise direction until a closed loop has been de fined. The objects selected may not be the complete object. The program makes clockwise turns based on the objects that are encountered when searching the area in question. When the search returns to the original object it started with, the boundary area is calculated and identified in a highlighted form.

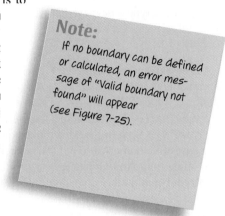

Note:

If no boundary can be defined or calculated, an error message of "Valid boundary not found" will appear (see Figure 7-25).

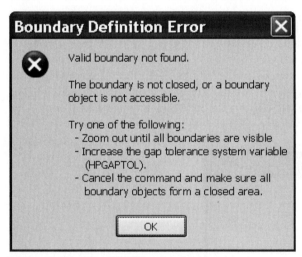

**Figure 7-25**    The HATCH error message

If no boundary is found, you will be allowed to select a second point or alternate boundary definition method. After one of the boundary methods has been calculated, you have the options to edit the boundary definition by removing objects identified during the creation process. By selecting the **Remove boundaries** button, you can select objects that make up the current boundary definition and have the objects removed from the current hatch boundary.

Now that two hatch issues have been addressed—the hatch pattern and the hatch boundary—you can use the **Preview** button in the lower left corner of the dialog box to preview the current hatching scenario. At this time you may choose to adjust two remaining areas in the **Hatch** dialog box. The **Scale** field adjusts the size of the pattern and the **Angle** field adjusts the rotation of the pattern.

In the **Scale** field a scale of 1.0 represents the pattern in its original defined size. A larger number enlarges the pattern, while a smaller number reduces the size of the pattern. In the **Angle** field, the number represents a rotational value, where 0 is in the East position, positive numbers rotate counterclockwise, and negative numbers rotate clockwise.

**Exercise 7-5:** Create and Hatch Items

- Start a new drawing.
- From the Draw menu, place a rectangle and a circle in the drawing area so that these entities intersect.
- From the Draw menu, access the HATCH command and place a different hatch pattern in each enclosed area.

## TEXT COMMANDS

### Creating Text

There are two methods for creating text with AutoCAD. Since this program is a vector-based system, creating text is slightly different than when using a typical word processor. The first method is referred to as **Single Line Text** or **Dynamic Text**. This command is found in the **Draw** menu and creates a string of text characters that act as one object. To execute this command from the command line, you type in **TEXT** or **DTEXT**. Although the command sounds like it only creates a single line of text, this is misleading. You can produce more than one line of text during a command sequence, with each line being treated as a single object regardless of how many characters are used. The procedure for **Single Line Text** will prompt you for three pieces of information. The text start position, the text height, and the text rotation all need to be established prior to typing the actual text string.

We now take a closer look at this sequence of prompts for **TEXT**. Upon entering the command you are prompted to Specify start point of text [Justify/Style]. By default, the insert or control point selected is the lower left corner of the first line of text. This is referred to as left justification. If you want to use the point selected with a different type of justification, you can execute the option of *justify* and select from a series of predefined justifications based on the point selected as the start point. Refer to Figure 7-26 for a description of each of the basic justification codes and the corresponding locations.

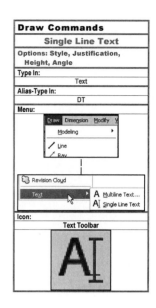

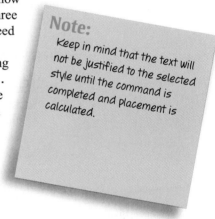

**Note:** Keep in mind that the text will not be justified to the selected style until the command is completed and placement is calculated.

justify: A method used to place text.

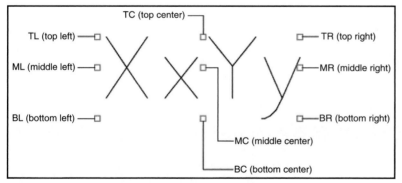

**Figure 7-26**    TEXT justification locations

Additional methods of justification for text include the following:

- **Align** With this option you select two points on the screen and the text is placed between the two points. The actual height and width of the text will depend on how many characters are in the string of text and the distance between the points.

- **Fit** With this option you select two points on the screen and the text is placed between the two points. The height of the text remains fixed, but the width of the characters depends on how many characters are in the string of text and the distance between the two points.

- **Center** This option calculates the center of the text string and places the bottom center of the text string on the point selected.
- **Middle** This option calculates the center of the text string along with the middle of the text height and places the text string on the point selected.
- **Right** This option places the lower right point on the end of the text string on the point selected.

The text's **Style** is another option in the command prompt and is used to establish the link to the numerous type fonts, special codes, letter width, and other special items. **TEXTSTYLE** in the **Format** menu is the command to create, view, and modify these items.

After selecting the starting point the command prompts you to Specify height <0.2000>. The current height is shown in the default brackets. This can be accepted by pressing the **Enter** key or changed by keying in a different value followed by the **Enter** key.

Once the height is established, you are prompted to Specify rotation angle of text <0>. The default angle of **0** produces a text string parallel to the X axis, moving from left to right. A positive angle rotates the text around the insert point counterclockwise. A negative angle rotates the text around the insert point clockwise.

After these three pieces of information are established, a text box with a flashing cursor shows up at the position selected for the start point. At this time you can input the characters for the string of **Text**. If multiple lines of **Text** are needed, you simply use the **Enter** key to start a new line of text. This creates a new line of text using all the same parameters established earlier in the command sequence. To end the command, you press the **Enter** key twice (once to end the current line of text and once to end the command). This completes the single line text command.

### Exercise 7-6: Placing TEXT in a Drawing

- Start a new drawing.
- From the Draw menu, access the TEXT command and choose Single Line Text from the cascading menu.
- Pick a location for the text with the mouse, enter .5 for the text height, and accept 0 for the angle by pressing the Enter key.
- Type in your name and address on three or four lines.
- Press the Enter key twice to complete the command.

### Creating Multiline Text

The second method for creating text is called **Multiline Text** or **MTEXT**. This command is more closely related to a word processing format than the **Single Line TEXT** command. It manipulates all the lines of text entered as a single object (see Figure 7-27), but also allows you to select any characters within the sequence for unique format changes.

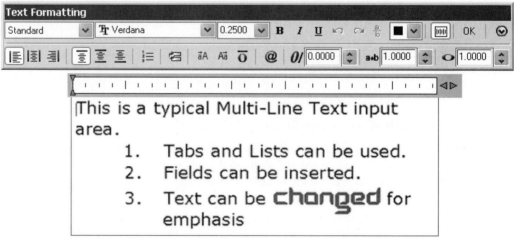

Figure 7-27    Multiline text command area

This command starts by having you create a **text box.** The box establishes the width of the text line and is expandable in the downward direction as shown by the arrow in the box. Once the text box has been established, two toolbars appear on the screen. The top toolbar has all the traditional text format options, such as text style, character font, height, bold, italicized, underlined, color, justification, and areas addressing several special characters. You can address any of these options during the creation of text, or highlight previously created text and alter the properties of the selected text as needed. The second toolbar, the **Ruler,** can be toggled on or off through an icon on the main multiline toolbar and is used to establish tab positions within the text window and the width of the text. When the **Ruler** is pulled wider, the text box will widen and all text will adjust to the new width. After establishing the text characteristics needed, all text characters are typed within the text box. When all text is completed, you can select the **OK** button to complete the command and place the contents of the text box into the file at the location established by the first point of the text box.

## Exercise 7-7: Creating Multiline Text

- Start a new drawing.
- From the Draw menu, access the TEXT command and choose Multiline Text from the cascading menu.
- Pick two points on the screen to represent the width of the text in your drawing.
- Enter your name and address using three or four lines for the information.
- Pick OK to complete the command.

## Editing Text

To edit text that has been placed within a drawing, you can double-click on the text object. Depending on the method used to create the text, this double-click action produces one of two results. If the text was created with a **Single Line TEXT** command, a text edit window appears as shown in Figure 7-28 with the selected string of text inside the edit window. At this time you can place the cursor location anywhere within the text string and alter the characters as needed. This method does not allow for the changing of text height, color, and font or style; only the characters of the text string. To change the other text characteristics, you have to use the **Properties** command and **Properties** palette in the **Modify** menu.

This is Single Line Text

**Figure 7-28**   Text edit window

From a productivity point of view, you can create large amounts of text in a word processor and drag or import them into the drawing file. Items such as general notes or product specifications can be externally referenced into a series of files for uniformity and ease of editing. Using common insertion points will increase the efficiency when placing or copying data from layout to layout.

If the text selected for editing is produced with the **multiline text** command, the double-click produces the multiline text box, with the text selected in the text box. At this time you can place the cursor anywhere within the box and make the changes needed. This method also allows you to highlight any series of characters and alter the properties of the selected contents such as text height, color, font, or style. To complete the editing session, select the **OK** button on the toolbar, and then all changes will be placed back into the drawing file.

## MODIFY COMMANDS

Now it is time to look at a few more commands found in the **Modify** menu (see Figure 7-29) that will help produce more geometry through objects already in the drawing file. Most of the following commands can also be found on the **Modify** toolbar (see Figure 7-30). Keep in

**Figure 7-30**    Modify toolbar

**Figure 7-29**    Modify menu

mind that during the execution of these commands you will be prompted to Select objects. You have to establish which objects you want to work with; the options available were discussed in Unit 3.

## OBJECT SELECTION METHODS

As we continue with the **Modify** menu, we can look at the additional methods of selecting objects. As discussed earlier there are two simple methods of selecting objects, the single-selection **pick box** and **implied windowing** (Window and Crossing Window).

The following are four additional methods that can be invoked at the Select objects prompt message.

- **All** This option selects all the objects in the current drawing file, whether they are visible on the screen, outside the current display screen, or on an **OFF** layer. The only objects exempted in this selection method are those on a layer that is currently frozen. This option is executed by typing in the word **All** when asked to Select objects.

- **Previous** This option calls back the previously defined or selected group of objects used in the last completed **Modify** command. This option is executed by typing in the letter **P** when asked to Select objects.

- **Last** This method selects only the last object added to the drawing file. It is executed by typing in the letter **L** when asked to Select objects.

- **Fence** The **Fence** option allows you to create a temporary line that acts in the same manner as a crossing window. Any object that comes in contact with the **Fence** will be in the selected set. This option is executed by typing in the letter **F** when asked to Select objects.

Although the use of these methods may be minimal, they are good to know when you are faced with a tricky selection set of objects to be made for a **Modify** command. A little practice with each of these methods will help you see their value.

## MODIFYING COMMANDS

Up to this point we have covered the basic commands within the **Modify** menu that will **MOVE, COPY,** or **ERASE** an object. We have discussed a series of commands that will produce more geometry from existing objects such as **OFFSET, MIRROR,** and **ARRAY.** Now it's time to look at a series of commands in the **Modify** menu that will alter the selected geometry in some form. As with most of the **Modify** commands, you are prompted to Select objects at the beginning of the command. The following commands will be asking you to select objects that have a special function pertaining to the execution of the command. Novice users should pay particular attention to the command prompt line, where extra information is displayed regarding the type of objects to be selected, the method of selection to be used, or the proper procedure for the command.

### Fillet

A **FILLET** command creates an arc that is tangent to two other entities at a specified radius. The simple concept of a fillet is to specify a **Radius** and then Select two objects. The command produces an arc based on the radius entered that is tangent to the objects selected, typically trimming off any extra portions of the selected objects to form a clean intersection at the tangent points (see Figure 7-31). When you first enter the **FILLET** command (see Figure 7-32), the current trim mode setting and radius value are listed in the prompt line.

Before  Fillet

After  Fillet

**Figure 7-31**    Fillet result

```
Command: _fillet
Current settings: Mode = TRIM, Radius = 0.0000
Select first object or [Undo/Polyline/Radius/Trim/Multiple]: r
Specify fillet radius <0.0000>: .5
Select first object or [Undo/Polyline/Radius/Trim/Multiple]:
Select second object or shift-select to apply corner:

Command:
```

| 11.4420, 2.7560, 0.0000 | SNAP | GRID | ORTHO | POLAR | OSNAP | OTRACK | DUCS | DYN | LWT | M |

**Figure 7-32**    FILLET command prompt

To establish the value of the radius you exercise the **Radius** option by entering an **R** and hitting the **Enter** key. At this time the program prompts you for a radius value. After entering a value and pressing the **Enter** key, the command resumes with the request to Select objects.

To change the **Trim** mode you follow a similar action. By entering a **T** you can adjust the trim mode from **Trim** to **No Trim.**

After addressing the desired options you are prompted to Select first object and then Select second object. You must keep in mind that the portion of the object selected is the portion retained after the command has completed trimming the entities. Once the second object is selected, the arc is constructed, and the objects are trimmed if this mode is set to the **Trim** value. At this time the command is complete and you are returned to the command prompt.

If you would like to create additional fillets, there is an option that can be set within the **FILLET** command called **Multiple.** This option allows you to select multiple sets of entities to fillet; you press the **Enter** key to complete the command.

### Exercise 7-8: Creating a Fillet on Two Objects

- Start a new drawing.
- From the Draw menu place two lines in the drawing that are roughly perpendicular.
- From the Modify menu pick the FILLET command.
- Type R and press the Enter key to set the radius at 0.5.
- Select each of the lines at the end to be modified. After picking the second object the fillet is created.

## Chamfer

The **CHAMFER** command creates an angled line that connects two other objects. The simplest concept with a chamfer is to specify a distance for each object and then select two objects. The command produces a line based on the distance entered from an intersection point between the two objects. It trims off any extra portions of the selected objects to form a clean intersection at the intersecting points (see Figure 7-33). When first entering the **CHAMFER** command the current settings are shown in the prompt line. There are two methods used to calculate a chamfer—distance and angle. By default the distance method is active with the two values for distance set to **0** (see Figure 7-34). You need to establish values for **Distance** on each object. These values determine the distance calculations for the chamfer placement. The connecting line is then generated. You can establish the values for **Distance** by entering a **D** at the first prompt, which is Select first line or <Undo/Polyline/Distance/Angle/Trim/mEthod/Multiple>.

Once the values for distances are established, you select the two objects. After the second object is selected the chamfer is produced. Keep in mind that the portion of the object selected is the portion retained after the command has completed trimming the entities.

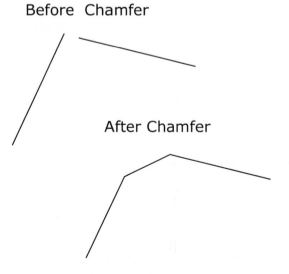

**Figure 7-33**   Chamfer results

```
Command: _chamfer
(TRIM mode) Current chamfer Dist1 = 0.0000, Dist2 = 0.0000
Select first line or [Undo/Polyline/Distance/Angle/Trim/mEthod/Multiple]: d
Specify first chamfer distance <0.0000>: .7
Specify second chamfer distance <0.7000>:
Select first line or [Undo/Polyline/Distance/Angle/Trim/mEthod/Multiple]:
Select second line or shift-select to apply corner:

Command:
```

```
10.6462, 1.5702, 0.0000    SNAP GRID ORTHO POLAR OSNAP OTRACK DUCS DYN LWT MODEL
```

Figure 7-34    CHAMFER command prompts

The **Angle** option uses the **Distance1** value and an **Angle** value to generate the connecting line. You still need to select two objects. The distance is calculated on the first object selected and the angle line then continues until it intersects the second object selected. Values for the distance and angle can be established through the **Angle** option. As with the **FILLET** command, the **Trim** option controls the cleanup of the objects selected, and the **Polyline** option applies the **Chamfer** values to all vertices capable of creating angle lines with the current settings.

### Exercise 7-9: Creating a Chamfer

- Start a new drawing.
- From the Draw menu place two lines in the drawing that are roughly perpendicular.
- From the Modify menu pick the CHAMFER command.
- Type a D and Enter the distances to be 0.75.
- Select each of the lines at the end to be modified. After picking the second object the chamfer will be created.

## Trim

Unlike the **ERASE** command, which removes an entire object, the **TRIM** command uses other pieces of geometry to act as a cutting edge or knife when you are removing only a portion of an object (see Figure 7-35). When starting the command, you select objects referred to as the cutting edges. In the command line you will see the following prompt:

```
Select cutting edges...
Select objects or <select all>:
```

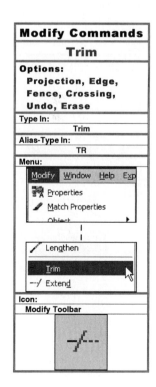

Any objects selected under this prompt are considered the "knife" or the objects to cause the cut. The geometry selected as the cutting edge has to come in contact with the object that will be trimmed. You can select several objects, or up to **All** objects, to act as cutting edges. You may even choose to simply hit the **Enter** key, which will select **All** the objects in the drawing file as cutting edges. To end this selection process hit the **Enter** key.

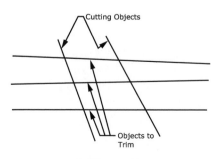

**Before Trim**

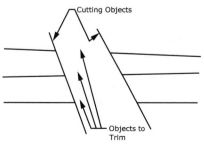

**After Trim**

Figure 7-35    The TRIM command

**Modify Commands**

**Extend**

**Options:**
Projection, Edge, Fence, Crossing, Undo

**Type In:**
Extend

**Alias-Type In:**
EX

**Menu:**

**Icon:**
Modify Toolbar

Following the selection of cutting edges, you then select the objects or parts of objects to trim away or remove. Keep in mind that the location used to touch the object will be the part of the object trimmed or removed. The selection of the **Objects to trim** can be made with a single-selection **pick box,** or you can choose to select multiple objects with the **Fence** or **Crossing** options. These two methods will only select multiple objects to **TRIM** at one time.

## Extend

The **EXTEND** command is basically the opposite of the **TRIM** command. **EXTEND** uses other pieces of geometry to act as a boundary edge when extending a portion of an object. When starting the command, you select objects referred to as boundary edges (see Figure 7-36). The command line shows the following prompt:

    Select boundary edges...
    Select objects or <select all>

The objects selected while this prompt message is active are considered the stop entity, the limit, or the objects to cause the extension to end. The geometry selected has to be in a direct path with the object that is extended. You can select several objects to act as **Boundary Edges.** You may even choose to simply hit the **Enter** key, which will select **All** the objects in the drawing file to act as boundary edges. To end this selection process for the boundaries you have to hit the **Enter** key.

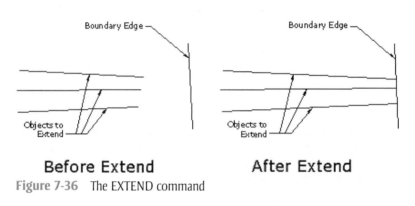

**Before Extend**     **After Extend**

**Figure 7-36**     The EXTEND command

**Modify Commands**

**Break**

**Options:**
First Point

**Type In:**
Break

**Alias-Type In:**
BR

**Menu:**

**Icon:**
Modify Toolbar

Following the selection of boundary edges, you then select the objects to **EXTEND**. Keep in mind the objects touched are the objects extended. The program does not add an additional entity for the extension, but it repositions the closest endpoint to intersect the new position defined by the extension. The selection of the **Objects to extend** can be made with a single-selection pick box or you can choose to select objects with the **Fence** or **Crossing** options. These two methods will select multiple objects to **EXTEND** at one time.

## Break

Similar to the **TRIM** command, **BREAK** removes a portion of an existing object. The difference between the two commands is that **BREAK** does not need other pieces of geometry to act as cutting edges. **BREAK** prompts you to Select objects. The object selected is the object that will be broken. The object's selected location automatically becomes the first break point. To complete the command you are prompted for a second break point. After the selection of the second break point, the portion of the object that lies between the two break points is removed. If you choose not to use the initial object selection point as the first break point, you can

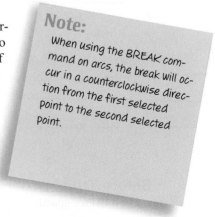

**Note:**
When using the BREAK command on arcs, the break will occur in a counterclockwise direction from the first selected point to the second selected point.

invoke a **First Point** option by typing in an **F** at the command prompt line after selecting the object (see Figure 7-37). This allows you to reposition the first break point to a new location, and continue on to select the second break point, thus completing the command. The **Object Snaps** such as **END**point, **INT**ersection, and **MID**point are available in the **BREAK** command to aid in the proper location of the **BREAK.**

```
Command:
Command:  _break Select object:
Specify second break point or [First point]:
Command:
```
```
3.7647, 5.1616, 0.0000    SNAP GRID ORTHO POLAR OSNAP OTRACK DUCS DYN L
```

**Figure 7-37**    BREAK command prompts

## Lengthen

Similar to the **EXTEND** command the **LENGTHEN** command increases (and may also decrease) the distance end to end of a selected object. If the object is selected before one of the following options, the current length is displayed as shown in Figure 7-38.

```
Command:   LENGTHEN
Select an object or [DElta/Percent/Total/DYnamic]: p
Enter percentage length <100.0000>: 125
Select an object to change or [Undo]:
Select an object to change or [Undo]:
Command:
```
```
22.8712, 0.6990 , 0.0000    SNAP GRID ORTHO POLAR OSNAP OTRACK DUCS DYN LWT
```

**Figure 7-38**    LENGTHEN command prompts

There are four options to determine how much the object is lengthened. They are as follows:

- The **Delta** option is executed by typing in a **DE** at the prompt line. This option allows you to select any two positions on the screen as a length value or enter a value at the command prompt. Next you are prompted to select the object to be lengthened. After the object is selected, the distance calculated between the first two points is added to the end closest to the object end that was selected.

- The **Percent** option is invoked by typing in a **P** on the command line. This option uses a percent value to increase or decrease the length of an object. The current length of the object is considered a value of 100 percent. Any value larger than 100 percent increases the object proportionally by that amount, and any value less than 100 percent decreases the length proportionally. After you have established the percentage needed, you are prompted to select the object to lengthen; the percentage is added to or subtracted from the closest chosen end of the object.

- The **Total** option uses the number entered as the new, current value of length of the object selected. The object is lengthened to or shortened from the closest endpoint selected, and the total length of the object equals the value of the length entered for the **Total.**

- The **Dynamic** option prompts you to select the object to be modified or lengthened. When you see a Dynamic link to the movement of the mouse, you can increase or decrease the length of the object by simply moving the mouse position to a desired location. This chosen length is then adjusted to the end closest to the original selection point.

## Stretch

The **STRETCH** command allows you to select objects and have the endpoints or control points of those objects relocated in such a manner that the objects are lengthened or shortened in any direction. As well, you can change the rotation angle of the objects. When using the **STRETCH** command, you must select the objects with a **Crossing Window** or a **Crossing Polygon.** Any other method of selecting the objects will result in a **MOVE** command, not a **STRETCH** command.

Once the object selection process (including hatches and dimensions) is complete, you are prompted to Specify a base point or displacement. You can enter a displacement value directly and the objects will **STRETCH** the corresponding distance and direction. If a base point is chosen, the command requests that you Specify a second point (see Figure 7-39). The objects selected are dynamically stretched to the new location prior to the selection of the second point (see Figure 7-40).

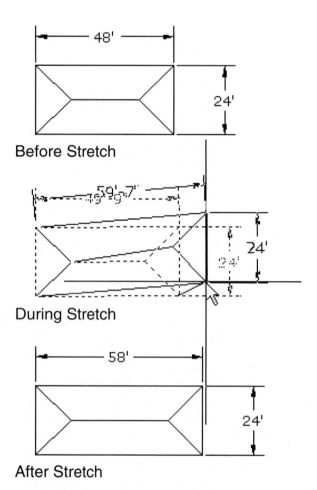

Before Stretch

During Stretch

After Stretch

**Figure 7-39**   Stretch the house 10′ or @ 10′, 0.

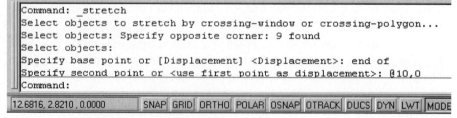

```
Command: _stretch
Select objects to stretch by crossing-window or crossing-polygon...
Select objects: Specify opposite corner: 9 found
Select objects:
Specify base point or [Displacement] <Displacement>: end of
Specify second point or <use first point as displacement>: @10,0
Command:
```

12.6816, 2.8210 , 0.0000     SNAP  GRID  ORTHO  POLAR  OSNAP  OTRACK  DUCS  DYN  LWT  MODE

**Figure 7-40**   STRETCH command prompt

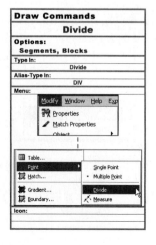

## Divide

The **DIVIDE** command allows you to create points or insert blocks at equal spaces along a selected object. Although the command may sound as if it will break the main objects into smaller objects, this is not true. The command places reference objects along the selected object that can be used as geometric references. The **DIVIDE** command is essentially a **Modify** command but is found in the **Draw** menu as one of the **Point** menu cascade options.

A proper application of the DIVIDE or the MEASURE commands gives you a series of points along an entity. This skill allows for accurate object snap positions.

Upon entering the command, you are prompted to `Select object to divide`. After the selection has been made you are prompted to `Enter the number of segments or [Block]`. If you enter a numeric value, the program places a point node at each proportioned location along the object. The actual shape of the symbol at the divided point node is controlled by the **PDMODE** system variable. By default the shape is a dot or period. This can be changed to a more recognizable symbol by changing the **PDMODE** value. See Figure 7-41 for values and related symbol results.

If you want to insert a block definition at each division location, you need to enter a **B** at the second prompt (`Enter the number of segments or [Block]`). You are then prompted for the block name including directory or folder path and whether you want the block aligned with the selected object. After entering the block information, you are prompted to `Enter the number of segments`. The symbol is placed along the object and at the proportional or division location as shown in Figure 7-42.

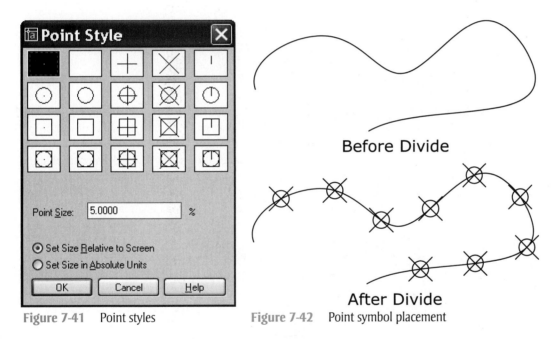

Figure 7-41    Point styles

Figure 7-42    Point symbol placement

## Measure

The **MEASURE** command is similar to the **DIVIDE** command. The difference is that the **MEASURE** command allows you to specify a distance that will be measured off as equal intervals from one end of a selected object. Similar to the **DIVIDE** command, this distance can be identified with points or blocks.

The starting point for the measurement will vary depending on the object selected. Lines or arcs will measure off the distance from the closest endpoint of the line or arc selected. For circles the starting point will be identified by the current snap angle. For example, if the snap angle is set to 90 degrees, the first point would be at the twelve o'clock position on the circle.

## Join

The **JOIN** command joins selected objects into a single unbroken object. Depending on the type of objects selected you see one of several prompts. There are certain restrictions to the objects eligible for this operation, as follows:

- If you select **LINES** for the objects to join, the lines must be collinear, although they may have gaps between the objects.
- If you select **ARCS**, the arcs must lie on the same imaginary circle, although they may have gaps between the objects. If you want a series of **ARCS** to form a closed circle you need to invoke the **Close** option from the command line.
- If you select **POLYLINES**, the polylines must be in the same XY plane, and there can be no gaps between the vertices of the polylines.
- Finally, if you select a series of **Splines,** they must be one continuous **Spline** joined end to end.

The **JOIN** command results in creating one single object of the same nature as the source objects selected, as shown in Figure 7-43. (This command was new in the 2006 version.)

## Before Join

## After Join

**Figure 7-43**   JOIN command

### Matching Properties

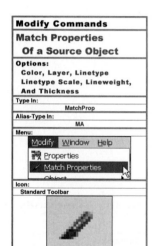

Proper drawing techniques use layers, colors, linetypes, and so on for specific definitions and meanings. In the process of creating and modifying entities in an AutoCAD drawing, object properties may not be properly defined, since an object may be drawn on the wrong layer or have the incorrect linetype. The MATCH PROPERTIES command allows you a quick way to change properties to match a properly defined object that already exists in the drawing.

The properties of an object as shown in Figure 7-44 include Color, Layer, Linetype, Lineweight, and Thickness. If a source object with the correct settings is already in the drawing

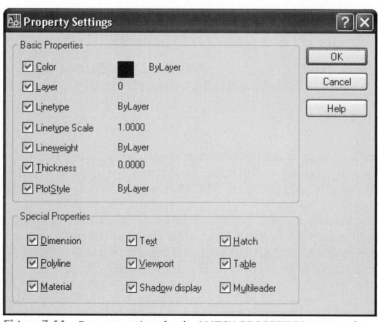

**Figure 7-44**   Property settings for the MATCH PROPERTIES command

it is easier to **Match Properties** than to **Modify Properties** within the **Modify** palette. Through the MATCH PROPERTIES command all changes are made at the same time. If not all the properties are to be transferred you can deselect or select the correct combination from the **Property Settings** dialog box (see Figure 7-44) while processing the command.

When the MATCH PROPERTIES command is invoked, you are requested to select a source object. Only one source object is allowed and therefore the only selection method is the pick box (see Figure 7-45). After the choice of the original object is made, the command prompt displays what settings for the matching are active and allows you to type an **S** to modify the current match settings (see Figure 7-46). Once the settings have been verified, destination objects or entities to be modified can then be chosen with any of the selection methods. The result is properly modified entities as shown in Figure 7-47.

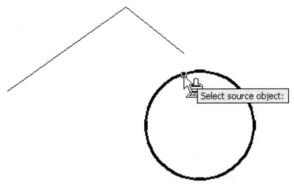

**Figure 7-45**    Selecting the source or original object for matching

```
Command: '_matchprop
Select source object:
Current active settings:  Color Layer Ltype Ltscale Lineweight Thickness
PlotStyle Dim Text Hatch Polyline Viewport Table Material Shadow display
Select destination object(s) or [Settings]:
Select destination object(s) or [Settings]:
Command:
```
-0.0026, 3.3428 , 0.0000        SNAP GRID ORTHO POLAR OSNAP OTRACK DUCS DYN LWT MODEL

**Figure 7-46**    The MATCH PROPERTIES command prompt

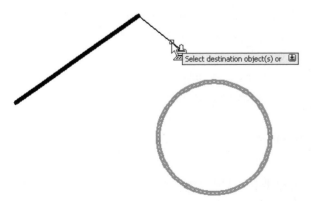

**Figure 7-47**    The result of the MATCH PROPERTIES command

# SUMMARY

In this unit, you advanced from using elementary AutoCAD commands in the draw-modify-dimension-print cycle to an intermediate skill level acquired through practice of what you have previously learned as well as an expansion of your knowledged of the **DRAW** and **MODIFY** commands. First, you learned some additional commands and options for creating various entities: circles **(2 Point; 3 Point; Tan, Tan, Radius; Tan, Tan, Tan)**; arcs (using various combinations of values for **Start** (first endpoint), **End** (second endpoint), **Center** (center point), **Angle** (included angle), **Radius, Length** (chord distance), **Direction** (starting tangent direction), and **Continue** (endpoint)); ellipses (**Center** method, **Axis, End** method, and **Arc** method); rectangles (**RECTANG** command with **Chamfer, Fillet, Elevation, Thickness, Width, Area, Dimension,** and **Rotation** options); and predefined and user-defined hatch patterns (**HATCH** command). Next, you learned how to create and edit **Single Line (Dynamic) Text** using the **TEXT** or **DTEXT** command, and **Multiline Text (MTEXT)** using the **MULTILINE TEXT** command. Finally, you were introduced to additional methods of object selection (**All, Previous, Last,** and **Fence**) and additional modifying commands (**FILLET, CHAMFER, TRIM, EXTEND, BREAK, LENGTHEN, STRETCH, DIVIDE, MEASURE, JOIN,** and **MATCH PROPERTIES**) from the **Modify** menu and toolbar.

# CHAPTER TEST QUESTIONS

## Multiple Choice

1. Which is **not** an option for creating a circle?
   a. Tan, Tan, Tan
   b. 3 Point
   c. 2 points and a Radius
   d. Tan, Tan, Radius

2. Which is **not** a valid selection option?
   a. Last
   b. Layer
   c. All
   d. Previous

3. Hatching will fill a boundary area with
   a. Solid Color
   b. Gradient
   c. Patterns
   d. All of the above

4. Single-line text produces text that will act as:
   a. Individual letters
   b. A paragraph
   c. A single line
   d. Individual words

5. The STRETCH command requires the objects to be selected with what method?
   a. Fence
   b. Window
   c. Crossing
   d. Previous

## Matching

a. _____ Join
b. _____ Break
c. _____ Trim
d. _____ Lengthen
e. _____ Last

1. Removes a portion of an object
2. Changes the endpoint distance
3. Connects multiple objects
4. Requires cutting edges
5. Selects the most current object created

## True or False

1. True or False: Multiline text acts more like a word processor than single-line text.

2. True or False: Offset will copy the properties of the selected object.

3. True or False: A Fillet radius cannot have a zero value.

4. True or False: The Polar ARRAY must have an angle input.

5. True or False: You can only use a single object as a cutting edge.

## CHAPTER PROJECTS

1. Research the size, and create a top view of a 54-tooth 8″ spur gear.
2. Develop a reflected ceiling plan for a 20′ × 20′ room using a traditional 2′ × 4′ fluorescent light fixture.
3. Develop a site plan of your campus showing buildings, parking, sidewalks, and so on.

## PRACTICE EXERCISES

### Practice Exercise 7-1: General Drawing

1. Start a new drawing with the **NEW** command in the **File** menu.
2. Enter 0,0 and 11, 8.5 as **DRAWING LIMITS** in the **Format** menu.
3. In the **View** menu pick **ZOOM/ALL** to reset the drawing area to the limits.
4. Create two layers, one for the part drawing and one for dimensions.
5. Draw a rectangle starting at **1,1** that is **5.5** units in the X direction and **4.0** units in the Y direction.
6. Using the **OFFSET, TRIM, EXTEND,** and other commands in this chapter, modify the rectangle to create the plate shown in Figure 7-48.

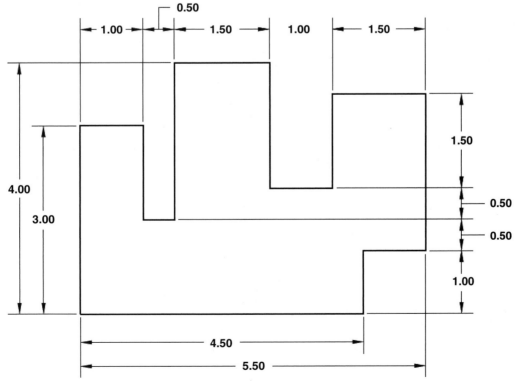

**Figure 7-48**    Drawing EX7-1

7. Using the **STRETCH** command, expand the right half of the drawing units to the right. Be sure to include all the dimensions in this operation.

8. Save the drawing in your **Workskills** folder as EX7-1.

Figures 7-49 to 7-59 represent typical general, architectural, civil, and mechanical drawings (and include dimensions, text, and other information) that can be created using the techniques and commands explained in this chapter.

- To begin the drawing process for each drawing, access the **File** menu and pick **NEW**. (Use the acad.dwt template if this is requested.)
- Then set the **Units** for the drawing if the drawing will use feet and inches or **Architectural** as **UNITS** for the input. This command is found in the **Format** menu.
- Next set **LIMITS** for the drawing to resize the screen to hold the drawing. This command is in the **Format** menu. The lower left corner should be set to 0,0 with the upper right set to numbers just beyond the maximum X,Y of the figure.
- Then process the **ZOOM ALL** command using the keyboard, **View** menu, or icon. This resizes the screen to view the complete drawing as described by the limits.
- Create layers for dimension, notes, text, and other information as well as layers for object lines, centerlines, hidden lines, and other linetypes that may be used.
- Access the **LINE** command to begin drawing the figure.
- Add dimensions, leaders, text, and other information on the drawings to make them complete.
- Remember to save your drawing every 10 to 15 minutes to avoid losing your work. Save the drawing in your **Workskills** folder with the figure number as the file name.

## Practice Exercise 7-2

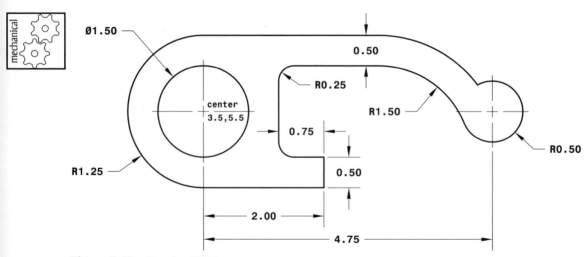

Figure 7-49     Drawing EX7-2

## Practice Exercise 7-3

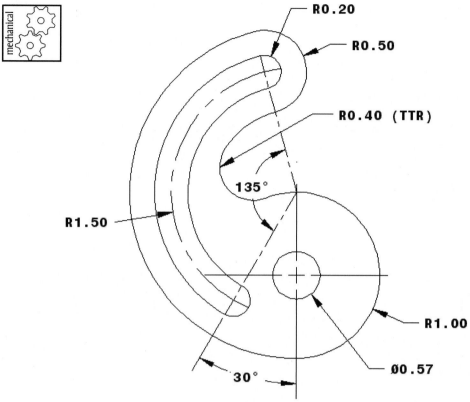

**Figure 7-50**    Drawing EX7-3

## Practice Exercise 7-4

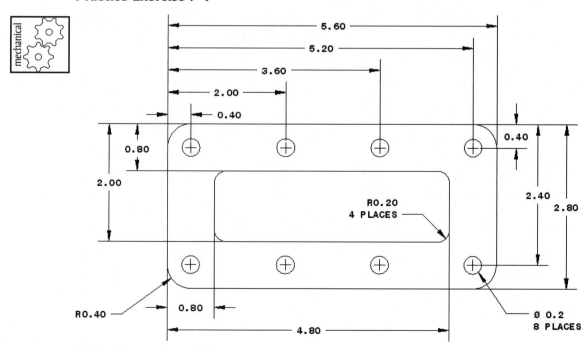

**Figure 7-51**    Drawing EX7-4

## Practice Exercise 7-5

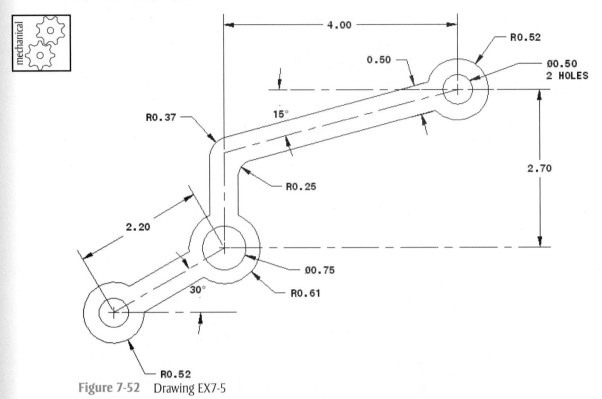

**Figure 7-52**   Drawing EX7-5

## Practice Exercise 7-6

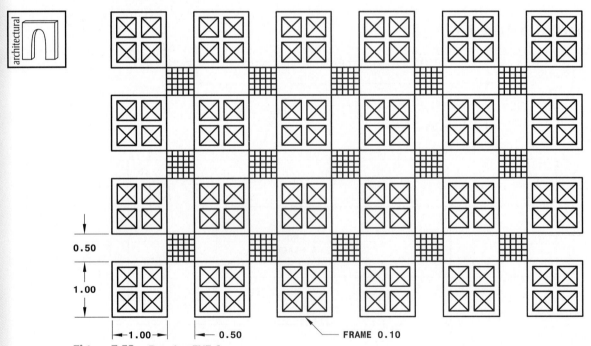

**Figure 7-53**   Drawing EX7-6

## Practice Exercise 7-7

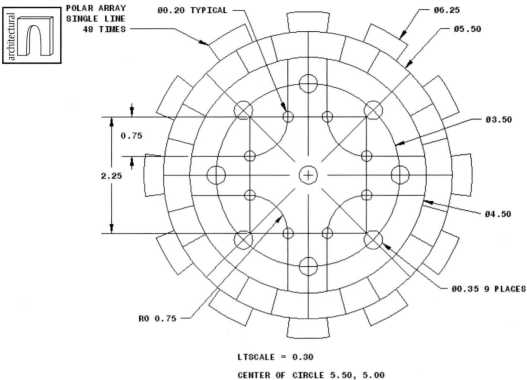

POLAR ARRAY
SINGLE LINE
48 TIMES

Ø0.20 TYPICAL

Ø6.25

Ø5.50

Ø3.50

0.75

2.25

Ø4.50

Ø0.35 9 PLACES

R0 0.75

LTSCALE = 0.30
CENTER OF CIRCLE 5.50, 5.00

Figure 7-54    Drawing EX7-7

## Practice Exercise 7-8

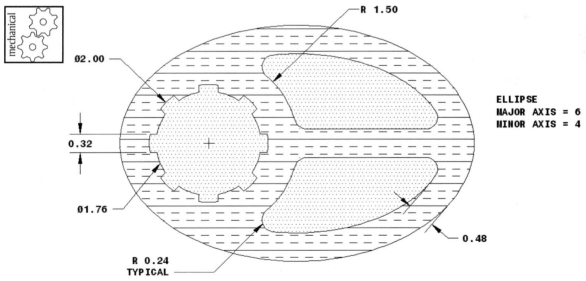

R 1.50

Ø2.00

ELLIPSE
MAJOR AXIS = 6
MINOR AXIS = 4

0.32

0.48

Ø1.76

R 0.24
TYPICAL

Figure 7-55    Drawing EX7-8

## Practice Exercise 7-9

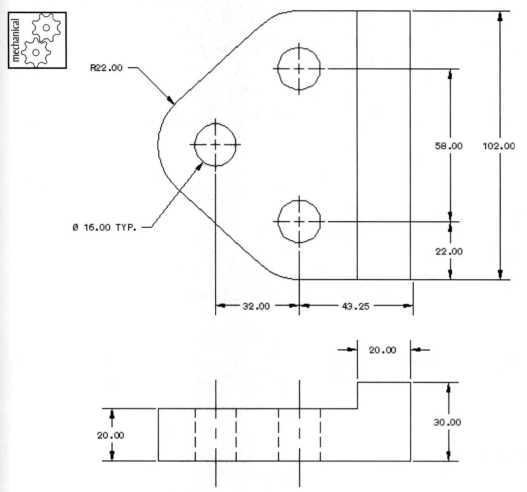

**Figure 7-56**    Drawing EX7-9

## Practice Exercise 7-10

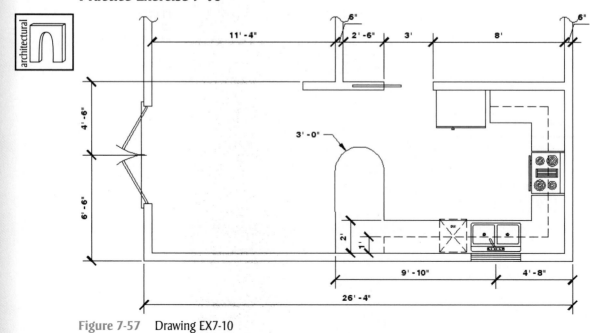

**Figure 7-57**    Drawing EX7-10

## Practice Exercise 7-11

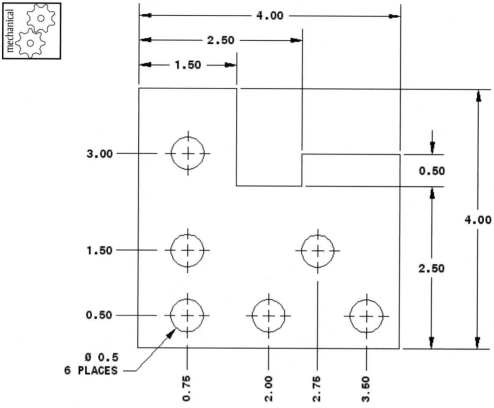

**Figure 7-58**    Drawing EX7-11

## Practice Exercise 7-12

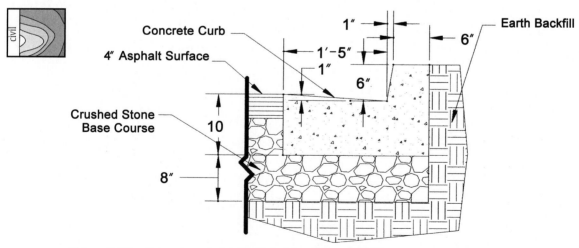

**Figure 7-59**    Concrete curb detail with hatch patterns; EX7-12

# 8

# Fundamentals of Layers, Groups, and Blocks

## *Chapter* Objectives

- Define layer properties.
- Create and manage groups.
- Create block definitions.
- Insert and manipulate blocks and external references.
- Use the DesignCenter™ for blocks and online objects.
- Use layers in the plotting process.

## INTRODUCTION

In Unit 2, we presented an introduction to the topic of layers. The general concept of layers was to use them to organize a drawing file. Commands such as **GROUP** and **BLOCK** will further these concepts of organization within a drawing file.

## LAYERS

When layering was introduced as an object's property, organization of a drawing suggested that similar objects are placed on individual layers. This discussion focuses on the creation of a layer and the explanation of a layer's properties and display controls. As already mentioned, the AutoCAD program does not automatically create layers in a drawing file. It is up to you to establish a *layering scheme.* In some cases the layering scheme is part of a defined series of office standards or standards set by a permitting agency. In other cases, it is simply personal preference based on experience.

**layering scheme:** A plan to create and manage a series of layers within a complex design.

The following discussion focuses on the implementation of a layering scheme and the fundamental practice operators use during a drawing session. You may want to revisit Unit 2 to review the explanation of the various options and display controls found in the **LAYER** command.

---

**FOR MORE DETAIL**

The U.S. National CAD Standards used by the Department of Defense and others establish a layering scheme that uses the American Institute of Architects (AIA) Layering Guidelines. For more information check www.aia.org and www. nationalcadstandard.org for more details.

## LAYER FUNCTIONS

You will address the layering topic in several types of commands. The definition of a series of layers and the ongoing placement of objects onto layers during a drawing session are the most basic command concerns of beginning users. As you learn to display a layer's content and control plotting through layers, you will discover the power of using layers. Keep in mind that the actual organization of specific objects on specific layers is governed by the type of drawing and the drawing's discipline.

Layering standards are being used in all disciplines of engineering. Whether your job uses office-developed standards or a national CAD standard for layering, you must be able to maintain these office practices by demonstrating a complete understanding of all layering concepts and commands.

## DIALOG BOX VERSUS TOOLBARS

On the initial creation of a layering scheme, there are two general thoughts for organizing information. You can define a series of layers that are property-based or you can organize information according to topic. Property-based layers can be defined by object lines, hidden lines, centerlines, dimensions, or text. A layering scheme using drawing topics might contain information for foundation plans, electrical plans, elevations, section views, or contour lines. In either case new layers are created with the **Layer Properties Manager** (see Figure 8-1). The manager is a dialog box that can be launched from the **Format** menu, the command line, or the **Layers** toolbar (see Figure 8-2). At the time a layer is created, you will give it a unique name, define the layer properties, and you may establish it to be the *current layer.*

current layer: The layer that is active to receive all newly created entities.

To complete this process using the **Layer Properties Manager,** you must click on the **Apply** or **OK** button in the lower left area of the dialog box. Failing to do this can result in the loss of the edited information.

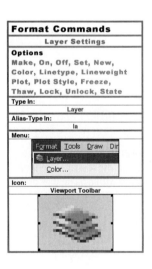

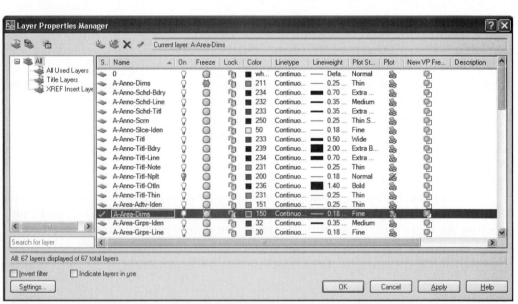

**Figure 8-1**   Typical AIA layers for a house drawing

**Figure 8-2**   Layers toolbar

After the layering scheme is created, all other **Layer** command options can be easily executed through the **Layers** toolbar. The ongoing issue when dealing with layers is to have the correct **Current Layer** when creating new objects, because objects take on the current layer as a property. Although this property can be changed after the creation of an object, it is better to pay attention to the Current Layer to make sure it is the one that your objects belong on. You can change the **Current Layer** by clicking on the down arrow in the **Layers** toolbar and simply selecting another layer name to be the next Current Layer. The visibility controls for a layer's content are found in this same drop-down list, represented by a lightbulb, a sun, and a padlock. Clicking on these icons executes the **On/Off** toggle options (see Figures 8-3, 8-4, 8-5, and 8-6) as well as

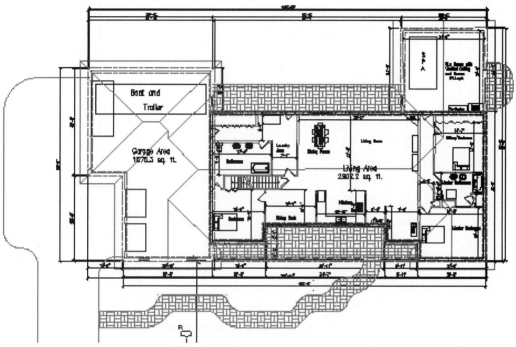

**Figure 8-3**    All layers are on and visible

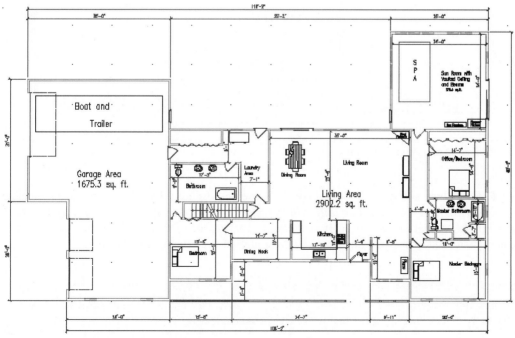

**Figure 8-4**    Floor plan with furniture layers on

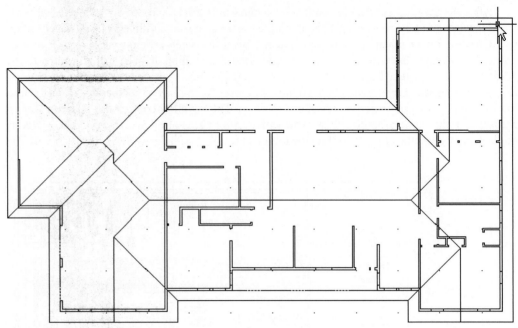

Figure 8-5     Roof plan layers only on

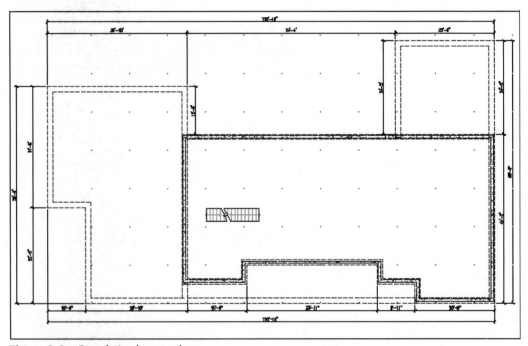

Figure 8-6     Foundation layers only on

the **Freeze/Thaw** and **Lock/Unlock** toggles. These options are referred to as the display-based options. Although these same options are available in the **Layer Properties Manager,** access through the toolbar can be faster. If you want to change one of the layer's properties (linetype, color, lineweight, plot style) this has to be done in the **Layer Properties Manager.**

Proper application of the No Plot layer property for temporary entities such as construction/layout geometry ensures that this data will not end up in a plotted drawing.

The **Layers** toolbar contains three commands that can only be found there. **Make Object's Layer Current, Layer Previous** and **Layerstate** are three additional methods for changing the **Current Layer.** With **Make Object's Layer Current,** you select an existing object, and the current layer is changed to the layer of the object that has been selected. The **Layer Previous** button changes the current layer back to its previous setting.

The **Layerstate** button will display a list of layer states saved within the drawing file. The **Layer State Manager** dialog box will allow you to create, rename, edit, or delete layer states. Layer states are a snapshot of the current conditions of the drawing layer's organization and display properties.

Paying attention to the current layer will make it easier to maintain an organized drawing file. As mentioned earlier, if needed, objects can be reassigned to other layers. If an object is placed on an incorrect layer, you simply select the object with the command prompt present (Grip the object), then move the cursor to the drop box in the **Layers** toolbar. Then, from the list, select the layer on which you want to place the object. Again, it is to your benefit to maintain an organized drawing. Using a logical layering scheme is a leading factor in a drawing's organization.

## ESTABLISHING AND WORKING WITH OBJECT GROUPS

*Groups* are formed from a selected set of objects and can be saved into a named set. This command is a simple way to organize objects into subsets that can be used to select multiple objects as well as manipulate those same objects as a single unit. **Groups** can be under continuous adjustment. Objects assigned to a group can be removed at any time and new objects can be added, making this an alternative method for drawing organization.

The **Object Grouping** dialog box (see Figure 8-7) is launched by typing in the word **GROUP** or entering a **G** at the prompt line. (No menu item or icon options are available with the standard installation of the AutoCAD program.) This dialog box allows you to define a group by establishing a **Group Name.** Next select the **New** button, which places you back into the drawing file to select the objects to be placed in the group. When a group is defined you must state whether the group is **Selectable.** If a group is labeled **Selectable,** selecting any object in the group results in selecting the entire group. The second option in the creation of a group is whether the group will be named. This option, when active, assigns a generic name to each group created if no name is input.

Once a group is defined, the same dialog box is used to adjust the members of the group. All defined groups are listed in the top area of the dialog box. When you select a name from this area, this activates the lower portion of the dialog box to allow for the editing of the **GROUP**

groups: A command used to manipulate a group of objects as if it was one.

| Commands |
|---|
| **Group** |
| **Options:** Add, Remove, Rename Re-order, Description, Selectable, Explode |
| **Type In:** Group |
| **Alias-Type In:** G |
| **Menu:** |
| **Icon:** |

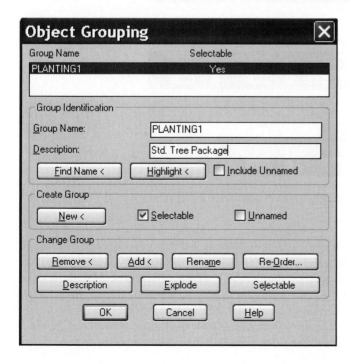

**Figure 8-7**   Object Grouping dialog box

definition. Editing of the group can include the adding or removing of objects, along with the explosion of the entire group definition. Groups that are created are saved with the drawing file and are available from one drawing session to another. The one disadvantage of Groups is that the Group definitions are not available to move from one drawing file to another drawing file to be used again. **Groups** can be made into **Block** as detailed next.

## FUNDAMENTALS OF MAKING BLOCKS

block: A series of objects in a drawing controlled as one entity.

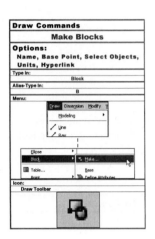

**Blocks** are similar to **Groups.** A *block* is a series of objects that is saved under a unique name in a drawing. The **Block** definition consists of the objects and their relationship at the time the objects are selected for the subset.

When the block is created the individual objects combine into one new object, which results in a smaller and more efficient object than the entities were individually. Blocks, by merging many into one, reduce the size of a set of objects by one-third to one-half (see Figure 8-8). The result is a more compact drawing that allows for faster selection of objects, faster pans and zooms, and an overall productivity improvement with every command. Also, any block can be exported and saved as a drawing and any existing drawing can be used as a block and placed in other drawings. The use of blocks increases consistency in a drawing file and throughout the organization, as more consistent symbols, details, and libraries are used.

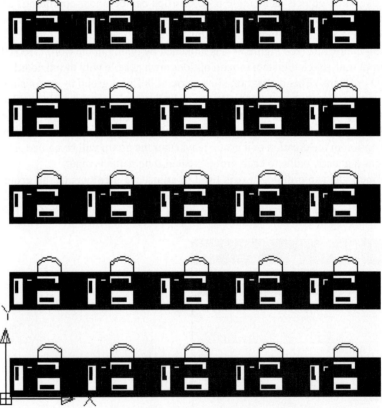

**Figure 8-8**    Classroom of 25 desks; drawing is 42% smaller when desks are blocks (33 kB versus 57 kB)

During the definition of the **Block** (see Figure 8-9), you need to define a control or **Base point,** which is used as the **Insert point** when the **Block** definition is located in a drawing file. Typically a **Block** definition will create and represent a symbol, detail, or **Group** that will be used again in the current drawing or in another drawing. By using the **Block** definition, you are placing the same series of objects through the same **Control point** every time the **Block** definition is inserted.

Selection of the **Block Make** command launches the **Block Definition** dialog box (shown in Figure 8-9). You need to do at least three things to define a block. You will enter a **Name** for the

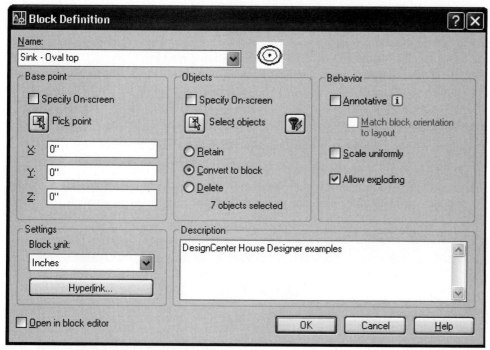

Figure 8-9    Block Definition dialog box

**Block** definition. This name should follow the same naming standards as other item definitions or standards related to AutoCAD drawings. After establishing the name, you will select the objects to be part of the definition. By selecting the **Select objects** icon in the upper right area of the **Block Definition** dialog box, you will be shifted back into the drawing file to use any of the **Select objects** methods discussed previously. The next item of the definition is to select a **Base point** for the control of the insert location relative to the future placement of this block definition. The **Base point** should be chosen with an **Object Snap** drawing aid to ensure accuracy and should be on or near the block. Figure 8-10 shows the possible locations of the **Base point** based

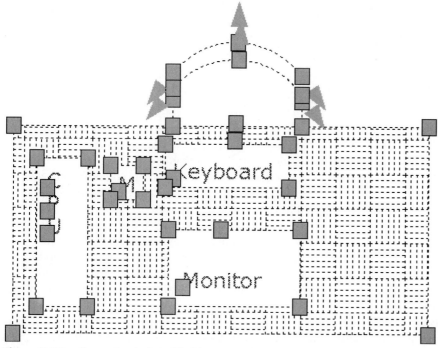

Figure 8-10    Computer desk as 16 objects

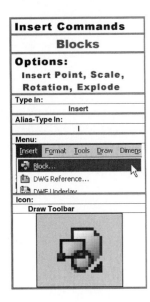

**Insert Commands**

**Blocks**

**Options:**

Insert Point, Scale,
Rotation, Explode

**Type In:**
Insert

**Alias-Type In:**
I

**Menu:**

Insert  Format  Tools  Draw  Dimens

Block...

DWG Reference...

DWF Underlay

**Icon:**
Draw Toolbar

on **Grips.** Using the typical default **Base point** with 0,0,0 as the coordinates is not recommended, as the **Base point** should be on or near the block to aid in placement. The blocks are created in the drawing units currently active. If you need to select a different type of unit, you can change the unit type in the **Block unit** area of the **Block Definition** dialog box.

After all the information is entered in the dialog box, you will finish the process by clicking on the **OK** button (see Figure 8-11). This writes the definition into the current drawing file for use and further placement in this drawing. Depending on the setting in the **Select objects** area of the dialog box, the objects selected may be treated as follows:

- **Converted** Selected entities become the new block definition.

- **Retained** Keep current form as separate objects.

- **Deleted** Removed from the drawing file as individual entities and retained only as a block in the drawing; with this option, the new block may be inserted in the drawing, if needed.

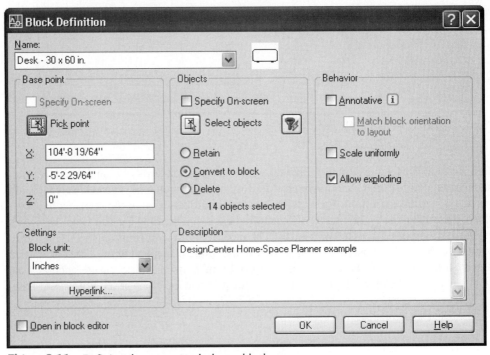

**Figure 8-11**    Defining the computer desk as a block

## INSERTING BLOCKS

insert: The process of merging a drawing file into the resident drawing file.

The process of placing a defined block in a drawing, or another drawing in the current drawing, is referred to as an *insert* operation. The **Insert** menu contains several commands that place various types of files into the current resident drawing file (see Figure 8-12).

The top selection in the **Insert** menu is **Block.** The selection of this command launches the **Insert** dialog box (see Figure 8-13). From this dialog box, you can select the **Block** definition to insert and control the location, scale, and rotation of the insertion.

To begin the insertion process, you select a block definition from the **Name** drop-down list at the top of the dialog box. All the block definitions that have been created in this drawing file or previously inserted into the drawing file will be found in this list. You may select to insert a complete drawing into the resident drawing file. To do this, you click on the **Browse** button. This launches the **Select Drawing File** dialog box (see Figure 8-14), allowing you to select any AutoCAD drawing file for insertion.

Once the **Block** definition is selected, you address three pieces of information to complete the process. The **Insertion point, Scale,** and **Rotation** must be specified through the supplied dialog box fields (see Figure 8-13), the command line, or on the drawing screen. A check mark

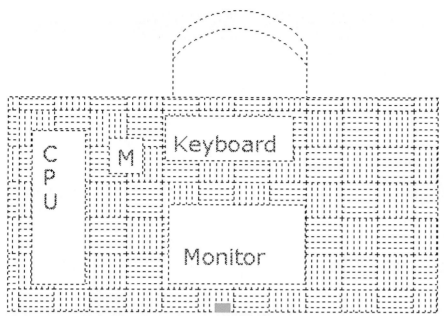

Figure 8-12    Computer desk as block showing base point

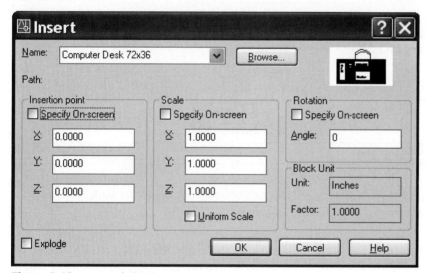

Figure 8-13    Insert dialog box

in any of the **Specify On-screen** boxes will cause this information to be entered on the drawing screen or in the command line (see Figure 8-15).

The **Insertion point,** which can be an absolute coordinate, is specified through the X, Y, and Z coordinate location. Use your cursor and an object snap override or other location method to specify the point on the drawing screen. The **Block** definition can be scaled on any one of the three axes (X, Y, or Z) by inputting a value in the **Scale** field. The default value or current scale of the definition is 1.0. To increase the size, you use a number larger than 1.0. To decrease the size you input a number less than 1.0. **Scale** can vary on one or more directions upon insertion. If you select the **Uniform Scale** check box, the value placed in the X scale field is applied to all scale fields. **Rotation** of the block definition is addressed in the third column. A value of zero inserts the block in the same orientation it was created in. Positive values rotate the **Block** definition counterclockwise, while negative values cause a clockwise rotation.

When all the fields in this dialog box have been addressed, click on the **OK** button. The **Block** definition will be inserted into the drawing file. If the **Insertion point** is to be specified on-screen, you will see a ghost image of the block definition attached at the cursor control

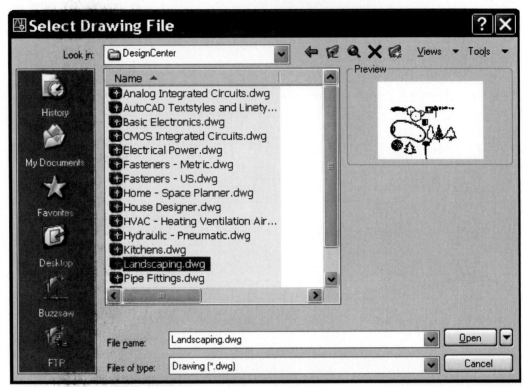

Figure 8-14    Browsing for a drawing to insert as a block

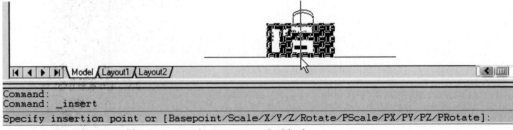

```
Command:
Command: _insert
Specify insertion point or [Basepoint/Scale/X/Y/Z/Rotate/PScale/PX/PY/PZ/PRotate]:
```

Figure 8-15    Command line prompts for insertion of a block

point in the drawing screen. The block will be placed in the file when the location is selected. This ghost image could take a few moments to appear depending on the complexity or size of the block.

Creating blocks, maintaining symbol libraries, and applying the various insertion options are daily activities for CAD operators. When you can demonstrate an understanding of these fundamental concepts, you will gain the productivity benefits offered by these commands.

## The EXPLODE Command

As mentioned earlier, a block definition comes into a file as one object regardless of how many objects make up the definition. By using the **EXPLODE** command, found in the **Modify** menu, you can choose to explode the block definition into the original objects. This breaks up only the block or blocks selected; it does not affect other similar blocks already in the drawing and does not destroy the original block definition. Exploding a block definition allows you to select the individual objects within a definition. Keep in mind that the block will no longer act as one object. But you will be able to insert additional versions of the definition when needed, since the original definition will still be valid and stays as part of the drawing database. A button in the lower left corner of the **Insert** dialog box lets you insert the block in an exploded format. This removes the benefits of a block.

Although a block is similar to a group, there are significant advantages to defining and inserting a block as opposed to a **group**. These include: smaller size, exploding only one not all, selectable control points, nonuniform scaling, and more. The biggest advantages are that blocks can be copied from drawing file to drawing file and can also become a drawing directly (through the **WBLOCK** command).

**Note:** *Block* has additional advantages as well. You can attach *Attributes* to block definitions, apply data-based searches for blocks, and edit blocks through dynamic global editing functions.

## DesignCenter Operations

An alternative method for block insertion is available through the *DesignCenter*. The **DesignCenter** palette allows definition-based objects to be copied, inserted, or dragged from file to file. A *palette* can be structured to open when active and close when inactive (through Auto-Hide). Palettes can be resized, moved, or docked. Some palettes can also have a level of transparency.

The **DesignCenter** allows you to search through other AutoCAD files and use drag-and-drop techniques to copy information from the selected file into the resident file. The type of information that is available for this operation is as follows:

- Blocks
- Dimstyles
- Layers
- Layouts

- Linetypes
- Tablestyles
- Textstyles
- External references

The **DesignCenter** palette (see Figure 8-16) is split into two sections, much like the Windows Explorer environment. The section on the left allows you to navigate directly to the category of interest in an AutoCAD drawing file or on the **DesignCenter (DC) Online** network. The four tabs at the top show the areas available in **DesignCenter.** With the first tab, you can select the type of information you are interested in from the various storage devices and network drives that can be accessed by your computer. You can quickly examine any currently open drawings or drawings recently accessed with the second and third tab, respectively. The fourth

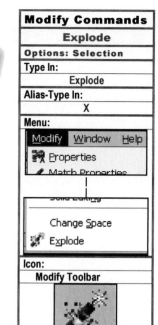

DesignCenter: A tool palette that allows you to drag and drop entities from other AutoCAD files into the current file.

palette: A special window that can access drawings, blocks, and commands in the AutoCAD environment.

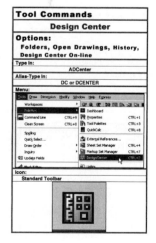

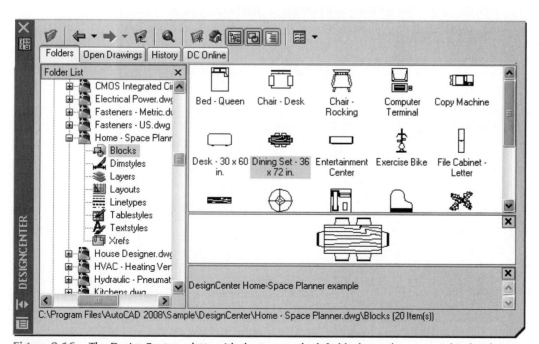

**Figure 8-16**    The DesignCenter palette with the tree on the left, blocks on the upper right, the chosen block detail in the center right, and descriptive information on the lower right

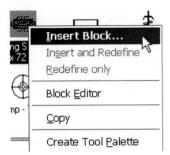

Figure 8-17    Right-click menu in the DesignCenter palette object viewer

tab leads to **DC Online,** an Internet-based service (Internet access must be available for this option) from Autodesk containing symbols, blocks, manufacturer materials, and more.

After the type of information is selected, the definitions found in the selected drawing file are listed on the right side of the dialog box. When an object is chosen a detail view is available in the middle right area and descriptive data are shown in the lower right window. You can select the items with the left mouse button depressed and drag them into the current drawing file, releasing the left mouse button when the cursor is over the resident drawing file for a 1:1 scale placement. Multiple items can be selected and copied at the same time, by adhering to the multiple selection methods of the Windows environment. If a different scale is desired, using the right mouse will provide the menu shown in Figure 8-17 to allow changes before placement. The **Insert Block** item shown leads to the **Insert** dialog box as seen in Figure 8-13, which allows precision placement, nonuniform scaling, rotation, and change of units.

**Note:**
From DesignCenter, items of interest can also be dragged and dropped onto a tool palette. Tool palettes have many of the same properties as DesignCenter. While tool palettes cannot be used to find items, they can be taken from drawing to drawing as part of a template and also exported for others to use. See Unit II for more information.

## EXTERNAL REFERENCES

External Reference: A special block that creates and maintains a live link between drawing files.

***External References,*** sometimes referred to as **Xrefs** can be a viable alternative command for the attachment of a selected drawing file to the resident drawing file. When a block is inserted into a drawing file, the process stores all the information regarding the definition in the active file, enlarging the resident file accordingly and thus maintaining no link to the original file. Therefore, if the original block file were to change, the block insertions in the active drawing would not.

The use of an **External Reference** brings in two distinct advantages. First, the externally referenced file is attached through a file-linking process from any location available to the computer (see Figure 8-18). This file-linking process does not bring the entire contents of the

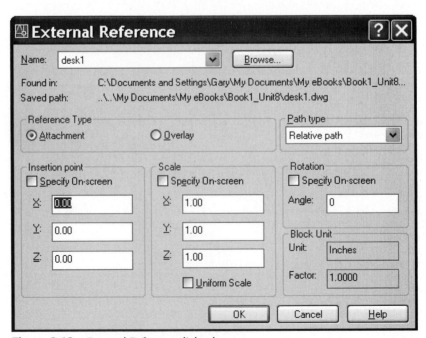

Figure 8-18    External Reference dialog box

definition into the resident file. It maintains a link to the file location and merely brings a display of the file's content to the resident drawing file on the opening of the resident file. This file-linking process leads to the second advantage. If the referenced original file were to change, the changes would be reflected in all the locations to which the External Reference is attached upon the next reload.

A single **External Reference** can be attached to multiple drawings at the same time and multiple external references can be attached to a single drawing file as well. Maintaining this link is an important concept because you are sure to be using the most current version of a drawing file (see Figure 8-19). This process also increases uniformity throughout an office when multiple operators use the same and most current version of the drawings.

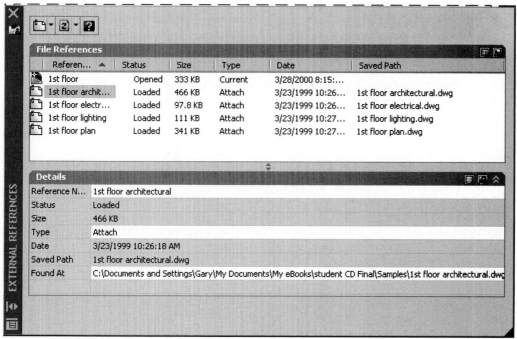

**Figure 8-19**    External References for AutoCAD 2008 as a palette

Another advantage of **Xrefs** is the access of the layers, to allow changes in visibility and color that can be assigned to that attachment or overlay (see Figure 8-20). This allows the first floor to be easily screened into a gray state, showing the second floor in the active colors to locate doors, walls, and windows more easily. Another example is to allow changing colors of existing contour lines from proposed lines for easier editing.

The attachment of an external reference is done through the **Insert** menu. In this menu you find the **EXTERNAL** or **DWG REFERENCE** command. Upon selecting this command, you will be prompted to `Select the referenced file` through a dialog box similar to the select file dialog box (see Figure 8-18). Once the file is selected, the **External Reference** dialog box appears. This box displays the file **Name** along with the file location path at the top of the dialog box. To maintain the intelligence of the

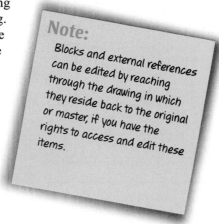

**Note:**

Blocks and external references can be edited by reaching through the drawing in which they reside back to the original or master, if you have the rights to access and edit these items.

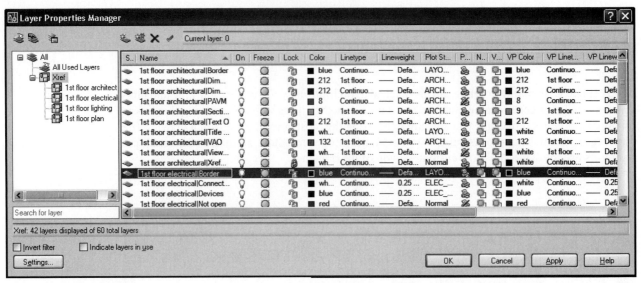

Figure 8-20    Layer Properties Manager showing externally referenced layers with the drawing name as a prefix

external reference the **Reference Type** should be an **Attachment** and the **Path type** should be **Full path.**

When you attach an external reference you have all the same options you had with block insertion. **Insertion point, Scale,** and **Rotation** act in the same manner as they did with the block insertion. When the command is complete the externally referenced drawing file is displayed at the insertion point location. This sequence is shown in Figures 8-21, 8-22, and 8-23.

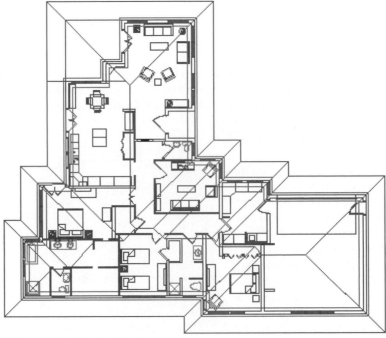

Figure 8-21    The house plan

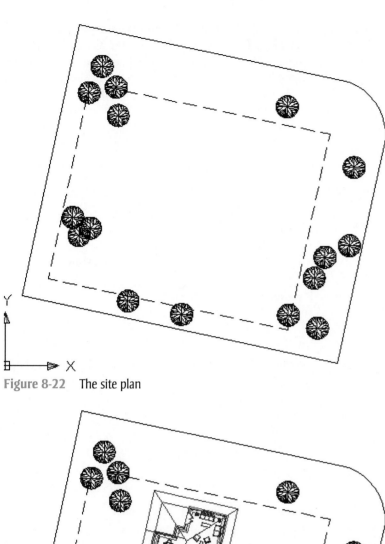

**Figure 8-22**   The site plan

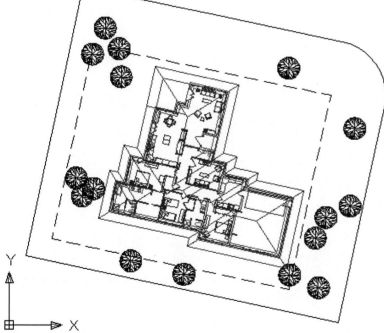

**Figure 8-23**   The site plan with the house plan as an external reference

# SUMMARY

This unit introduced you to the use of layers, groups, and blocks for organizing AutoCAD drawings. First, you learned how to implement a layering scheme by creating layers with the **Layer Properties Manager,** giving them unique names, and defining their properties, as well as how to modify layers with the **Layers** toolbar and its commands (drop-down menu icons, **Make Object's Layer Current, Layer Previous,** and **Layerstate**). Then you learned how to organize selected sets of objects into groups using the **Object Grouping** dialog box, a process that enables you to manipulate the objects as a single unit. Subsequently, you were introduced to the creation and manipulation of block using the **Block Definition** and **Insert** dialog boxes, the **EXPLODE** command, and the **DesignCenter** palette. Blocks are series of objects, saved under unique names that may be used repeatedly in a drawing. Using block results in more compact, consistent drawings that allow commands to be executed quickly, improving productivity. Finally,

you learned how to attach **External References (Xrefs)** from the **Insert** menu (**EXTERNAL** or **DWG REFERENCE** command). Xrefs are special blocks that create and maintain live links between drawing files, enabling the contents of externally referenced file(s) to be displayed in the resident file and providing multiple operators with the same and most current version of drawing files.

## CHAPTER TEST QUESTIONS

### Multiple Choice

1. Properties of a layer can include all the following except:
   a. Color
   b. Linetype
   c. Coordinates
   d. Lineweight

2. Which of the following is not a display control for a layer?
   a. On/Off
   b. Freeze/Thaw
   c. Lock/Unlock
   d. Plot/No Plot

3. A group is a named set of
   a. Entities
   b. Menu commands

   c. System variables
   d. Layers

4. To place a block in a drawing file which command would you use?
   a. Import
   b. Open
   c. Merge
   d. Insert

5. Which of the following cannot be brought in through the DesignCenter?
   a. Layers
   b. Blocks
   c. Dimension Styles
   d. System Variables

### Matching

a. _____ Block
b. _____ Base point
c. _____ Overlay
d. _____ Layer
e. _____ Bind

1. A way of using an external reference
2. To make an external reference a permanent part of a drawing file
3. A form of a drawing's organization
4. The control point of a block
5. The result of combining many entities into one object

### True or False

1. True or False: Layers can only be created in the **Layer Manager** dialog box.

2. True or False: Groups must have a unique control point.

3. True or False: Blocks are the opposite of Groups.

4. True or False: The DesignCenter allows you to grab layers and blocks from other drawing files.

5. True or False: External references maintain a link to the original file.

## CHAPTER PROJECTS

### Chapter Project 8-1

Interview various consultants, government agencies, manufacturing companies, architects, and other CAD users about the following:
a. Storage of drawings and naming conventions
b. Storage of blocks and naming conventions
c. Use of external references
d. Use of layer standards

### Chapter Project 8-2

Make a presentation to the class on "How I Store My Drawings and Blocks."

### Chapter Project 8-3

Download various items from the DC Online to add to your library and show the class. Explain why you chose these items.

## TUTORIALS

### Tutorial 8-1: Bedroom Drawing

1. Start a new drawing.
2. Drawing units **Length Type** should be set to **Architectural** (see Figure 8-24).

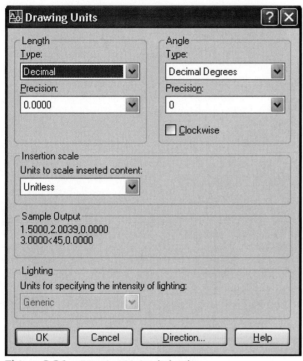

**Figure 8-24**    Drawing Units dialog box

3. Draw a **RECTANG**le that is 15′ × 13′ and save the drawing as **My Bedroom** in your **Workskills** folder (see Figure 8-25).

**Figure 8-25**    Your bedroom drawing

4. Start **DesignCenter** and navigate to the following folders:
   **C:\Program Files\AutoCAD 2008\Sample\DesignCenter\**
   **Home-Space Planner.dwg.HouseDesigner.dwg,** and **Kitchen.**
   **dwg** and the DC Online.
5. To complete the drawing drag and drop your bedroom furniture
   (see Figure 8-26). Remember to show a door and windows.
6. Save your drawing in your **Workskills** folder.

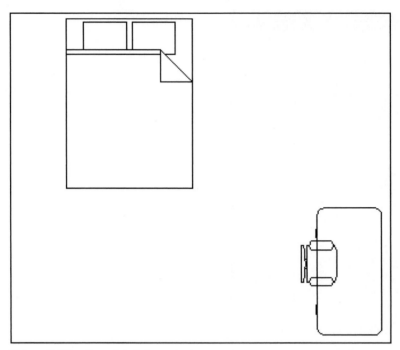

**Figure 8-26**   Completed dream bedroom

## Tutorial 8-2: Creating a Site Plan

1. Open the **Site** drawing from the Student CD.
2. **Zoom Extents** to fill the screen with the display (see Figure 8-27).

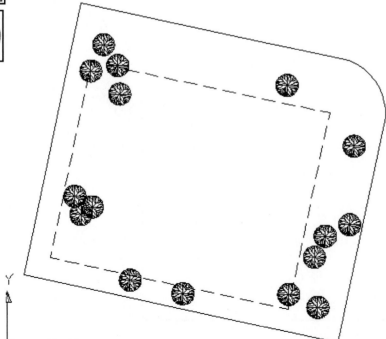
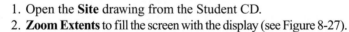

**Figure 8-27**   Site drawing

3. From the **Format** menu pick **Drawing Units** and be sure the **Insertion scale** is set to Feet, as the **Site** drawing from the surveyor team is in Feet (see Figure 8-28).

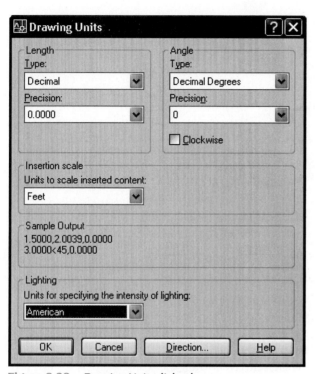

**Figure 8-28**    Drawing Units dialog box

4. From the **Insert** menu browse to find the "house" drawing (see Figure 8-29), and insert it in a good location (see Figure 8-30). You may need to move and rotate the house to fit on the site plan inside the dashed lines (setbacks) and away from trees.

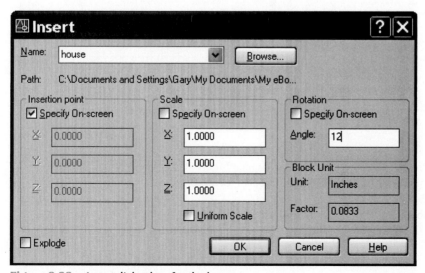

**Figure 8-29**    Insert dialog box for the house

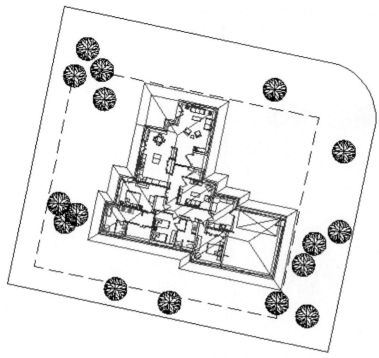

**Figure 8-30**    House inserted as block into site plan

5. Examine the **Layer Properties Manager** (see Figure 8-31) and see what layers are available for control.
6. Save the drawing as **Site1** in the **Workskills** folder.
7. Erase the "house" and remove all unused layers from the **Layer Properties Manager.**

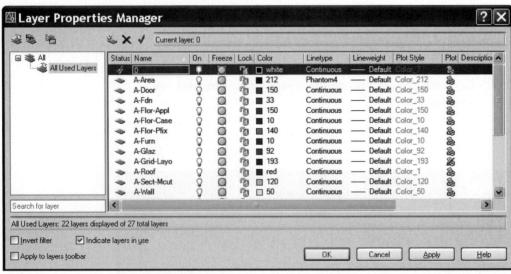

**Figure 8-31**    Layers with house as block

8. Insert the "house" as an external reference (see Figure 8-32) to result in basically the same image (see Figure 8-33) as Figure 8-30.
9. Examine the **Layer Properties Manager** (see Figure 8-34) and notice the difference in the layer names, control, and visibility.

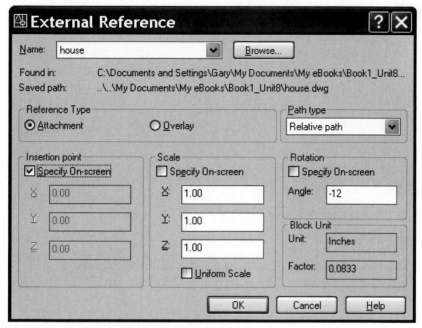

Figure 8-32    External Reference dialog box

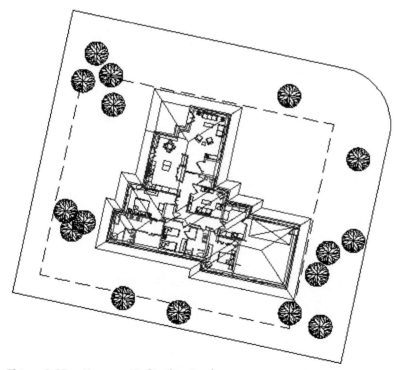

Figure 8-33    House as Xref in the site plan

10. Save your drawing as **Site2** in the **Workskills** folder.
11. Turn On/Off various layers and change the colors of the externally referenced layers and watch the change to the drawing.
12. Close the drawing and end the work session.

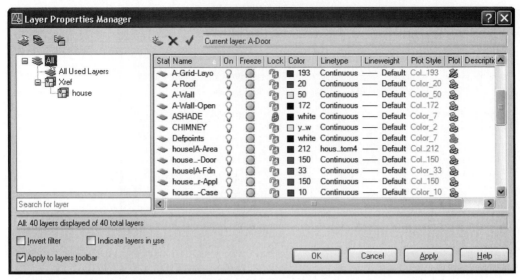

**Figure 8-34**    Typical layers using an external reference

## Tutorial 8-3: Creating a Basic Circuit

The following tutorial creates the basic circuit drawing shown in Figure 8-35. The process for creating this drawing is as follows:

- First make three block definitions.
- Insert the symbols in the drawing.
  1. Open the **Mechanical Block Tutorial** drawing (see Figure 8-36) from the Student CD.
  2. In the **Draw** menu, select the **Block** cascading menu and choose the **MAKE** command.

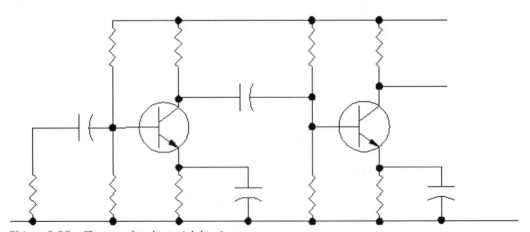

**Figure 8-35**    The completed tutorial drawing

3. In the **Block Definition** dialog box (see Figure 8-37), enter the word "RESISTOR" in the **Name** field.
4. Click on the **Select objects** icon. This sends you back to the drawing screen to select the entities that make up the block. Place a selection window, either a **CROSSING** or **WINDOW** version, around the entities that form the resistor

TRANSISTOR          RESISTOR          CAPACITOR

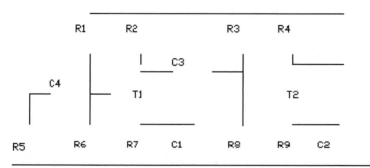

**Figure 8-36**   The initial drawing

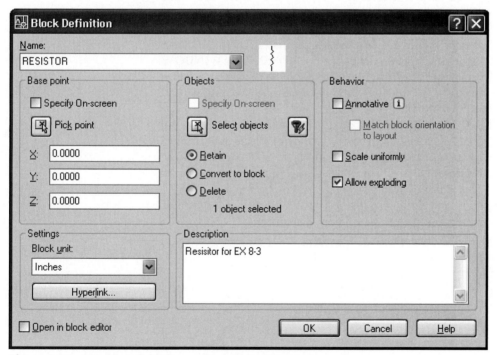

**Figure 8-37**   The Block Definition or Block Make dialog box

(see Figure 8-38). Hit **<Enter>** to complete the selection process and return to the **Block Definition** dialog box.

5. Select the **Pick point** icon. This sends you back to the drawing screen to select a control point for the block. Select the point marked with the **X** in Figure 8-38. Be sure to use the **ENDpoint OBJECT SNAP** when selecting the control point. This increases accuracy when inserting the block.

6. Finish the Block definition procedure by clicking on the **OK** button near the bottom of the dialog box. Although there are

a few other areas to the **Block Definition** dialog box, the default values for these other areas will work fine for this tutorial. Now let's repeat these steps to make two other blocks.

7. In the **Draw** menu, select the **Block** cascading menu and choose the **MAKE** command.

8. In the **Block Definition** dialog box, enter the word "CAPACITOR" in the **Name** field.

9. Click on the **Select objects** icon. This sends you back to the drawing screen to select the entities that make up the block. Place a selection window, either a **CROSSING** or **WINDOW** version, around the entities that form the capacitor (see Figure 8-39). Hit **Enter** to complete the selection process and return to the **Block Definition** dialog box.

10. Select the **Pick point** icon. This sends you back to the drawing screen to select a control point for the block. Select the point marked with the **X** in Figure 8-39. Be sure to use **ENDpoint Object Snap** when selecting the control point. This increases accuracy when inserting the block.

11. Finish the block definition procedure by clicking on the **OK** button near the bottom of the dialog box.

12. In the **Draw** menu, select the **Block** cascading menu and choose the **MAKE** command.

13. In the **Block Definition** dialog box, enter the word "TRANSISTOR" in the **Name** field.

14. Click on the **Select objects** icon. This sends you back to the drawing screen to select the entities that make up the block. Place a selection window, either a **CROSSING** or **WINDOW** version, around the entities that form the transistor (see Figure 8-40). Hit **Enter** to complete the selection process and return to the **Block Definition** dialog box.

15. Select the **Pick point** icon. This sends you back to the drawing screen to select a control point for the block. Select the point marked with the **X** in Figure 8-40. Be sure to use **ENDpoint Object Snap** when selecting the control point. This increases accuracy when inserting the block.

16. Finish the block definition procedure by clicking on the **OK** button near the bottom of the dialog box.

With the blocks defined the next steps are to place the blocks in the drawing as shown in Figure 8-41.

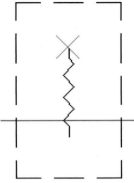

**Figure 8-38**   The objects that define the resistor

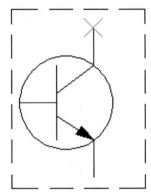

**Figure 8-39**   The objects that define the capacitor

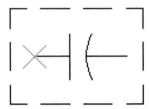

**Figure 8-40**   The objects that define the transistor

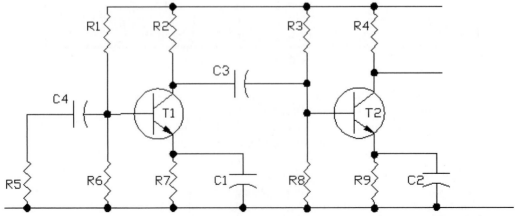

**Figure 8-41**   The completed drawing; the text represents ID tags to aid in placement of the blocks

17. From the **Insert** menu select **Block** (see Figure 8-42). This brings up the **Insert** dialog box (see Figure 8-43).

Figure 8-42    Insert Block menu

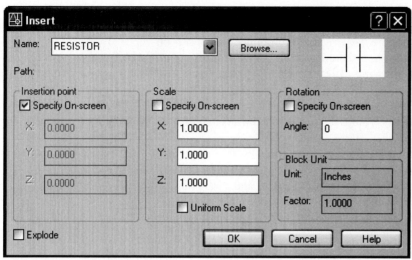

Figure 8-43    The Insert dialog box

18. From the **Name** drop-down list select "RESISTOR."
19. Select the **OK** button to return to the drawing screen.
20. Using the **ENDpoint Object Snap** insert the **R1** resistor into the circuit drawing as shown in Figure 8-41. Make the connection based on the control point and the correct endpoint of the lines in the tutorial file.
21. Repeat Steps 18–20 to insert the remaining eight resistors. Keep in mind there are **ENDpoints** in the locations where the resistors will be connecting, too.
22. From the **Insert** menu select **Block** (see Figure 8-42). This brings up the **Insert** dialog box (see Figure 8-43).
23. From the **Name** drop-down list select "CAPACITOR." In the **Rotation** area of the dialog box, enter a value of **−90** for the **Angle.**
24. Select the **OK** button to return to the drawing screen.
25. Using the **ENDpoint Object Snap** insert the **C1** capacitor as shown in Figure 8-41. Make the connection based on the control point and the correct endpoint of the lines in the tutorial file.
26. Repeat Steps 22–25 to insert the **C2** capacitor. Keep in mind there are **ENDpoints** in the locations where the capacitors will be connecting.
27. From the **Insert** menu select **Block** (see Figure 8-42). This brings up the **Insert** dialog box (see Figure 8-43).
28. From the **Name** drop-down list select "CAPACITOR."
29. Select the **OK** button to return to the drawing screen.
30. Using the **ENDpoint Object Snap** insert the **C3** capacitor as shown in Figure 8-41. Make the connection based on the control point and the correct endpoint of the lines in the tutorial file.
31. Repeat Steps 27–30 to insert the **C4** capacitor.
32. From the **Insert** menu select **Block** (see Figure 8-42). This brings up the **Insert** dialog box (see Figure 8-43).

33. From the **Name** drop-down list select "TRANSISTOR."
34. In the **Scale** area of the dialog box, turn on the **Uniform Scale** option by placing a check mark in the box; enter a value of **.75** for the **X** value.
35. Select the **OK** button to return to the drawing screen.
36. Using the **ENDpoint Object Snap** insert the **T1** transistor as shown in Figure 8-41. Make the connection based on the control point and the correct endpoint of the lines in the tutorial drawing file. Keep in mind there are **ENDpoints** in the locations where the transistors will be connecting, too.
37. Repeat this process (Steps 32–36) to insert the remaining **T2** transistor.
38. The solder joints can be created by using a **DONUT** command. From the **Draw** menu select the **DONUT** command.
39. Enter a value of **0** for the inside diameter and a value of **.05** for the outside diameter. Then **Object Snap** to the locations that show a solder joint symbol. Refer to Figure 8-44 for the solder joint locations.
40. Save your drawing as **T8-3** in your **Workskills** folder.

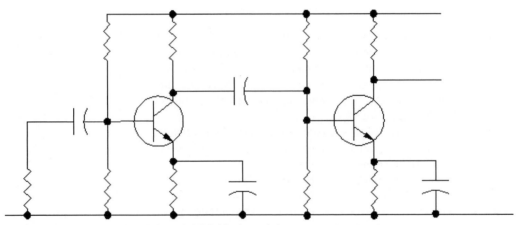

**Figure 8-44**   The completed drawing with blocks and donuts

# PRACTICE EXERCISES

## Practice Exercise 8-1

1. Create a classroom similar to the one in Figure 8-8 by first building a block consisting of a 60″ × 30″ desk that holds a computer system and books with a chair using new or existing blocks from the DesignCenter library at **C:\Program Files\AutoCAD 2008\Sample\ DesignCenter\Home - Space Planner.dwg.**
2. Save the desk block as **Desk6030.**
3. Save your drawing as **Classroom1** in the **Workskills** folder.

## Practice Exercise 8-2

1. Open the drawing **Civil1** from your Student CD (see Figure 8-45).

Figure 8-45    The Civil1 drawing

2. Attach as external references the drawings "Pond Contours," "Roads," and "Existing Contours" to make the complete drawing (see Figure 8-46).

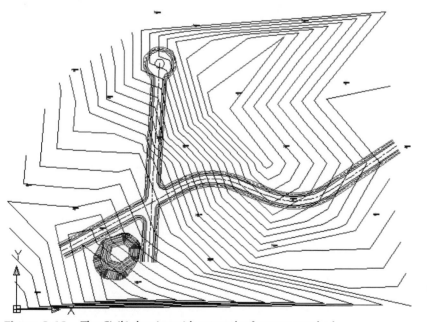

Figure 8-46    The Civil1 drawing with external references attached

3. Review the layers to avoid color conflicts and change as needed (see Figure 8-47).
4. Save the drawing as **Civil Complete** in your **Workskills** folder.

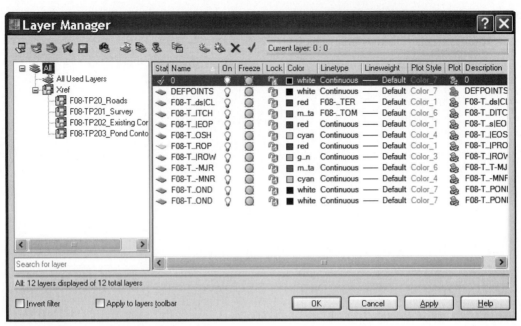

**Figure 8-47**     The Civil1 drawing layer list

# Editing with Grips

# 9

## *Chapter* Objectives

- Demonstrate grip editing techniques.
- Identify grip options.
- Recognize the grip control points for all objects.
- Improve productivity with grips.
- Edit object properties through grips.
- Identify additional right-click options.

## INTRODUCTION

*Grips* are often referred to as automatic editing. The AutoCAD program, in general, is command-driven. This means you pick a command first (verb), and then the object for the operation (noun). Grips reverse the process to allow you to choose the object first (noun) and then select the action or command (verb).

**grip:** A predefined control point used for editing the selected object.

## ELEMENTARY CONCEPT OF GRIP EDITING

Through the **Grips** series of commands, you can execute the five basic editing commands: **STRETCH, MOVE, ROTATE, MIRROR**, and **SCALE.** The **Copy** and **Basepoint** options can accompany any of these commands. This series of commands expedites the traditional commands through the use of predefined control points known as **Grips.** The execution of a grip command presents you with a series of predefined control point boxes.

The advent of the Grips series of commands greatly increased the productivity of the basic modify commands. An understanding of their accessibility and simple execution is a job skill that will increase speed, accuracy, and consistency within a drawing file.

Each entity has the same predefined grips, which can be shown as colored boxes. **Grips** is a system variable that will enable grips (if set to 1) or disable grips (if set to 0). It is reflected in the check mark next to **Enable grips** in the **Options** dialog box under the **Selection** tab (see Figure 9-1).

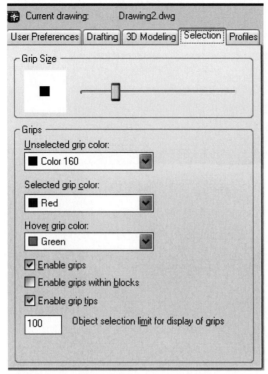

**Figure 9-1**   Grips dialog area of the Selection tab in the Options dialog box

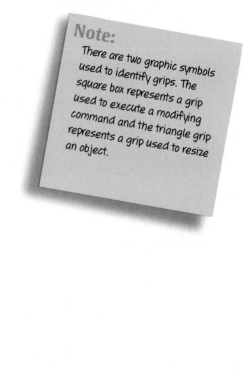

## GRIP CONTROL POINTS

**grip box:** Graphic symbol used to show grip control points.

**grip control points:** Predefined locations on an entity used to modify the selected object.

*Grip boxes* are shown at the same location for each of the entities. A line has three ***grip control points***—each endpoint and the midpoint of the line (see Figure 9-2). An arc has three grip control points—at the endpoints of the arc and the midpoint of the arc—plus three directional control points and a center control point for a total of seven (see Figure 9-2). A circle has five grip control points—one at each quadrant point and one at the center point of the circle (see Figure 9-2). Single-line text has a grip control point at the insertion point of the text (see Figure 9-2), while **MTEXT** has control points at the corners of the text box (see Figure 9-3). The polylines (see Figure 9-3) and splines have a control point on each vertex of the polyline. Dimensions have five grip control points—two control the extension line locations, two control the dimension line locations, and one control point controls the dimension text location (see Figure 9-3). Leader lines have three grip control points (see Figure 9-4). Finally, a block definition can have a single control point at the insertion point of the block (see Figure 9-5), or you can show all the grips for each object that make up the block definition (see Figure 9-6). This is controlled through the **Options**

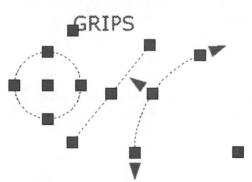

**Figure 9-2**   View of grips on line, arc, circle, and single-line text

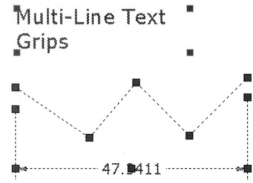

**Figure 9-3**   View of grips on multiline text (4), polylines (at each vertex), and dimensions (5)

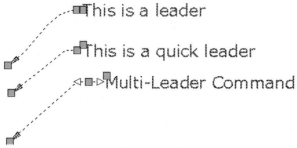

**Figure 9-4**    Grips on the various leader lines

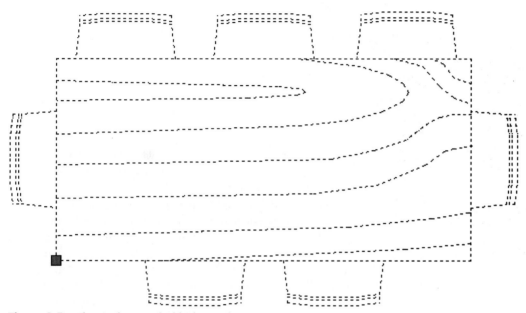

**Figure 9-5**    The single grip of a block is at the insert point

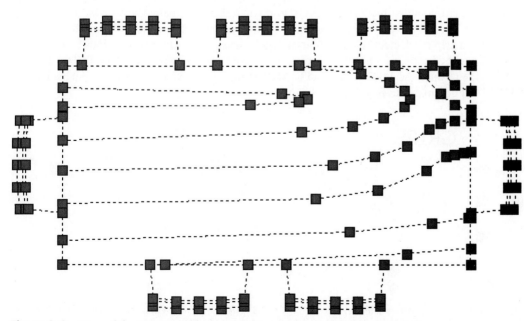

**Figure 9-6**    View of the Figure 9-5 block with internal grips displayed and selected

dialog box under the **Selection** tab as seen in Figure 9-1. The maximum number of grips that can be displayed is set by the **GRIPOBJLIMIT** system variable, and its default value is 100.

## MODIFYING OBJECTS WITH GRIPS

Before selecting or gripping an object, AutoCAD 2008 highlights the object as the cursor passes over it as shown in Figure 9-7. This rollover feature previews an entity before it is chosen to verify it is the one you want. This feature helps to avoid errors and confusion in the object selection process.

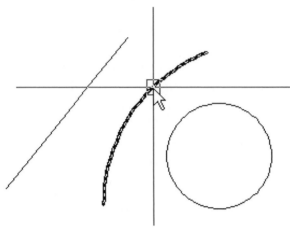

**Figure 9-7**    Rollover highlighting of an entity in the drawing before selection

**unselected grip:** The status of a grip control point identifying an object.

**selected grip:** The status of a grip control point involved in an editing function.

**hover grip:** The status of a grip control point when there are multiple choices in a grip location.

**Grips** are activated when an object is selected with the command prompt in place and no command is currently running. At that time the entity goes into a highlighted mode (the object will be shown as a dashed, or highlighted entity) and the grip control points appear as blue boxes (default setting is color 160, or blue). **Grips** have three stages—unselected, selected, and hover. In an ***unselected grip,*** the object is first selected and shows the entity in a highlighted mode with blue boxes. In a ***selected grip,*** you click on one of the blue boxes, which then becomes a red box (see Figure 9-8). At the time a grip is in a selected state, you can then cycle through the choices of available editing commands. Objects that are in a selected state are directly affected by the grip editing function, as are objects in an unselected state, except when you are using the **STRETCH** option of the grip commands.

If the cursor is held over an unselected grip, the color changes to green, indicating a ***hover grip.*** Hover grips aid in the correct selection of a grip when there are many grips in one location (see Figure 9-9). They can display preview menus of activities that can be done with that chosen grip.

When a grip is selected (red box) you can cycle through the editing commands by hitting the space bar on the keyboard. The cycle is always the same, starting with the **STRETCH** command and moving through the **MOVE, ROTATE, MIRROR,** and **SCALE** commands, and back to the **STRETCH** command, to begin the cycle again.

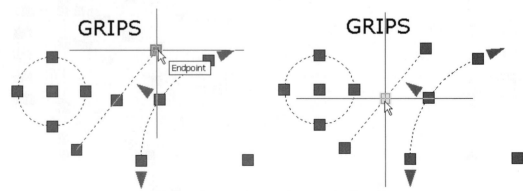

**Figure 9-8**    The red grip is selected

**Figure 9-9**    The cursor is placed over a grip and hovers

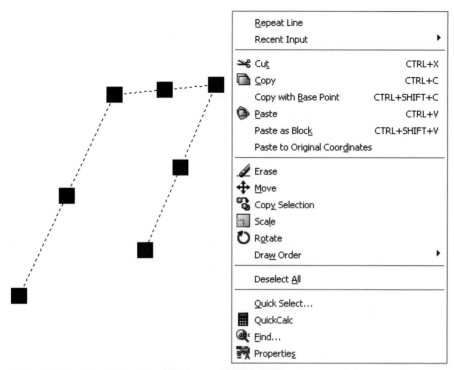

**Figure 9-10**    The right-click menu for unselected grips

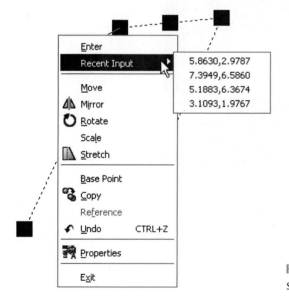

**Figure 9-11**    The right-click menu for a selected grip

A second method to select the **Grip** editing commands is to execute a right mouse click when a grip is in either the unselected or selected stage. This executes a **Grip** pop-up menu (see Figure 9-10 for an unselected grip, Figure 9-11 for a selected grip) at the current location of the cursor, from which you can choose the editing command you wish to use. To **Exit,** or **Cancel,** a grip function, hit the **Esc** key at any time, use the **Exit** or **Deselect** menu items, or begin another AutoCAD command from a menu or toolbar.

## OBJECTS, GRIPS, AND HOVERING FOR MENUS AND MORE

As more software is developed using object technology, grips are becoming more intelligent, as shown in Figure 9-12 from the Autodesk Architectural Desktop software.

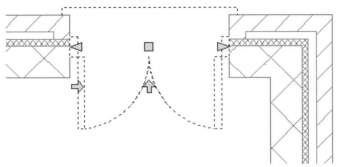

**Figure 9-12** A door object showing grips (from Autodesk's Architectural Desktop software)

Notice the door object has the basic three grips of a line. The two ends show directional operations while the other two directional grips are used to flip the hinge point and thus the door. When you "hover" over an object's grip, tip boxes may appear to explain its operation. Some object-oriented grips have menus of operations as shown in Figure 9-13 from the Architectural Desktop program. More software will in time take advantage of this technology to enhance the productivity with this kind of automated editing.

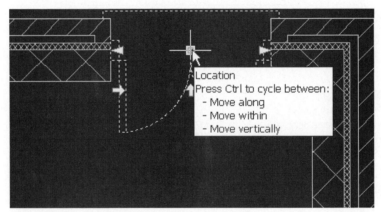

**Figure 9-13** A door object showing grips and the menu (from Autodesk's Architectural Desktop software)

## GRIP OPTIONS

Along with the editing commands, there are a few options within the execution of the grip commands that you may choose to exercise. Each command has a **Copy** option, which creates a new entity of the current selection set, based on the editing function. For instance, you can **MOVE** and **Copy** an entity, or you can **ROTATE** and **Copy** an entity. Along with the **Copy** option, you have the option to redefine the operation's **Base Point** with any of the grip editing commands. By default, the **Selected Grip** (red box) is used as the **Base Point** for the execution of the command. If you choose not to use this selected grip as the control point, you can select the **Base Point** option and redefine the **Base Point** to any other grip or select any point by coordinates, object snap, or other methods on the screen.

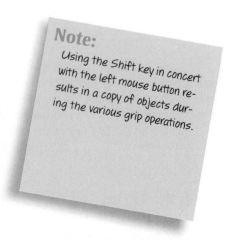

**Note:**
Using the Shift key in concert with the left mouse button results in a copy of objects during the various grip operations.

The editing commands of **ROTATE** and **SCALE** also have an option of **Reference** available. This option allows you to select two points on the screen that define a line, and then specify a rotation degree based on the AutoCAD 360° increment (0° is east and counterclockwise is positive). Upon execution, the objects are rotated, pointing the defined reference line to that degree in space.

The final four options available on the shortcut, pop-up menu are always available. They are **Undo,** to reverse the previous function, **Properties,** which launches the properties panel displaying the properties of the selected entities and **Exit,** or **Cancel,** which returns you to the command prompt.

The following operations are available with each grip editing command.

- **STRETCH** When a grip is selected, it can be moved to a new location, changing the dimension of the entity (see Figure 9-14). When a midpoint grip, a centerpoint grip, a text grip, or a block reference grip is selected, the resulting action is a **MOVE** command instead of a **STRETCH** command.

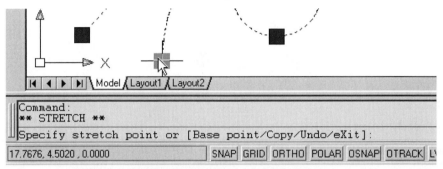

**Figure 9-14**    The Grip STRETCH command line and prompts

- **MOVE** This option moves the selected entity, using the selected grip as a base point (see Figure 9-15), to a new location specified by a second selected point. This command also moves all entities that are currently in the unselected state. If you want the original entities to remain in the original location, you can select the **Copy** option, which creates a second set of entities at the new location. If you choose not to use the selected grip as the base point, you may select the **Base Point** option to select a different point as the control point.

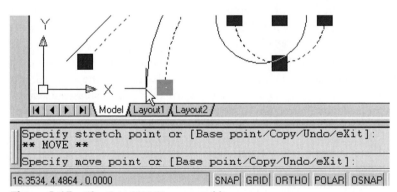

**Figure 9-15**    The Grip MOVE command line

- **ROTATE** The **ROTATE** command (see Figure 9-16) rotates the entity around the **Selected Grip Point** by selecting a new point for the direction of rotation that you specify. An alternate method to the dragging operation is to specify the amount of rotation through a keyboard entry. As in the previous commands, the options of **Base Point** and **Copy** are available for the selection of a new control point or the creation of multiple copies of the entities around the rotation point.

- **SCALE** This command changes the size of an entity, or entities, relative to a base point (see Figure 9-17). If you move a grip control point outward, the entity increases in size, whereas if you move the point inward, the entity decreases in size. You can also choose to enter a value through a keyboard entry for a relative scale factor. The original object size

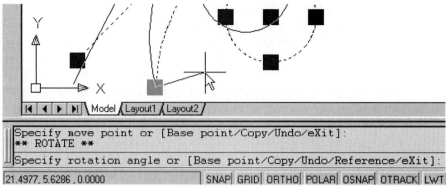

Figure 9-16     The Grip ROTATE command prompts

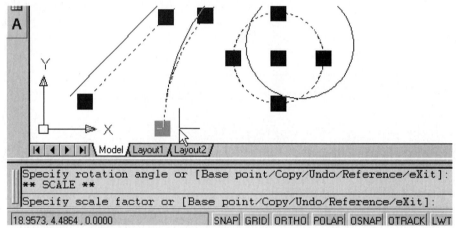

Figure 9-17     The Grip SCALE command prompts

has a value of 1.0. Entering a 2.0 doubles the size of the object. Entering a 3.0 triples the size. To decrease size, you put in a decimal value such as 0.5, which decreases the object by half. The **SCALE** command uses the **Selected Grip** (red box) as the base point. All scaling operations are relative to that base point. You can choose a different base point through the **Base Point** option and then execute a **Copy** option, leaving the original entities unchanged but still scaling the copied entities.

- **MIRROR** The **MIRROR** command (see Figure 9-18) inverts an entity over a temporary mirror line. By default, one end of the mirror line is at the location of the selected grip while the other end is defined by the operator. The use of **ORTHO** increases accuracy when mirroring in an orthogonal direction (horizontal or vertical only). The **Base Point**

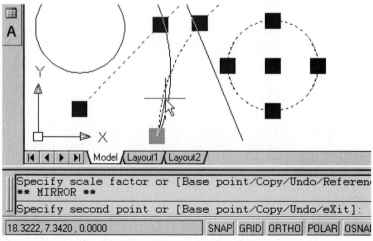

Figure 9-18     The Grip MIRROR command prompts

option allows for the repositioning of the first **Endpoint** of the mirror line, while a **Copy** option creates a second copy of the entity, leaving the original in place.

- **Delete** When using grips to delete entities, you will not encounter questions about deleting source objects. They will simply be deleted when the **Delete** key is pressed.

- **Grip Snap Setting** Grips have the ability to create a temporary snapping distance based on the first copy's input when it is created. To activate the snapping distance, simply hold down the **Shift** key when placing additional copies. The future copies will be controlled in the same fashion as the **SNAP** function in the status line. The snapping distance is equal to the original distance made from the first copy, and has the same value in all directions. As shown in Figures 9-19 and 9-20, a circle is to be located 10 units away from its current location. You enter **C** for copies of the entities and **@10,0** to establish the distance for the **Grip SNAP** as shown in Figure 9-19. The result is shown in Figure 9-20. By holding down

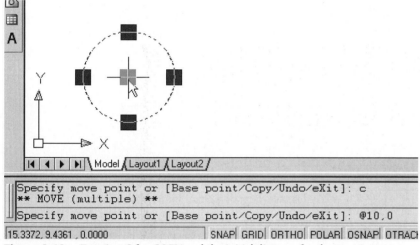

**Figure 9-19**    Entering C for COPY and the initial distance for the next insert location and establishing the Grip SNAP temporary distance

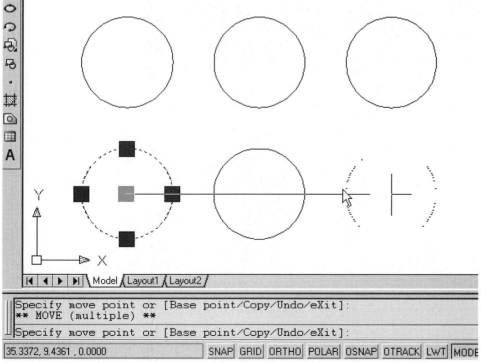

**Figure 9-20**    With the Shift key depressed, the relative dimension input is repeated in all directions as a SNAP; picking with the left mouse places another copy of the entity

the **Shift** key and picking locations with the pick button on the mouse, the copies are placed 10 units apart in the X and/or Y directions.

Control of most grip system variables is located in the **Options** dialog box under the **Selection** tab shown in Figure 9-1. Here you can turn grips on or off, change the size of grip boxes, and alter the color of grips at the different stages.

# SUMMARY

The editing of objects in AutoCAD is usually command-driven, requiring the user to pick a specific editing command first, and then the object(s) to be edited. Grips, which consist of predefined control points, reverse this process, allowing the user to pick the object first, then select one of the five basic editing commands (**STRETCH, MOVE, ROTATE, MIRROR,** and **SCALE**) from a preview or a pop-up (right mouse button) menu. In this unit you have learned how to use grip control points to modify objects such as lines, arcs, circles, single-line and multiline text, polylines and splines, dimensions, leader lines, and block definitions. You also learned about the increasingly intelligent nature of grips (e.g., tip boxes and menus that appear when the mouse cursor "hovers" over an object's grips) with improvements in software technology. Finally, you learned about the options (**Copy, Base Point, Undo, Properties, Exit,** and **Cancel**) you can use together with the grip editing commands as well as the delete and grip snap setting operations.

# CHAPTER TEST QUESTIONS

## Multiple Choice

1. Which of the following is **not** a type of grip?

   a. Hover
   b. Selected
   c. Unselected
   d. Floating

2. To continually copy a gripped object, what key would you use?

   a. ALT
   b. Shift
   c. CTRL
   d. Space bar

3. To cycle through the automated editing options, what key would you use?

   a. ALT
   b. Shift

   c. CTRL
   d. Space bar

4. The function of a **Base Point** option is to:

   a. Redefine the base point
   b. Measure from the base point
   c. Delete the symbol
   d. Launch an Options menu

5. Settings for the **Grip** commands can be found in what dialog box?

   a. Format
   b. Configure
   c. Options
   d. SetVAR

## Matching

a. _____ Hot Grip

b. _____ Reference

c. _____ **GRIPOBJLIMIT**

d. _____ Hover Grip

e. _____ Warm Grip

1. An aid in the correct placement

2. Unselected grip

3. Scale option

4. Selected grip

5. Maximum number of grips

## True or False

1. True or False: A right mouse click will access the **Grip** shortcut menu.

2. True or False: Grips are on all the time and can never be shut off.

3. True or False: Grips have no control over the properties of an object.

4. True or False: A second point location can be established with relative (@x,y) coordinates.

5. True or False: Grips will allow you to select the object first, then the command.

## CHAPTER PROJECTS

### Chapter Project 9-1

Explain the following setting variables and their relationship to grips:

a. PICKFIRST
b. GRIPBLOCK
c. GRIPSIZE
d. GRIPOBJLIMIT
e. GRIPTIPS
f. GRIPCOLOR
g. GRIPHOT
h. GRIPHOVER

### Chapter Project 9-2

List three production advantages when using grips.

### Chapter Project 9-3

List three disadvantages of using grips.

## TUTORIALS

### Tutorial 9-1: Basic Operations with Grips

1. Start AutoCAD.
2. Pick the **File** menu and choose **Open.**
3. Using the drop-down area at the top of the **Select File** dialog box, maneuver to the **C:\Program Files\AutoCAD 2008\Samples** folder or access the sample folder on the Student CD.
4. Scroll through the list of drawing files **(.dwg)** and choose one to open by picking the **Open** button in the lower right of the dialog box:
   a. **Architectural Drawings**—8th Floor, Hotel, Hummer, Stadium, Taisei, or Wilhome
   b. **Building Services**—8th Floor
   c. **Civil Drawings**—Hotel or SPCA Site Plan
   d. **Facilities Management**—Db_samp
   e. **Landscaping**—SPCA Site Plan
   f. **Mechanical**—Oil Module, Welding Fixture 1, or Welding Fixture Model
   g. **Presentation**—Hotel, Hummer, Stadium, or Welding Fixture Model
   h. **Process Piping**—Oil Module
   i. **Structural**—MKMPlan or Oil Module
5. Practice placing **Grips** on various entities in these drawings. Remember that **<Esc>** will cancel the grips.
6. Access the various **Grip** command options with these entities and watch the command line for instructions. Feel free to press **<Esc>** to cancel any operation.
7. To end your work session on a drawing, go to the **File** menu and pick **Close.** Pick the answer **No** so no modifications are saved at this time. If you want to open and examine another drawing go back to Step 4.
8. To end your AutoCAD session, go to the **File** menu and pick **Exit.** If a drawing is active, pick the answer **No** so no modifications are saved at this time. The program will then end.

## Tutorial 9-2: Creating a Storage Warehouse Plan

Create a storage warehouse plan that has six rows of 10′ × 10′ storage spaces that are in 160′ long buildings.

1. Start a new drawing or use the architectural template created in Unit 2, Practice Exercise 2-2.
2. In the **Format** menu set the following parameters:
   a. **LAYERS:** Current: WALLS—color = cyan
      DOORS—color = red
      DIMS—color = magenta
   b. Drawing **UNITS:** Length = Architectural
   c. Drawing **LIMITS:** Lower Left—0′,0′
      Upper Right—200′,200′
3. Process a **ZOOM ALL** command to reset the display screen to the above drawing limits.
4. Draw a rectangle by choosing the icon (see Figure 9-21) (or using another method) with the first point at **10′,10′** and the other corner at **20′,20′,** as shown in Figure 9-22. This unit represents the lower left storage area for the site.

**Figure 9-21**   The Draw/Rectangle command icon

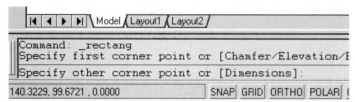

**Figure 9-22**   Typical inputs for the creation of a rectangle

5. Using the **Grip MOVE** with **Copy** option and **Grip SNAP,** copy the first unit at 30′, 40′, 70′, 80′, and 110′ to the right to make the first row of the storage units as shown in Figure 9-23.

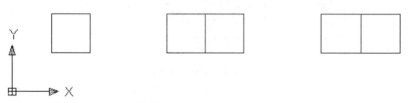

**Figure 9-23**   First row of the warehouse plan

6. Using the **Grip MIRROR** with **Copy** option on all the rectangles, create a second row of units (see Figure 9-24).

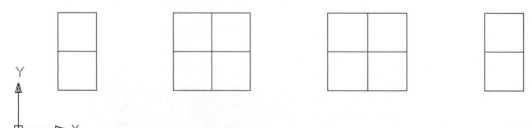

**Figure 9-24**   Creating the second row of storage rooms

7. Using the **Grip MIRROR** with **Copy** option on all the rectangles, create the third and fourth rows of units (see Figure 9-25).
8. Using the **Grip MIRROR** with **Copy** option on all the rectangles, create the fifth, sixth, seventh, and eighth rows of units.

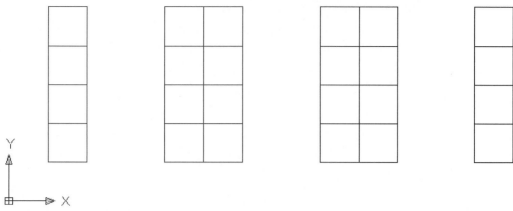

**Figure 9-25**    The plan after the creation of rows 3 and 4

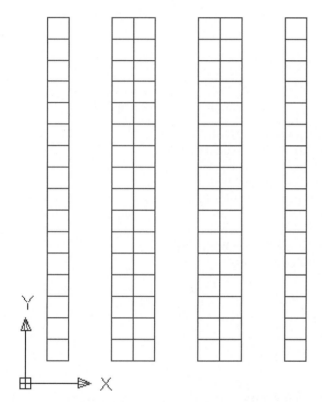

**Figure 9-26**    Completed warehouse plan

9. Using the **Grip MIRROR** with **Copy** option on all the rectangles, create the final eight rows of units. After this operation, the basic layout is complete for the storage center as shown in Figure 9-26.

10. Add some overall dimensions to complete this basic drawing. Remember to change to the correct layer for Dimensions.

11. **Save** the drawing as **T9-2.**

There are at least two other methods using grips and grip commands to create this drawing. What are the other procedures? Which do you think is the most efficient? Why?

## Tutorial 9-3: Modifying Contour Lines with Grips

Create a final grading plan (contour map) for a 100′ by 100′ building pad that is set back 30′ from the front lot line (the property line that is labeled with the distance and bearing).

1. From the **File** menu pick **Open** and load the **T9-3** drawing from the Student CD.

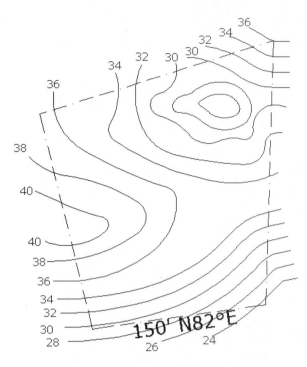

**Figure 9-27**   Drawing T9-3

2. Examine the contour lines as shown in Figure 9-27.
3. From the **Modify** menu pick the **OFFSET** command and enter **30** for the offset distance.
4. Pick the Front Lot Line and the line will go to highlight mode.
5. Pick anywhere above the Front Lot line to establish the Set Back Line as shown in Figure 9-28.
6. Change the color of this line to red by gripping the new line (see Figure 9-29) and then moving to the **Object Properties** color drop-down to choose **Red** (see Figure 9-30).

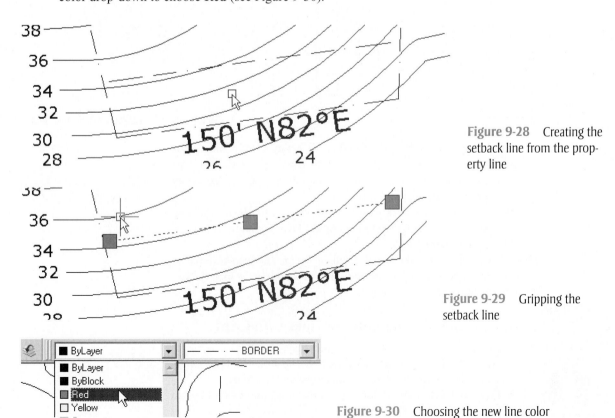

**Figure 9-28**   Creating the setback line from the property line

**Figure 9-29**   Gripping the setback line

**Figure 9-30**   Choosing the new line color

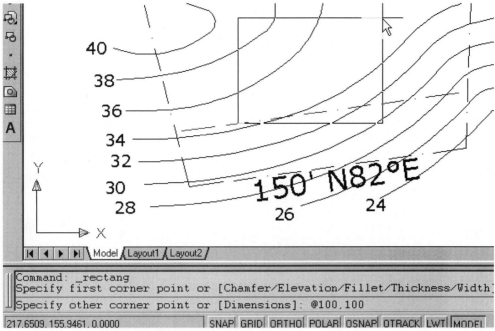

**Figure 9-31**    Placing the building pad

7. Press <**Esc**> to clear the grips.
8. Draw a rectangle and with the mouse pick one corner on the red Set Back Line. Type in **@100,100** for the second corner of the rectangle and end the command, as shown in Figure 9-31.
9. Grip the rectangle, select the lower left grip to make it hot, and use the space bar to proceed to the **Rotate** option (see Figure 9-32).

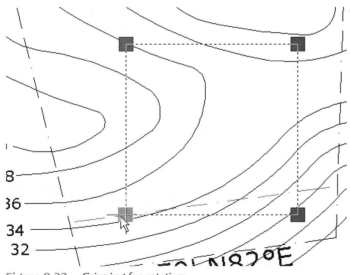

**Figure 9-32**    Gripping for rotation

10. Enter **8** for the rotation angle as this will align the building area to the front lot line. The result should look like Figure 9-33.
11. If the building area is not centered, grip it and move it to a position similar to Figure 9-33.
12. Based on the drawing in Figure 9-33 a decision is made to put the building area at an elevation of 35 feet. Grip each contour line (see Figure 9-34) and move the vertices appropriately to create the new contours (see Figure 9-35). Remember that

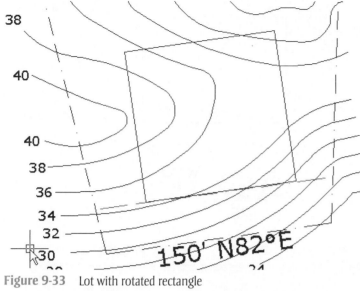

**Figure 9-33**    Lot with rotated rectangle

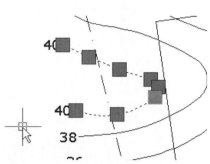

**Figure 9-34**    A gripped contour line

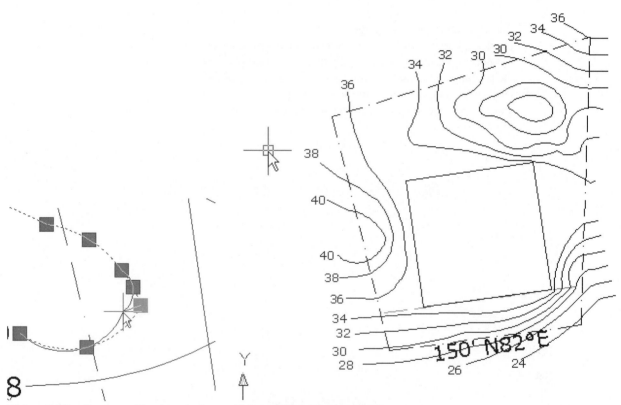

**Figure 9-35**    Contour with selected grip in STRETCH mode

**Figure 9-36**    Drawing T9-3A

contour lines *do not cross* as no location can have two elevations.

13. Continue gripping and stretching the contour lines to finish the drawing similar to the drawing in Figure 9-36.

14. **Save** the drawing in your **Workskills** folder as **T9-3A.**

## PRACTICE EXERCISES

### Practice Exercise 9-1: Using Grips with Stretch, Grip Snaps, and OSNAPs

1. From the **File** menu pick **New** to start a new drawing, or use one of your templates.
2. Verify that **SNAP, GRID, ORTHO, POLAR, OSNAP,** and **OTRACK** are **off** in the status line.
3. Check to be sure that **Grips** are **enabled** in the **Options** dialog box with the **Selection** tab.
4. Draw a line with **1,2** and **4,7** as coordinates.
5. Grip this line and select the upper right point to make it **Active** or **Hot** (red box).
6. Move the mouse and see how the line moves with the cursor.
7. Type in **6,10** and this endpoint of the line will move to this location.
8. Press <**Esc**> to remove the grips.
9. Draw a circle with center at **8,5** and a radius of **2.**
10. Grip the circle and Select the center grip to make it **Active** or **Hot (red box).**
11. Move the mouse and see how the circle moves with the cursor and stays the same size.
12. Press <**Esc**> to remove the grips.
13. Grip the circle and Select the north quadrant point to make it **Active.**
14. Move the mouse and see the circle changing radius but not location.
15. Type in **8,9** and the circle will enlarge. What is the radius?
16. Press <**Esc**> to remove the grips.
17. Grip the line and the circle. Select the north **Quadrant** point on the circle to make it **Active.**
18. Move the cursor to the upper-right line grip and pick. Notice that the **Quadrant** point and the **Endpoint** snap together.
19. Press <**Esc**> to remove the grips.
20. Grip the line and select the upper right end to make it **Active.**
21. Type in **CEN** and press <**Enter**>. Then move across the circle and the centerpoint **Osnap** will appear. Move the mouse to the center and pick. The line will connect to the center of the circle.
22. Save your drawing as **EX9-1** in your **Workskills** folder.

### Practice Exercise 9-2: Using Grips with Move, Copy, and Auxiliary Grids

1. From the **File** menu pick **New** to start a new drawing, or use one of your templates.
2. Verify that **SNAP, GRID, ORTHO, POLAR, OSNAP,** and **OTRACK** are **off** in the status line.
3. Check to be sure that **Grips** are **enabled** in the **Options** dialog box with the **Selection** tab.
4. Draw a line with **2,1** and **7,4** as coordinates.
5. Draw a circle with the center at **5,2** and a radius of **1.**
6. Grip the line and the circle.
7. Make the middle grip on the line **Active** and press <**Enter**> to get to the **Move** option in the **Grips** command series.
8. Type in **@1<135** and press <**Enter**> to move the entities **1** unit at an angle of **135.**

9. Make the middle grip on the line **Active** and press **<Enter>** to get to the **Move** option in **Grips.**

10. Type a **C** and press **<Enter>** to use the copy mode.

11. Type in **@2<315** and press **<Enter>** to copy the entities **2** units at an angle of **315.** Now a second line and the circle should appear.

12. Repeat Step 11 three more times, typing in **@2<45, @2<135,** and **@2<225.**

13. Draw an arc in the center area of the drawing.

14. Grip the arc and select a triangular grip on one end to **Activate.** As you move the mouse, the arc is extended or shortened, keeping the same radius.

15. Make each grip on the arc active and test the action under the **STRETCH** mode.

16. Press **<Enter>** and see the different actions under the **MOVE** mode.

17. **Save** the drawing as **EX9-2** in your **Workskills** folder.

## Practice Exercise 9-3: Using Grips with Rotate, Scale, and Mirror

1. From the **File** menu pick **New** to start a new drawing, or use one of your templates.

2. Verify that **SNAP, GRID, ORTHO, POLAR, OSNAP,** and **OTRACK** are **off** in the status line.

3. Check to be sure that **Grips** are **enabled** in the **Options** dialog box with the **Selection** tab.

4. Draw a line with **2,2** and **2,7** as coordinates.

5. Grip the line and make the bottom or lower grip **Active.**

6. Press **<Enter>** twice to access the **ROTATE** mode.

7. Type a **C** to go to the **Copy** operation.

8. Enter **15** at the command prompt to create a line 15° on the counterclockwise rotation.

9. Continue by entering **30, 45, 60, 75,** and **90** to complete lines in this quadrant.

10. Grip the second, fourth, and sixth lines and make the base grip **Active.**

11. Press **<Enter>** three times to be in **SCALE** mode.

12. Enter **.7** as the scale factor to reduce these lines to 70 percent of their original size.

13. Press **<Esc>** to clear the grips.

14. Grip all lines and make the bottom of the first line **Active.**

15. Press **<Enter>** four times to be in **MIRROR** mode.

16. Type a **C** to go to the **Copy** operation.

17. Move the mouse to the grip box furthest to the west or left. This defines a mirror line for the reflection to be done.

18. Grip all lines and make the bottom of the first line **Active.**

19. Press **<Enter>** four times to be in **MIRROR** mode.

20. Type a **C** to go to the **Copy** operation.

21. Move the mouse to the grip box, to the grip furthest down. This defines a mirror line for the reflection.

22. **SAVE** your drawing as **EX9-3** in your **Workskills** folder (see Figure 9-37).

## Practice Exercise 9-4: Using Grips to Modify Object Properties

1. From the **File** menu pick **Open** and load drawing **T9-3** from the Student CD (see Figure 9-38).

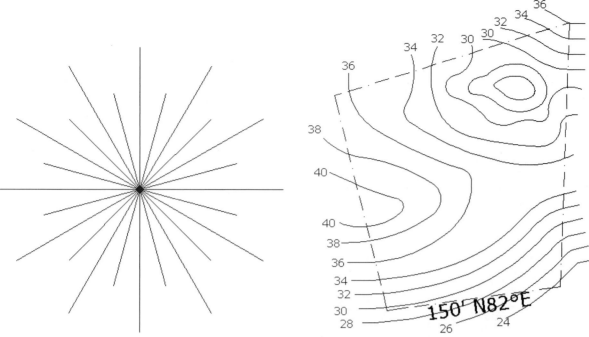

**Figure 9-37**    Drawing EX9-3

**Figure 9-38**    Drawing T9-3

2. Verify that **SNAP, GRID, ORTHO, POLAR, OSNAP**, and **OTRACK** are **off** in the status line.
3. Check to be sure that **Grips** are enabled in the **Options** dialog box in the **Selection** tab.
4. **Grip** the **40′** contour line as shown in Figure 9-39.
5. Go to the **Color** drop-down and pick **Magenta** as the new color for this object as shown in Figure 9-40.
6. Proceed with the same operation (Steps 4 and 5) on the 30′ contour lines.

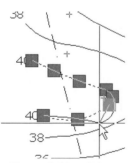

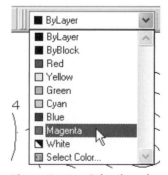

**Figure 9-39**    Grips on the 40′ contour line

**Figure 9-40**    Color drop-down

7. When completed, the drawing should look like Figure 9-41.
8. **Save** your drawing as **EX9-4** in your **Workskills** folder.

## Practice Exercise 9-5: Using Grips to Complete the GROFFICE Plan

1. Open the **GROFFICE** drawing as shown in Figure 9-42 from the Student CD.
2. Using only **Grips** and the related commands, complete the drawing approximately as shown in Figure 9-43.
3. **Save** your completed drawing in your **Workskills** folder as **EX9-5.**

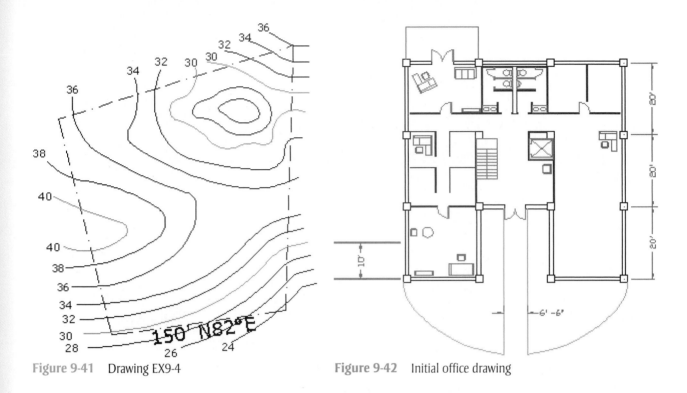

**Figure 9-41** Drawing EX9-4

**Figure 9-42** Initial office drawing

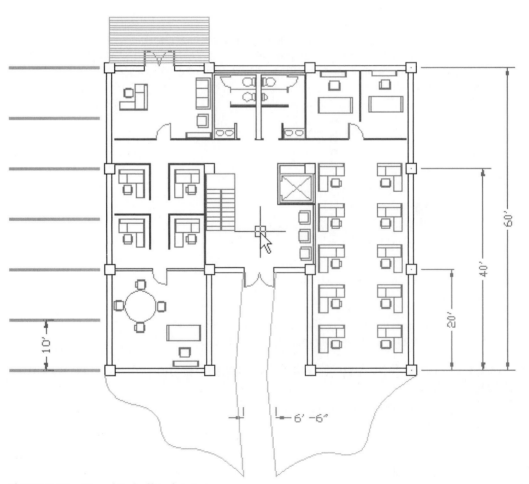

**Figure 9-43** Completed office drawing

# Tables, Cells, and Fields Fundamentals

# 10

## *Chapter* Objectives

- Create a table using Table Styles.
- Edit table elements.
- Edit cells in a table.
- Create and edit table styles.
- Distinguish the categories related to fields.
- Insert fields in a drawing.
- Update fields in a drawing.
- Use fields across drawings.

## INTRODUCTION

Drawings show the size and shape of an object. In many cases more information is needed. One such way to present an enhanced version of the information is by adding text to the drawing, which was discussed in Unit 7. Another way to present this additional information is in the form of a table, schedule, or spreadsheet. Cells are the individual items of data in the table. Fields are information taken from the drawing such as area or attribute data. Fields can also be a direct input.

## AUTOCAD TABLES

Tables are used to present information in an organized, efficient, and easy-to-read format (see Figure 10-1). Schedules and spreadsheets are additional examples of tables. In many cases there are many options or pieces of information to describe an object in a drawing, and it is not possible to place this information as text or attribute data near the object. To avoid confusion and increase understanding a key code or symbol is placed near the object to be described. This code or symbol is then placed in the table to create the connection of the information or data to the object.

---

All engineering disciplines make use of a table format when displaying certain types of information. Whether it be a door and window schedule, a room finish schedule, or a bill of materials/parts list, these items will be easier to create and maintain if they are developed using the table, cells, and field commands offered in AutoCAD.

## Plant Table

Broadleaf Deciduous

| Quantity | Symbol | Scientific Name |
|---|---|---|
| 1 | | Cercis canadensis |

Broadleaf Evergreen

| Quantity | Symbol | Scientific Name |
|---|---|---|
| 13 | | Grevillea 'Noellii' |
| 1 | | Grevillea 'Noellii' |
| 36 | | Nandina domestica 'Nana' |
| 10 | | Podocarpus macrophyllus |
| 11 | | Raphiolepis indica |
| 15 | | Rhododendron indicum |
| 6 | | Thevetia peruviana |

Perennial

| Quantity | Symbol | Scientific Name |
|---|---|---|
| 12 | | Heuchera sanguinea |
| 60 | | Heuchera sanguinea |

Shrub

| Quantity | Symbol | Scientific Name |
|---|---|---|
| 5 | | Camellia japonica |

**Figure 10-1**   Typical plant table

**cell:** A box in the table for data.

Tables have rows and columns that form ***cells,*** which can contain repetitive or similar information. For example, a door schedule (see Figure 10-2) typically has columns showing the door dimensions, finish, lock and key, and more. A plant table (see Figure 10-1) shows quantities, names of plants, size, and more. A dimension table (see Figure 10-3) shows the dimension relationships of a part, based on parametric modeling procedures.

| DOOR SCHEDULE | | | | |
|---|---|---|---|---|
| **Code** | **Height** | **Width** | **Finish** | **Handle** |
| D101 | 8' | 3' | Exterior Glazed | Bar with Lock |
| D102 | 6'-8' | 8' | Exterior Sliding | Locking |
| D103 | 6'-8" | 3' | White | Locking |

**Figure 10-2**   Typical architectural door schedule

| Case Dimensions | | | | | | |
|---|---|---|---|---|---|---|
| **Shaft Size** | **A** | **B** | **C** | **D** | **E** | **F** |
| 3/8" | 4-1/2 | 3-3/4 | 2-1/8 | 5-5/8 | 1-1/2 | 6-3/4 |
| 1/2" | 4-3/4 | 3-3/4 | 2-1/4 | 5-7/8 | 1-3/8 | 7 |
| 5/8" | 4-7/8 | 4 | 2-3/8 | 6 | 1-1/4 | 7-1/4 |
| 3/4" | 5 | 4 | 2-1/2 | 6-1/8 | 1-1/8 | 7-1/2 |
| 7/8" | 5-1/8 | 4-1/4 | 2-5/8 | 6-3/8 | 1 | 7-3/4 |

**Figure 10-3**   Typical parametric dimension table

Tables use a row and column layout to create the basic layout size. A column header row and a title row can be added to enhance the table. Tables are set up based on the table styles defined in the current drawing template or defined by the user. Tables can have the numbers of rows and columns defined when they are inserted. The row and column format creates a matrix of the information in cells.

## Inserting a Table

If a table is to be used, the style will dictate the look of the table. The size of the table (the number of rows and columns) as well as the column width and row height are selected when you insert the table. If a title row and column header row are desired, the style should reflect this choice.

To place a table in the drawing, choose **Table** from the **Draw** menu. This results in the dialog box shown in Figure 10-4. After specifying the needed information, you can specify an insertion point or choose the opposite corners of the window to fit the table. The table appears with the **Text Formatting** bar displayed above it as shown in Figure 10-5. The **Text Formatting** bar helps you with the placement, size, font, color, emphasis, and other parameters of the text in the table.

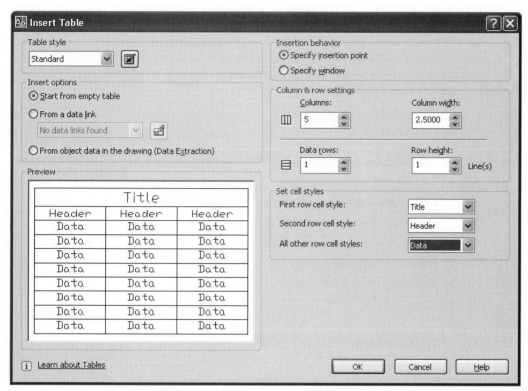

**Figure 10-4**    Insert Table dialog box

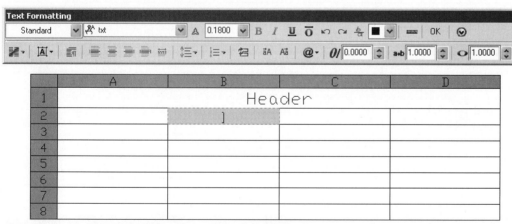

**Figure 10-5**    Initial table for data entry and text completion

To move around the table the following methods may be employed:

*   Use the left mouse button to choose the cell for input of information.
*   Use the **Arrow** keys to move around the table from cell to cell.
*   Use the **Enter** key to move to the next cell (moving to the right or down depending on the initial style setting).

### Exercise 10-1: Table Operations

■ Start AutoCAD and open the UNIT10 drawing from the Student CD.
■ Verify the current layer is TABLE and that all other layers are off.
■ Access the Draw menu and choose Table.
■ Insert a table with the following specifications:
  Rows: 7
  Columns: 6
  Column Width: 2″
  Row Height: 2 lines
■ Put your name in the Title Area (i.e., _____'s Table). Place your year of graduation as the center column header. Place the years before this date as column headers to the left and after this date as column headers to the right.
■ Save the drawing as UNIT10-1.

The cells in a table can contain alphanumeric text, numeric data, symbols, blocks, fields, and attribute data (see Figure 10-6). Information in a cell can be rotated using the standard AutoCAD angles. Information will word-wrap if two or more lines are needed because the column width will not change. Once the table is placed in the drawing, there are five ways to modify the table and its content:

• Use the **Table Formating bar** by gripping a cell (see Figure 10-7).
• Use the **Text Formatting bar** by double clicking in a cell (see Figure 10-8).
• Use the drop-down menu from the button on the **Text Formatting** bar (see Figure 10-9).
• Use the **Right Mouse Button** menu (see Figure 10-10).
• Use the **Properties** palette (see Figure 10-11).

| Title Area | | | | |
|---|---|---|---|---|
| Header 1 | Header 2 | Header 3 | Header 4 | Header 5 |
| A | 1 | 2 | 3 | 4 |
| B | 5 | 6 | 7 | 8 |
| C | 9 | 10 | 11 | 12 |
| D | 13 | 14 | 15 | 16 |
| E | 17 | 18 | 19 | 20 |
| F | 21 | 22 | 23 | 24 |

**Figure 10-6**   Typical AutoCAD table with sample information

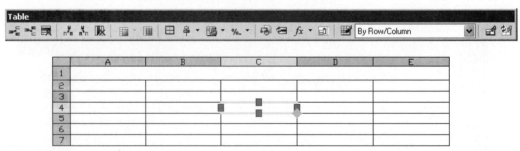

**Figure 10-7**

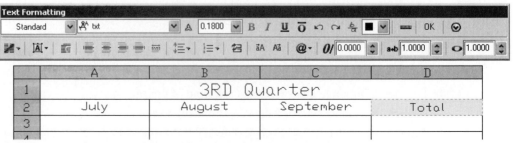

**Figure 10-8**   Editing of a cell in a table with the Text Formatting bar present

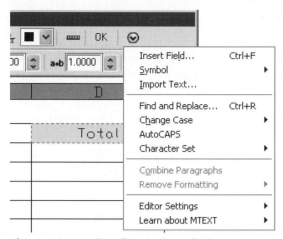

| | | |
|---|---|---|
| Insert Field... | | Ctrl+F |
| Symbol | ▶ | |
| Import Text... | | |
| Find and Replace... | | Ctrl+R |
| Change Case | ▶ | |
| AutoCAPS | | |
| Character Set | ▶ | |
| Combine Paragraphs | | |
| Remove Formatting | ▶ | |
| Editor Settings | ▶ | |
| Learn about MTEXT | ▶ | |

**Figure 10-9** Edit Cell menu from the button on the Text Format bar

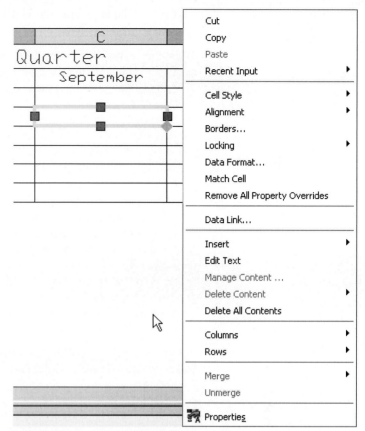

| | |
|---|---|
| Cut | |
| Copy | |
| Paste | |
| Recent Input | ▶ |
| Cell Style | ▶ |
| Alignment | ▶ |
| Borders... | |
| Locking | ▶ |
| Data Format... | |
| Match Cell | |
| Remove All Property Overrides | |
| Data Link... | |
| Insert | ▶ |
| Edit Text | |
| Manage Content ... | |
| Delete Content | ▶ |
| Delete All Contents | |
| Columns | ▶ |
| Rows | ▶ |
| Merge | ▶ |
| Unmerge | |
| Properties | |

**Figure 10-10** Edit Cell menu from the right mouse button when a cell is active

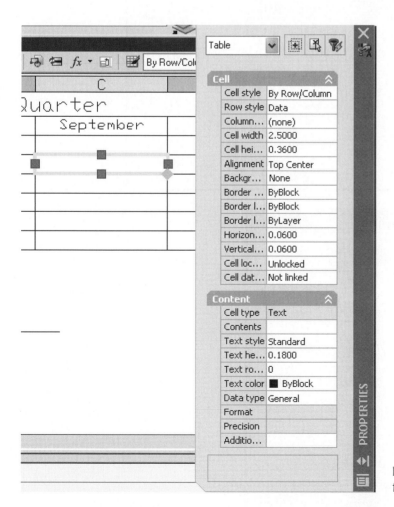

**Figure 10-11** Properties palette for active table cells

When the keyboard is touched for entering information into a cell the **Text Formatting** bar will appear to aid in entering the information in the correct format. To enter information into a cell or to edit information, choose the cell to make it active (with grips) and enter the new text or data.

An understanding of Quick Calc and transparent 'cal command will allow you to work out complicated calculations and copy the results to the prompt line as expressions. Engineering formulas are often needed in the design process. The application of these commands increases a drawing's accuracy.

You can also right-mouse-click to bring forward a menu (see Figure 10-10) with more options, or display these other options by clicking on the button in the upper right area of the text bar, as shown in Figure 10-9. While some of these menu items are the same, many are different and offer additional options as well. Many of these items and actions are straightforward to understand such as Insert Field, Delete, Justification, Change Case, Find and Replace, Cell Borders, and so on. A few of these items are highlighted below.

Further formatting control of the cells in a table can include single and double line borders (see Figure 10-12) and various data formats (see Figure 10-13). These formats include currency,

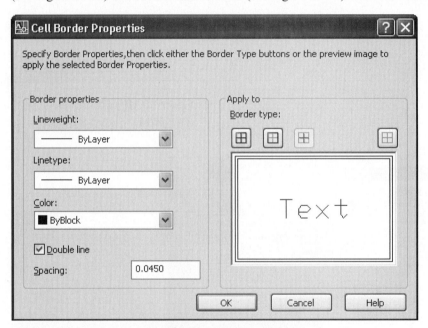

**Figure 10-12**

**Figure 10-13**

**Figure 10-14**

whole numbers, angles, percentages, dates, and text. New for AutoCAD 2008, the table can contain and have a dynamic link with other files such as Excel spreadsheets, Word documents, and other similar objects that can be embedded and linked. The link is named and established using the **Select a Data Link** dialog box as shown in Figure 10-14.

FOR MORE DETAIL   The insertion of fields in a cell of a table is discussed later in this chapter.

## Merge Cells

If more than one cell is highlighted by gripping, those cells can be merged into one cell encompassing the same space as the original highlighted cells and in the same location in the table. This merge operation can be done using all cells highlighted or by merging them as rows or columns. The data is preserved and placed in the merged cell using the same alignment and justification as the original cell (see Figures 10-15 and 10-16).

## Symbols

The ability to add special symbols to information in a cell is available through the @ symbol or through the **Options** button drop-down, both of which are in the **Text Formatting** bar. The list of symbols available in the menu is shown in Figure 10-17. The chosen symbol is placed at the current location of the blinking cursor.

## Insert Formula

Through the use of the **Right Mouse Button** menu, when a cell is highlighted (see Figure 10-18) various mathematical operations can be assigned to that cell. For these operations you pick inside the range of cells to be considered for this action. You can also type the operation and the range with relative or absolute locations (using a $ sign). The result is a formula similar to an Excel® spreadsheet when in Edit mode and the answer to the formula when in normal view (see Figures 10-19, 10-20, and 10-21). In the Formula option (Figure 10-22), the equation

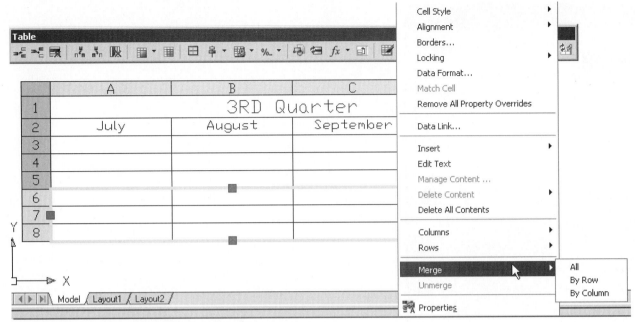

**Figure 10-15**    Cells highlighted before the merge operation

**Figure 10-16**    Cell after merge

**Figure 10-17**    Symbols available in tables through the Text Formatting bar

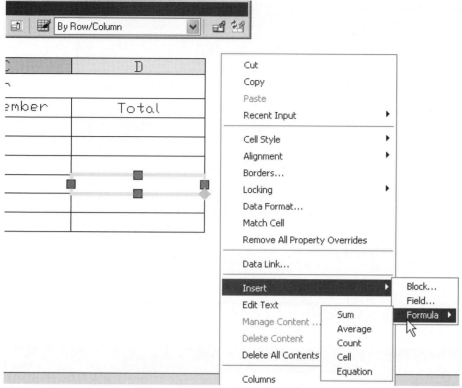

**Figure 10-18**    Cell math formula that can be used for higher-level information

**Figure 10-19**    Sum formula example

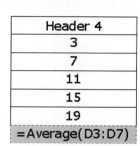

**Figure 10-20**    Average formula example

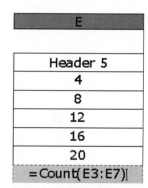

**Figure 10-21**    Count formula example

must begin with an equals sign (=). Formulas can use addition (+), subtraction (−), multiplication (*), division (/), and exponential (^). Parentheses "()" can be used to show hierarchy in the formula and a colon is used to define a range of cells. A comma can be used to list individual cells.

## Exercise 10-2: Table with Formulas

■ Continue with the UNIT10 drawing or open this drawing from the Student CD.
■ Make the TABLE2 Layer current and on. Turn off any other layers.
■ Randomly enter numbers between 1 and 50 in the empty cells except for the bottom row.
■ In the bottom row of cells use the following formulas:
  • Column 2—use the Sum of the column
  • Column 3—use the Average of the column
  • Column 4—use the Count of the column
  • Column 5—use the formula "= (B8+C8)*D8/2"
  • Column 6—use the same as cell E8
■ Save the drawing as UNIT10-2.

## TABLE STYLES

As with many objects in the AutoCAD program, tables can be predefined as a style. The initial style in the AutoCAD template drawing is called Standard and this can be used as a basis for other styles. From the **Format** menu you can access **Table Styles** or call upon another method as shown (see Figure 10-23). Initially the standard-style table includes a title, column headers, and data cells. To **Modify** the table or to create a **New** style, pick the appropriate tab on the right side of the dialog box.

For a new table, choose a name as well as a base table to begin the design. Toggles are available to include the title row and the column header row in a new table.

**Figure 10-22**    Another formula example

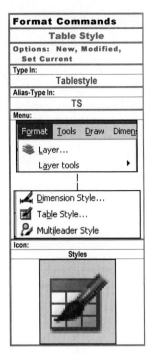

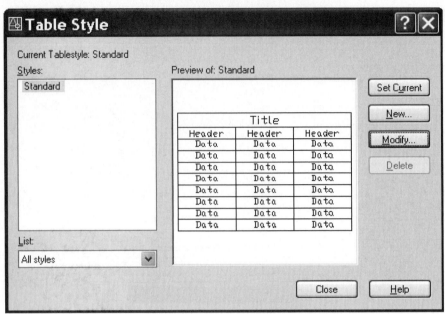

Figure 10-23    Table Style dialog box

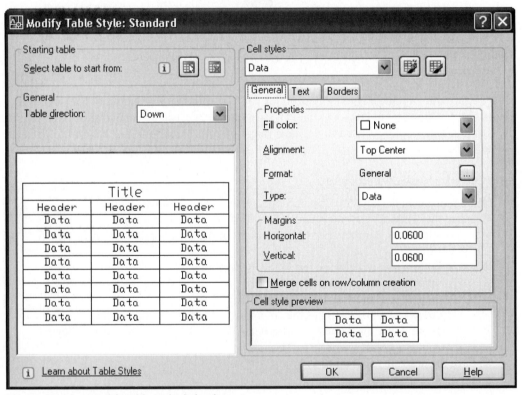

Figure 10-24    Modify Table Style dialog box

The **Modify Table Style** dialog box (see Figure 10-24) gives you the ability to change any of the areas addressing the format of a table. You will be able to change the table direction in the **General** area; change the style of a cell that contains data, header information, or title information in the **Cell styles** area; or select one of the three tabs addressing the properties of the table in the right side of the dialog box. the three tabs in this area are **General** for color, alignment, format, and type; the **Text** tab, which addresses text characteristics; and the **Borders** tab, which allows you to change the lineweight, linetype, and color of lines along with line spacing. This dialog box also contains two preview windows to see what effect your change(s) will have on the table.

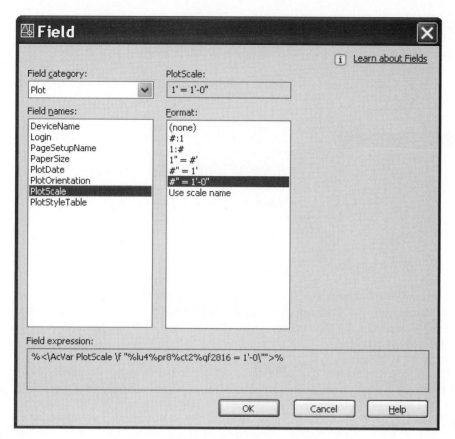

**Figure 10-25**    The Field dialog box

# FIELDS

Fields are an enhancement to multiline text and allow for use of information contained in the drawing. This data can be placed in a field or can stand alone if so desired (see Figure 10-25). For example, a field can display the current date in a title block, show the area of a closed polyline, or show the current plot scale of a layout window on the paper. There are hundreds of options in creating a freestanding field or using it in a multiline text environment. If the drawing information changes, fields can be automatically updated to reflect the current level of data. Fields can also come from drawings in a sheet set.

## Categories of Fields

Due to the many possibilities available as fields, categories have been developed to aid in quickly locating the appropriate field to insert. The categories (see Figure 10-26) are as follows:

- **All** Shows all fields available (see Figure 10-26)
- **Date & Time** (see Figure 10-27)
- **Document** Keywords, title, author, etc. (see Figure 10-28)
- **Linked** Hyperlinks (see Figure 10-29)
- **Objects** Entities in the drawings, formula equation, and blocks (see Figure 10-30)
- **Other** System variables and diesel expressions (see Figure 10-33)
- **Plot** Plot scale, Plot date, paper size, and others (see Figure 10-34)
- **Sheet Set** Current Sheet Set data and Placeholders (see Figure 10-35)

Once the category is chosen, you select from the **Field name** list below the category field. Field names vary based on the category chosen as shown in the following figures. Many of the names are self-explanatory and are entered in various parts of the AutoCAD program or set by the profile, template, or options. A further explanation of some field categories follows.

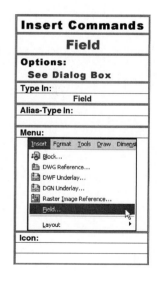

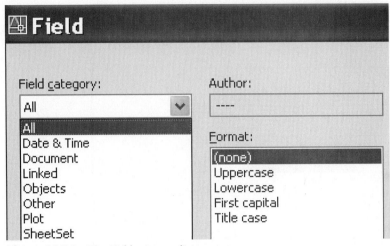

**Figure 10-26**    The Field category list

*Date & Time*    In the **Data & Time** category (see Figure 10-27), many examples are presented for the four field names available. Hints are provided to aid in picking the correct format for the field to be inserted. Except for the **CreateDate** of the drawing, the other options update to the current date of the activity involved.

*Document*    Most of these fields (see Figure 10-28) are defined in the **Drawing Properties** dialog boxes from the **File** menu. Various formats are available for the display of this information as a field.

*Linked*    Hyperlinks can connect an object in a drawing to an Internet website, an intranet site, or another object to further define the object or to be used as an aid in specifying the correct item. This link can also connect to a graphic, picture, or video file. For example, in Figure 10-29, the desk identified can link to an office supply website that shows the desk desired, its price, and other specifications.

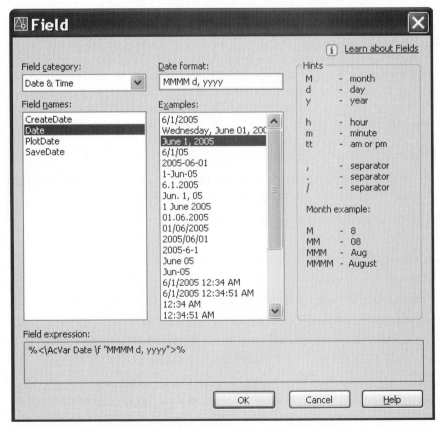

**Figure 10-27**    Date and time field options

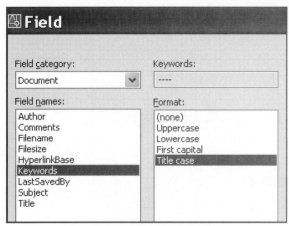

**Figure 10-28**    The Document field options

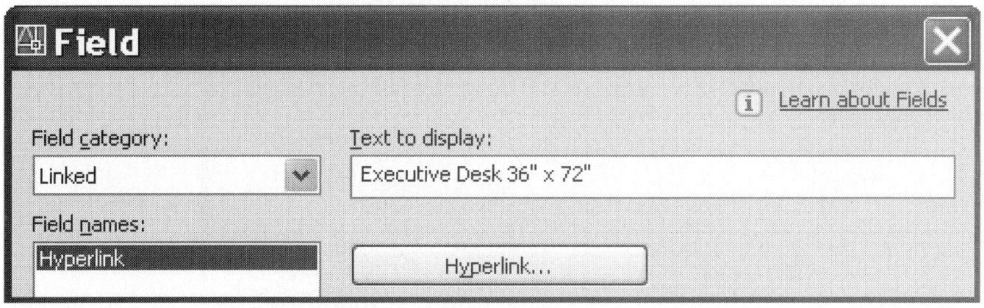

**Field**

Field category:        Text to display:
Linked                 Executive Desk 36" x 72"

Field names:
Hyperlink              Hyperlink...

**Figure 10-29**    The Linked field option

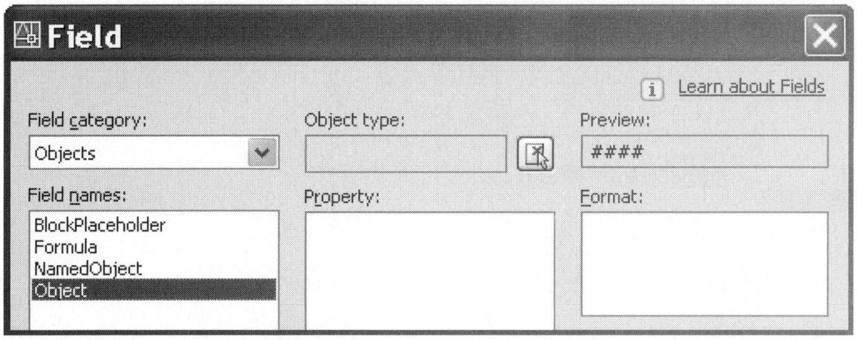

**Field**

Field category:        Object type:        Preview:
Objects                                     ####

Field names:           Property:           Format:
BlockPlaceholder
Formula
NamedObject
Object

**Figure 10-30**    The Field dialog box

*Objects*    Various objects in the drawing have properties that can be accessed and used as fields (see Figure 10-30). Typically you choose the precise object via the pick box that will supply data to the inserted field. Once the object is chosen, a list of properties is displayed in the center column.

The list of objects is extensive; you can choose virtually any entity currently in the drawing. You cannot choose an object type directly as it must exist in the drawing for entity properties to be used. For example, in Figure 10-31, a polyline is the object selected using the pick symbol at the top right of the middle column. Once chosen, the properties available are displayed in the middle column. After choosing a property value to display, the value is shown in the third column and you can choose the proper format of those shown. The **Field Format** button leads to options regarding conversion factors, zero suppression, numerical separators, the prefix phase, and the suffix phase. For Figure 10-32, the object chosen is a circle. Some of the properties available are the same as for the polyline and some are different. You should examine numerous objects and review the properties available for fields in various formats.

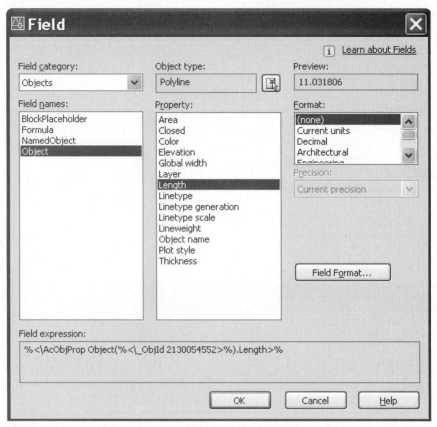

**Figure 10-31**    Field properties available for a closed polyline

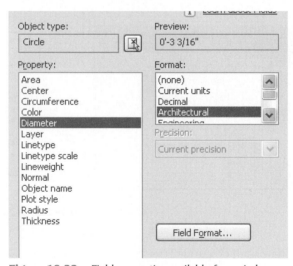

**Figure 10-32**    Field properties available for a circle

*Other*    The **Other** category focuses on system variables and diesel expression values (see Figure 10-33). The **System variable** values are set in the drawing template, profiles, customized programming, and other locations throughout the AutoCAD program. These fields can be used to inform others of certain "standard" values used in the current drawing. If this value has differing formats available, the third column will display the possibilities for format. You should examine various options and see the current values and format options.

*Plot*    The **Plot** category (see Figure 10-34) offers fields that relate to layout and plotting settings. These values can be used to inform others of the settings needed for the proper plotting and presentation of the drawing. The device name present for these items is based on the current

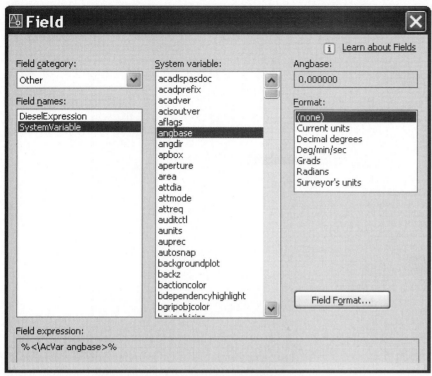

**Figure 10-33**    Typical system variable dialog for fields

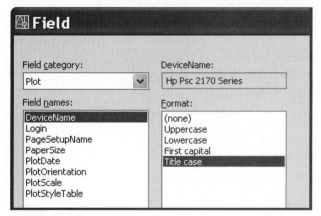

**Figure 10-34**    Insert fields available in the Plot category

default printer. It is not possible to change the device name in this dialog box; this needs to be changed before accessing this command.

*Sheet Sets*    The **SheetSet** category (see Figure 10-35) offers values that can be used related to sheet sets. Sheet sets allow the organization of multiple drawings and their corresponding layouts into a set for plotting, view control, and the relationship of details.

To determine who has locked a sheet set, simply hover the mouse over the icon and the user's name will appear in a tooltip box.

## Using Fields in Tables

As shown earlier in this chapter, tables can be used to present a large amount of data in an organized form. Fields showing drawing information can also be inserted in a table in various methods. A cell in the table must be active to place a field as part of the table. Using the **FIELD** command

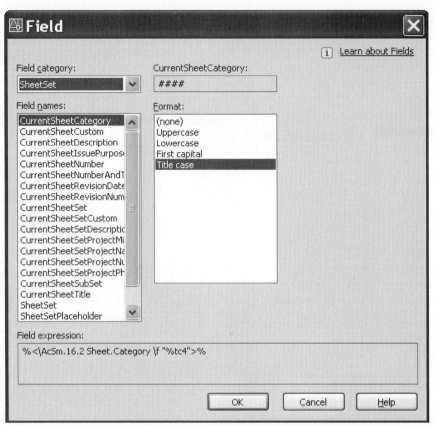

**Figure 10-35**    Sheet set fields available

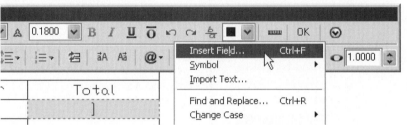

**Figure 10-36**    Inserting a field in a table from the Options drop-down arrow in the Text Formatting bar

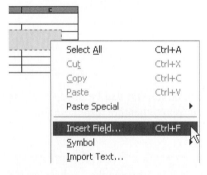

**Figure 10-37**    Inserting a field in a table from the right-click menu

does not place a field inside the cell, but the command can be used to place a field in a location on the drawing, which could be in the table.

To place a field in the drawing, you can activate the cell by clicking in it. The field insert dialog can be accessed by the following methods:

- Use the **Options** arrow at the right end of the **Text Formatting** bar as shown in Figure 10-36.
- Use the **Right-Click** menu as shown in Figure 10-37 when the **Text Formatting** bar is active.
- After gripping a cell, use the **Right-Click** menu as shown in Figure 10-38.

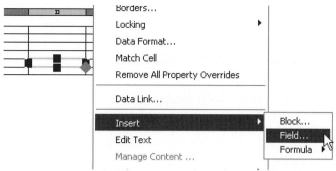

**Figure 10-38**    Right-click menu when a table cell is gripped

After choosing **Insert Field** from the preceding methods, the **Field** dialog screen is present. This allows you to pick the field category and proceed as discussed previously in this chapter to complete the field placement in the cell of the table. Care should be taken in placing fields in tables so that updates to field information do not modify the table disproportionately by the adjustment of cell size; you don't want to make the table difficult to read and understand.

# SUMMARY

Often, more information than the size and shape of an object is needed in an AutoCAD drawing. In this unit, you learned how to incorporate tables, cells (individual items of data in tables), and fields (information taken from the drawing) into AutoCAD drawings to supply additional information. After being introduced to the basic layout of AutoCAD tables (including schedules and spreadsheets), you learned how to insert a table into a drawing (using the **Table** item from the **Draw** menu) and modify and format the table and the contents of its cells (**Table Formatting bar, Text Formatting bar, Right Mouse Button** menu, and **Properties** palette). Then

you learned how to perform various operations on table cells (merging, adding special symbols to information, and inserting mathematical formulas). Then you were introduced to the topic of defining and modifying table styles using the various options available in the **Table Style** and **Modify Table Style** dialog boxes. Finally, you learned the advantages and use of automatically updateable data fields (either freestanding or in a multiline text environment), some of their various categories (**Date & Time, Document, Linked, Objects, Other, Plot, SheetSet**), and their use in tables.

# CHAPTER TEST QUESTIONS

## Multiple Choice

1. Which of the following is **not** allowed in a cell?

   a. Formula
   b. LINE command
   c. Sum
   d. Count

2. Tables styles:

   a. Must have a Header row
   b. Must have a Title row
   c. Must have four rows
   d. Require a name

3. Fields cannot contain:

   a. Commands
   b. Dates

   c. Drawing information
   d. Hyperlinks

4. Fields are _____ into the drawing.

   a. Drawn
   b. Modified
   c. Inserted
   d. Added

5. Initial settings for the AutoCAD standard table come from the:

   a. Toolbars
   b. Template
   c. Aliases
   d. Standards

## Matching

a. _____ Table

b. _____ Cell

c. _____ Table styles

d. _____ Formulas

e. _____ Field

1. Can contain alphanumeric characters

2. Can contain entity property data

3. Can be created in a cell

4. Contains rows and columns

5. Can be established in the drawing

## True or False

1. True or False: Fields are updated automatically.

2. True or False: Tables can only contain numeric data.

3. True or False: Cells can be merged.

4. True or False: Fields can contain symbols.

5. True or False: Using a $ in a cell formula means the formula is using absolute cell locations.

## CHAPTER PROJECTS

### Chapter Project 10-1

Measure your house on a room-by-room basis and create a chart showing the dimensions, color, wall coverings, and so on.

### Chapter Project 10-2

Create a chart of your class schedule. Is each day different? What does this mean in making a table?

### Chapter Project 10-3

Visit a home development center or home construction company and ask to see a set of plans. Examine the plans, especially the schedules of doors, finishes, and windows. Report to the class on the information shown.

## TUTORIALS

### Tutorial 10-1: Creating Tables for Doors and for Windows

1. Start AutoCAD.
2. Open drawing **T10-1** (shown in Figure 10-39) from the Student CD.

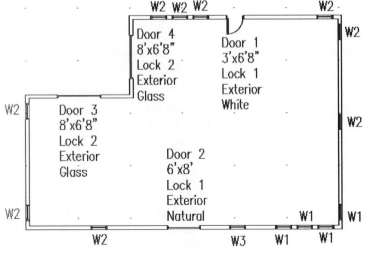

**Figure 10-39**    Drawing T10-1

3. From the **Draw** menu insert a **Table** with four rows and six columns as shown in Figure 10-40 to be the **Door Schedule.** Fill in the information as shown.

| Door Schedule | | | | | |
|---|---|---|---|---|---|
| Description | Height | Width | Type | Finish | Lock # |
| Door 1 | 6' - 8" | 3' - 0" | Exterior | White | 1 |
| Door 2 | 8' - 0" | 6' - 0" | Exterior | Natural | 1 |
| Door 3 | 6' - 8" | 8' - 0" | Exterior | Glass | 2 |
| Door 4 | 6' - 8" | 8' - 0" | Exterior | Glass | 2 |

**Figure 10-40**    The completed table for the door schedule

4. From the **Draw** menu insert a **table** with three rows and six columns as shown in Figure 10-41 to be the window schedule. Fill in the information as shown.

| Window Schedule | | | | | |
|---|---|---|---|---|---|
| Code/ID | Height | Width | Type | Finish | Sill Height |
| W1 | 5' - 0" | 3' - 0" | Double Pane | Wood | 2' - 0" |
| W2 | 4' - 0" | 3' - 0" | Casement | Aluminum | 3' - 0" |
| W3 | 3' - 0" | 3' - 0" | Hexagon | Fixed | 4' - 0" |

**Figure 10-41**    The completed table for the window schedule

5. Modify the drawing to reflect the addition of the tables and save as T10-1A in your **Workskills** folder (see Figure 10-42).

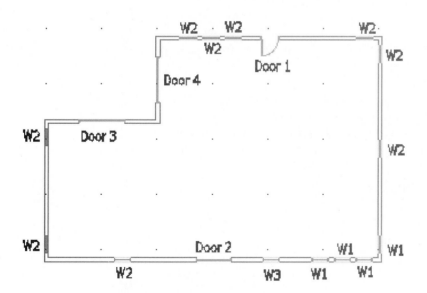

| Window Schedule | | | | | |
|---|---|---|---|---|---|
| Code/ID | Height | Width | Type | Finish | Sill Height |
| W1 | 5' - 0" | 3' - 0" | Double Pane | Wood | 2' - 0" |
| W2 | 4' - 0" | 3' - 0" | Casement | Aluminum | 3' - 0" |
| W3 | 3' - 0" | 3' - 0" | Hexagon | Fixed | 4' - 0" |

| Door Schedule | | | | | |
|---|---|---|---|---|---|
| Description | Height | Width | Type | Finish | Lock # |
| Door 1 | 6' - 8" | 3' - 0" | Exterior | White | 1 |
| Door 2 | 8' - 0" | 6' - 0" | Exterior | Natural | 1 |
| Door 3 | 6' - 8" | 8' - 0" | Exterior | Glass | 2 |
| Door 4 | 6' - 8" | 8' - 0" | Exterior | Glass | 2 |

**Figure 10-42**    Drawing T10-1A

## Tutorial 10-2: Adding Fields to Properties

1. Start AutoCAD.
2. Open drawing **T10-2** (see Figure 10-43) from the Student CD.
3. Add multiline text to the drawing, including the area field for each lot (these are polyline objects). See Figure 10-44.

**Figure 10-43**    Drawing T10-2

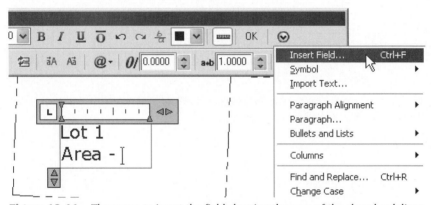

**Figure 10-44**    The menu to insert the field showing the area of the closed polylines

4. The field to insert is an object (using the polyline that defines the lot) in the **Object** category. After choosing the polyline, the property is **Area,** the **Format** is **Decimal,** and **Precision** should be **0.** The preview box should show **24000** as the value. See Figure 10-45.

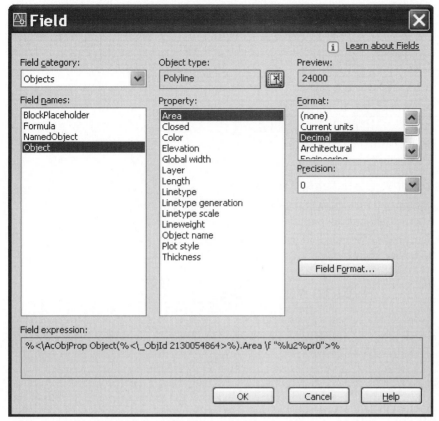

**Figure 10-45**    The Field dialog box

5. Repeat this procedure to label the other lots as shown in Figure 10-46.
6. Save the finished drawing as **T10-2A** in your folder.

**Figure 10-46**    Text with Area fields for the completed drawing

## PRACTICE EXERCISES

### Practice Exercise 10-1: Basic Table Creation 1

Create a table of information related to cars such as gas mileage, length, wheelbase, engine size, interior size, or other data. Use the Internet, magazines, or other sources for this information. See Figure 10-47.

| Car Comparison | | | | | |
|---|---|---|---|---|---|
| Description | Ford | Chevrolet | Dodge | Honda | Toyota |
| Item 1 | | | | | |
| Item 2 | | | | | |
| Item 3 | | | | | |
| Item 4 | | | | | |
| Item 5 | | | | | |
| Item 6 | | | | | |

**Figure 10-47**    Sample table for Practice Exercise 10-1

## Practice Exercise 10-2: Basic Table Creation 2

Create a table based on information collected from people around you (family, friends, instructors, fellow students, etc.) based on their current age. With a formula cell calculate the year of birth for all in the table. See Figure 10-48.

| Birth Year Table | | | | |
|---|---|---|---|---|
| | Friend 1 | Friend 2 | Friend 3 | Friend 4 |
| Current Age | | | | |
| Current Year | | | | |
| Year of Birth | | | | |

**Figure 10-48**    Sample table for Practice Exercise 10-2

## Practice Exercise 10-3: Table Creation for Room Finishes

Assume a house has three bedrooms, two bathrooms, a kitchen, a dining room, a living room, and a family room. Create a table showing room finishes for each wall in each room.

## Practice Exercise 10-4: Table Creation for Machine Equipment

Create a table showing information on lathes such as speed, bar sizes, number of tools, horsepower, torque, and so on. Information can be found on the Internet regarding the various manufacturers and models.

## Practice Exercise 10-5: Table Creation for Volume Calculations

Create a table that summarizes and calculates the Earthwork Volume of Cut and Fill for the 20′ × 20′ grid shown in Figure 10-49. The number in each grid area is the average depth in feet for Cut (C) or for Fill (F). The table should calculate the final volumes in cubic yards.

| C=1.6 | C=0.4 | C=1.5 | C=0.6 | F=0.3 | F=0.6 | C=0.3 | C=0.5 | C=1.4 | C=0.5 |
| C=2.1 | C=0.8 | F=1.2 | F=2.3 | F=3.1 | F=3.2 | F=2.9 | F=1.2 | C=0.3 | C=1.2 |
| C=3.3 | C=2.5 | C=0.5 | F=2.1 | F=3.9 | F=3.8 | F=3.5 | F=1.4 | F=0.6 | C=1.5 |
| C=4.2 | C=3.6 | C=1.3 | F=1.5 | F=3.2 | F=4.1 | F=3.8 | F=1.2 | C=0.4 | C=1.8 |
| C=4.1 | C=3.9 | C=1.5 | C=0.5 | F=1.4 | F=1.7 | F=1.2 | F=0.6 | C=1.2 | C=1.4 |
| C=4.6 | C=4.2 | C=5.1 | C=3.1 | C=2.3 | C=1.8 | C=2.2 | C=1.7 | C=2.3 | C=2.1 |

**Figure 10-49**    Cut and fill grid for earthwork volume calculations

# More about AutoCAD Screens and Commands

# 11

## Chapter Objectives

- Organize toolbars.
- Use tool palettes.
- Define special properties offered by tool palettes.
- Create additional command aliases.
- Use templates to aid startup.
- Explain the Dashboard feature.

## INTRODUCTION

In the previous units of this book, the focus has been on commands and their operations. This unit focuses on additional ways to become a more efficient and productive user of AutoCAD. The topics presented can improve your operation of the program and create a more consistent workspace. The use of customized toolbars and palettes can add uniformity to your office by convenient placement of often-used commands and blocks for quick access and insertion.

## USING COMMANDS

As you have seen from the command graphics, there are generally four ways to activate a command. For example, the **LINE** command is available by using the following methods:

- Type **LINE** in the command prompt area and press the **Enter** key.
- Type the alias, **L,** in the command prompt area and press the **Enter** key.
- Choose the **Draw** menu drop-down and then choose **LINE** from the menu.
- Pick the **LINE** command icon in the **Draw** toolbar.
- Pick the **LINE** command icon from the **Commands** tool palette (this feature was new in the 2006 version).

In addition, if a **LINE** command has just been processed, three more options are available:

- Press the **Enter** key to repeat the **LINE** command just completed.
- Use the **Right Mouse Button** menu to repeat the **LINE** command just completed.
- Use the **Right Mouse Button's Recent Input** menu to access the previous **LINE** command.
- Pick the **LINE** command icon from the **2D Draw** panel in the dashboard.

This gives you much flexibility to work in the most efficient way by using any or all of the above methods, and to develop a flow in drawing creation and modification. In addition, commands can be customized, scripted together to form a process, and moved around in the menus.

3D Navigation
CAD Standards
Camera Adjustment
Dimension
Draw
Draw Order
Inquiry
Insert
✔ Layers
Layers II
Layouts
Lights
Mapping
Modeling
Modify
Modify II
Multileader
Object Snap
Orbit
✔ Properties
Refedit
Reference
Render
Solid Editing
✔ Standard
Standard Annotation
✔ Styles
Text
UCS
UCS II
View
Viewports
Visual Styles
Walk and Fly
Web
✔ Workspaces
Zoom

Lock Location     ▶
Customize...

**Figure 11-1**     Toolbar list

**Figure 11-2**     Floating
Draw toolbar

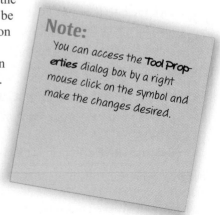

# TOOLBAR ORGANIZATION

Toolbars offer single-click icons of various commands, thereby providing quick access to the command desired. Some toolbars (see Figure 11-1) are typically placed around the AutoCAD workspace or docked; others can float around the screen (see Figure 11-2). As mentioned in Unit 1, floating toolbars can be docked in a location around the edge, or they can be pulled off the edge to float with the double bars at the end of the icons. When toolbars are floating they will show a title bar and name and their shape can be changed by grabbing an edge and moving as shown by the double arrow.

The standard list of toolbars (see Figure 11-1) contains commands that are generally related. Toolbars already in view have a check mark present in the list, and this list acts as a toggle to turn the toolbars on and off. The **Draw** toolbar contains many of the DRAW commands; the **Modify** toolbar contains many of the MODIFY commands. Typically, the toolbars offer only one option of the command and do not have every command in that category. For example, in the **Draw** toolbar the **Circle** icon defaults to the **Center, Radius** option, the **Arc** icon defaults to the **3 Point Arc,** and the **Point** icon defaults to the **Multiple Points** option. In the same regard, the **Draw** toolbar does not contain **Multiline, Donut,** and **Ray,** which are found in the **Draw** menu.

Toolbars can also be customized to maximize productivity by mixing various commands on a new toolbar. This can aid the access to commands by putting your most frequently accessed commands together and closer to the area of the drawing activity.

### Exercise 11-1: Insert a Toolbar

- Start AutoCAD and open the UNIT11 drawing on the Student CD.
- Right-mouse-click on any icon to bring up the toolbar list shown in Figure 11-1.
- Left-mouse-click on Render to put the Render toolbar in the drawing area.
- Hold the left mouse button while pointing at the title of the toolbar. Move around the screen. Dock and undock the toolbar.
- Save as UNIT11-1.

# TOOL PALETTES

**Tool** palettes were initially established as a way to store blocks and hatch patterns for quick access, review, and insertion. When the **Tool** palette is activated, various named tabs are present to expedite finding the block or hatch you want (see Figure 11-3). These can be named Doors, Tables, Bolts, Kitchen, Plants, Trees, and so on. You can easily add new palettes. Then you can drag blocks from the DesignCenter and other sources onto the appropriate palette or create the correct hatch settings.

**Tool** palette items can be assigned properties as shown in Figure 11-4; these will be put into play when the palette item is placed in the drawing. This allows presetting of layers, color, and more as you select an object or hatch from the palette. These properties must be set in advance and already be defined to work properly. For example, if a hatch pattern is to go on the **Steel** layer in the color **Red,** the layer **Steel** must be defined in the **Layer** set. Then it can be assigned to the palette item properties. The resulting icon displays the color, scale, pattern, and other settings.

In addition to blocks and hatches, tool palettes can also host commands for quicker access (see Figure 11-5). As with a toolbar, the icon is a single-click to activate the command. The appropriate prompts and requests for information proceed as with any other method to access that command. As already mentioned, properties can also be preset so that a line or text is placed on the pre-defined and/or preset layer, has a preset linetype, assigns the preset color, and other attributes as shown in Figure 11-6.

**Note:**
You can access the **Tool Properties** dialog box by a right mouse click on the symbol and make the changes desired.

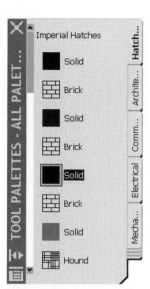

**Figure 11-3** Basic Tool palette showing tabs

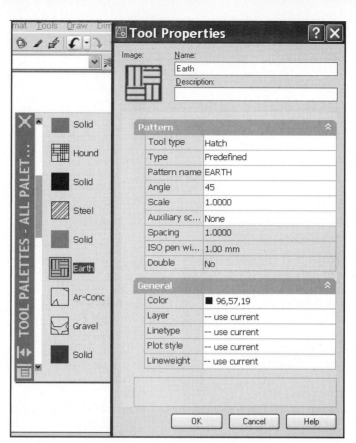

**Figure 11-4** Tool Properties dialog box

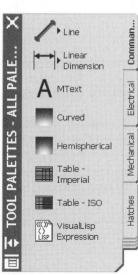

**Figure 11-5** Command palette

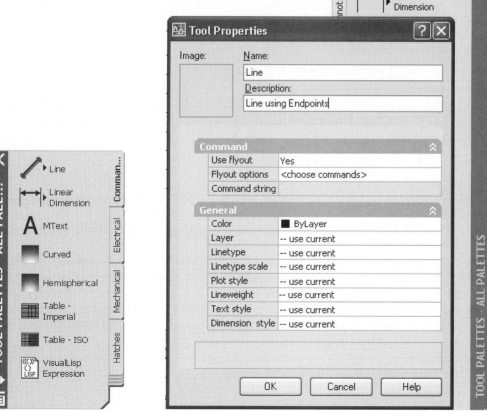

**Figure 11-6** Tool Properties dialog for a Tool palette command

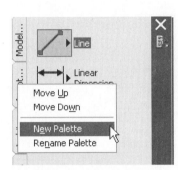

**Figure 11-7**   Tool palette right-click menu from the tab

**Figure 11-8**   Tool palettes main menu

You can arrange the order of the tool palettes as shown in Figure 11-7. This menu also allows for the creation of new palettes, the renaming of palettes, and the removal of palettes. A right-mouse-click on the menu symbol at the bottom of the title bar on the tool palette brings up the menu shown in Figure 11-8. Some of the same options appear along with others. For example, one menu item is for hiding (opening and closing of the window), another for the transparency (being able to see through the palette), and a third for docking. Tool palettes can also be exported and imported through the **Customize** option in this menu by assigning names with an .xtp extension.

The use of customized toolbars and tool palettes will simplify the screen layout. You will benefit by organizing the commands used most often within these custom toolbars and palettes. This will also allow you to close the traditional toolbar and palettes to maximize the screen drawing area to its largest possible size.

**Exercise 11-2:** Create a Palette and Add Commands and Blocks

- ■ Start AutoCAD and open the UNIT11 drawing from the Student CD.
- ■ Type TP to access the Tool Palettes window. Right-mouse-click on one of the tabs of a Tool palette to bring up the menu.
- ■ Left-mouse-click to create a new palette and enter your name as the name of the palette.
- ■ With the new palette active, right-mouse-click and choose Customize Commands from the menu.
- ■ In the Customize User Interface dialog box highlight the Modify toolbar in the Categories drop-down list, and pick and drag the Copy icon onto the palette. Add two other command icons to the palette. Close the Customize window.
- ■ In the drawing pick the Motor and copy it to the clipboard. Move the mouse to the palette and right-mouse-click to paste the block into the palette. Select two other blocks to copy and paste onto the palette.
- ■ Open DesignCenter and access blocks in a drawing. Using the left mouse button, pick a block and—holding the left mouse button—drag the block onto the palette. Select two other blocks to drag and drop onto the palette.
- ■ Save the drawing as UNIT11-2.

## CREATING AND USING DRAWING TEMPLATES

AutoCAD drawing templates are empty drawings with all the layers, linetypes, text styles, dimension styles, table styles, units, drawing limits, layouts, plot scales, toolbars, tool palettes, and other settings in place. By initiating the proper template (see Figure 11-9), you are ready to draw at a higher productivity level, since no creation of the preceding items is needed.

The AutoCAD program has a default template named acad.dwt. This file is empty of the items previously mentioned. AutoCAD provides a special folder that contains predefined templates for standard drawings, along with various international formats recognized by the engineering world. These templates can be modified to include additional items and saved as .dwt files (AutoCAD template files) in this special folder with descriptive names for future use (see Figure 11-10).

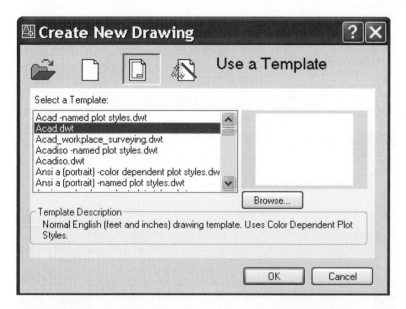

Figure 11-9   Using a template to begin a new drawing

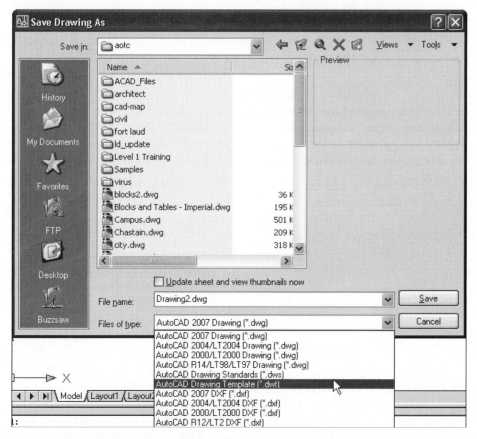

Figure 11-10   Saving as a template

| Single-Character Aliases (Typical) | |
|---|---|
| A | ARC |
| B | BLOCK |
| C | CIRCLE |
| D | DIMSTYLE |
| E | ERASE |
| F | FILLET |
| G | GROUP |
| H | BHATCH |
| I | INSERT |
| J | JOIN |
| L | LINE |
| M | MOVE |
| O | OFFSET |
| P | PAN |
| R | REDRAW |
| S | STRETCH |
| T | MTEXT |
| U | UNDO |
| V | VIEW |
| W | WBLOCK |
| X | EXPLODE |
| Z | ZOOM |

Table 11-1

Another approach to creating templates is to begin with a completed project drawing and erase all the drawing entities. This leaves all the defined layers, styles, layouts, and so on in the drawing ready to use. This "empty" drawing can then be saved in the template folder (see Figure 11-11) as a .dwt file. It can then be accessed by anyone starting a new drawing through the new drawing dialog box as shown in Unit 2 of this book.

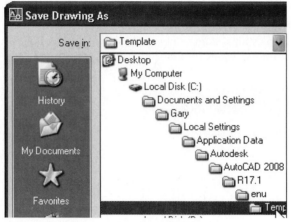

Figure 11-11     Path to the template folder

### Exercise 11-3: Saving as a Template

■ Start AutoCAD and open the UNIT11-Template drawing from the Student CD.
■ Examine the drawing for layers, text styles, and dimension styles. Add two more linetypes to this drawing.
■ From the File menu, pick Save As and change the File type to AutoCAD drawing template (.DWT) at the bottom of the window. Notice the Save In folder change.
■ Save as AATemplate in the template folder.

## MORE ALIAS AND KEYBOARD SHORTCUTS

In Unit 1 the concept of command aliases and keyboard shortcuts was introduced. These items are designed to increase your productivity by giving you a quicker method to initiate a command. Generally, the toolbar icon is the fastest way to start a command. Using a single-character alias (as shown in Table 11-1) is also a quick way to start a command. Many two-character aliases can also be an efficient aid to increase productivity (see Table 11-2). In Appendix C a more complete list of aliases is presented.

Experienced users generally employ keyboard shortcuts and command aliases as these have been very consistent in every version of AutoCAD. Since menus and toolbars are usually modified in new versions of the program, learning these shortcuts allows you to work more easily on any version of the AutoCAD program.

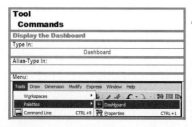

## THE AUTOCAD DASHBOARD

The **DASHBOARD** (Figures 11-12 and 11-13) is a special form of the tool palette. It displays more information than a typical palette as there are display windows for styles, states, and other information as well as more commands and command flyouts. When floating, the Dashboard can be transparent and auto-hide as do other palettes. Unlike palettes with commands, however, no

| Two-Character Aliases (Typical) | |
|---|---|
| DC | DesignCenter |
| DL | Dimension Linear |
| EX | Extend |
| HE-1 | Hatch Editing |
| LA | Layer |
| LI, LS | List |
| OS | Object Snap |
| PL | Polyline |
| QC | Quick Calc |
| RO | Rotate |
| SC | Scale |
| SP | Spell |
| ST | Style |
| TB | Table |
| TP | Tool Palette |
| TO | Toolbar |
| TR | Trim |

**Table 11-2**

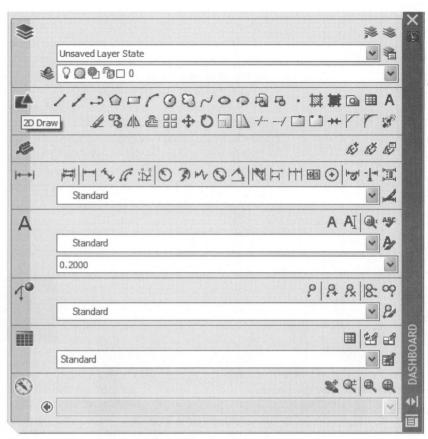

**Figure 11-12**    Floating Dashboard

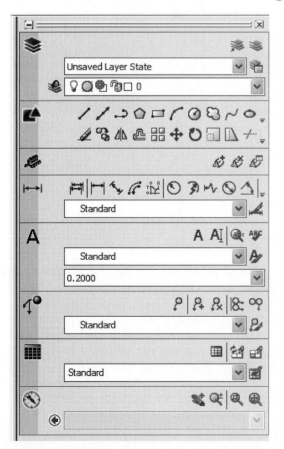

**Figure 11-13**    Docked Dashboard

options for changing entity properties can be applied. Therefore, the icons in the Dashboard are the same as icons in a toolbar.

The Dashboard reduces the clutter caused by displaying many toolbars, presents a single location and interface for information and for icons, and allows you to maximize the drawing area.

If more icons are present on the Dashboard than are able to be displayed, an overflow or fly-out button in the lower right will be present as shown in Figure 11-14. The flyout requires you to hold down the left mouse button and move to the command you wish to activate. Letting go of the mouse will start the command.

The display of a panel is set by the **Control** icon, which is the stand-alone icon on the left. When you left-mouse-click on the **Control** icon, a related tool palette will be displayed. When you left-mouse-click on the other icons, the command is activated. When you right-mouse-click on any icon, a menu is displayed. Most of the menu items are easily recognizable. Accessing the **Control panels** submenu from this main menu shows the list of dashboard palettes available (Figure 11-15). Those with check marks are already being displayed in the Dashboard, and all of them can be toggled on and off.

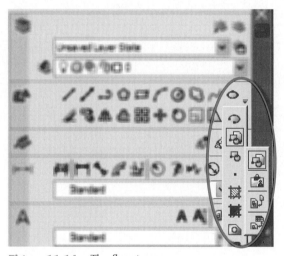

**Figure 11-14**    The flyout menus

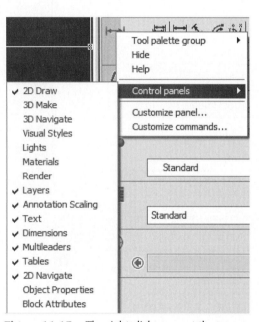

**Figure 11-15**    The right-click menu at the proson

# SUMMARY

In the final unit of this text, we have presented various methods that will enable you to use the AutoCAD program more efficiently and productively. First, you learned how to use the **Enter** key, the **Right Mouse Button** menu, and the **Right Mouse Button's Recent Input** menu to repeat previously executed commands, thereby saving time in drawing creation and modification. You also learned how to customize the organization and arrangement of floating and docked toolbars and tool palettes; this eases access to frequently used commands by placing them closer to the area of the drawing activity and makes the use of drawing space more efficient. Then you were introduced to the use and creation of AutoCAD drawing templates (empty drawings with predefined layers, linetypes, text styles, etc.) for saving the drawing time that otherwise would be consumed in the creation of these items. Keyboard shortcuts and command aliases were then presented to allow you to work more quickly on any version of the Auto-CAD program. Finally, you were introduced to the AutoCAD Dashboard, a special form of the tool palette that maximizes the drawing area by presenting a single location and interface for information and icons, thereby decreasing the number of toolbars displayed.

## CHAPTER TEST QUESTIONS

### Multiple Choice

1. Which of the following is **not** an alias?
   a. H
   b. DL
   c. Undo
   d. E

2. Templates have a ____ extension in their name.
   a. .dwg
   b. .dwt
   c. .dws
   d. .xtp

3. Tool palettes cannot contain:
   a. Commands
   b. Blocks
   c. Hatches
   d. Templates

4. The tool palette properties can place the object:
   a. At a scale
   b. On a specified layer
   c. With a plot style
   d. All of the above

5. Initial settings for the AutoCAD Drawing come from the:
   a. Toolbars
   b. Template
   c. Aliases
   d. Standards

### Matching

| | |
|---|---|
| a. _____ .dwg | 1. AutoCAD template |
| b. _____ .xtp | 2. Used to access a command |
| c. _____ Transparency | 3. Exported tool palette |
| d. _____ .dwt | 4. AutoCAD drawing file |
| e. _____ Icon | 5. The setting to see through the object to the drawing underneath |

### True or False

1. True or False: Using the menu is always faster than using an icon.

2. True or False: Templates are essentially empty drawings.

3. True or False: Aliases can only be one character long.

4. True or False: Toolbars must be docked to be usable.

5. True or False: Templates are stored in the same place as AutoCAD Drawings.

## CHAPTER PROJECTS

### Chapter Project 11-1

Examine Appendix C. Develop a list of at least five changes to the aliases that you would recommend to "your boss" and explain why these changes should be made.

### Chapter Project 11-2

Develop three templates that reflect the disciplines of architecture, civil engineering, and mechanical engineering. Explain what is common to all three and what the differences are.

### Chapter Project 11-3

Discuss within your team and with other professional users of AutoCAD which commands are better as menu items, aliases, in toolbars, or on palettes. Is there a pattern based on discipline (architectural, civil, mechanical, etc.) or on the level of drawing detail? What else may determine the best placement of commands and blocks?

### Chapter Project 11-4

Check with area companies on the use of customized toolbars and palettes. Make a presentation to the class on the findings.

## Tutorial 11-1: Creating a Toolbar

- From the **File** menu, pick **New** to begin a new drawing.
- From the **Tools** menu, pick **CUSTOMIZE** and then pick **INTERFACE** from the menus that appear. The result should be the **Customize User Interface** dialog box as shown in Figure 11-16. Be sure the **Customize** tab is active.

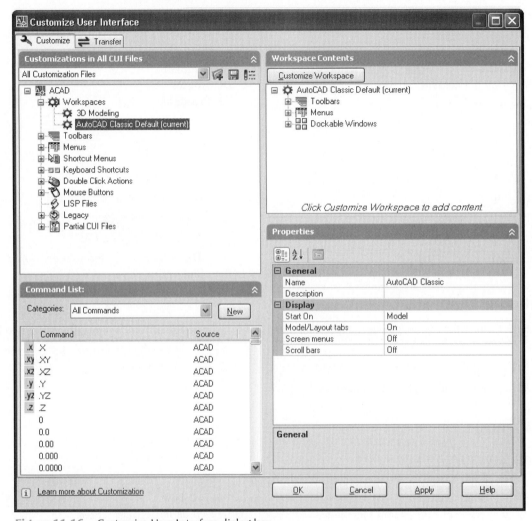

**Figure 11-16**   Customize User Interface dialog box

- Using the right mouse, pick on the word **Toolbars** in the upper left area of the dialog box and pick **New** (see Figure 11-17) to create a new toolbar for this interface.
- Right-mouse-click on the new toolbar and **Rename** it **11Special** (see Figure 11-18).
- From the lower left of the **Customize User Interface** dialog box find the commands listed below and drag and drop them to the new toolbar. The upper right area will show the icons as the toolbar is constructed (see Figure 11-18).

  - **LINE** command
  - **POLYLINE** command
  - **ERASE** command

**Figure 11-17**  Creating the new toolbar

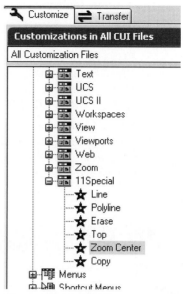

**Figure 11-18**  Toolbar commands

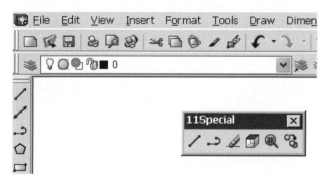

**Figure 11-19**  Completed toolbar

**Figure 11-20**  Create the new palette

- **COPY** command
- **TOP** View command
- **ZOOM CENTER** command
- Close the Customize User Interface dialog box and the new toolbar created should be on the list of toolbars as well as in the screen (see Figure 11-19).
- Save the drawing in your **Workskills** folder as **T11-1.**

### Tutorial 11-2: Creating a Tool Palette

- From the **File** menu pick **New** to begin a new drawing.
- From the **Tools** menu, pick the **Palettes** and then pick **Tool Palettes** to bring the **Tool** palettes forward into the drawing area.
- Right-mouse-click on one of the tabs of the **Tool** palettes to generate the **New Palette** menu item (see Figure 11-20).
- Rename the new tool palette **11Special.**
- Right-mouse-click on the new palette to access the **Customize Commands** menu item (see Figure 11-21).

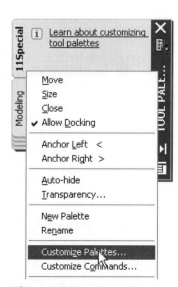

**Figure 11-21**  Customize menu for the new palette

- With the **Customize User Interface** dialog box open, drag and drop the commands listed below from their location on the various toolbars around the drawing area as shown in Figure 11-22:
  - **LINE** command
  - **POLYLINE** command
  - **ERASE** command
  - **COPY** command
  - **LAYER PROPERTIES** command
- Close the **Customize** dialog box to stop adding commands to the palette (see Figure 11-23).
- On the new **11Special** palette, right-click on the **LINE** command and pick **Copy** (see Figure 11-24).

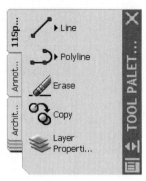

**Figure 11-22** Commands on the new palette

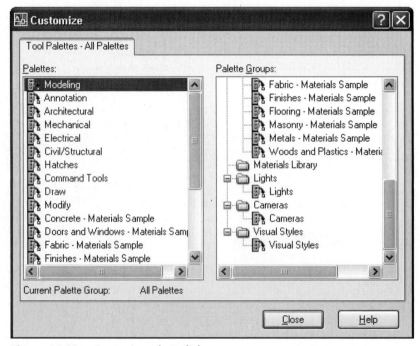

**Figure 11-23** Customize palette dialog

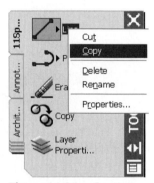

**Figure 11-24** Creating copies of the LINE command

- Right-click in an open area on the **11Special** palette and **PASTE** the **LINE** command on the current palette twice.
- Right-click on the second copy of the **LINE** command and choose **Properties** (see Figure 11-25).
- Edit the **Name** of the command to be **Red Line** and modify the color to **Red** (see Figure 11-26).
- Right-click on the third copy of the **LINE** command and choose **Properties.**
- Edit the **Name** of the command to be **Yellow Line** and modify the color to **Yellow,** similar to what is shown in Figure 11-26.
- Click on each LINE command in the palette (see Figure 11-27) and draw a few line segments in the drawing. While only color was changed in this tutorial, more properties could have been changed. Tailoring your commands in this way can result in more productive drawing sessions.
- Save the drawing in your **Workskills** folder as **T11-2.**

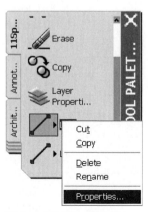

**Figure 11-25** Modify properties of the command

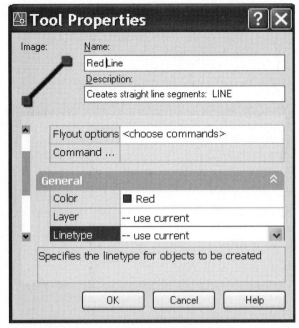

Figure 11-26    Properties for the Red Line

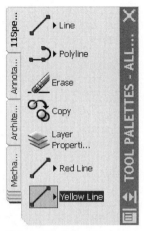

Figure 11-27    Final palette for Tutorial 11-2

## PRACTICE EXERCISES

### Practice Exercise 11-1: Creating Toolbars

Create a toolbar with at least six of the commands that you use most often. Name this toolbar with your name or initials. Save the drawing in your **Workskills** folder as **EX11-1.**

### Practice Exercise 11-2: Creating Palettes

Create a palette with at least six of the commands that you use most often. Modify properties on some of the commands based on the usage of the commands. Also add four of the blocks you created or used in the Unit 8 Tutorials to this palette by accessing those saved drawings with DesignCenter (**CTRL+2** or the alias **DC**). Being able to combine commands and blocks with customized properties offers you great productivity in creating drawings. Use the commands in the palette to draw a few items, and place a few blocks from the palette in the drawing. Save the drawing in your **Workskills** folder as **EX11-2.**

# AutoCAD Commands

**A**

3D
3DALIGN
3DARRAY
3DCLIP
3DCONFIG
3DCORBIT
3DDISTANCE
3DDWF
3DDWFPUBLISH
3DFACE
3DFLY
3DFORBIT
3DMESH
3DMOVE
3DORBIT
3DORBITCTR
3DPAN
3DPOLY
3DROTATE
3DSIN
3DSOUT
3DSWIVEL
3DWALK
3DZOOM

ABOUT
ACISIN
ACISOUT
ADCCLOSE
ADCENTER
ADCNAVIGATE
ALIGN
AMECONVERT
ANIPATH
ANNORESET
ANNOUPDATE
APERTURE
APPLOAD
ARC
ARCHIVE
AREA
ARRAY
ARX
ATTACHURL

ATTDEF
ATTDISP
ATTEDIT
ATTEXT
ATTIPEDIT
ATTREDEF
ATTSYNC
AUDIT
AUTOPUBLISH

BACKGROUND
BACTION
BACTIONSET
BACTIONTOOL
BASE
BASSOCIATE
BATTMAN
BATTORDER
BAUTHORPALLETTE
BAUTHORPALLETTECLOSE
BCLOSE
BCYCLEORDER
BEDIT
BGRIPSET
BHATCH
BLIPMODE
BLOCK
BLOCKICON
BLOOKUPTABLE
BMPOUT
BOUNDARY
BOX
BPARAMETER
BREAK
BREP
BROWSER
BSAVE
BSAVEAS
BVHIDE
BVSHOW
BVSTATE

CAL
CAMERA

CHAMFER
CHANGE
CHECKSTANDARDS
CHPROP
CHSPACE
CIRCLE
CLEANSCREENOFF
CLEANSCREENON
CLOSE
CLOSEALL
COLOR
COMMANDLINE
COMMANDLINEHIDE
COMPILE
CONE
CONVERT
CONVERTCTB
CONVERTOLDLIGHTS
CONVERTOLDMATERIALS
CONVERTPSTYLES
CONVTOSOLID
CONVTOSURFACE
COPY
COPYBASE
COPYCLIP
COPYHIST
COPYLINK
COPYTOLAYER
CUI
CUIEXPORT
CUIIMPORT
CUILOAD
CUIUNLOAD
CUSTOMIZE
CUTCLIP
CYLINDER

DASHBOARD
DASHBOARDCLOSE
DATAEXTRACTION
DATALINK
DATALINKUPDATE
DBCONNECT
DBLIST

| | | |
|---|---|---|
| DDEDIT | ELLIPSE | LAYCUR |
| DDPTYPE | ERASE | LAYDEL |
| DDVPOINT | ETRANSMIT | LAYER |
| DELAY | EXPLODE | LAYERP |
| DETACHURL | EXPORT | LAYERPMODE |
| DGNADJUST | EXPORTTOAUTOCAD | LAYERSTATE |
| DGNATTACH | EXTEND | LAYFRZ |
| DGNCLIP | EXTERNALREFERENCES | LAYISO |
| DGNEXPORT | EXTERNALREFERENCES- | LAYLCK |
| DGNIMPORT | CLOSE | LAYMCH |
| DIM | EXTRUDE | LAYMCUR |
| DIM1 | | LAYMGR |
| DIMALIGNED | FIELD | LAYOFF |
| DIMANGULAR | FILL | LAYON |
| DIMARC | FILLET | LAYOUT |
| DIMBASELINE | FILTER | LAYOUTWIZARD |
| DIMBREAK | FIND | LAYTHW |
| DIMCENTER | FLATSHOT | LAYTRANS |
| DIMCONTINUE | FOG | LAYULK |
| DIMDIAMETER | FREESPOT | LAYUNISO |
| DIMDISASSOCIATE | FREEWEB | LAYVPI |
| DIMEDIT | | LAYWALK |
| DIMINSPECT | GEOGRAPHICLOCATION | LEADER |
| DIMJOGGED | GOTOURL | LENGTHEN |
| DIMJOGLINE | GRADIENT | LIGHT |
| DIMLINEAR | GRAPHSCR | LIGHTLIST |
| DIMORDINATE | GRID | LIGHTLISTCLOSE |
| DIMOVERRIDE | GROUP | LIMITS |
| DIMRADIUS | | LINE |
| DIMREASSOCIATE | HATCHEDIT | LINETYPE |
| DIMREGEN | HATCH | LIST |
| DIMSPACE | HELIX | LIVESECTION |
| DIMSTYLE | HELP | LOAD |
| DIMTEDIT | HIDE | LOFT |
| DIST | HLSETTINGS | LOGFILEOFF |
| DISTANTLIGHT | HYPERLINK | LOGFILEON |
| DIVIDE | HYPERLINKOPTIONS | LSEDIT |
| DONUT | | LSLIB |
| DRAGMODE | ID | LSNEW |
| DRAWINGRECOVERY | IMAGEADJUST | LTSCALE |
| DRAWINGRECOVERYHIDE | IMAGEATTACH | LWEIGHT |
| DRAWORDER | IMAGECLIP | |
| DSETTINGS | IMAGEFRAME | MARKUPCLOSE |
| DSVIEWER | IMAGE | MARKUP |
| DVIEW | IMAGEQUALITY | MASSPROP |
| DWFADJUST | IMPORT | MATCHCELL |
| DWFATTACH | IMPRINT | MATCHPROP |
| DWFCLIP | INSERT | MATERIALATTACH |
| DWFLAYERS | INSERTOBJ | MATERIALMAP |
| DWGPROPS | INTERFERE | MATERIALS |
| DXBIN | INTERSECT | MATERIALSCLOSE |
| | ISOPLANE | MATLIB |
| EATTEDIT | | MEASURE |
| EATTEXT | JOGSECTION | MENU |
| EDGE | JOIN | MENULOAD |
| EDGESURF | JPGOUT | MENUUNLOAD |
| ELEV | JUSTIFYTEXT | MINSERT |

MIRROR3D
MIRROR
MLEADER
MLEADERALIGN
MLEADERCOLLECT
MLEADEREDIT
MLEADERSTYLE
MLEDIT
MLINE
MLSTYLE
MODEL
MOVE
MREDO
MSLIDE
MSPACE
MTEDIT
MTEXT
MULTIPLE
MVIEW
MVSETUP

NETLOAD
NEW
NEWSHEETSET

OBJSCALE
OFFSET
OLELINKS
OLESCALE
OOPS
OPENDWFMARKUP
OPEN
OPENSHEETSET
OPTIONS
ORTHO
OSNAP

PAGESETUP
PAN
PARTIALOAD
PARTIALOPEN
PASTEASHYPERLINK
PASTEBLOCK
PASTECLIP
PASTEORIG
PASTESPEC
PCINWIZARD
PEDIT
PFACE
PLAN
PLANESURF
PLINE
PLOT
PLOTSTAMP
PLOTSTYLE
PLOTTERMANAGER
PNGOUT

POINT
POINTLIGHT
POLYGON
POLYSOLID
PRESSPULL
PREVIEW
PROPERTIESCLOSE
PROPERTIES
PSSETUPIN
PSFACE
PUBLISH
PUBLISHTOWEB
PURGE
PYRAMID

QCCLOSE
QDIM
QLEADER
QNEW
QSAVE
QSELECT
QTEXT
QUICKCALC
QUICKCUI
QUIT

RAY
RECOVER
RECOVERALL
RECTANG
REDEFINE
REDO
REDRAWALL
REDRAW
REFCLOSE
REFEDIT
REFSET
REGENALL
REGENAUTO
REGEN
REGION
REINIT
RENAME
RENDER
RENDERCROP
RENDERENVIRONMENT
RENDERPRESETS
RENDERWIN
RENDSCR
REPLAY
RESETBLOCK
RESUME
REVCLOUD
REVOLVE
REVSURF
RMAT
ROTATE3D

ROTATE
RPREF
RPREFCLOSE
RSCRIPT
RULESURF

SAVEAS
SAVEIMG
SAVE
SCALE
SCALELISTEDIT
SCALETEXT
SCRIPT
SECTION
SECTIONPLANE
SECURITYOPTIONS
SELECT
SETBYLAYER
SETIDROPHANDLER
SETUV
SETVAR
SHADEMODE
SHAPE
SHEETSETHIDE
SHEETSET
SHELL
SHOWMAT
SIGVALIDATE
SKETCH
SLICE
SNAP
SOLDRAW
SOLID
SOLIDEDIT
SOLPROF
SOLVIEW
SPACETRANS
SPELL
SPHERE
SPLINEDIT
SPLINE
SPOTLIGHT
STANDARDS
STATUS
STLOUT
STRETCH
STYLESMANAGER
STYLE
SUBTRACT
SUNPROPERTIES
SUNPROPERTIESCLOSE
SWEEP
SYSWINDOWS

TABLE
TABLEDIT
TABLEEXPORT

TABLESTYLE
TABLET
TABSURF
TARGETPOINT
TASKBAR
TEXTSCR
TEXT
TEXTTOFRONT
THICKEN
TIFOUT
TIME
TINSERT
TOLERANCE
TOOLBAR
TOOLPALETTESCLOSE
TOOLPALETTES
TORUS
TPNAVIGATE
TRACE
TRANSPARENCY
TRAYSETTINGS
TREESTAT
TRIM

U
UCS
UCSICON

UCSMAN
UNDEFINE
UNDO
UNION
UNITS
UPDATEFIELD
UPDATETHUMBSNOW

VBAIDE
VBALOAD
VBAMAN
VBARUN
VBASTMT
VBAUNLOAD
VIEW
VIEWPLOTDETAILS
VIEWRES
VISUALSTYLES
VISUALSTYLESCLOSE
VLISP
VPCLIP
VPLAYER
VPMAX
VPMIN
VPOINT
VPORTS
VSCURRENT

VSLIDE
VSSAVE
VTOPTIONS

WALKFLYSETTINGS
WBLOCK
WEBLIGHT
WEDGE
WHOHAS
WIPEOUT
WMFIN
WMFOPTS
WMFOUT
WORKSPACE
WSSAVE
WSSETTINGS

XATTACH
XBIND
XCLIP
XEDGES
XLINE
XOPEN
XPLODE
XREF

ZOOM

# Menus and Toolbars

## MENUS

### Insert menu

### File menu

### Layout menu

### Drawing Utilities menu

### Edit menu

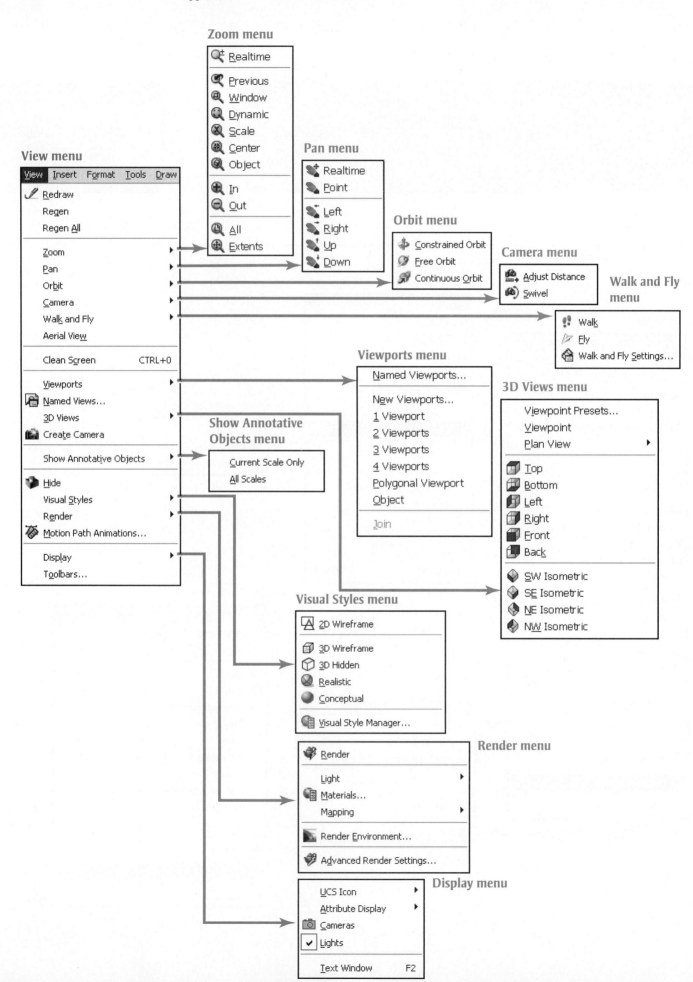

**Zoom menu**

- Realtime
- Previous
- Window
- Dynamic
- Scale
- Center
- Object
- In
- Out
- All
- Extents

**Pan menu**

- Realtime
- Point
- Left
- Right
- Up
- Down

**Orbit menu**

- Constrained Orbit
- Free Orbit
- Continuous Orbit

**Camera menu**

- Adjust Distance
- Swivel

**Walk and Fly menu**

- Walk
- Fly
- Walk and Fly Settings...

**View menu**

View  Insert  Format  Tools  Draw

- Redraw
- Regen
- Regen All
- Zoom
- Pan
- Orbit
- Camera
- Walk and Fly
- Aerial View
- Clean Screen          CTRL+0
- Viewports
- Named Views...
- 3D Views
- Create Camera
- Show Annotative Objects
- Hide
- Visual Styles
- Render
- Motion Path Animations...
- Display
- Toolbars...

**Show Annotative Objects menu**

- Current Scale Only
- All Scales

**Viewports menu**

- Named Viewports...
- New Viewports...
- 1 Viewport
- 2 Viewports
- 3 Viewports
- 4 Viewports
- Polygonal Viewport
- Object
- Join

**3D Views menu**

- Viewpoint Presets...
- Viewpoint
- Plan View
- Top
- Bottom
- Left
- Right
- Front
- Back
- SW Isometric
- SE Isometric
- NE Isometric
- NW Isometric

**Visual Styles menu**

- 2D Wireframe
- 3D Wireframe
- 3D Hidden
- Realistic
- Conceptual
- Visual Style Manager...

**Render menu**

- Render
- Light
- Materials...
- Mapping
- Render Environment...
- Advanced Render Settings...

**Display menu**

- UCS Icon
- Attribute Display
- Cameras
- ✓ Lights
- Text Window          F2

**Format menu**

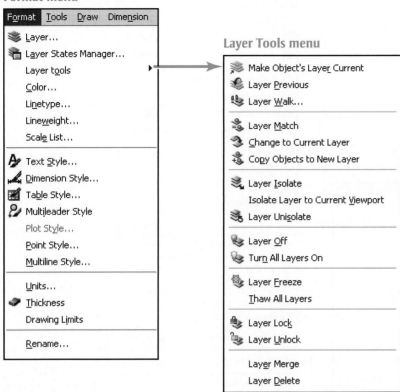

**Layer Tools menu**

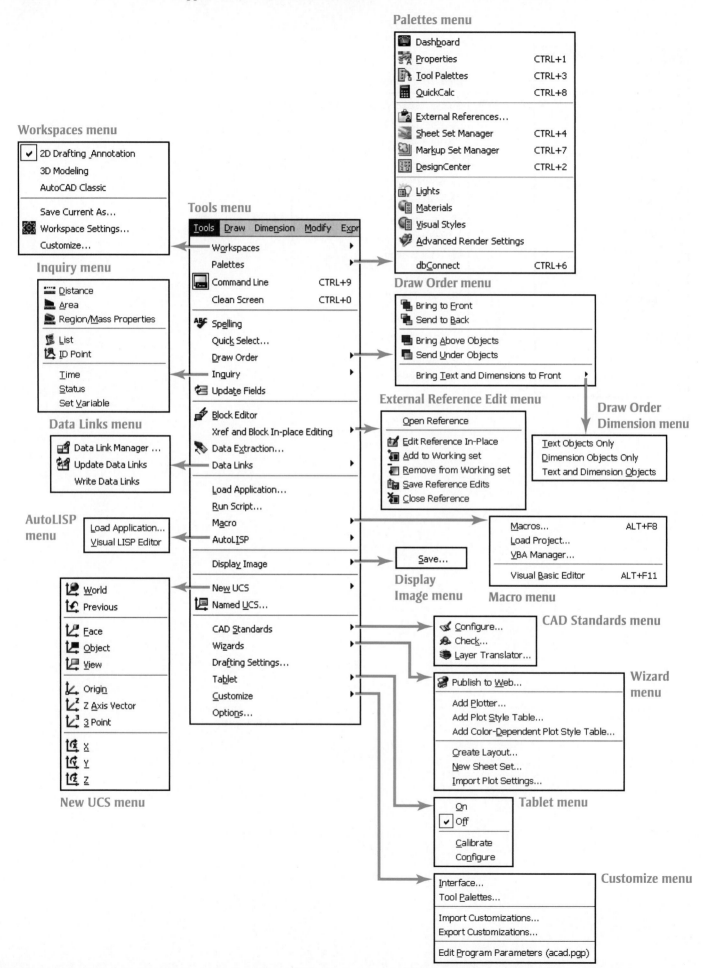

**Palettes menu**

| | | |
|---|---|---|
| | Dashboard | |
| | Properties | CTRL+1 |
| | Tool Palettes | CTRL+3 |
| | QuickCalc | CTRL+8 |
| | External References... | |
| | Sheet Set Manager | CTRL+4 |
| | Markup Set Manager | CTRL+7 |
| | DesignCenter | CTRL+2 |
| | Lights | |
| | Materials | |
| | Visual Styles | |
| | Advanced Render Settings | |
| | dbConnect | CTRL+6 |

**Workspaces menu**

| | |
|---|---|
| ✓ | 2D Drafting _Annotation |
| | 3D Modeling |
| | AutoCAD Classic |
| | Save Current As... |
| | Workspace Settings... |
| | Customize... |

**Tools menu**

Tools  Draw  Dimension  Modify  Expr
- Workspaces ▶
- Palettes ▶
- Command Line          CTRL+9
- Clean Screen          CTRL+0
- Spelling
- Quick Select...
- Draw Order ▶
- Inquiry ▶
- Update Fields
- Block Editor
- Xref and Block In-place Editing ▶
- Data Extraction...
- Data Links ▶
- Load Application...
- Run Script...
- Macro ▶
- AutoLISP ▶
- Display Image ▶
- New UCS ▶
- Named UCS...
- CAD Standards ▶
- Wizards ▶
- Drafting Settings...
- Tablet ▶
- Customize ▶
- Options...

**Inquiry menu**

- Distance
- Area
- Region/Mass Properties
- List
- ID Point
- Time
- Status
- Set Variable

**Data Links menu**

- Data Link Manager ...
- Update Data Links
- Write Data Links

**AutoLISP menu**

- Load Application...
- Visual LISP Editor

**New UCS menu**

- World
- Previous
- Face
- Object
- View
- Origin
- Z Axis Vector
- 3 Point
- X
- Y
- Z

**Draw Order menu**

- Bring to Front
- Send to Back
- Bring Above Objects
- Send Under Objects
- Bring Text and Dimensions to Front ▶

**Draw Order Dimension menu**

- Text Objects Only
- Dimension Objects Only
- Text and Dimension Objects

**External Reference Edit menu**

- Open Reference
- Edit Reference In-Place
- Add to Working set
- Remove from Working set
- Save Reference Edits
- Close Reference

**Display Image menu**

- Save...

**Macro menu**

| | |
|---|---|
| Macros... | ALT+F8 |
| Load Project... | |
| VBA Manager... | |
| Visual Basic Editor | ALT+F11 |

**CAD Standards menu**

- Configure...
- Check...
- Layer Translator...

**Wizard menu**

- Publish to Web...
- Add Plotter...
- Add Plot Style Table...
- Add Color-Dependent Plot Style Table...
- Create Layout...
- New Sheet Set...
- Import Plot Settings...

**Tablet menu**

| | |
|---|---|
| | On |
| ✓ | Off |
| | Calibrate |
| | Configure |

**Customize menu**

- Interface...
- Tool Palettes...
- Import Customizations...
- Export Customizations...
- Edit Program Parameters (acad.pgp)

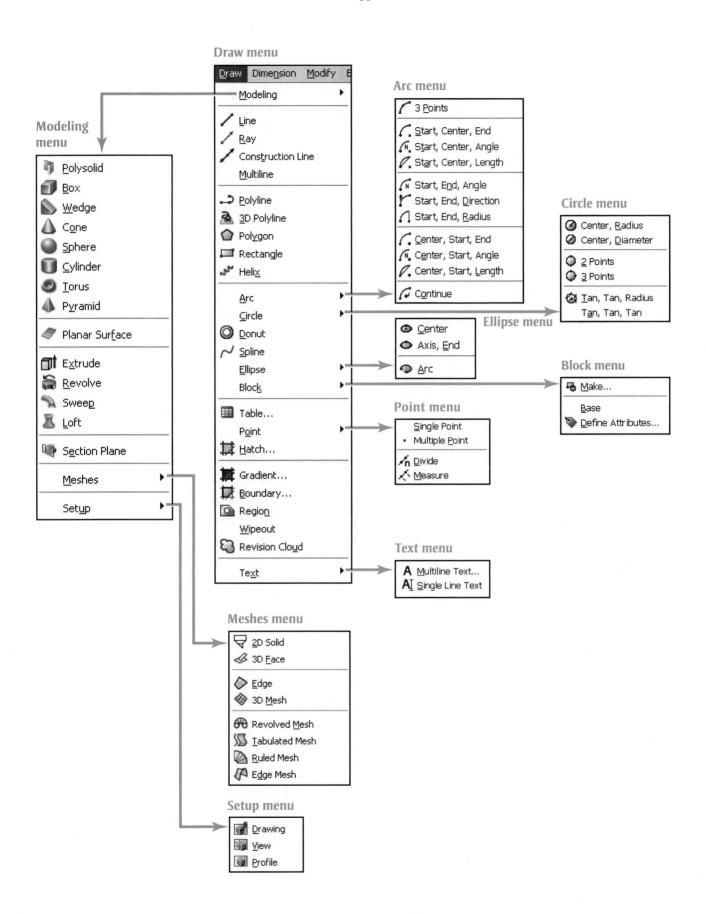

**Draw menu**

**Modeling menu**

**Arc menu**

**Circle menu**

**Ellipse menu**

**Block menu**

**Point menu**

**Text menu**

**Meshes menu**

**Setup menu**

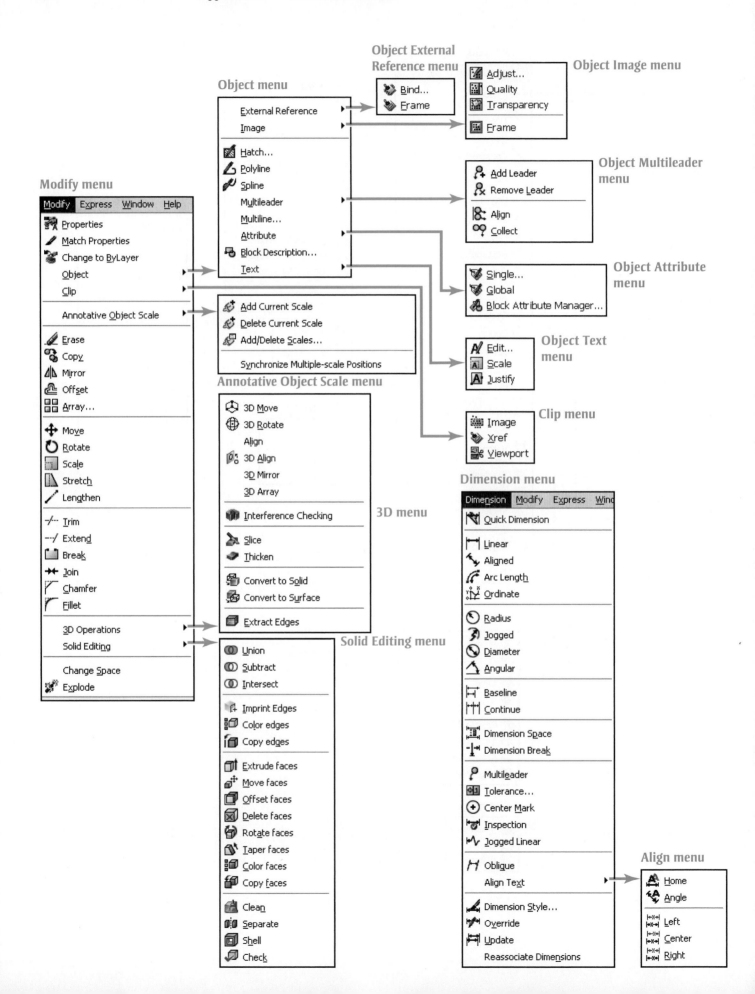

**Object External Reference menu**

**Object Image menu**

**Object menu**

**Object Multileader menu**

**Modify menu**

**Object Attribute menu**

**Object Text menu**

**Annotative Object Scale menu**

**Clip menu**

**3D menu**

**Dimension menu**

**Solid Editing menu**

**Align menu**

**Window menu**

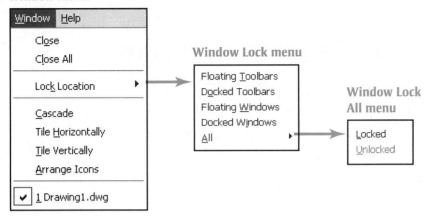

**Help menu**

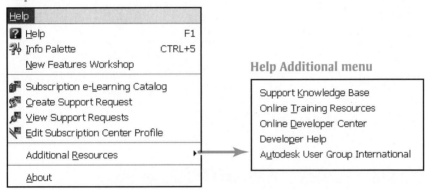

# TOOLBARS

### 3D Navigation

### CAD Standards

### Camera Adjustments

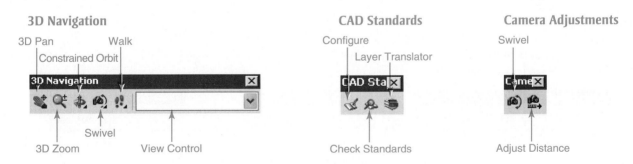

## Dimension

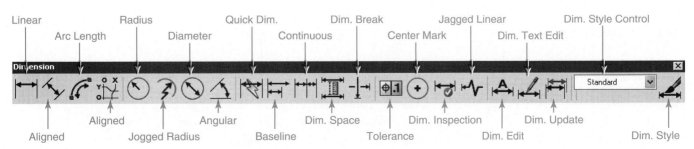

**Draw**

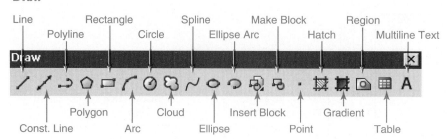

**Draw Order**          **Inquiry**          **Insert**

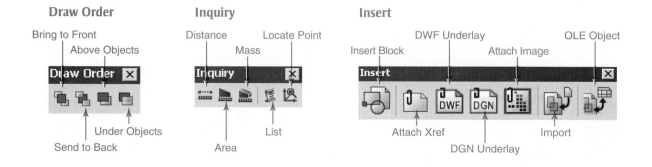

**Layers**

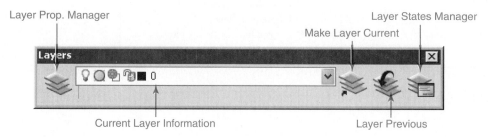

**Layers II**                    **Layouts**          **Lights**

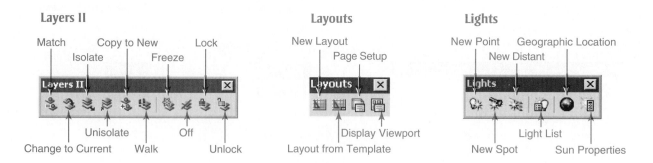

**Mapping**          **Modeling**

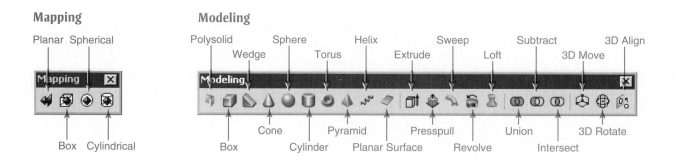

## Modify

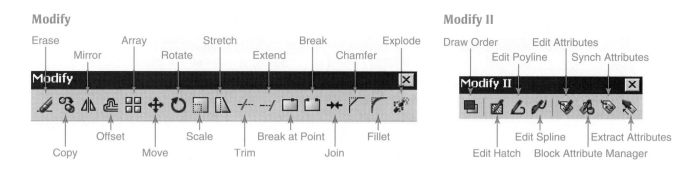

## Modify II

## Multileader

## Object Snap

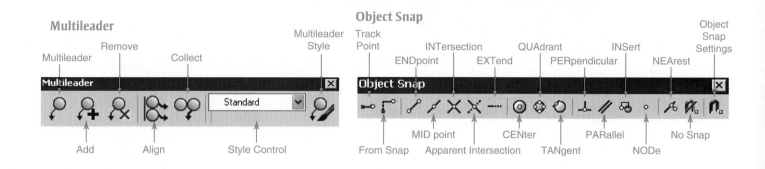

## Orbit

## Properties

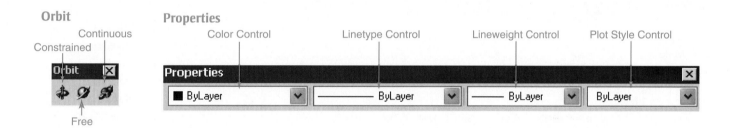

## External Reference and Block Edit

## External Reference and Image (Reference)

## Render

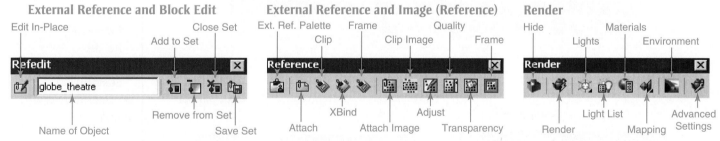

## Solids Editing

## Standard

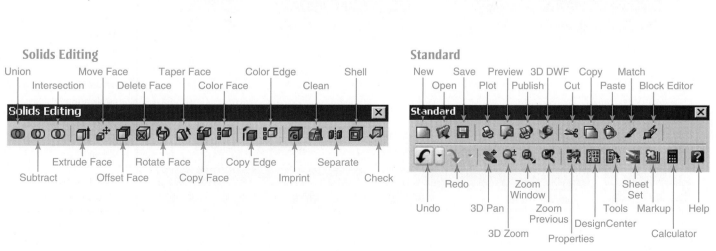

## Styles

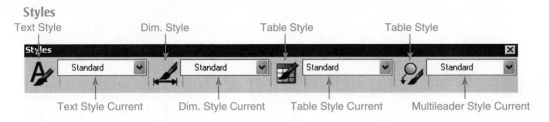

Text Style    Dim. Style    Table Style    Table Style

Text Style Current    Dim. Style Current    Table Style Current    Multileader Style Current

## Text

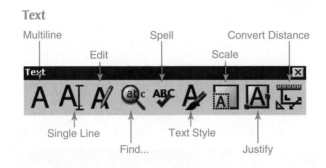

Multiline    Spell    Convert Distance
Edit    Scale
Single Line    Text Style
Find...    Justify

## UCS

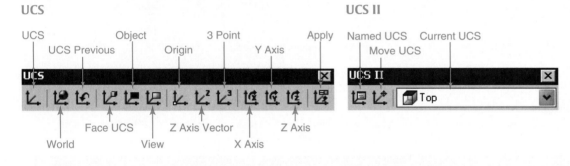

UCS    Object    3 Point    Apply
UCS Previous    Origin    Y Axis
Face UCS    Z Axis Vector    Z Axis
World    View    X Axis

## UCS II

Named UCS    Current UCS
Move UCS

## View

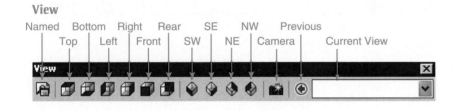

Named    Bottom    Right    Rear    SE    NW    Previous
Top    Left    Front    SW    NE    Camera    Current View

## Viewports

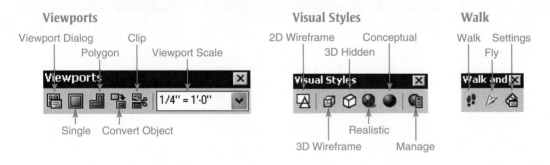

Viewport Dialog    Clip
Polygon    Viewport Scale
Single    Convert Object

## Visual Styles

2D Wireframe    Conceptual
3D Hidden
Realistic
3D Wireframe    Manage

## Walk

Walk    Settings
Fly

## Web

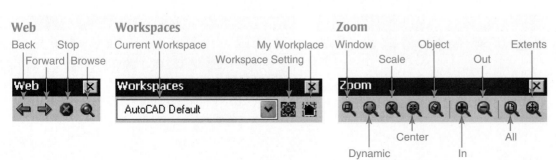

Back    Stop
Forward    Browse

## Workspaces

Current Workspace    My Workplace
Workspace Setting

AutoCAD Default

## Zoom

Window    Object    Extents
Scale    Out
Dynamic    Center    In    All

3D Navigation
CAD Standards
Camera Adjustment
Dimension
✔ Draw
Draw Order
Inquiry
Insert
✔ Layers
Layers II
Layouts
Lights
Mapping
Modeling
✔ Modify
Modify II
Multileader
Object Snap
Orbit
✔ Properties
Refedit
Reference
Render
Solid Editing
Standard
✔ Standard Annotation
✔ Styles
Text
UCS
UCS II
View
Viewports
Visual Styles
Walk and Fly
Web
✔ Workspaces
Zoom

Lock Location    ▶
Customize...

# Command Alias List

C

| Alias | Command (Standard) | Alternate Alias | Command Line Version Only |
|---|---|---|---|
| **Single Stroke (Most Used)** | | | |
| A | ARC | | |
| B | BLOCK | -B | -BLOCK |
| C | CIRCLE | | |
| D | DIMSTYLE | | |
| E | ERASE | | |
| F | FILLET | | |
| G | GROUP | -G | -GROUP |
| H | BHATCH | -H | -HATCH |
| I | INSERT | -I | -INSERT |
| J | JOIN | | |
| L | LINE | | |
| M | MOVE | | |
| O | OFFSET | | |
| P | PAN | -P | -PAN |
| R | REDRAW | | |
| S | STRETCH | | |
| T | MTEXT | -T | -MTEXT |
| U | UNDO | | |
| V | VIEW | -V | -VIEW |
| W | WBLOCK | -W | -WBLOCK |
| X | EXPLODE | | |
| Z | ZOOM | | |
| **Block and Xref Commands** | | | |
| AC | BACTION | | |
| ATT | ATTDEF | -ATT | -ATTDEF |
| ATE | ATTEDIT | -ATE | -ATTEDIT |
| ATI | ATTIPEDIT | | |
| ATTE | -ATTEDIT | | |
| B | BLOCK | -B | -BLOCK |
| BC | BCLOSE | | |
| BE | BEDIT | | |
| BS | BSAVE | | |
| BVS | BVSTATE | | |
| ED | DDEDIT | | |
| ER | EXTERNALREFERENCES | | |
| I | INSERT | -I | -INSERT |
| PA | PASTESPEC | | |
| PARAM | BPARAMETER | | |
| W | WBLOCK | -W | -WBLOCK |
| XA | XATTACH | | |
| XB | XBIND | -XB | -XBIND |
| XC | XCLIP | | |
| XR | XREF | -XR | -XREF |

| Alias | Command (Standard) | Alternate Alias | Command Line Version Only |
|---|---|---|---|
| **Draw Commands** | | | |
| 3F | 3DFACE | | |
| 3P | 3DPOLY | | |
| A | ARC | | |
| BH | BHATCH | | |
| BO | BOUNDARY | -BO | -BOUNDARY |
| C | CIRCLE | | |
| CYL | CYLINDER | | |
| DO | DONUT | | |
| DT | TEXT | | |
| EL | ELLIPSE | | |
| EXT | EXTRUDE | | |
| GD | GRADIENT | | |
| H | HATCH | -H | -HATCH |
| L | LINE | | |
| ML | MLINE | | |
| MT | MTEXT | | |
| PL | PLINE | | |
| PO | POINT | | |
| POL | POLYGON | | |
| PSOLID | POLYSOLID | | |
| PYR | PYRAMID | | |
| REC | RECTANG | | |
| REG | REGION | | |
| SO | SOLID | | |
| SPL | SPLINE | | |
| T | MTEXT | -T | -MTEXT |
| TB | TABLE | | |
| TOR | TORUS | | |
| WE | WEDGE | | |
| XL | XLINE | | |
| **Dimension Commands** | | | |
| D | DIMSTYLE | | |
| DAL | DIMALIGNED | | |
| DAN | DIMANGULAR | | |
| DAR | DIMARC | | |
| DBA | DIMBASELINE | | |
| DCE | DIMCENTER | | |
| DCO | DIMCONTINUE | | |
| DDA | DIMDISASSOCIATE | | |
| DDI | DIMDIAMETER | | |
| DED | DIMEDIT | | |
| DJL | DIMJOGLINE | | |
| DJO | DIMENSIONJOGGED | | |
| DLI | DIMLINEAR | | |
| DOR | DIMORDINATE | | |
| DOV | DIMOVERRIDE | | |
| DRA | DIMRADIUS | | |
| DRE | DIMREASSOCIATE | | |
| DST | DIMSTYLE | | |
| JOG | DIMJOGGED | | |
| LE | QLEADER | | |
| MLA | MLEADERALIGN | | |
| MLC | MLEADERCOLLECT | | |
| MLD | MLEADER | | |
| MLE | MLEADEREDIT | | |
| MLS | MLEADERSTYLE | | |
| TOL | TOLERANCE | | |

| Alias | Command (Standard) | Alternate Alias | Command Line Version Only |
|---|---|---|---|
| **File Commands** | | | |
| AECTOACAD | EXPORTTOAUTOCAD | | |
| DRM | DRAWINGRECOVERY | | |
| EXIT | QUIT | | |
| EXP | EXPORT | | |
| IMP | IMPORT | | |
| IO | INSERTOBJ | | |
| LO | -LAYOUT | | |
| PARTIALOPEN | -PARTIALOPEN | | |
| PRE | PREVIEW | | |
| PRINT | PLOT | | |
| PTW | PUBLISHTOWEB | | |
| SSM | SHEETSET | | |
| **Format Commands** | | | |
| COL | COLOR | COLOUR | COLOR |
| CT | CTABLESTYLE | | |
| D | DIMSTYLE | | |
| DST | DIMSTYLE | | |
| LA | LAYER | -LA | -LAYER |
| LAS | LAYERSTATE | | |
| LMAN | LAYERSTATE | | |
| LT | LINETYPE | -LT | -LINETYPE |
| LTYPE | LINETYPE | -LTYPE | -LINETYPE |
| LTS | LTSCALE | | |
| LW | LWEIGHT | LINEWEIGHT | LWEIGHT |
| ST | STYLE | | |
| STA | STANDARDS | | |
| TH | THICKNESS | | |
| TS | TABLESTYLE | | |
| UN | UNITS | -UN | -UNITS |
| **Image Commands** | | | |
| IAD | IMAGEADJUST | | |
| IAT | IMAGEATTACH | | |
| ICL | IMAGECLIP | | |
| IM | IMAGE | -IM | -IMAGE |
| **Modify Commands** | | | |
| 3A | 3DARRAY | | |
| 3AL | 3DALIGN | | |
| 3DMIRROR | MIRROR3D | | |
| 3M | 3DMOVE | | |
| 3R | 3DROTATE | | |
| AL | ALIGN | | |
| AR | ARRAY | -AR | -ARRAY |
| BR | BREAK | | |
| CH | PROPERTIES | -CH | CHANGE |
| CHA | CHAMFER | | |
| CO | COPY | | |
| CP | COPY | | |
| DIV | DIVIDE | | |
| E | ERASE | | |
| ED | DDEDIT | | |
| EX | EXTEND | | |
| F | FILLET | | |
| G | GROUP | -G | -GROUP |
| GD | GRADIENT | | |
| HE | HATCHEDIT | | |
| IN | INTERSECT | | |

| Alias | Command (Standard) | Alternate Alias | Command Line Version Only |
|---|---|---|---|
| INF | INTERFERE | | |
| J | JOIN | | |
| LEN | LENGTHEN | | |
| M | MOVE | | |
| MA | MATCHPROP | | |
| ME | MEASURE | | |
| MI | MIRROR | | |
| MO | PROPERTIES | | |
| O | OFFSET | | |
| PE | PEDIT | | |
| PR | PROPERTIES | | |
| PRCLOSE | PROPERTIESCLOSE | | |
| PROPS | PROPERTIES | | |
| PU | PURGE | -PU | -PURGE |
| REN | RENAME | -REN | -RENAME |
| REV | REVOLVE | | |
| RO | ROTATE | | |
| S | STRETCH | | |
| SC | SCALE | | |
| SEC | SECTION | | |
| SL | SLICE | | |
| SP | SPELL | | |
| SPE | SPLINEDIT | | |
| SPLANE | SECTIONPLANE | | |
| SU | SUBTRACT | | |
| TR | TRIM | | |
| UNI | UNION | | |
| X | EXPLODE | | |

**Tool Commands**

| Alias | Command (Standard) | Alternate Alias | Command Line Version Only |
|---|---|---|---|
| AA | AREA | | |
| ADC | ADCENTER | | |
| AL | ALIGN | | |
| AP | APPLOAD | | |
| CHK | CHECKSTANDARDS | | |
| CLI | COMMANDLINE | | |
| DBC | DBCONNECT | | |
| DC | ADCENTER | DCENTER | ADCENTER |
| DI | DIST | | |
| DL | DATALINK | | |
| DLU | DATALINKUPDATE | | |
| DR | DRAWORDER | | |
| DS | DSETTINGS | | |
| DX | DATAEXTRACTION | | |
| FI | FILTER | | |
| GEO | GEOGRAPHICLOCATION | | |
| GR | DDGRIPS | | |
| LI | LIST | | |
| LS | LIST | | |
| MSM | MARKUP | | |
| NORTH | GEOGRAPHICLOCATION | | |
| NORTHDIR | GEOGRAPHICLOCATION | | |
| OP | OPTIONS | | |
| OS | OSNAP | -OS | -OSNAP |
| QC | QUICKCALC | | |
| QCUI | QUICKCUI | | |
| SCR | SCRIPT | | |
| SE | DSETTINGS | | |

| Alias | Command (Standard) | Alternate Alias | Command Line Version Only |
|---|---|---|---|
| SET | SETVAR | | |
| SN | SNAP | | |
| TA | TABLET | | |
| TO | TOOLBAR | | |
| TP | TOOLPALETTES | | |
| **View Commands** | | | |
| 3DNAVIGATE | 3DWALK | | |
| 3DO | 3DORBIT | | |
| 3DW | 3DWALK | | |
| CAM | CAMERA | | |
| DV | DVIEW | | |
| FREEPOINT | POINTLIGHT | | |
| FSHOT | FLATSHOT | | |
| HI | HIDE | | |
| LO | -LAYOUT | | |
| MAT | MATERIALS | | |
| MS | MSPACE | | |
| MV | MVIEW | | |
| ORBIT | 3DORBIT | | |
| P | PAN | -P | -PAN |
| PS | PSPACE | | |
| R | REDRAW | | |
| RA | REDRAWALL | | |
| RC | RENDERCROP | | |
| RE | REGEN | | |
| REA | REGENALL | | |
| RP | RENDERPRESETS | | |
| RPR | RPREF | | |
| RR | RENDER | | |
| RW | RENDERWIN | | |
| SHA | SHADEMODE | | |
| TI | TILEMODE | | |
| UC | UCSMAN | | |
| V | VIEW | -V | -VIEW |
| VP | DDVPOINT | -VP | VPOINT |
| VS | VSCURRENT | | |
| VSM | VISUALSTYLES | -VSM | -VISUALSTYLES |
| XC | XCLIP | | |
| Z | ZOOM | | |

# AutoCAD Setting Variables (with Typical Initial or Default Values)

D

| Variable Name | Value | |
|---|---|---|
| 3DCONVERSIONMODE | 1 | |
| 3DDWFPREC | 2 | |
| 3DSELECTIONMODE | 1 | |
| ACADLSPACDOC | 0 | |
| ACADPREFIX | "C:\Documents and Settings\ username\Application\data\ Autodesk\Aut..." | (read only) |
| ACADVER | "17.0s (LMS Tech)" | (read only) |
| ACISOUTVER | 70 | |
| AFLAGS | 16 | |
| ANGBASE | 0 | |
| ANGDIR | 0 | |
| ANNOALLVISIBLE | 1 | |
| ANNOAUTOSCALE | −4 | |
| ANNOTATIVEDWG | 0 | |
| APBOX | 0 | |
| APERTURE | 10 | |
| AREA | 0.0000 | (read only) |
| ATTDIA | 0 | |
| ATTIPE | 0 | |
| ATTMODE | 1 | |
| ATTMULTI | 1 | |
| ATTREQ | 1 | |
| AUDITCTL | 0 | |
| AUNITS | 0 | |
| AUPREC | 0 | |
| AUTODWFPUBLISH | 0 | |
| AUTOSNAP | 55 | |
| BACKGROUNDPLOT | 2 | |
| BACKZ | 0.0000 | (read only) |
| BACTIONCOLOR | "7" | |
| BDEPENDENCYHIGHLIGHT | 1 | |
| BGRIPOBJCOLOR | "141" | |
| BGRIPOBJSIZE | 8 | |
| BINDTYPE | 0 | |
| BLIPMODE | 0 | |
| BLOCKEDITLOCK | 0 | |
| BLOCKEDITOR | 0 | (read only) |
| BPARAMETERCOLOR | "7" | |
| BPARAMETERFONT | "Simplex.shx" | |
| BPARAMETERSIZE | 12 | |
| BTMARKDISPLAY | 1 | |
| BVMODE | 0 | |
| CALCINPUT | 1 | |
| CAMERADISPLAY | 0 | |
| CAMERAHEIGHT | 0.0000 | |

| Variable Name | Value | |
|---|---|---|
| CANNOSCALE | "1:1" | |
| CANNOSCALEVALUE | 1.000000000 | (read only) |
| CDATE | 20050915.01344651 | (read only) |
| CECOLOR | "BYLAYER" | |
| CELTSCALE | 1.0000 | |
| CELTYPE | "BYLAYER" | |
| CELWEIGHT | −1 | |
| CENTERMT | 0 | |
| CHAMFERA | 0.0000 | |
| CHAMFERB | 0.0000 | |
| CHAMFERC | 0.0000 | |
| CHAMFERD | 0 | |
| CHAMMODE | 0 | |
| CIRCLERAD | 0.0000 | |
| CLAYER | "0" | |
| CLEANSCREENSTATE | 0 | (read only) |
| CLISTATE | 0 | |
| CMATERIAL | "ByLayer" | |
| CMDACTIVE | 1 | (read only) |
| CMDDIA | 1 | |
| CMDECHO | 1 | |
| CMDINPUTHISTORYMAX | 20 | |
| CMDNAMES | "SETVAR" | (read only) |
| CMLJUST | 0 | |
| CMLSCALE | 1.0000 | |
| CMLSTYLE | "STANDARD" | |
| COMPASS | 0 | |
| COORDS | 0 | |
| CPLOTSTYLE | "ByColor" | |
| CPROFILE | "standard" | (read only) |
| CROSSINGAREACOLOR | 3 | |
| CSHADOW | "Cast And Receive Shadows" | |
| CTAB | "Model" | |
| CTABLESTYLE | "Standard" | |
| CURSORSIZE | 25 | |
| CVPORT | 2 | |
| DATE | 2453629.06584183 | (read only) |
| DBCSTATE | 0 | |
| DBLCLKEDIT | ON | |
| DBMOD | 4 | (read only) |
| DCTCUST | "C:\Documents and Settings\ username\Application\Data\ Autodesk\Aut..." | |
| DCTMAIN | "enu" | |
| DEFAULTLIGHTING | 1 | |
| DEFAULTLIGHTINGTYPE | 1 | |
| DEFLPLSTYLE | "ByColor" | |
| DEFPLSTYLE | "ByColor" | |
| DELOBJ | 1 | |
| DEMANDLOAD | 3 | |
| DIASTAT | 1 | (read only) |
| DIMADEC | 0 | |
| DIMALT | OFF | |
| DIMALTD | 2 | |
| DIMALTF | 25.4000 | |
| DIMALTRND | 0.0000 | |
| DIMALTTD | 2 | |
| DIMALTTZ | 0 | |
| DIMALTU | 2 | |
| DIMALTZ | 0 | |

| Variable Name | Value | |
|---|---|---|
| DIMANNO | 0 | (read only) |
| DIMAPOST | "" | |
| DIMARCSYM | 0 | |
| DIMASO | ON | |
| DIMASSOC | 2 | |
| DIMASZ | 0.1800 | |
| DIMATFIT | 3 | |
| DIMAUNIT | 0 | |
| DIMAZIN | 0 | |
| DIMBLK | "" | |
| DIMBLK1 | "" | |
| DIMBLK2 | "" | |
| DIMCEN | 0.0900 | |
| DIMCLRD | 0 | |
| DIMCLRE | 0 | |
| DIMCLRT | 0 | |
| DIMDEC | 4 | |
| DIMDLE | 0.0000 | |
| DIMDLI | 0.3800 | |
| DIMDSEP | "." | |
| DIMEXE | 0.1800 | |
| DIMEXO | 0.0625 | |
| DIMFIT | 3 | |
| DIMFRAC | 0 | |
| DIMFXL | 1.0000 | |
| DIMFXLON | OFF | |
| DIMGAP | 0.0900 | |
| DIMJOGANG | 45 | |
| DIMJUST | 0 | |
| DIMLDRBLK | "" | |
| DIMLFAC | 1.0000 | |
| DIMLIM | OFF | |
| DIMLTEX1 | "" | |
| DIMLTEX2 | "" | |
| DIMLTYPE | "" | |
| DIMLUNIT | 2 | |
| DIMLWD | −2 | |
| DIMLWE | −2 | |
| DIMPOST | "" | |
| DIMRND | 0.0000 | |
| DIMSAH | OFF | |
| DIMSCALE | 1.0000 | |
| DIMSD1 | OFF | |
| DIMSD2 | OFF | |
| DIMSE1 | OFF | |
| DIMSE2 | OFF | |
| DIMSHO | ON | |
| DIMSOXD | OFF | |
| DIMSTYLE | "Standard" | (read only) |
| DIMTAD | 0 | |
| DIMTDEC | 4 | |
| DIMTFAC | 1.0000 | |
| DIMTFILL | 0 | |
| DIMTFILLCLR | 0 | |
| DIMTIH | ON | |
| DIMTIX | OFF | |
| DIMTM | 0.0000 | |
| DIMTMOVE | 0 | |
| DIMTOFL | OFF | |
| DIMTOH | ON | |

| Variable Name | Value | |
|---|---|---|
| DIMTOL | OFF | |
| DIMTOLJ | 1 | |
| DIMTP | 0.0000 | |
| DIMTSZ | 0.0000 | |
| DIMTVP | 0.0000 | |
| DIMTXSTY | "Standard" | |
| DIMTXT | 0.1800 | |
| DIMTZIN | 0 | |
| DIMUNIT | 2 | |
| DIMUPT | OFF | |
| DIMZIN | 0 | |
| DISPSILH | 0 | |
| DISTANCE | 0.0000 | (read only) |
| DONUTID | 0.5000 | |
| DONUTOD | 1.0000 | |
| DRAGMODE | 2 | |
| DRAGP1 | 10 | |
| DRAGP2 | 25 | |
| DRAGVS | "" | |
| DRAWORDERCTL | 3 | |
| DTEXTED | 2 | |
| DWFFRAME | 2 | |
| DWFOSNAP | 1 | |
| DWGCHECK | 1 | |
| DWGCODEPAGE | "ANSI_1252" | (read only) |
| DWGNAME | "Drawing1.dwg" | (read only) |
| DWGPREFIX | "C:\Documents and Settings\ username\My Documents\" | (read only) |
| DWGTITLED | 0 | (read only) |
| DXEVAL | 12 | |
| DYNDIGRIP | 31 | |
| DYNDIVIS | 1 | |
| DYNMODE | −3 | |
| DYNPICOORDS | 0 | |
| DYNPIFORMAT | 0 | |
| DYNPIVIS | 1 | |
| DYNPROMPT | 1 | |
| DYNTOOLTIPS | 1 | |
| EDGEMODE | 0 | |
| ELEVATION | 0.0000 | |
| ENTERPRISEMENU | "." | (read only) |
| EXPERT | 0 | |
| EXPLMODE | 1 | |
| EXTMAX | −1.0000E+20,−1.0000E+20,−1.0000E+20 | (read only) |
| EXTMIN | 1.0000E+20,1.0000E+20,1.0000E+20 | (read only) |
| EXTNAMES | 1 | |
| FACETRATIO | 0 | |
| FACETRES | 0.5000 | |
| FIELDDISPLAY | 1 | |
| FIELDEVAL | 31 | |
| FILEDIA | 1 | |
| FILLETRAD | 0.0000 | |
| FILLMODE | 1 | |
| FONTALT | "txt" | |
| FONTMAP | "C:\Documents and Settings\username\ Application\Data\ Autodesk\Aut..." | |
| FRONTZ | 0.0000 | (read only) |
| FULLOPEN | 1 | (read only) |
| FULLPLOTPATH | 1 | |
| GFANG | 0 | |

| Variable Name | Value | |
|---|---|---|
| GFCLR1 | "RGB:000,000,255" | |
| GFCLR2 | "RGB:255,255,153" | |
| GFCLRLUM | 1.000000000 | |
| GFCLRSTATE | 1 | |
| GFNAME | 1 | |
| GFSHIFT | 0 | |
| GRIDDISPLAY | 2 | |
| GRIDMAJOR | 5 | |
| GRIDMODE | 0 | |
| GRIDUNIT | 0.5000,0.5000 | |
| GRIPBLOCK | 0 | |
| GRIPCOLOR | 160 | |
| GRIPDYNCOLOR | 140 | |
| GRIPHOT | 1 | |
| GRIPHOVER | 3 | |
| GRIPOBJLIMIT | 100 | |
| GRIPS | 1 | |
| GRIPSIZE | 9 | |
| GRIPTIPS | 1 | |
| GTAUTO | 1 | |
| GTDEFAULT | 0 | |
| GTLOCATION | 0 | |
| HALOGAP | 0 | |
| HANDLES | 1 | (read only) |
| HIDEPRECISION | 0 | |
| HIDETEXT | ON | |
| HIGHLIGHT | 1 | |
| HPANG | 0 | |
| HPASSOC | 1 | |
| HPBOUND | 1 | |
| HPDOUBLE | 0 | |
| HPDRAWORDER | 3 | |
| HPGAPTOL | 0.0000 | |
| HPINHERIT | 0 | |
| HPMAXLINES | 1000000 | |
| HPNAME | "ANSI31" | |
| HPOBJWARNING | 10000 | |
| HPORIGIN | 0.0000,0.0000 | |
| HPORIGINMODE | 0 | |
| HPSCALE | 1.0000 | |
| HPSEPARATE | 0 | |
| HPSPACE | 1.0000 | |
| HYPERLINKBASE | "" | |
| IMAGEHLT | 0 | |
| IMPLIEDFACE | 1 | |
| INTERFERECOLOR | "1" | |
| INTERFEREOBJVS | "Realistic" | |
| INTERFEREVPVS | "3D Wireframe" | |
| INDEXCTL | 0 | |
| INETLOCATION | "http://www.autodesk.com" | |
| INPUTHISTORYMODE | 15 | |
| INSBASE | 0.0000,0.0000,0.0000 | |
| INSNAME | "" | |
| INSUNITS | 1 | |
| INSUNITSDEFSOURCE | 1 | |
| INSUNITSDEFTARGET | 1 | |
| INTELLIGENTUPDATE | 20 | |
| INTERSECTIONCOLOR | 257 | |
| INTERSECTIONDISPLAY | OFF | |
| ISAVEBAK | 1 | |

| Variable Name | Value | |
|---|---|---|
| ISAVEPERCENT | 50 | |
| ISOLINES | 4 | |
| LASTANGLE | 0 | (read only) |
| LASTPOINT | 0.0000,0.0000,0.0000 | |
| LASTPROMPT | "LASTANGLE 0 | (read only) |
| LATITUDE | 37.7950 | |
| LAYEREVAL | 1 | |
| LAYERFILTERALERT | 2 | |
| LAYERNOTIFY | 15 | |
| LAYLOCKFADECTL | 50 | |
| LAYOUTREGENCTL | 2 | |
| LEGACYCTRPICK | 0 | |
| LENSLENGTH | 50.0000 | (read only) |
| LIGHTGLYPHDISPLAY | 10 | |
| LIGHTINGUNITS | 2 | |
| LIGHTSINBLOCKS | 1 | |
| LIMCHECK | 0 | |
| LIMMAX | 12.0000,9.0000 | |
| LIMMIN | 0.0000,0.0000 | |
| LINEARBRIGHTNESS | 0 | |
| LINEARCONTRAST | 0 | |
| LOCALE | "ENU" | (read only) |
| LOCALROOTPREFIX | "C:\Documents and Settings\ username\Local Settings\ application\Da..." | (read only) |
| LOCKUI | 0 | |
| LOFTANG1 | 90 | |
| LOFTANG2 | 90 | |
| LOFTMAG1 | 0.0000 | |
| LOFTMAG2 | 0.0000 | |
| LOFTNORMALS | 1 | |
| LOFTPARAM | 7 | |
| LOGEXPBRIGHTNESS | 65.0 | |
| LOGEXPCONTRAST | 50.0 | |
| LOGEXPDAYLIGHT | 2 | |
| LOGEXPMIDTONES | 1.00 | |
| LOGEXPPHYSICALSCALE | 1500.000 | |
| LOGFILEMODE | 0 | |
| LOGFILENAME | "C:\documents and settings\ username\local settings\ application\da..." | (read only) |
| LOGFILEPATH | "C:\documents and settings\ username\local settings\ application\da..." | |
| LOGINNAME | "UserName" | (read only) |
| LONGITUDE | −122.3940 | |
| LTSCALE | 1.0000 | |
| LUNITS | 2 | |
| LUPREC | 4 | |
| LWDEFAULT | 25 | |
| LWDISPLAY | OFF | |
| LWUNITS | 1 | |
| MAXACTVP | 64 | |
| MAXSORT | 1000 | |
| MBUTTONPAN | 1 | |
| MEASUREINIT | 0 | |
| MEASUREMENT | 0 | |
| MENUCTL | 1 | |
| MENUECHO | 0 | |

| Variable Name | Value | |
|---|---|---|
| MENUNAME | "C:\Documents and Settings\ username\Application\Data\ \Autodesk\Aut..." | (read only) |
| MIRRTEXT | 0 | |
| MODEMACRO | "" | |
| MSOLESCALE | 1.0000 | |
| MTEXTED | "Internal" | |
| MTEXTFIXED | 2 | |
| MTJIGSTRING | "abc" | |
| MYDOCUMENTSPREFIX | "C:\Documents and Settings\ username\My Documents" | (read only) |
| NOMUTT | 0 | |
| NORTHDIRECTION | 0 | |
| OBSCUREDCOLOR | 257 | |
| OBSCUREDLTYPE | 0 | |
| OFFSETDIST | 1.0000 | |
| OFFSETGAPTYPE | 0 | |
| OLEFRAME | 2 | |
| OLEHIDE | 0 | |
| OLEQUALITY | 3 | |
| OLESTARTUP | 0 | |
| ORTHOMODE | 0 | |
| OSMODE | 183 | |
| OSNAPCOORD | 2 | |
| OSNAPHATCH | 0 | |
| OSNAPZ | 0 | |
| OSOPTIONS | 3 | |
| PALETTEOPAQUE | 0 | |
| PAPERUPDATE | 0 | |
| PDMODE | 0 | |
| PDSIZE | 0.0000 | |
| PEDITACCEPT | 0 | |
| PELLIPSE | 0 | |
| PERIMETER | 0.0000 | (read only) |
| PERSPECTIVE | 0 | |
| PERSPECTIVECLIP | 5.0000 | |
| PFACEVMAX | 4 | (read only) |
| PICKADD | 1 | |
| PICKAUTO | 1 | |
| PICKBOX | 5 | |
| PICKDRAG | 0 | |
| PICKFIRST | 1 | |
| PICKSTYLE | 1 | |
| PLATFORM | "Microsoft Windows NT Version 5.1 (x86)" | (read only) |
| PLINEGEN | 0 | |
| PLINETYPE | 2 | |
| PLINEWID | 0.0000 | |
| PLOTOFFSET | 0 | |
| PLOTROTMODE | 2 | |
| PLQUIET | 0 | |
| POLARADDANG | "0" | |
| POLARANG | 90 | |
| POLARDIST | 0.0000 | |
| POLARMODE | 0 | |
| POLYSIDES | 4 | |
| POPUPS | 1 | (read only) |
| PREVIEWEFFECT | 2 | |
| PREVIEWFILTER | 7 | |
| PROJECTNAME | "" | |

| Variable Name | Value | |
|---|---|---|
| PROJMODE | 1 | |
| PROXYGRAPHICS | 1 | |
| PROXYNOTICE | 1 | |
| PROXYSHOW | 1 | |
| PROXYWEBSEARCH | 0 | |
| PSLTSCALE | 1 | |
| PSOLHEIGHT | 4.0000 | |
| PSOLWIDTH | 0.2500 | |
| PSPROLOG | "" | |
| PSQUALITY | 75 | |
| PSTYLEMODE | 1 | (read only) |
| PSTYLEPOLICY | 1 | |
| PSVPSCALE | 0.00000000 | |
| PUBLISHALLSHEETS | 1 | |
| PUBLISHCOLLATE | 1 | |
| PUCSBASE | "" | |
| QTEXTMODE | 0 | |
| RASTERDPI | 300 | |
| RASTERPERCENT | 20 | |
| RASTERPREVIEW | 1 | |
| RASTERTHRESHOLD | 20 | |
| RECOVERYMODE | 2 | |
| REFEDITNAME | "" | (read only) |
| REGENMODE | 1 | |
| REMEMBERFOLDERS | 1 | |
| RENDERUSERLIGHTS | 1 | |
| REPORTERROR | 1 | |
| ROAMABLEROOTPREFIX | "C:\Documents and Settings\ username\Application\Data\ Autodesk\Aut..." | (read only) |
| RTDISPLAY | 1 | |
| SAVEFIDELITY | 1 | |
| SAVEFILE | "" | (read only) |
| SAVEFILEPATH | "C:\Documents and Settings\ username\Local Settings\Temp\" | |
| SAVENAME | "" | (read only) |
| SAVETIME | 10 | |
| SCREENBOXES | 0 | (read only) |
| SCREENMODE | 3 | (read only) |
| SCREENSIZE | 937.0000,485.0000 | (read only) |
| SELECTIONANNODISPLAY | 1 | |
| SELECTIONAREA | 1 | |
| SELECTIONAREAOPACITY | 25 | |
| SELECTIONPREVIEW | 3 | |
| SETBYLAYERMODE | 127 | |
| SHADEDGE | 3 | |
| SHADEDIF | 70 | |
| SHADOWPLANELOCATION | 0.0000 | |
| SHORTCUTMENU | 11 | |
| SHOWHIST | 1 | |
| SHOWLAYERUSAGE | 0 | |
| SHPNAME | "" | |
| SIGWARN | 1 | |
| SKETCHING | 0.1000 | |
| SKPOLY | 0 | |
| SNAPANG | 0 | |
| SNAPBASE | 0.0000,0.0000 | |
| SNAPISOPAIR | 0 | |
| SNAPMODE | 0 | |
| SNAPSTYL | 0 | |

| Variable Name | Value | |
|---|---|---|
| SNAPTYPE | 0 | |
| SNAPUNIT | 0.5000,0.5000 | |
| SOLIDCHECK | 1 | |
| SOLIDHIST | 1 | |
| SORTENTS | 127 | |
| SPLFRAME | 0 | |
| SPLINESEGS | 8 | |
| SPLINETYPE | 6 | |
| SSFOUND | "" | (read only) |
| SSLOCATE | 1 | |
| SSMAUTOOPEN | 1 | |
| SSMPOLLTIME | 60 | |
| SSMSHEETSTATUS | 2 | |
| STANDARDSVIOLATION | 2 | |
| STARTUP | 1 | |
| STEPSIZE | 6.0000 | |
| STEPSPERSEC | 2.0000 | |
| SUNSTATUS | 0 | |
| SURFTAB1 | 6 | |
| SURFTAB2 | 6 | |
| SURFTYPE | 6 | |
| SURFU | 6 | |
| SURFV | 6 | |
| SYSCODEPAGE | "ANSI_1252" | (read only) |
| TABLEINDICATOR | 1 | |
| TABLETOOLBAR | 1 | |
| TABMODE | 0 | |
| TARGET | 0.0000,0.0000,0.0000 | (read only) |
| TDCREATE | 2453629.06304220 | (read only) |
| TDINDWG | 0.00123557 | (read only) |
| TDUCREATE | 2453629.22970887 | (read only) |
| TDUPDATE | 2453629.06304220 | (read only) |
| TDUSRTIMER | 0.00123128 | (read only) |
| TDUUPDATE | 2453629.22970887 | (read only) |
| TEMPOVERRIDES | 1 | |
| TEMPPREFIX | "C:\Documents and Settings\ username\Local Settings\Temp\" | (read only) |
| TEXTEVAL | 0 | |
| TEXTFILL | 1 | |
| TEXTOUTPUTFILEFORMAT | 0 | |
| TEXTQLTY | 50 | |
| TEXTSIZE | 0.2000 | |
| TEXTSTYLE | "Standard" | |
| THICKNESS | 0.0000 | |
| TILEMODE | 1 | |
| TIMEZONE | −8.0000 | |
| TOOLTIPMERGE | 0 | |
| TOOLTIPS | 1 | |
| TRACEWID | 0.0500 | |
| TRACKPATH | 0 | |
| TRAYICONS | 1 | |
| TRAYNOTIFY | 1 | |
| TRAYTIMEOUT | 0 | |
| TREEDEPTH | 3020 | |
| TREEMAX | 10000000 | |
| TRIMMODE | 1 | |
| TSPACEFAC | 1.0000 | |
| TSPACETYPE | 1 | |
| TSTACKALIGN | 1 | |
| TSTACKSIZE | 70 | |

| Variable Name | Value | |
| --- | --- | --- |
| UCSAXISANG | 90 | |
| UCSBASE | "" | |
| UCSDETECT | 0 | |
| UCSFOLLOW | 0 | |
| UCSICON | 3 | |
| UCSNAME | "" | (read only) |
| UCSORG | 0.0000,0.0000,0.0000 | (read only) |
| UCSORTHO | 1 | |
| UCSVIEW | 1 | |
| UCSVP | 1 | |
| UCSXDIR | 1.0000,0.0000,0.0000 | (read only) |
| UCSYDIR | 0.0000,1.0000,0.0000 | (read only) |
| UNDOCTL | 21 | (read only) |
| UNDOMARKS | 0 | (read only) |
| UNITMODE | 0 | |
| UPDATETHUMBNAIL | 15 | |
| VIEWCTR | 8.7025,4.5000,0.0000 | (read only) |
| VIEWDIR | 0.0000,0.0000,1.0000 | (read only) |
| VIEWMODE | 0 | (read only) |
| VIEWSIZE | 9.0000 | (read only) |
| VIEWTWIST | 0 | (read only) |
| VISRETAIN | 1 | |
| VPLAYEROVERRIDES | 0 | (read only) |
| VPLAYEROVERRIDESMODE | 1 | |
| VPMAXIMIZEDSTATE | 0 | (read only) |
| VSBACKGROUNDS | 1 | |
| VSEDGECOLOR | "ByEntity" | |
| VSEDGEJITTER | −2 | |
| VSEDGEOVERHANG | −6 | |
| VSEDGES | 1 | |
| VSEDGESSMOOTH | 1 | |
| VSFACECOLORMODE | 0 | |
| VSFACEHIGHLIGHT | −30 | |
| VSFACEOPACITY | −60 | |
| VSFACESTYLE | 0 | |
| VSHALOGAP | 0 | |
| VSHIDEPRECISION | 0 | |
| VSINTERSECTIONCOLOR | "7(white)" | |
| VSINTERSECTIONEDGES | 0 | |
| VSINTERSECTIONLTYPE | 1 | |
| VSICONTOP | 0 | |
| VSLIGHTINGQUALITY | 1 | |
| VSMATERIALMODE | 0 | |
| VSMAX | 52.2149,27.0000,0.0000 | (read only) |
| VSMIN | −34.8099,−18.0000,0.0000 | (read only) |
| VSMONOCOLOR | "RCB:255,255,255" | |
| VSOBSCUREDCOLOR | "ByEntity" | |
| VSOBSCUREDEDGES | 1 | |
| VSOBSCUREDLTYPE | 1 | |
| VSSHADOWS | 0 | |
| VSSILHEDGES | 0 | |
| VSSILHWIDTH | 5 | |
| VTDURATION | 750 | |
| VTENABLE | 3 | |
| VTFPS | 7 | |
| WHIPARC | 0 | |
| WINDOWAREACOLOR | 5 | |
| WMFBKGND | OFF | |
| WMFFOREGND | OFF | |
| WORLDUCS | 1 | (read only) |

| Variable Name | Value | |
|---|---|---|
| WORLDVIEW | 1 | |
| WRITESTAT | 1 | (read only) |
| WSCURRENT | "" | |
| XCLIPFRAME | 0 | |
| XEDIT | 1 | |
| XFADECTL | 50 | |
| XLOADCTL | 2 | |
| XLOADPATH | "C:\Documents and Settings\ username\Local Settings\Temp\" | |
| XREFCTL | 0 | |
| XREFNOTIFY | 2 | |
| XREFTYPE | 0 | |
| ZOOMFACTOR | 60 | |
| ZOOMWHEEL | 0 | |

# Glossary*

**absolute coordinate system** Coordinate values measured from a coordinate system's origin point. *See also* origin, relative coordinates, user coordinate system (UCS), world coordinates, and world coordinate system (WCS).

**acquired point** In the tracking or object snap tracking methods of locating a point, an intermediate location used as a reference.

**acquisition marker** During tracking or object snap tracking, the temporary plus sign displayed at the location of an acquired point.

**action** Defines how the geometry of a dynamic block reference will move or change when the custom properties of a block reference are manipulated in a drawing. A dynamic block definition usually contains at least one action that is associated with a parameter. (BACTION)

**activate** Part of the Autodesk software registration process. It allows you to run a product in compliance with the product's end-user license agreement.

**adaptive sampling** A method to accelerate the anti-aliasing process within the bounds of the sample matrix size. *See also* anti-aliasing.

**adjacent cell selection** A selection of table cells that share at least one boundary with another cell in the same selection.

**affine calibration** A tablet calibration method that provides an arbitrary linear transformation in two-dimensional space. Affine calibration requires three calibration points to allow a tablet transformation that combines translation, independent X and Y scaling, rotation, and some skewing. Use affine calibration if a drawing has been stretched differently in the horizontal or vertical direction. (TABLET)

**alias** A shortcut for a command. For example, CP is an alias for COPY, and Z is an alias for ZOOM. You define aliases in the acad.pgp and aclt.pgp file.

**aliasing** The effect of discrete picture elements, or pixels, aligned as a straight or curved edge on a fixed grid appearing to be jagged or stepped. *See also* anti-aliasing.

**aligned dimension** A dimension that measures the distance between two points at any angle. The dimension line is parallel to the line connecting the dimension's definition points. (DIMALIGNED)

**aligned system** A dimension style where all the text entities are written in line with or parallel to the dimension line and are read from the bottom and/or right-hand side of the paper.

**alpha channel** Alpha is a type of data, found in 32-bit bitmap files, that assigns transparency to the pixels in the image. A 24-bit truecolor file contains three channels of color information: red, green, and blue, or RGB. Each channel of a truecolor bitmap file is defined by 8 bits, providing 256 levels of intensity. The intensity of each channel determines the color of the pixel in the image. Thus, an RGB file is 24-bit with 256 levels each of red, green, and blue. By adding a fourth, alpha channel, the file can specify the transparency, or opacity, of each of the pixels. An alpha value of 0 is transparent, an alpha value of 255 is opaque, and values in between are semi-transparent. An RGBA file (red, green, blue, alpha) is 32-bit, with the extra 8 bits of alpha providing 256 levels of transparency. To output a rendered image with alpha, save in an alpha-compatible format such as PNG, TIFF, or Targa.

**ambient color** A color produced only by ambient light. Ambient color is the color of an object where it is in shadow. This color is what the object reflects when illuminated by ambient light rather than direct light.

**ambient light**  Light that illuminates all surfaces of a model with equal intensity. Ambient light has no single source or direction and does not diminish in intensity over distance.

**angular dimension**  A dimension that measures angles or arc segments and consists of text, extension lines, and leaders.

**angular unit**  The unit of measurement for an angle. Angular units can be measured in decimal degrees, degrees/minutes/seconds, grads, and radians.

**annotation scale**  A setting that is saved with model space, layout viewports, and model views. When you create annotative objects, they are scaled based on the current annotation scale setting and automatically displayed at the correct size.

**annotations**  Text, dimensions, tolerances, symbols, notes, and other types of explanatory symbols or objects that are used to add information to your model.

**anonymous block**  An unnamed block created by a number of features, including associative and nonassociative dimensions.

**ANSI**  (American National Standards Institute). Coordinator of voluntary standards development for both private and public sectors in the United States. Standards pertain to programming languages, Electronic Data Interchange (EDI), telecommunications, and the physical properties of diskettes, cartridges, and magnetic tapes.

**anti-aliasing**  A method that reduces aliasing by shading the pixels adjacent to the main pixels that define a line or boundary. *See also* aliasing.

**approximation points**  Point locations that a B-spline must pass near, within a fit tolerance. *See also* fit points and interpolation points.

**arc**  A portion of a circle that forms a curve.

**array**  1. Multiple copies of selected objects in a rectangular or polar (radial) pattern. (ARRAY) 2. A collection of data items, each identified by a subscript or key, arranged so a computer can examine the collection and retrieve data with the key.

**arrowhead**  A terminator, such as an arrowhead, slash, or dot, at the end of a dimension line showing where a dimension begins and ends.

**ASCII**  For American Standard Code for Information Interchange. A common numeric code used in computer data communications. The code assigns meaning to 128 numbers, using seven bits per character with the eighth bit used for parity checking. Nonstandard versions of ASCII assign meaning to 255 numbers.

**aspect ratio**  Ratio of display width to height.

**associative dimension**  A dimension that automatically adapts as the associated geometry is modified. Controlled by the DIMASSOC system variable. *See also* nonassociative dimension and exploded dimension.

**associative hatch**  Hatching that conforms to its bounding objects such that modifying the bounding objects automatically adjusts the hatch. (BHATCH)

**associative property**  The ability to connect entities together so that when changes are made the changes will be reflected in the new edited dimension.

**attenuation**  The diminishing of light intensity over distance.

**attribute definition**  An object that is included in a block definition to store alphanumeric data. Attribute values can be predefined or specified when the block is inserted. Attribute data can be extracted from a drawing and inserted into external files. (ATTDEF)

**attribute extraction file**  A text file to which extracted attribute data is written. The contents and format are determined by the attribute extraction template file. *See also* attribute extraction template file.

**attribute extraction template file** An ASCII text file that determines which attributes are extracted and how they are formatted when written to an ASCII attribute extraction file. *See also* attribute extraction file.

**attribute prompt** The text string displayed when you insert a block with an attribute whose value is undefined. *See also* attribute definition, attribute tag, and attribute value.

**attribute tag** A text string associated with an attribute that identifies a particular attribute during extraction from the drawing database. *See also* attribute definition, attribute prompt, and attribute value.

**attribute value** The alphanumeric information associated with an attribute tag. *See also* attribute definition, attribute prompt, and attribute tag.

**AutoCAD Library search path** The search order for a support file: current directory, drawing directory, directory specified in the support path, and directory containing the executable file, acad.exe.

**AutoCAD window** The drawing area, its surrounding menus, and the command line.

**axis tripod** Icon with X, Y, and Z coordinates that is used to visualize the viewpoint (view direction) of a drawing without displaying the drawing. (VPOINT)

**B-spline curve** A blended piecewise polynomial curve passing near a given set of control points. *See also* Bezier curve. (SPLINE)

**back face** The opposite side of an object's normal face. Back faces are not visible in a rendered image. *See also* normal faces.

**BAK** A standard file name extension used by many programs to be the last saved version of a document, drawing, or spreadsheet before the most recently saved version.

**base point** A control point within several applications. 1. In the context of editing grips, the grip that changes to a solid color when selected to specify the focus of the subsequent editing operation. 2. A point for relative distance and angle when copying, moving, rotating, scaling, and other modifications to objects. 3. The insertion base point of the current drawing. (BASE) 4. The insertion base point for a block definition. (BLOCK)

**baseline** An imaginary line on which text characters appear to rest. Individual characters can have descenders that drop below the baseline. *See also* baseline dimension.

**baseline dimension** Multiple dimensions measured from the same datum location on an object. Also called parallel dimensions. *See also* baseline.

**Bezier curve** A polynomial curve defined by a set of control points, representing an equation of an order one less than the number of points being considered. A Bezier curve is a special case of a B-spline curve. *See also* B-spline curve.

**bitmap** The digital representation of an image having bits referenced to pixels. In color graphics, a different value represents each red, green, and blue component of a pixel.

**blips** Temporary screen markers displayed in the drawing area when you specify a point or select objects. (BLIPMODE)

**block** A generic term for one or more objects that are combined to create a single object. Commonly used for either block definition or block reference. *See also* block definition and block reference. (BLOCK)

**Block Authoring palettes** Tool palettes used in the Block Editor to add actions and parameters to dynamic block definitions.

**Block Authoring tools** Actions, parameters, and parameter sets on the tabs of the Block Authoring palettes window. Used in the Block Editor to create dynamic blocks.

**block definition** The name, base point, and set of objects that are combined and stored in the symbol table of a drawing. *See also* block and block reference.

**block definition table** The nongraphical data area of a drawing file that stores block definitions. *See also* named object.

**block instance** *See* block reference.

**block reference** A compound object that is inserted in a drawing and displays the data stored in a block definition. Also called *instance*. *See also* block and block definition. (INSERT)

**bump map** A map in which brightness values are translated into apparent changes in the height of the surface of an object.

**button menu** The menu for a pointing device with multiple buttons. Each button on the pointing device (except the pick button) can be defined in the customization file (acad.cui).

**BYBLOCK** A special object property used to specify that the object inherits the color or linetype of any block containing it. *See also* BYLAYER.

**BYLAYER** A special object property used to specify that the object inherits the color or linetype associated with its layer. *See also* BYBLOCK.

**callout block** A block used as symbol to reference another sheet. Callout blocks have many industry-specific terms, such as reference tags, detail keys, detail markers, and so on. *See also* label block.

**camera** Defines the current eye-level position in a 3D model. A camera has a location *XYZ* coordinate, a target *XYZ* coordinate, and a field of view or lens length, which determines the magnification or zoom factor.

**camera target** Defines the point you are viewing by specifying the coordinate at the center of the view.

**candela** The SI unit of luminous intensity (perceived power emitted by a light source in a particular direction) (Symbol: cd). Cd/Sr

**Cartesian coordinate system** A three-dimensional coordinate system where the X axis or direction is typically horizontal and increasing to the right, the Y axis or direction is vertical and increasing upward, and the Z axis or direction follows the right-hand rule. The origin of the system is the intersection of the three axes and is called 0,0,0.

**category** *See* view category.

**cell** A box or location in a table.

**cell boundary** The four gridlines surrounding a table cell. An adjacent cell selection can be surrounded with a cell boundary.

**cell style** A style that contains specific formatting for table cells.

**chain actions** In a dynamic block definition, a property of point, linear, polar, XY, and rotation parameters. When set to Yes, a change in an action that contains the parameter in the action's selection set triggers any actions associated with that parameter, just as if you had edited the parameter in the block reference through a grip or custom property.

**circle** An unbroken line that has no angles and is drawn around a center point where every point is the same distance from the center point.

**circular external reference** An externally referenced drawing (xref) that references itself directly or indirectly. The xref that creates the circular condition is ignored.

**circumscribed** An option to construct an entity on the outside of a circle.

**clipping planes** The boundaries that define or clip the field of view. (DVIEW)

**CMYK** For cyan, magenta, yellow, and key color. A system of defining colors by specifying the percentages of cyan, magenta, yellow, and the key color, which is typically black.

**Color bleed scale** Increases or decreases the saturation of the reflected color from the material.

**color map** A table defining the intensity of red, green, and blue (RGB) for each displayed color.

**column** A vertically adjacent table cell selection spanning the height of the table. A single column is one cell in width.

**command line** A text area reserved for keyboard input, prompts, and messages.

**composite solid** A solid created from two or more individual solids. (UNION, SUBTRACT, INTERSECT)

**computer-aided drafting (CAD)** The process of producing engineering drawings and documentation through a computer system.

**construction plane** A plane on which planar geometry is constructed. The XY plane of the current UCS represents the construction plane. *See also* elevation and user coordinate system (UCS).

**continued dimension** A type of linear dimension that uses the second extension line origin of a selected dimension as its first extension line origin, breaking one long dimension into shorter segments that add up to the total measurement. Also called chain dimension. (DIMCONTINUE)

**control frame** A series of point locations used as a mechanism to control the shape of a B-spline. These points are connected by a series of line segments for visual clarity and to distinguish the control frame from fit points. The SPLFRAME system variable must be turned on to display control frames.

**control panel** An area on the dashboard that contains related tools and controls. *See also* dashboard and slide-out panel.

**control point** *See* control frame.

**coons patch** In 3D surface meshes, the bi-cubic surface (one curved in the M direction and another in the N direction) interpolated between four edges.

**coordinate filters** Functions that extract individual X, Y, and Z coordinate values from different points to create a new, composite point. Also called X,Y,Z point filters.

**cross sections** Generally, curves or lines that define the profile (shape) of a lofted solid or surface. Cross sections can be open or closed. A lofted solid or surface is drawn in the space between the cross sections. (LOFT)

**crosshairs** A type of cursor consisting of two lines that intersect.

**crossing window** A rectangular area drawn to select objects fully or partly within its borders.

**CTB file** A color-dependent plot style table.

**current layer** The layer that is active to receive all newly created entities.

**cursor** *See* pointer and crosshairs.

**cursor menu** *See* shortcut menu.

**custom grips** Found in a dynamic block reference, used to manipulate the geometry and custom properties.

**custom object** A type of object that is created by an ObjectARX application and that typically has more specialized capabilities than standard objects. Custom objects include parametric solids (Autodesk Mechanical Desktop), intelligently interactive door symbols (Autodesk Architectural Desktop), polygon objects (Autodesk Map®), and associative dimension objects (AutoCAD and AutoCAD LT®). *See also* proxy object and object enabler.

**customization (CUI) file** An XML-based file that stores customization data. You modify a customization file through the Customize User Interface dialog box. CUI files replace MNU, MNS, and MNC files that were used to define menus in releases prior to AutoCAD 2006.

**dashboard** A special palette that displays buttons and controls used primarily for 3D modeling, viewing, and rendering. *See also* control panel and slide-out panel. (DASHBOARD)

**data link** A connection between a table and an external source of data.

**default** A predefined value for a program input or parameter. Default values and options for commands are denoted by angle brackets (< >).

**default drawing** *See* initial environment.

**default lighting** The lighting in a shaded viewport when the sun and user lights are turned off. Faces are lighted by two distant light sources that follow the viewpoint as you move around the model.

**definition points** Points for creating a dimension. The program refers to the points to modify the appearance and value of a nonassociative dimension when the dimensioned object is modified. Also called defpoints and stored on the special layer DEFPOINTS.

**definition table** The nongraphical data area of a drawing file that stores block definitions.

**delta distance** The horizontal or vertical measured distance between two points.

**dependency highlighting** In a dynamic block definition, how associated objects are displayed when you select a parameter, grip, or action.

**dependent named objects (in xrefs)** Named objects brought into a drawing by an external reference.

**dependent symbols** *See* dependent named objects (in xrefs).

**DesignCenter** A tool palette that allows you to drag and drop definition-based entities from other AutoCAD files into the resident file.

**desktop** The initial screen of a Windows operating system.

**DGN underlay** *See* underlay.

**dialog box** A window that appears on top of the drawing screen allowing for random input of command data and options.

**DIESEL** For Direct Interpretively Evaluated String Expression Language. A macro language for altering the status line with the MODEMACRO system variable and for customizing menu items.

**diffuse color** An object's predominant color.

**dimension line arc** An arc (usually with arrows at each end) spanning the angle formed by the extension lines of an angle being measured. The dimension text near this arc sometimes divides it into two arcs. *See also* angular dimension.

**dimension style** A named group of dimension settings that determines the appearance of the dimension and simplifies the setting of dimension system variables. (DIMSTYLE)

**dimension text** The measurement value of dimensioned objects.

**dimension variables** A set of numeric values, text strings, and settings that control dimensioning features. (DIMSTYLE)

**direct distance entry** A method to specify a second point by first moving the cursor to indicate direction and then entering a distance.

**directory** A location on a disk for saving existing files, sometimes referred to as a folder.

**dithering** Combining color dots to give the impression of displaying more colors than are actually available.

**dockable window** A user interface element that can be either docked or floating in the drawing area. Dockable windows include the command window, tool palettes, Properties palette, and so on.

**drawing aids** A series of on/off toggles such as SNAP, GRID, ORTHO, and POLAR that assist with input.

**drawing area** The area in which your drawings are displayed and modified. The size of the drawing area varies, depending on the size of the AutoCAD window and on how many toolbars and other elements are displayed. *See also* AutoCAD window.

**drawing extents** The smallest rectangle that contains all objects in a drawing, positioned on the screen to display the largest possible view of all objects. (ZOOM)

**drawing limits** A defined area within model space used to control drawing area size. *See* grid limits.

**drawing scale** A mathematical ratio between the design's full size or real size and the size needed to fit on the piece of paper.

**drawing set** A collection of drawings assembled using the Publish dialog box.

**drawing template** A drawing file with preestablished settings for new drawings such as acad.dwt, aclt.dwt or acadiso.dwt, acltiso.dwt; however, any drawing can be used as a template. *See also* initial environment.

**drop-down list** A selection method for a list of options within a dialog box.

**DSD** For drawing set descriptions. A file format for saving a description of a drawing set that has been assembled using the Publish dialog box.

**DST** For sheet set data. The XML file format used to store the associations and information that define a sheet set.

**DWF™** Design Web Format. A highly compressed file format that is created from a DWG file, DWF files are easy to publish and view on the Web. *See also* DWG and DXF.

**DWG** Standard file format for saving vector graphics in AutoCAD. *See also* DWF and DXF.

**DWF underlay** *See* underlay

**DXF™** For drawing interchange format. An ASCII or binary file format of a drawing file for exporting drawings to other applications or for importing drawings from other applications. *See also* DWF and DWG.

**edge** The boundary of a face.

**edge modifiers** Effects such as overhang and jitter that control how edges are displayed in a shaded model.

**electronic drawing set** The digital equivalent of a set of plotted drawings. You create an electronic drawing set by publishing drawings to a DWT file.

**elevation** The default Z value above or below the XY plane of the current user coordinate system, which is used for entering coordinates and digitizing locations. (ELEV)

**ellipse** A closed curve that is shaped like an egg where the sum of the squares of the projected distances equals a constant.

**embed** To use object linking and embedding (OLE) information from a source document in a destination document. An embedded object is a copy of the information from a source document that is placed in the destination document and has no link to the source document. *See also* link.

**enterprise customization file** A CUI file that is typically controlled by a CAD manager. It is often accessed by many users and is stored in a shared network location. The file is read-only to users to prevent the data in the file from being changed. A CAD manager creates an enterprise CUI file by modifying a main CUI file and then saving the file to the support location defined in the Options dialog box, Files tab.

**environment map** A bitmap that is used to simulate reflections in materials that have reflective properties. The map is "wrapped" around the scene and any reflective object will show the appropriate portion of the map in the reflective parts of its material.

**environment variable** A setting stored in the operating system that controls the operation of a program.

**explode** To disassemble a complex object, such as a block, dimension, solid, or polyline, into simpler objects. In the case of a block, the block definition is unchanged. The block reference is replaced by the components of the block. *See also* block, block definition, and block reference. (EXPLODE)

**exploded dimension**  Independent objects that have the appearance of a dimension but are not associated with the dimensioned object or each other. Controlled by the DIMASSOC system variable. *See also* associative dimension, nonassociative dimension, and explode. (EXPLODE)

**extents**  *See* drawing extents.

**external reference (xref)**  An alternative method to the insertion of a block that creates and maintains a link between the two drawing files. A drawing file referenced by another drawing. (XREF)

**extrude**  A 3D solid created by sweeping an object that encloses an area along a linear path.

**face**  A triangular or quadrilateral portion of a surface object.

**face color mode**  A setting in the visual style that controls how color is displayed on a face.

**face style**  A setting in the visual style that defines the shading on a face.

**feature control frame**  The tolerance that applies to specific features or patterns of features. Feature control frames always contain at least a geometric characteristic symbol to indicate the type of control and a tolerance value to indicate the amount of acceptable variation.

**fence**  A multisegmented line specified to select objects it passes through.

**field**  A specialized text object set up to display data that may change during the life cycle of the drawing. When the field is updated, the latest value of the field is displayed. (FIELD)

**file management**  The process of saving, copying, moving, and deleting the files produced by a computer system.

**fill**  A solid color covering an area bounded by lines or curves. (FILL)

**filters**  *See* coordinate filters.

**final gathering**  Final gathering is an optional, additional step to calculating global illumination. Using a photon map to calculate global illumination can cause rendering artifacts such as dark corners and low-frequency variations in the lighting. You can reduce or eliminate these artifacts by turning on final gathering, which increases the number of rays used to calculate global illumination. Final gathering can greatly increase rendering time. It is most useful for scenes with overall diffuse lighting, less useful for scenes with bright spots of indirect illumination. You turn on final gathering on the Advanced Render Settings palette. *See also* global illumination.

**fit points**  Locations that a B-spline must pass through exactly or within a fit tolerance. *See also* interpolation points and approximation points.

**fit tolerance**  The setting for the maximum distance that a B-spline can pass for each of the fit points that define it.

**floating viewports**  *See* layout viewports.

**font**  A character set, comprising letters, numbers, punctuation marks, and symbols of a distinctive proportion and design.

**footcandle**  The American unit of illuminance (symbol: fc). Lm/ft^2

**frame**  An individual, static image in an animated sequence. *See also* motion path.

**freeze**  A setting that suppresses the display of objects on selected layers. Objects on frozen layers are not displayed, regenerated, or plotted. Freezing layers shortens regenerating time. *See also* thaw. (LAYER)

**front faces**  Faces with their normals pointed outward.

**full size/full scale**  Creating a drawing where 1″=1″, 1″=1″, 1 m = 1 m, 1 km = 1 km, etc. making the drawing the true size of the object.

**function keys**  The 10 or 12 programmable keys typically across the top of the keyboard.

**geometry** All graphical objects such as lines, circles, arcs, polylines, and dimensions. Nongraphical objects, such as linetypes, lineweights, text styles, and layers are not considered geometry. *See also* named object.

**gizmo** Some modifiers display in viewports as a box-like apparatus called a gizmo, which initially surrounds the selected object. A gizmo acts like a kind of container that transfers the modification to the object to which it's attached.

**global illumination** An indirect illumination technique that allows for effects such as color bleeding. As light hits a colored object in the model, photons bounce to adjacent objects and tint them with the color of the original object.

**Gooch shading** A type of shading that uses a transition from cool to warm colors rather than from dark to light.

**graphics area** *See* drawing area.

**graphics screen** *See* drawing area

**graphics window** *See* AutoCAD window and drawing area.

**grid** An area covered with regularly spaced dots to aid drawing. The spacing between grid dots is adjustable. Grid dots are not plotted. *See also* grid limits. (GRID)

**grid limits** The user-defined rectangular boundary of the drawing area covered by dots when the grid is turned on. Also called drawing limits. (LIMITS)

**grip box** Graphic symbol used to show grip control points.

**grip control points** Predefined locations on an entity used to modify the selected object.

**grip modes** The editing capabilities activated when grips are displayed on an object: stretching, moving, rotating, scaling, and mirroring.

**grip tool** An icon that you use in a 3D view to easily constrain the movement or rotation of a selection set of objects to an axis or a plane. (3DMOVE, 3DROTATE)

**grips** A small square that appears on objects you select. After selecting the grip, you edit the object by dragging it with the pointing device instead of entering commands.

**ground plane** The XY plane of the user coordinate system when perspective projection is turned on. The ground plane displays with a color gradient between the ground horizon (nearest to the horizon) and the ground origin (opposite the horizon). *See also* sky and underground.

**groups** A command used to manipulate a group of objects as if it was one. (GROUP)

**guide curves** Lines or curves that intersect each cross section of a lofted solid or surface and that define the form by adding additional wireframe information to the object. (LOFT)

**handle** A unique alphanumeric tag for an object in the program's database.

**hatch** A pattern of lines or symbols used to fill a closed boundary of a shape to identify parts of a drawing.

**HDI** For Heidi® Device Interface. An interface for developing device drivers that are required for peripherals to work with the program and other Autodesk products.

**helix** An open 2D or 3D spiral. (HELIX)

**HLS** Hue, Luminance, and Saturation. A system of defining color by specifying the amount of hue, luminance, and saturation.

**home page** The main navigating screen for a website.

**horizontal landing** An optional line segment connecting the tail of a leader line with the leader content.

**hover grip** The status of a grip control point when there are multiple choices in a grip location.

**icon** A small picture or symbol used as a shortcut to launch a command.

**i-drop**® A method by which a drawing file, object, or entity can be dragged from a Web page and inserted into a drawing.

**IGES** For Initial Graphics Exchange Specification. An ANSI-standard format for digital representation and exchange of information between CAD/CAM systems. *See also* ANSI.

**illuminance** In photometry, illuminance is the total luminous flux incident on a surface per unit area.

**indirect bump scale** Scales the effect of the base material's bump mapping in areas lit by indirect light.

**indirect illumination** Illumination techniques such as global illumination and final gathering, that enhance the realism of a scene by simulating radiosity, or the interreflection of light between objects in a scene.

**initial environment** The variables and settings for new drawings as defined by the default drawing template, such as acad.dwg, aclt.dwg or acadiso.dwg, acltiso.dwg. *See also* template drawing.

**input property** In a dynamic block definition, a parameter property other than that of a lookup, alignment, or base point parameter that you can add as a column to a lookup table. When the parameter values in a dynamic block reference match a row of input property values, the corresponding lookup property values in that table row are assigned to the block reference. (BLOOKUPTABLE)

**inquiry** The process of retrieving information from a drawing file.

**inscribed** An option to construct an entity inside a circle.

**insert** The process of merging an object (drawing, block, image, etc.) into the resident drawing file.

**interface element** A user interface object that can be customized, such as a toolbar, pull-down menu, shortcut key, dockable window, and so on.

**interpolation points** Defining points that a B-spline passes through. *See also* approximation points and fit points.

**island** An enclosed area within another enclosed area. Islands may be detected as part of the process of creating hatches, polylines, and regions. (BHATCH, BOUNDARY)

**ISO** (International Standards Organization). The organization that sets international standards in all fields except electrical and electronics. Headquartered in Geneva, Switzerland.

**isometric snap style** A drafting option that aligns the cursor with two of three isometric axes and displays grid points, making isometric drawings easier to create.

**justify** A method used to place text.

**key point** In a dynamic block definition, the point on a parameter that drives its associated action when edited in the block reference.

**label block** A block used to label views and details. Labels contain data, such as a title, view number, and scale, that is associated with the referenced view. *See also* callout block.

**landing** The portion of a leader object that acts as a pointer to the object being called out. A landing can be either a straight line or a spline curve.

**Landing gap** An optional space between a leader tail and the leader content.

**layer** A logical grouping of data that are like transparent acetate overlays on a drawing. You can view layers individually or in combination. (LAYER)

**layer index** A list showing the objects on each layer. A layer index is used to locate what portion of the drawing is read when you partially open a drawing. Saving a layer index with a drawing also enhances performance when you work with external references. The INDEXCTL system variable controls whether layer and spatial indexes are saved with a drawing.

**layer translation mappings** Assignments of a set of layers to another set of layers that defines standards. These standards include layer names and layer properties. Also called layer mappings.

**layering scheme** A plan to create and manage a series of layers within a complex design.

**layout** The tabbed environment in which you create and design paper space layout viewports to be plotted. Multiple layouts can be created for each drawing.

**layout space** One of two spaces in which entities can be created. Layout space is used for creating finished views of a design with annotations. It is used for printing or plotting, as opposed to doing design work.

**layout viewports** Objects that are created in layout space that display views of your model. *See also* paper space. (VPORTS)

**leader** A text-based entity used to add clarification to a detail through a dimensioning function.

**leader tail** The portion of a leader line that is connected to the annotation.

**lens length** Defines the magnification properties of a camera's lens. The greater the lens length, the narrower the field of view.

**light glyph** The graphic representation of a point light or a spotlight.

**limits** *See* drawing limits.

**line font** *See* linetype.

**linear dimension** A projected straight line distance between two points in space parallel to the X, Y, or Z axis.

**linetype** The display of a line or curve. For example, a continuous line has a different linetype than a dashed line. Also called line font. (LINETYPE)

**lineweight** A width value that can be assigned to all graphical objects except TrueType® fonts and raster images.

**link** To use object linking and embedding (OLE) to reference data in another file. When data is linked, any changes in the source document are automatically updated in any destination document. *See also* embed.

**lofted solid/surface** A solid or surface that is drawn through a set of two or more cross-section curves. The cross sections define the profile (shape) of the resulting solid or surface. Cross sections (generally, curves or lines) can be open or closed. (LOFT)

**lookup property** In a dynamic block definition, a lookup parameter that you add to a lookup table. The lookup parameter label is used as the property name. When the parameter values in a dynamic block reference match a row of input property values, the corresponding lookup property values in that table row are assigned to the block reference. (BLOOKUPTABLE)

**lookup table** Defines properties for and assigns property values to a dynamic block. Assigns property values to the dynamic block reference based on how the block is manipulated in a drawing. (BLOOKUPTABLE)

**lumen** The SI unit of luminous flux (Symbol: lm). Cd * Sr

**luminaire** This refers to the aggregation of a lamp or lamps and its fixture. The fixture may be a simple can or a complex armature with constrained joints.

**luminance** Luminance is the value of light reflected off a surface. It is a measure of how bright or dark we perceive the surface.

**luminous flux** The perceived power per unit of solid angle. The total luminous flux for a lamp is the perceived power emitted in all directions.

**lux** The SI unit of illuminance (symbol: lx). $Lm/m^2$

**main customization file** A writable CUI file that defines most of the user interface elements (including the standard menus, toolbars, keyboard accelerators, and so on). The acad.cui file (the default main CUI file) is automatically loaded when you start AutoCAD.

**markup** A single comment or a redline geometry correction inserted into a DWF file using Autodesk® DWF™ Composer.

**markup set** A group of markups contained within a single DWF file.

**merge** In tables, an adjacent cell selection that has been combined into a single cell.

**mirror** To create a new version of an existing object by reflecting it symmetrically with respect to a prescribed line or plane. (MIRROR)

**mode** A software setting or operating state.

**model** A two- or three-dimensional representation of an object.

**model space** One of the two primary spaces in which objects reside. Typically, a geometric model is placed in a three-dimensional coordinate space called model space. A final layout of specific views and annotations of this model is placed in layout space. *See also* paper space or layout space. (MSPACE)

**model viewports** A type of display that splits the drawing area into two or more adjacent rectangular viewing areas. *See also* layout viewports, TILEMODE, and viewport. (VPORTS)

**motion path** Defines the path or target of a camera. A path can be a line, arc, elliptical arc, circle, polyline, 3D polyline, or spline.

**multileader** A leader object that creates annotations with multiple leader lines.

**multisheet DWF** A DWF file that contains multiple sheets.

**named object** Describes the various types of nongraphical information, such as styles and definitions, stored with a drawing. Named objects include linetypes, layers, dimension styles, text styles, block definitions, layouts, views, and viewport configurations. Named objects are stored in definition (symbol) tables.

**named path** A saved motion path object that is linked to a camera or target.

**named range** In Microsoft Excel, a cell or cell range that is given an alphanumeric name.

**named view** A view saved for restoration later. (VIEW)

**node** An object snap specification to locate points, dimension definition points, and dimension text origins.

**nonassociative dimension** A dimension that does not automatically change as the associated geometry is modified. Controlled by the DIMASSOC system variable. *See also* associative dimension and exploded dimension.

**normal** A vector that is perpendicular to a face.

**noun-verb selection** Selecting an object first and then performing an operation on it rather than entering a command first and then selecting the object.

**NURBS** For nonuniform rational B-spline curve. A B-spline curve or surface defined by a series of weighted control points and one or more knot vectors. *See also* B-spline curve.

**object** One or more graphical elements, such as text, dimensions, lines, circles, or polylines, treated as a single element for creation, manipulation, and modification. Formerly called entity.

**object enabler** A tool that provides specific viewing and standard editing access to a custom object when the ObjectARX application that created the custom object is not present. *See also* custom object and proxy object.

**Object Snap mode** Method for selecting predefined positions on an object while you create or edit a drawing. *See also* running object snap and object snap override.

**object snap override** Turning off or changing a running Object Snap mode for input of a single point. *See also* Object Snap mode and running object snap.

**ObjectARX® (AutoCAD Runtime Extension)** A compiled-language programming environment for developing AutoCAD applications.

**OLE** For object linking and embedding. An information-sharing method in which data from a source document can be linked to or embedded in a destination document. Selecting the data in the destination document opens the source application so that the data can be edited. *See also* embed and link.

**opacity map** Projection of opaque and transparent areas onto objects, creating the effect of a solid surface with holes or gaps.

**operating system** The code that runs all commands for the computer system.

**ordinate dimension** A method of dimensioning that describes the X and Y locations of a feature based on a fixed origin.

**origin** The point where coordinate axes intersect. For example, the origin of a Cartesian coordinate system is where the X, Y, and Z axes meet at 0,0,0.

**ORTHO** A drawing aid to create objects at right angles.

**Ortho mode** A setting that limits pointing device input to horizontal or vertical (relative to the current snap angle and the user coordinate system). *See also* snap angle and user coordinate system (UCS).

**orthogonal** Having perpendicular slopes or tangents at the point of intersection.

**page setup** A collection of plot device and other settings that affect the appearance and format of the final output. These settings can be modified and applied to other layouts.

**palette** A special window that can access drawings, blocks, and commands in the AutoCAD environment.

**pan** To shift the view of a drawing without changing magnification. (PAN)

**paper space** One of two primary spaces in which objects reside. Paper or layout space is used for creating a finished layout for printing or plotting, as opposed to doing drafting or design work. You design your paper space viewports using a layout tab. Model space is used for creating the drawing. You design your model using the Model tab. *See also* model space and viewpoint. (PSPACE)

**parameter** In a dynamic block definition, defines custom properties for the dynamic block by specifying positions, distances, and angles for geometry in the block.

**parameter set** A tool on the Parameter Sets tab of the Block Authoring palettes window that adds one or more parameters and one or more associated actions to the dynamic block definition.

**partial customization file** Any CUI file that is not defined as the main CUI file. You can load and unload partial CUI files as you need them during a drawing session.

**path curve** Defines the direction and length that a profile curve is lofted, swept, or extruded to create a solid or surface. (SWEEP, LOFT, EXTRUDE)

**PC2 file** Complete plotter configuration file. PC2 files contain all plot settings and device-specific settings that were saved in previous versions. *See also* PCP file and PC3 file.

**PC3 file** Partial plotter configuration file. PC3 files contain plot settings information such as the device driver and model, the output port to which the device is connected, and various device-specific settings, but do not include any custom plotter calibration or custom paper size information. *See also* PMP file, STB file, and CTB file.

**PCP file** Partial plotter configuration file. PCP files contain basic plot specifications and pen parameters that were saved in previous versions. Plot settings that are stored in a PCP file include pen assignments, plotting units, paper size, plot rotation, plot origin, scale factor, and pen optimization level. *See also* PC2 file and PC3 file.

**personalization** Customizes the executable file acad.exe and aclt.exe during installation, by entering the user name, company, and other information.

**perspective view** Objects in 3D seen by an observer positioned at the viewpoint looking at the view center. Objects appear smaller when the distance from the observer (at the view point) to the view center increases. Although a perspective view appears realistic, it does not preserve the shapes of objects. Parallel lines seemingly converge in the view, so measurements cannot be made to scale from perspective views. The program has perspective view settings for VPORTS table entries as well as viewport objects. When you are looking at a viewport with a perspective view, the UCS icon has a different appearance.

**photometric lights** Photometric lights are physically correct lights. Physically correct lights attenuate as the square of the distance. Photometry is the science of measurement of visible light in terms of its perceived brightness.

**photon map** A technique to generate the indirect illumination effects of global illumination used by the renderer. When it calculates indirect illumination, the renderer traces photons emitted from a light. The photon is traced through the model, being reflected or transmitted by objects, until it strikes a diffuse surface. When it strikes a surface, the photon is stored in the photon map.

**photorealistic rendering** Rendering that resembles a photograph.

**pick button** The button on a pointing device that is used to select objects or specify points on the screen. For example, on a two-button mouse, it is the left button.

**plan view** A view orientation from a point on the positive Z axis toward the origin (0,0,0). (PLAN)

**planar face** A flat face that can be located anywhere in 3D space.

**planar projection** Mapping of objects or images onto a plane.

**planar surface** A flat surface that can be located anywhere in 3D space. (PLANESURF)

**PLINE** *See* polyline.

**plot** The process of printing through a CAD system.

**plot style** An object property that specifies a set of overrides for color, dithering, gray scale, pen assignments, screening, linetype, lineweight, endstyles, joinstyles, and fill styles. Plot styles are applied at plot time.

**plot style table** A set of plot styles. Plot styles are defined in plot style tables and apply to objects only when the plot style table is attached to a layout or viewport.

**plug-ins** *Plug-ins* are libraries of reuseable content that extend the functionality of AutoCAD. Plug-ins are created by third party developers and can be accessed from the Featured Technologies and Content channel of the Communications Center.

**PMP file** Plot Model Parameter. File containing custom plotter calibration and custom paper size information associated with plotter configuration file.

**point** 1. A location in three-dimensional space specified by X, Y, and Z coordinate values. 2. An object consisting of a single coordinate location. (POINT)

**point filters** *See* coordinate filters.

**pointer** A cursor on a video display screen that can be moved around to place textual or graphical information. *See also* crosshairs.

**polar array** A pattern of objects copied around a specified center point a specified number of times. (ARRAY)

**polar coordinate system** Input method based on an angle and a distance.

**polar snap**  A precision drawing tool used to snap to incremental distances along the polar tracking alignment path. *See also* polar tracking.

**polar tracking**  A precision drawing tool that displays temporary alignment paths defined by user-specified polar angles. *See also* polar snap.

**polygon window selection**  A multi-sided area specified to select objects. *See also* crossing window and window selection.

**polyline**  An object composed of one or more connected line segments or circular arcs treated as a single object. Also called pline. (PLINE, PEDIT)

**polysolid**  A swept solid that is drawn the same way you draw a polyline or that is based on an existing line. By default, a polysolid always has a rectangular profile. You can specify the height and width of the profile. (POLYSOLID)

**primary table fragment**  The fragment of a broken table that contains the beginning set of rows up to the first table break.

**procedural materials**  Materials that generate a 3D pattern in two or more colors, and apply it to an object. These include marble, granite, and wood. Also called template materials.

**profile curve**  An object that is swept, extruded, or revolved and defines the shape of the resulting solid or surface. (SWEEP, EXTRUDE, REVOLVE)

**prompt**  A message on the command line that asks for information or requests action such as specifying a point.

**proxy object**  A substitute for a custom object when the ObjectARX application that created the custom object is not available. *See also* custom object and object enabler.

**PWT**  A template file format used to publish drawings to the Web.

**ray-traced shadows**  A way that the renderer can generate shadows. Ray tracing traces the path of rays sampled from the light source. Shadows appear where rays have been blocked by objects. Ray-traced shadows have sharp edges. Ray-traced shadows are active when Shadow Map is turned off on the Advanced Render Settings palette.

**ray tracing**  The renderer can generate reflections and refractions. Ray tracing traces the path of rays sampled from the light source. Reflections and refractions generated this way are physically accurate. You turn on ray tracing on the Advanced Render Settings palette.

**radial dimension**  A dimension style that describes the center point and radius/diameter of a circle or an arc.

**radio buttons**  A series of buttons used to select a single option as an input method in a dialog box.

**rectangle**  A four-sided geometric shape with equal-length opposite sides and right angles in each corner.

**rectangular break**  To break a table into multiple parts that are evenly spaced and set at a user-specified height using the table breaking grips.

**REDRAW**  To quickly refresh or clean up blip marks in the current viewport without updating the drawing's database. *See also* regenerate. (REDRAW)

**reference**  A definition, known as an external reference or block reference, that is used and stored in the drawing. *See also* block (BLOCK) and external reference. (XREF)

**reflectance scale**  Increases or decreases the amount of energy the material reflects.

**reflection color**  The color of a highlight on shiny material. Also called specular color.

**reflection line**  In a dynamic block reference, the axis about which a flip action's selection set flips when the associated parameter is edited through a grip or the Properties palette.

**reflection mapping**  Creates the effect of a scene reflected on the surface of a shiny object.

**refraction**  How light distorts through an object.

**regenerate**  To update a drawing's screen display by recomputing the screen objects and coordinates from the database. *See also* redraw. (REGEN)

**regular polygon**  A multisided closed figure where all sides and interior angles are equal.

**relative coordinate system**  Coordinates specified in relation to previous coordinates or an object.

**relative polar coordinate system**  Coordinates specified in relation to previous coordinates based on an angle and a distance.

**resource drawing**  A drawing that is used as a data resource for the sheet set. You can place a saved model space view from a resource drawing onto a sheet.

**return button**  The button on a pointing device used to accept an entry. For example, on a two-button mouse, it is the right button.

**reverse lookup**  Adds a lookup grip to a dynamic block reference. When you click this grip, a drop-down list of the lookup values for that lookup property (column in the lookup table) is displayed. When you select a value from the list, the corresponding input property values are assigned to the block reference. Depending on how the block was defined, this usually results in a change in the block reference's geometry. (BLOOKUPTABLE)

**RGB**  For red, green, and blue. A system of defining colors by specifying percentages of red, green, and blue.

**roughness**  Value to simulate how light hitting a face is reflected back to the user. A high roughness value simulates a non-shiny or rough object (sandpaper/carpet). A low roughness value simulates a very shiny object (metals, some plastics.)

**row**  A horizontally adjacent table cell selection spanning the width of the table. A single row is one cell in height.

**RSS feed**  Information published by a website to which you subscribe. Usually allows users to receive notifications when new content (articles) are posted. RSS stands for Rich Site Summary (or Really Simple Syndication).

**rubber-band line**  A line that stretches dynamically on the screen with the movement of the cursor. One endpoint of the line is attached to a point in your drawing, and the other is attached to the moving cursor or crosshairs.

**running object snap**  Setting an Object Snap mode so it continues for subsequent selections. *See also* Object Snap mode and object snap override. (OSNAP)

**sampling**  Sampling is an antialiasing technique. It provides a "best guess" color for each rendered pixel. The renderer first samples the scene color at locations within the pixel or along the pixel's edge, then uses a filter to combine the samples into a single pixel color.

**save back**  To update the objects in the original reference (external or block reference) with changes made to objects in a working set during in-place reference editing.

**scale representation**  The display of an annotative object based on the annotation scales that the object supports. For example, if an annotative object supports two annotation scales, it has two scale representations.

**script file**  A set of commands executed sequentially with a single SCRIPT command. Script files are created outside the program using a text editor, saved in text format, and stored in an external file with the file extension .scr.

**secondary table fragment**  Any fragment of a broken table that does not contain the beginning set of rows.

**selected grip**  The status of a grip control point involved in an editing function.

**selection set**  One or more selected objects that a command can act upon at the same time. In a dynamic block definition, the geometry associated with an action.

**shadow maps** A shadow map is a bitmap that the renderer generates during a pre-rendering pass of the scene. Shadow maps don't show the color cast by transparent or translucent objects. On the other hand, shadow maps can have soft-edged shadows, which ray-traced shadows cannot. Shadow mapped shadows provide softer edges and can require less calculation time than ray-traced shadows, but are less accurate. On the Advanced Render Settings palette, shadow mapped shadows are active when Shadow Map is turned on.

**ShapeManager** The technology used to produce 3D solids.

**sheet** A layout selected from a drawing file and assigned to a sheet set. *See also* sheet set.

**sheet list table** A table listing all sheets in a sheet set. A sheet list table can be generated automatically with the Sheet Set Manager.

**sheet selection** A named selection of sheets in a sheet set that can be conveniently recalled for archiving, transmitting, and publishing operations.

**sheet set** An organized and named collection of sheets from several drawing files. *See also* sheet. (SHEETSET)

**shortcut keys** Keys and key combinations that start commands; for example, CTRL+S saves a file. The function keys (F1, F2, and so on) are also shortcut keys. Also known as accelerator keys.

**shortcut menu** The menu displayed at your cursor location when you right-click your pointing device. The shortcut menu and the options it provides depend on the pointer location and other conditions, such as whether an object is selected or a command is in progress.

**sky** The background color of the drawing area when perspective projection is turned on. The sky displays with a color gradient between the sky horizon (nearest to the horizon) and the sky zenith (opposite the horizon). *See also* ground plane.

**slide file** A file that contains a raster image or snapshot of the objects displayed in the drawing area. Slide files have the file extension .sld. (MSLIDE, VSLIDE)

**slide library** A collection of slide files organized for convenient retrieval and display. Slide library names have the extension .slb and are created with the slidelib.exe utility.

**slide-out panel** An area on the dashboard associated with a control panel. A slide-out panel contains additional tools and controls, and it can be displayed or hidden by clicking the large icon at the left side of the control panel. *See also* control panel and dashboard.

**smooth shading** Smoothing of the edges between polygon faces.

**snap** The ability to exactly choose a known location.

**snap angle** The angle that the snap grid is rotated.

**snap grid** The invisible grid that locks the pointer into alignment with the grid points according to the spacing set by Snap. Snap grid does not necessarily correspond to the visible grid, which is controlled separately by GRID. (SNAP)

**Snap mode** A mode for locking a pointing device into alignment with an invisible rectangular grid. When Snap mode is on, the screen crosshairs and all input coordinates are snapped to the nearest point on the grid. The snap resolution defines the spacing of this grid. *See also* Object Snap mode.

**snap resolution** The spacing between points of the snap grid.

**software** Programs that control the operations of a computer and its peripherals.

**solid history** A property of a solid that allows you to see and modify the original forms of the solid.

**solid object** An object that represents the entire volume of an object, for example a box.

**solid primitive** A basic solid form. Solid primitives include: box, wedge, cone, cylinder, sphere, torus, and pyramid.

**spatial index**  A list that organizes objects based on their location in space. A spatial index is used to locate what portion of the drawing is read when you partially open a drawing. Saving a spatial index with a drawing also enhances performance when working with external references. The INDEXCTL system variable controls whether layer and spatial indexes are saved with a drawing.

**specular reflection**  The light in a narrow cone where the angle of the incoming beam equals the angle of the reflected beam.

**status bar**  A series of readouts and on/off buttons, for drawing aids, located on the bottom of the screen.

**STB file**  For plot style table file. Contains plot styles and their characteristics.

**stretch frame**  In a dynamic block definition that contains a stretch action or a polar stretch action, determines how the objects within or crossed by the frame are edited in the block reference.

**Subscription Center**  A resource available from the Help menu for subscription members to access the latest releases of Autodesk software, incremental product enhancements, personalized web support, and self-paced e-learning.

**subobject**  Any part of a solid: a face, an edge, or a vertex. Also, an original individual form that is part of a composite solid.

**subset**  A named collection of sheets in a sheet set that is often organized by discipline or work-flow stage. *See also* view category.

**surface normal**  Positive direction perpendicular to the surface of an object.

**swept solid/surface**  A solid or surface created in the shape of the specified profile (the swept object) swept along the specified path. (SWEEP)

**symbol**  A representation of an item commonly used in drawings. Symbols are inserted in drawings as blocks.

**symbol library**  A collection of block definitions stored in a single drawing file.

**system variable**  A name that is recognized as a mode, size, or limit. Read-only system variables, such as DWGNAME, cannot be modified directly by the user.

**table**  A rectangular array of cells that contain annotation, primarily text but also blocks. In the AEC industry, tables are often referred to as "schedules" and contain information about the materials needed for the construction of the building being designed. In the manufacturing industry, they are often referred to as "BOM" (bills of materials). (TABLE)

**table break**  The point at the bottom of a table row where the table will be split into a supplementary table fragment.

**table style**  A style that contains a specific table format and structure. A table style contains at least 3 cell styles.

**tangent**  A location on a circle where a line and a circle touch at one point and only one point.

**template/template drawing**  A drawing file with preestablished settings for new drawings such as *acad.dwt* and *acadiso.dwt;* however, any drawing can be used as a template. *See also* initial environment.

**temporary files**  Data files created during an program session. The files are deleted by the time you end the session. If the session ends abnormally, such as during a power outage, temporary files might be left on the disk.

**tessellation lines**  Lines that help you visualize a curved surface.

**text screen (text window)**  One of two screens within AutoCAD. This screen houses the history of the current drawing session.

**text style**  A named, saved collection of settings that determines the appearance of text characters—for example, stretched, compressed, oblique, mirrored, or set in a vertical column.

**texture map** The projection of an image (such as a tile pattern) onto an object (such as a chair).

**thaw** A setting that displays previously frozen layers. *See also* freeze.

**thickness** The distance certain objects are extruded to give them a 3D appearance. (PROPER-TIES, CHPROP, ELEV, THICKNESS)

**tiled viewports** *See* model viewports.

**TILEMODE** A system variable that controls whether viewports can be created as movable, resizable objects (layout viewports), or as non-overlapping display elements that appear side by side (model viewports). *See also* viewport.

**toolbar** Part of the interface containing icons that represent commands.

**tracking** A way to locate a point relative to other points on the drawing.

**translucency** How light is scattered through an object.

**transmittance scale** Increases or decreases the amount of energy a transparent material transmits out to the scene.

**transparency** A quantity defining how much light is let through an object.

**transparent command** A command started while another is in progress. Precede transparent commands with an apostrophe.

**two sided material** The positive and negative normal of the material will be considered during the rendering process.

**UCS** *See* user coordinate system (UCS).

**UCS icon** An icon that indicates the orientation of the UCS axes. (UCSICON)

**underground** The XY plane of the user coordinate system when perspective projection is turned on and when viewed from below ground. The underground plane displays with a color gradient between the earth horizon (nearest to the horizon) and the earth azimuth (opposite the horizon). *See also* ground plane and sky.

**underlay** A DWF or DGN file used to provide visual context in a drawing file. Underlays cannot be edited, and do not provide the full range of notification. Underlays cannot be bound to a drawing. *See also* external reference (xref).

**unidirectional system** A dimensional system where all text entities are placed parallel to the X axis and read from the bottom of the document.

**unselected grip** The status of a grip control point identifying an object.

**user coordinate system (UCS)** A user-defined coordinate system that defines the orientation of the X, Y, and Z axes in 3D space. The UCS determines the default placement of geometry in a drawing. *See also* world coordinate system (WCS).

**UVW** The material's coordinate space. Used instead of XYZ because that is usually reserved for the world coordinate system (WCS). Most material maps are a 2D plane assigned to a 3D surface. The U, V, and W coordinates parallel the relative directions of X, Y, and Z coordinates. If you look at a 2D map image, U is the equivalent of X, and represents the horizontal direction of the map. V is the equivalent of Y, and represents the vertical direction of the map. W is the equivalent of Z and represents a direction perpendicular to the UV plane of the map.

**value set** In a dynamic block definition, a range or list of values specified for a linear, polar, XY, or rotation parameter.

**vector** A mathematical object with precise direction and length but without specific location.

**vertex** A location where edges or polyline segments meet.

**view** A graphical representation of a model from a specific location (viewpoint) in space. *See also* viewpoint and viewport. (VPOINT, DVIEW, VIEW)

**view category** A named collection of views in a sheet set that is often organized by function. *See also* subset.

**viewpoint** The location in 3D model space from which you are viewing a model. *See also* view and viewport. (DVIEW, VPOINT)

**viewport** A bounded area that displays some portion of the model space of a drawing. The TILEMODE system variable determines the type of viewport created. When TILEMODE is off (0), viewports are objects that can be moved and resized on a layout. (MVIEW) When TILE-MODE is on (1), the entire drawing area is divided into nonoverlapping model viewports. *See also* TILEMODE, view, and viewpoint. (VPORTS)

**viewport configuration** A named collection of model viewports that can be saved and restored. (VPORTS)

**virtual screen display** The area in which the program can pan and zoom without regenerating the drawing.

**visibility mode** Displays or does not display geometry (in a dimmed state) that is invisible for a visibility state. (BVMODE)

**visibility state** In a dynamic block, a custom property that allows only specified geometry to display in the block reference. (BVSTATE)

**visual style** A collection of settings that control the display of edges and shading in a viewport.

**volumetric shadows** A photorealistically rendered volume of space cast by the shadow of an object.

**WCS** *See* world coordinate system (WCS).

**window selection** A rectangular area specified in the drawing area to select multiple objects at the same time. *See also* crossing selection, polygon window selection.

**wipeout object** A polygonal area that masks underlying objects with the current background color. This area is bounded by the wipeout frame, which you can turn on for editing and turn off for plotting.

**wireframe model** The representation of an object using lines and curves to represent its boundaries.

**Wizard** A tool that uses a step-by-step routine to establish a series of drawing settings.

**working drawing** A drawing for manufacturing or building purposes.

**working set** A group of objects selected for in-place reference editing.

**workplane** Another name for the XY plane of the user coordinate system. *See also* elevation and user coordinate system (UCS).

**workspace** A set of menus, toolbars, and dockable windows (such as the Properties palette, DesignCenter, and the Tool palettes window) that are grouped and organized so that you can work in a custom, task-oriented drawing environment.

**world coordinate system (WCS)** A coordinate system used as the basis for defining all objects and other coordinate systems. *See also* user coordinate system (UCS).

**world coordinates** Coordinates expressed in relation to the world coordinate system (WCS).

**WYSIWYG** What You See Is What You Get.

**X,Y,Z point filters** *See* coordinate filters.

**xref** *See* external reference.

**zoom** To reduce or increase the apparent magnification of the drawing area. (ZOOM)

# Index